GEORGE ROGERS CLARK
His Life and Public Services

GENERAL GEORGE ROGERS CLARK

1752   1818

The Son of Virginia   The Sword of Kentucky
The Conqueror of the Illinois
His Prophetic Vision Gave to Civilization its Richest Empire
A Tribute to Foresight, Courage and Fortitude
Erected by the State of Illinois, 1909

GEORGE ROGERS CLARK

His Life and Public Services

BY

TEMPLE BODLEY

BOSTON AND NEW YORK

HOUGHTON MIFFLIN COMPANY

The Riverside Press Cambridge

1926

The Riverside Press
CAMBRIDGE · MASSACHUSETTS
PRINTED IN THE U.S.A.

PREFACE

FOR over a hundred years most of the facts about George Rogers Clark have lain buried in the unpublished and widely scattered records of his time. His outstanding early military services have often been described; but later ones, hardly less important and demanding far more of patriotic sacrifice, have rarely or never been noticed. Excepting his well-known 'Mason' and 'Memoir' letters, describing his conquest of the British posts north of the Ohio during the Revolutionary War, almost none of his extensive correspondence ever appeared in print until very recently, and much of it still remains unpublished; yet it throws a flood of light not only upon his military movements, but upon the conditions under which he labored and upon his motives and character.

During many years of painstaking search and study of the source materials of the history of our first great West — the Revolutionary West — I became, I think, pretty familiar with Clark as the military leader there and as a man; and this volume, if I know myself, has been written to give the record truth about him. It has been prepared under many difficulties, a chief one being defective sight, which has often necessitated the use of other eyes than my own in gathering and arranging many of the materials.

I wish here to acknowledge my indebtedness to a number of friends for valuable aid in my search-work, and others in the preparation of this book. To Mr. R. C. Ballard Thruston, president of the Filson Club of Louisville, I owe much. His extensive and valuable private collection of historic publications, original manuscripts, and photostat reproductions of others (including many from the Draper Collection and the Virginia State Library), he has placed at my service as freely as if it were my own. He has also found for me a number of exceedingly valuable papers and works which I should otherwise never have secured; and his intelligent suggestions and constant encouragement have helped me greatly.

To Mrs. Henry L. Cook, of Milwaukee, I am indebted for early stimulating my active interest in Clark's career and for help in finding many source materials concerning him. Some years before my investigations began, hers had been carried on, and for several years we coöperated in gathering and exchanging manuscripts; while duplicates of such as she had previously gathered and her knowledge of the facts about Clark's career were put at my service. Her investigations have extended over a wide and varied range of early American history; but, like many other painstaking investigators, she has written almost nothing for publication.

To Mr. William Warner Bishop (both while he was in active charge of the Library of Congress, and since he became Librarian of his *alma mater*, the University of Michigan) I am also deeply indebted. It was through him that I secured first access to the valuable Shelburne Papers, recently purchased by him for the Clements Library of American History at Ann Arbor.

To Dr. McIlwaine, Librarian, and Dr. Eckenrode, former Archivist, of the Virginia State Library at Richmond, I am indebted for many courtesies and for assistance in exploring that priceless mine of source materials illustrating our early western history. To Mr. William A. Richardson for his long and excellent search-work for me amongst the archives of the Virginia State Library, in the Library of Congress, and in the State Department at Washington, I owe many valuable 'finds' and suggestions. To my former assistants, Mr. John D. Kemper, now of Chicago, and Mrs. Mary Crume, of Louisville, and to my present secretary, Mr. Alvin L. Prichard, I cannot sufficiently express my thanks for their keen interest and competent assistance in my work. I also wish to acknowledge very valuable suggestions concerning its scope and general character from my friends Mr. Wm. W. Thum of Louisville and Mr. Malcolm Ross of New York.

If the life-story told in this book has been relieved of the heavy lawyer-like style in which it was first written, and now makes entertaining reading, it is because my manuscript has undergone frank and trenchant criticism from my daughter, Mrs. William A. Stuart, and has been revised in accordance with her better literary taste.

As Volume VIII of the *Illinois Historical Collections*, containing the *George Rogers Clark Papers*, gives many of the source materials concerning Clark, prior to October, 1781, which I had previously collected, and as that excellent work by Professor James Alton James is widely distributed, readily accessible, and remarkably accurate, both in transcribing the original documents and indicating where they may be found, I have made my references to it wherever I could in the following pages. His second volume, continuing the *Clark Papers* after October, 1781 (Volume XIX of the *Illinois Historical Collections*), was not issued until after the present work was in the hands of the publishers. It contains a much smaller part, however, of the source materials referred to in this book concerning Clark during the twenty-seven years of his life after that date.

LOUISVILLE, KENTUCKY

CONTENTS

CONTENTS

CONTENTS

INTRODUCTION

In all American history it would be hard to find a more dramatic career than that of the young Virginia surveyor whose life will be sketched in the following pages — George Rogers Clark. In spectacular settings, in strongly contrasted actors, in tense situations and thrilling actions, it seems unique. Its scenes take in the old colonial life of Tidewater Virginia; the wilderness of the Mississippi Valley; the far-away Kentucky settlements with pioneers living in rude cabins or log forts: the ever picturesque Indians; the French Creoles of varied grades in the old Illinois and Wabash towns; the Spanish officials and motley population of early St. Louis; the Canadian French, and the highly disciplined British redcoats of the 'King's Own Regiment.'

No true and adequate life of Clark can be written without presenting many of these dramatic scenes, but that is not the aim of this book. It is one product of many years of careful search and study of the numerous extant source materials — most of them unpublished — in preparation for writing a history of the Revolutionary West, and it aims to give the facts about him as disclosed in those records.

For over fifty years after the Revolutionary War its western phase was rarely mentioned in our histories. They were nearly all written by eastern men who were naturally more interested and better informed about the events and men in their own sections than about those in the far western wilderness. They did not realize, as historians now do, that both the winning and the value of American independence hung upon the successful conduct of the war in the west, as well as along the Atlantic seaboard. The result was that generations of American readers of history were left ignorant of the fact that in the Mississippi Valley there was a struggle for independence and empire which, although the numbers engaged were small, was far more desperate than the eastern conflict and hardly less significant in the upbuilding of this nation. In that western war, as all historians agree, the out-

standing figure was George Rogers Clark. Our successful
warfare to drive the British from the trans-Allegheny country
was carried on by Virginia, and, throughout, he was in chief
command.

To judge the national significance of Clark's service, one
not only must know the part he took in winning that region,
but also what the possession of the region has meant to the
nation. Since Professor Frederick J. Turner first duly emphasized its importance, our westward-moving frontier has
come to be regarded as 'the most constant and potent force in
our history.' American democracy is the child of that moving
frontier; but it would have come into the world still-born had
our frontier been limited by the Alleghenies, with no room
to move west with the sun.

We made our first stride to territorial greatness by securing the Revolutionary West. It laid the foundation for the
Louisiana Purchase and of all our latter expansion to Mexico,
the Pacific, and beyond. It also yielded priceless benefits
entirely aside from territorial bigness. It gave the financially
exhausted states a vast area of fertile lands in the Northwest
Territory, the anticipated value of which furnished them their
one basis of public credit and saved them from bankruptcy
and continued dependence on France. The public lands did
more. At the critical time when the Confederation was falling
to pieces, those jointly owned lands furnished the jealous
states a sorely needed bond of union. It has been well said:
'In the possession of the public lands the old states found a
common tie which bound them permanently together. However widely political ideas might differ, however much economic interests might antagonize sections, however greatly social institutions and customs might vary, there remained back
of the Alleghenies a vast tract of fallow land in the settlement
and disposition of which all the states found a common interest.
That interest bound them together in a territorial commonwealth. The public lands were the backbone of the United
States. The history of their constitutional government cannot be understood without a study of the land question.'[1]
To the same effect Fiske, in his *Critical Period of American*

[1] Shosuke Sato, *History of the Land Question in the United States*, in *Johns Hopkins University Studies in Historical and Political Science*, Series 4, vii–ix. (Baltimore, 1886.)

History, says: 'The creation of a national domain laid the corner stone of the Federal Union.'

Certainly the winning of the trans-Allegheny wilderness was fundamental in the making of this nation; and the story of Clark's large part in the winning must be worth knowing.

GEORGE ROGERS CLARK

CHAPTER I

CHILDHOOD AND YOUTH

GEORGE ROGERS CLARK's parents were Virginia planter-people with comfortable means and good social position in the old tide-water county of King-and-Queen. The father, John Clark, when a young man of twenty-three, married his second cousin, Ann Rogers, a girl of fifteen, and soon afterward removed to the newly created frontier county of Albemarle. There, some twelve miles east of the beautiful Blue Ridge, they made their home on a four hundred acre tract of fertile land on the Rivanna River, and there George Rogers Clark was born, November 19, 1752. On the adjoining tract lived the parents of Thomas Jefferson, who had been born there nine years before. The region was then a primitive and sparsely settled one, and the Jeffersons no doubt warmly welcomed the young Clarks as next neighbors, and saw much of them. Certainly Thomas Jefferson became the lifelong friend of George Rogers. Little did any one then dream that to these two children of the Virginia frontier this nation would mainly owe its possession of the priceless empire extending from the Alleghenies to the Mississippi.

Albemarle County is now noted for its beauty, as Jefferson's birthplace, and as the seat of his favorite creation, the University of Virginia. It is hard to realize how different the region must have been in 1752, when few people had ventured to live so far west. Perhaps nineteen-twentieths of the British colonists then lived in the tide-water country along the bays and rivers near the Atlantic. West of the Blue Ridge the Valley of Virginia was still a nearly unbroken forest, with here and there the clearings of a few pioneers. Men who were still not old remembered seeing Governor Spottswood leading his 'Knights of the Golden Horseshoe' on their way to the crest of the range to overlook the great valley for the first time.

It was not until just before the outbreak of the French and
Indian War, in 1754, that Governor Dinwiddie of Virginia,
in order to bridle the French, caused a small log fort to be
built at Pittsburg — then far out in the western wilds and
thought to be within the bounds of the Old Dominion. The
whole Mississippi Valley was claimed by France and, excepting that one crude little British outpost, the French were
the only civilized people who occupied it. They had old and
thriving towns at Detroit, at New Orleans, at Vincennes on
the Wabash, in what is now southwestern Indiana, at Kaskaskia in Illinois near the Mississippi, and at Cahokia, sixty
miles farther up the river.

Such was the situation when the clash of war came — a
war which was to determine whether the region between the
Alleghenies and the Mississippi should be French or British.
At first the tide ran strongly against the British colonists.
From New England to Georgia the Indian allies of the French
played havoc along the frontiers, and many settlers there fled
for safety to the tide-water country. The third year of the war
Mr. Clark and his wife removed with their four small children
to Caroline County (formerly part of King-and-Queen), where
he had become owner of the plantation of a deceased uncle.
There they had many relatives and friends, and the children
had school and social advantages not to be found in Albemarle.

For an insight into George Rogers' character and career,
it is of course well to know the associations and opportunities
of his early life; yet to this day printed history has given almost no information about them. Of the life of the Clarks in
Albemarle little is known, but in Caroline it appears to have
been a very happy one. Fortunately there is an exceedingly
interesting and informing diary, kept by George Rogers'
brother, Jonathan, which sheds much light upon many of the
social and other conditions surrounding the family in Caroline,
and recalls many of the people amongst whom the children
grew up. The diary consists of seventeen closely and beauti-
fully written little pocket volumes, beginning shortly before
Jonathan's twentieth birthday, June 1, 1770, continuing with
hardly a break for over forty years, and ending only the day
before his death, in 1811. It gives a pretty fair idea of the
care-free life of a young Virginian during the five years before
the Revolution. Visiting then was a large part of one's oc-

cupation, for, having few neighbors but great abundance of provisions and trained servants, planters and their wives gladly welcomed many guests. At first the diary shows Jonathan visiting amongst the well-known families of Caroline and adjacent counties, attending parties, church meetings, the high court at Richmond, or the theater at Fredericksburg. Other glimpses of his daily life were of dances, funerals, weddings, barbecues, fox chases, shooting matches, deerhunts, and cockfights; while several times fights between neighbors are mentioned.

As Jonathan and George Rogers were chums of nearly the same age, and lived together — probably sharing the same room and bed — until the latter went west, they must have had many friends in common, shared many sports, visited the same girls, attended the same parties, and, with other laced and queued planters' sons, danced many a stately minuet and merry reel with panniered and powdered young ladies of the neighborhood. Unfortunately, however, the diary was merely intended for a weather record and as a reminder of Jonathan's whereabouts. It rarely mentions George Rogers, or any of the many visitors to his father's home, but gives only his own movements, the houses where he lay overnight, and sometimes particular incidents that he wished to recall. Although it does mention hundreds of events of historic significance, its omissions are most disappointing. For example, he was a member of the famous Virginia Revolutionary Convention of 1775 and, in the little church at Richmond, heard Patrick Henry's immortal 'Give me liberty, or give me death' speech — perhaps the most telling ever made in America — yet the diary only says: 'Clear: at Richmond; the Convention continued: lay Capt Gunn's.'

Mr. Clark appears to have been a quiet, peace-loving man, moderately well educated according to the very indifferent standard then prevailing amongst Virginia planters, and indeed nearly everywhere in the colonies. His letters show constant solicitude for the welfare of his children, not only in this world, but the next; for he and his wife were deeply religious in an age when religion had a very strong hold upon the minds and conduct of believers. All were Episcopalians. Jonathan was a regular attendant on church services and long a vestryman; while George Rogers, through all the strain and rough associations of pioneer life and Indian war, clung to the faith he had received from his parents. At the height of his success, writing to his father, he attributed it to the providence of God, and said: 'Fortune in every respect as yet hath hovered around me, as if determined to direct me. You may judge, Sir, what impression it must have on a grateful Brest whose greatest glory is to addore the Supreme director of all things.'

That after a hundred and fifty years John and Ann Rogers Clark are still mentioned in history has been due to the distinction won by their descendants. Six of their ten children were sons, of whom five became officers in the Revolutionary War. The oldest two, Jonathan and George Rogers, became generals, the next a captain, the other two lieutenants. The sixth son, William — a small lad during the Revolution — also became a general and the first governor of Missouri, but won main distinction while a captain in the Lewis and Clark Expedition to the Pacific.[1]

Both Jonathan and George Rogers attended the school of a noted Scotch educator of the time, Mr. Donald Robertson, who had married their mother's sister and, it is said, was a graduate of the University of Edinburgh and a cousin of the distinguished historian. Another pupil at the same time was James Madison, afterwards President. It is uncertain how long the two brothers remained at school. Jonathan, who was two years the older, and perhaps the more diligent scholar, became a man of affairs, note, and wealth. George Rogers became proficient in mathematics and was fond of geography, history, and especially of nature study, which held great interest for him throughout life.[2] He also became

[1] It is almost impossible to trace the remote ancestry of one bearing a name common to so many families as Clark. Our first census in 1790 gave 2442 heads and 11,324 members of families in the United States of that name, in its two spellings, Clark and Clarke. Of the European forebears of the family we only know that their surname shows them English. Tradition says the original immigrant was John Clark, and his wife a 'red-haired Scotch beauty.' Then followed four generations of paternal ancestors named successively Jonathan (I), John (II), Jonathan (II) and John (III) who was the father of George Rogers. Of the original immigrant and his son nothing definite is known. John (II) seems to have had extensive land interests, and his son Jonathan (II) to have been a well-to-do planter of Caroline.

[2] *Draper MSS.* 10 J 8, and 231-A. 'I learned from his mother, with whom I lived a great deal, that General Clark was very fond of history and geography, and the study of nature from his earliest youth. When I lived with him he used to caution me against novel reading and urged me to read history. The first book he ever gave me was the Spectator. I heard his mother say he was the arbiter

expert in surveying, which he first studied and practised under his grandfather Rogers. During childhood and early youth, it is not likely that he was required to spend many hours out of school in the study of books, but was given much freedom for play. It must not be hastily inferred, however, that his educational advantages were poor, for education is not gained only from books. Like the ancient Greeks, most people in his day learned far less from what they read than from what they heard; and the art of instructive conversation was not then a lost one. Often when a family and guests were gathered by fireside they had both leisure and desire for talk about subjects worth knowing; and on such occasions a great variety of topics were discussed, some entertainingly, some instructively, — politics, agriculture, recent inventions, shipping methods and commerce, a play at Fredericksburg, the Sunday sermon, the latest news from London, the report of some trader from the wilderness with a tale of the wonders he saw there, or a story of the Indians. During these gatherings many a listening boy's receptive mind took in much of value and was stimulated to a wider range of thinking. George Rogers must have heard many such discussions and learned from them lessons more valuable than many taught him in school. His appreciation of the precepts impressed upon him in his youth by the eminent George Mason, he gratefully acknowledged in later years.[1]

The educational advantages of a planter's son were by no means limited, however, to what he learned in these ways. His outdoor life had great part in his mental as well as physical development and discipline. Sports — especially hunting when alone — trained him in close observation, self-reliance, courage, and endurance. In a day's deer hunt in wild woods, a boy would sometimes encounter more danger and fatigue, and exercise more resourcefulness to extricate himself from awkward predicaments, than a soldier in a day's forced march; and all this taught him forethought and alertness.

George Rogers' schooling was also of another kind, for he

of the boys in disputes at school.' (Mrs. Diana Gwathmey Bullitt, General Clark's niece, *Draper MSS. 10 J 176-A.*)

[1] *Illinois Historical Collections*, VIII, 114. Colonel Mason, who lived at Gunston Hall in the adjoining county of Stafford, was one of Virginia's ablest and best men. He was Mr. Clark's friend, took much interest in his sons, and largely influenced George Rogers' career. The two families were intimate and Jonathan's diary repeatedly mentions visits for days at a time at the Mason home.

early learned to earn his own spending money. When he was only fifteen years old, he was charged in his father's well-kept account book [1] with the cost of clothes and other articles bought for him, and credited with the proceeds of a crop of tobacco. Next year he raised both corn and tobacco and sold them for nearly thirty pounds — equivalent in purchasing power, perhaps, to five hundred dollars at the present time.

In 1763, six years after the Clarks removed from Albemarle to Caroline and when George Rogers was eleven years of age, the French and Indian War ended, and France lost. By the treaty of Paris she surrendered to Great Britain Canada, and all the country she had claimed east of the centre line of the Mississippi, except New Orleans and a small area east of it, which, along with the great region between that river and the Rocky Mountains, she gave by secret treaty to her ally, Spain. At the same time Spain ceded Florida to Great Britain, in exchange for Cuba, which the British had captured.

When this treaty was made, the western country between the Alleghenies and the Mississippi was nearly all a vast wilderness, most of it covered by a dense forest, and abounding in buffalo, deer, and other game. It was also the home of many ferocious animals, the most dreaded being the panther; but far more dangerous were thousands of warlike Indians living in scattered villages north of the Ohio and south of the Tennessee. Between those rivers was a fertile but uninhabited region separating the northern and southern tribes. As already seen, however, not all the western region was wild, nor were all its inhabitants savages; for in and about the old French towns of the Illinois and Wabash were some inhabitants of quite respectable antecedents and culture. The French were singularly successful in winning the confidence and even affection of the Indians, and their merchants there carried on an extensive fur trade in the Indian country, and sent large quantities of flour, pork, and other products to New Orleans and live-stock to Detroit.

The British colonists west of the Alleghenies were very few and widely scattered — most of them living along the streams flowing from those mountains into the upper Ohio. Pittsburg was new, crude, and small, containing only about thirty

[1] *Author's MSS.*

houses.[1] Far to the south of it, along the Holston River, in what are now southwestern Virginia and northeastern Tennessee, were many small settlements, known collectively as 'The Holston.' Kentucky, the favorite hunting ground and often the fighting ground of the many tribes living north and south of it, was well called the 'Dark and Bloody Ground.' Because it was uninhabited, it made an entering wedge for pioneer settlement, separating these northern and southern Indians — a fact of very great importance in the coming Revolutionary War, since the savages were exposed to flank attack from Kentucky if they dared leave their homes to fall upon the Allegheny frontiers.

[1] *Journal of Nicholas Cresswell* (Dial Press, 1924), pp. 65.

CHAPTER II

YOUNG PIONEER, SURVEYOR, AND SOLDIER

THREE years before the Revolution, George Rogers Clark left his father's home to see the great West and perhaps live and find fortune there. He was then a tall, slender, blue-eyed youth of nineteen, with clear complexion and sandy hair. In his father's account book these two charges are entered against him:

1772 April 13	To Surveyors Instruments	£ 7. 0. 0.
" "	Euclid's elements	12. 0.

Thus equipped for surveying, he set out, crossing the Blue Ridge and Alleghenies and descending the Monongahela River to Pittsburg.

Of the young explorer's first venture into the western wilderness nearly all we know appears in the journal of the Reverend David Jones, later a chaplain in Washington's army, who wrote:

'I left Fort Pitt on Tuesday June 9, 1772, in company with George Rogers Clark, a young gentleman from Virginia, who, with several others, inclined to make a tour of this new world. We traveled by water in a canoe, and as I laboured none, I had an opportunity of making my remarks on the many creeks which empty into the Ohio, as also the courses of said river. [Some days later they approached a village inhabited by some mongrel Indians] but as they have a name for plundering canoes we passed them quickly as possible and were so happy as not to be discovered by any of them. ...[Thirty miles farther down they stopped near the mouth of Grave Creek.] It was in the night when we came; instead of feathers, my bed was gravel stones by the river side. From Fort Pitt to this place we were only in one place where white people live.' [1]

The explorers continued down the Ohio to the mouth of the Great Kanawha, whence they returned home through the tangle of rugged mountains. Two months later George Rogers, evidently enthusiastic about the western country he had seen, returned there with a young neighbor and a couple of negro slaves. This time his father accompanied him, to see him settled 'on a bottom of fine land on the Ohio, about forty

[1] *Draper MSS.* 1 L 9; English's *Conquest of the Northwest*, 60.

miles below Wheeling.'[1] Here the youthful pioneer cleared his land for farming, and engaged in profitable surveying. By the next year, (1773) the swelling tide of emigration had carried the white settlements along the Ohio some 353 miles below Fort Pitt. Several Virginian surveying parties went 245 miles farther, to the Falls of Ohio, and others up the Kentucky River to the fertile 'Bluegrass Region.' In another direction, settlers from Virginia, Maryland, and Pennsylvania trekked southwestwardly up the Valley of Virginia to the Holston settlements on the headwaters of the Tennessee. George Rogers wrote Jonathan: 'I had an offer of a very considerable sum for my place. I get a good deal of cash by surveying on this river, ... and drive on pretty well as to clearing, hoping by spring to get a full crop. ... Corn is in some parts 7/6 pr Bushel, but I have got great plenty.'[2]

This summer he made a short visit to his parents, probably to get funds for land-entry fees. Just before he returned to the west his father wrote the letter printed below, saying he was uneasy lest his boy meet danger in the 'back country.'[3] There was good cause for this uneasiness, for the Shawnees and other Indian tribes north of the Ohio were in an angry mood. For ten years after the French and Indian War the tribes near the upper Ohio had refrained from open warfare; but they saw their lands being steadily encroached upon, their hunting grounds invaded, and the game upon which they relied for food being killed or driven away by white hunters; and the relations between them and the colonists along the border soon reached the breaking point.

Early in 1774, despite signs of Indian war, settlers still streamed over the mountains. All went south of the Ohio,

[1] John Roy to Jonathan Clark, *Draper MSS.* 1 L 8.
[2] *Draper MSS.* 1 L 8.
[3] CAROLINE COUNTY *ye 23rd Sepbr*
1773

DEAR SON: —
This leaves us well, I thank God; but we are under some onease [uneasy] apprehensions at your not coming down & at your brothers setting out for the back country. He purposes to leave us tomorrow, in company with Col? Muse and Wm. Higgins. If you cannot com down, shall be glad you let us know by the first opportunity how you do; but hope that it will sute you to come by ye

20th of next month, October, at which time we expect your sister will be married to Owen Gwathmey. We intend to have a weding, but the satisfaction will be small unless you are with us. As I expect to see you soon, I conclud without entering into perticklers, as I should on expecting a long absence. We all joine in affentions to you & will have the greatest expectations to see you.
From your affectionate Father
JOHN CLARK

To Mr. Jonathan Clark
Woodstock, Dunmore
(*Draper MSS.* 1 L 12.)

for they dared not venture north of the river, where, in what is now southeastern Ohio, were the Shawnees and Delawares, and, farther west and northwest, many other tribes. (Their locations are indicated in the footnote.[1] For convenience, regions will often be indicated by the names of states not created until years afterward.) One party of about fifty Virginians, led by James Harrod, went down the Ohio and up into central Kentucky. There they laid out a town called Harrodsburg, where they erected some forty log cabins and started to build a fort; but their work was soon stopped, for the Shawnees and their allies were on the war path. The Harrodsburg builders hurried back again to the upper Ohio to handle rifles instead of axes. Young Clark was there, busily engaged in surveying and 'engrossing' rich lands; but such pacific pursuits were rudely disturbed by the Indian warwhoop and tomahawk, and the butchery of his fellow pioneers changed the whole course of his career and made him a soldier. Few of the new settlers had experienced Indian warfare, and nearly all abandoned their clearings and fled back over the mountains. In the Pittsburg region 'the panic became contagious. There was a rapid retreat across the Monongahela; more than a thousand are said to have passed over in one day.' [2]

The Indian warfare to which the pioneers were exposed was not only dreadful in its cruelty, but probably the most effective ever waged by equal bodies of uncivilized men.

---

[1] A short distance below Pittsburg was the town of a motley gathering of Shawnees, Delawares, Mingoes, and other tribesmen called the 'Loggstown Indians.' Lower down, in the valley of the Muskingum, were the Delawares. Early during the Revolution they migrated to central Indiana. Farther west, on the waters of the Scioto, were the main towns of the Shawnees. Northwest of them, on two rivers bearing their names and flowing into the Ohio, were part of the Miamis, also called Wyandots. These Indians lived within what is now the state of Ohio, as did others near Lake Erie. In northeastern Indiana were the main settlements of the Miamis, near the site of Fort Wayne. West of them, on the upper Wabash River, were the Ouiatenans — sometimes called 'Ouias' or 'Weas.'

Lower on that river, near Vincennes, were the Piankeshaws, whose chief was known as 'The Grand Door of the Wabash.' In Illinois were various nations. Their chief gathering place, and a main center of Indian trade, was Cahokia on the Mississippi, a short distance below the mouth of the Missouri. It was nearly opposite St. Louis, the main trading post of Spanish upper Louisiana. In southwestern Michigan were the Pottawatomies, north of them the Ottawas and Saginaws, as well as part of the Chippewas. The main body of Chippewas were west of Lake Michigan, as were the Sacs and Foxes. There too were Sioux, who spread over a large region, especially west of the Mississippi.

[2] Thwaites and Kellogg's *Revolution on the Upper Ohio*, 13.

The Indian was a born warrior; his ambition centered in war; his standing in his tribe, his winning of his bride, his own self-esteem, and even, he believed, his reception after death by his departed ancestors depended on his prowess in war. The proudest adornment he could wear was a string of the bloody scalps of enemies of his tribe; and the scalp of a helpless old man, or of a woman or child, was counted as well as that of an able-bodied man. Crafty, inured to hardship, rapid and tireless travelers, requiring little food and trusting to find that on their way, the Indians were masters of the arts of woodcraft, hiding, and stealthy attack. They preferred to divide their forces and go to war in small bands. Striking where the enemy was weakest and most damage could be done, they would vanish before any formidable foe, and often, in an incredibly short time, reappear at a distance to carry havoc to a new settlement. A single small band would thus seem to be at half a dozen places at nearly the same time, and would spread terror, even amongst the sturdy frontier people, over miles of country; and everywhere they went they left their bloody trail of scalped and mutilated bodies and burned homes, and carried away their helpless captives for slavery or merciless torture.

White men were usually more or less bewildered in the tangled forest, but the Indians were as much at home there as any wild animal. In the wooded country where they usually fought, they were, man for man, far more than a match in battle for any but the most skillful pioneers. They kept in touch with their comrades, passed signals, and preserved a long and rapidly changing battle line with great skill. Yet they labored under several disadvantages. In marksmanship they were inferior to experienced pioneers, for their guns were oftenest poor, while, to save their powder supply, they rarely engaged in target practice, and also undercharged their rifles, thus reducing both range and accuracy of fire.[1] Their most serious shortcomings as warriors, however,

---

[1] The 'Kentucky Rifle,' as the best weapon of that day came to be known, was a remarkably accurate weapon, although its range and power were very limited. The use of the flint lock and powder-pan detracted greatly from its reliability as compared with modern weapons, but in the hands of a practiced pioneer this disadvantage was more than made up by the weight of the long barrel, its inappreciable recoil, and the 'hair-trigger' then used. Its accuracy varied much according to the skill of the gun-maker, and great care was often taken to get rifles from the best makers, of whom Deckard was the most famous.

were lack of subordination and perseverance; owing to which many well-planned raids would be abandoned and victories lost that they might certainly have won. Their aversion to pitched battles was a very reasonable one, for they knew they were greatly outnumbered by the whites and could not afford to lose men. Because of this, and because they sought to attack the weak and not the strong, and would frequently retire before enemies much inferior to themselves in number, especially if entrenched, many have thought they lacked steady courage; but never was a greater mistake. They simply joined caution to bravery.

Lacking a commissariat, the Indians rarely made long sieges, for they could not depend for food on the game about a beleaguered fort, since it was usually scarce before their arrival, and certain to vanish when they appeared. It was this lack of food, rather than the guns of the whites, which oftenest compelled besieging Indians to retire and saved the garrison. When, however, several hundred savages would attack a fort containing not a tenth of their own number of fighting men, and, failing to take it promptly, would retire, the white defenders were apt to think highly of their own prowess and belittle that of their foes. Because the Indians loved the sport and plunder of offensive war and planned to strike only a weaker enemy, they were usually ready to be led on forays, however distant, if they felt that their homes were left safe. It was there that they were vulnerable, for they dreaded to leave their wives, children, and old people, and their food crops, liable to destruction by an enemy. While a foe was within striking distance of their towns they could seldom be induced to go far from them.[1]

The Indians were unfamiliar with cannon, and greatly feared them because of the great noise they made and the havoc they sometimes caused.

[1] It is quite usual to attribute great superiority in courage and military skill to certain Indian nations because they fought more successfully or with more determination than others; when in truth they were simply better supplied with arms and ammunition, or had stronger motives for fighting. Those with whom the early seaboard colonists came into conflict had nothing better than bow and arrow with which to meet the powder and ball of the whites. During the Revolution, although all the tribes used firearms, some were much better equipped than others. Thus the northwestern Indians were usually well supplied from the many British posts near them; those near the Mississippi trade routes were also; but the Cherokees and Creeks, being far removed from their white allies, were very ill furnished. This, far more than any inferiority in warlike qualities, explains the fact that, excepting the Chickasaws living by the Mississippi, the southern Indians carried on a much less vigorous warfare during

At the time of the Indian outbreak, in 1774, western Pennsylvania, it should be understood, was claimed and governed by Virginia, [1] and on May 14th Lord Dunmore appointed Clark 'Captain of the Militia of Pittsburg and its Dependencies.' [2] What led to this appointment is unknown. *Cresap's War* and *McDonald's Expedition* against the Shawnees followed, and Clark took part in both; but neither was more than a minor incident preliminary to *Dunmore's War*. *Cresap's War* owes its place in history almost entirely to the Mingo chief, Logan, and his famous speech. He was a noble example of Indian manhood — dignified, brave, and kindly. Even at the risk of being thought unfaithful to his own race, he had always been friendly toward the white people, and had used his influence with the tribes to preserve peace. While surveying, Clark became well acquainted with him, and evidently respected him highly. Across the Ohio from Logan's hunting camp was the trading house of a border ruffian named Greathouse; and one day, while all Logan's near relatives, including his father, brother, and sister, were making a friendly visit there, they were murdered in cold blood. The fury of Logan was mighty. From a true friend of the whites, he became their dreaded scourge; half civilized before, he became the blood-thirsty savage, demanding ten lives for one, until a long string of gory scalps hung from his belt. Then he said he was satisfied. [3]

By autumn the Indian war assumed much larger proportions. Under Dunmore's order, General Andrew Lewis marched with some eleven hundred frontiersmen against the Shawnees and their allies, and, on October 6th, camped

---

the Revolution than the tribes north of the Ohio.

Again, the success of particular tribes of Indians in war depended very much on the fighting qualities of the whites who opposed them; and in this respect the whites of different sections varied greatly. Thus, in the pioneers of the Ohio Valley, during the Revolution, the Indians found foes who had lived with their rifles from boyhood and were almost as expert in forest warfare as themselves; whereas the Six Nation Iroquois, in their destructive raids in New York and Pennsylvania, fell upon a population comparatively ignorant of Indian warfare and much more easily slaughtered.

[1] Crumrine's *Old Virginia Court House at Augusta Town;* Lord Dartmouth to Dunmore, June 1, 1774, *British Museum MSS.*

[2] A facsimile of the commission appears in Thwaites and Kellogg's *Dunmore's War*, 156.

[3] Judge Henry Jolly, an eye witness, said 'that this same Logan, who a few days before was so pacific, raised the hatchet, with a declaration, that he will not Ground it, untill he has taken ten for one, which I believe he completely fulfilled, by taking thirty scalps and prisoners in the sumer of '74.' (*Dunmore's War,* 13.)

on a point of land, called Point Pleasant, at the junction of the Kanawha and Ohio. Meantime, Dunmore, accompanied by Clark, was marching another army, by a more northerly route, into the enemy's country, where it was planned that Lewis should join him. The Shawnee chief, Cornstalk, resolved to strike Lewis before his junction with Dunmore. With some six hundred warriors he crossed the Ohio a short distance above the camp, and formed a battle line from river to river. Early next morning he skillfully decoyed nearly half the whites out of their camp and within a few minutes killed the two commanding colonels, four captains, and about forty other men, and wounded many more. More of the whites then joining their comrades, the battle continued until sunset. In the night Cornstalk withdrew across the Ohio, leaving not a single Indian prisoner or corpse.[1] It was perhaps the greatest and, on the part of the Indians, the best-planned and best-conducted battle that had ever occurred between the red men and white. Although often extolled as a great victory for the Virginians, they were in fact out-generaled, outfought, and nearly crushed by an inferior force.

Cornstalk, foiled in his attempt to destroy one army, saw it would be useless to fight two, and therefore concluded to make a treaty of peace with Lord Dunmore before Lewis could join him. Logan was invited to the treaty meeting, but would not attend. Clark, who was present, afterward said: 'I was acquainted with him and wished to know the reason. The answer was that "he was like a mad dog, his bristles had been up and were not quite fallen, but the good talk now going on might allay them."' It was then that Logan sent Dunmore his famous speech (given below [2]), which has

---

[1] For details see varying reports in *Dunmore's War*, 253–344. That of Floyd (266) was probably the most reliable.

[2] 'I appeal to any white man to say if he ever entered Logan's cabin hungry and he gave him no meat; if he ever came cold and naked and he clothed him not. During the course of the last long and bloody war, Logan remained idle in his cabin and was an advocate of peace. Such was my love for the whites that my countrymen pointed as they passed and said "Logan is the friend of the white man." I had even thought to have lived with you, but for the injuries of one man.

Col. Cresap, the last spring, in cold blood and unprovoked, murdered all the relatives of Logan. This called on me for revenge. I have sought it. I have killed many. I have fully glutted my vengeance. For my country I rejoice at the beams of peace, but do not harbor the thought that mine is the joy of fear. Logan never felt fear. He will not turn on his heel to save his life. Who is there to mourn for Logan? Not one!' Jefferson, in his *Notes of Virginia*, says: 'I may challenge the whole orations of Demosthenes and Cicero, to produce a single passage superior to the speech of Logan, a Mingo chief, to Lord Dunmore.'

been declared the most eloquent and pathetic ever made by an Indian. By their treaty with Dunmore the Shawnees yielded all claim to lands south of the Ohio, agreed not to go there; and, as security for their good faith, delivered hostages to Dunmore, Cornstalk himself being one.[1]

Peace now seeming assured, the next year, 1775, opened with bright prospects for western settlement, and many who had fled from their homes the year before now returned. The chief immigration was to Kentucky, which was the El Dorado of that day. A prominent Virginia divine wrote: 'What a Buzzel is this, amongst the People, about Kentucky? To hear people speak of it, one would think it was a new found Paradise, and I doubt not, if such a place as you represented, but Ministers will lose their congregations. But why need I fear that? Ministers are movable goods as well as others and stand [as much] in need of good land as any do, for they are bad farmers.' [2] In the bottom lands on the Monongahela, Kanawha, and other tributaries of the upper Ohio, axemen were busily felling great trees and making flatboats and 'dugout' canoes to carry intending settlers and land traders to Kentucky. James Harrod reformed his party of the year before and, with about fifty others, returned to Harrodsburg. In March they completed their log cabins and fort, and established the first settlement in Kentucky.[3]

While their work at Harrodsburg was going on, a meeting which was to concern them greatly was held on the Holston River. At this meeting a group of North Carolina men, headed by Colonel Richard Henderson and commonly called Henderson & Company, got from the Cherokees a land grant covering all of Kentucky and Tennessee between the Kentucky

---

[1] Cornstalk soon escaped. Draper says he gave many proofs of his desire to maintain peace with the Americans during the Revolution, and went to Pittsburg as a mediator; but he was killed there by lawless American soldiers.

[2] Thwaites and Kellogg's *Revolution on the Upper Ohio*, 10.

[3] A persistent popular belief attributes to Daniel Boone not only the first settlement of Kentucky, but its first exploration, and the leadership of the pioneers there in war. In fact, the region was partially explored by Doctor Thomas

Walker for a Virginia land company in 1750 — nineteen years before Boone entered it for the first time on one of his trapping trips. Many others preceded Boone, who was unexcelled as a hunter and woodsman, and was a skillful small-scale Indian fighter, but was always in secondary or lower military position and took no noteworthy part either in planning or executing any important military movement. His fame is mainly due to the first Kentucky historian, John Filson, who, following the custom of writers of his time, made Boone's career as romantic and heroic as he could.

and Cumberland Rivers. They named the region 'Transylvania,' and sent Boone with a party of axemen to open a pack-horse road from Cumberland Gap, at the southeast corner of Kentucky, to a point on the south side of the Kentucky River, where they built a fort and founded a town which they called Boonesborough. In part Boone's road — now famous as the 'Wilderness Road' — followed a 'buffalo trace,' which was a path trampled by herds of buffalo in their yearly migrations between Kentucky and the Valley of East Tennessee.[1]

Henderson himself soon followed Boone to organize a proprietary government over Transylvania and sell its lands. On his arrival he found Harrod's party occupying and claiming to own a considerable part of the country under the laws of Virginia. Not without cause, he feared they would oppose his company's claim of ownership; for they were sturdy men, not likely to surrender claims of their own which they considered just and could maintain by force of arms. The Colonel was an interesting character, amusingly pompous, but withal a worthy man. Born in Virginia, he was taken while young to North Carolina, where he rose to be an associate judge of the Superior Court. During what he called his 'Expedition to Caintuckey,' he kept a journal which is not only interesting, but gives the best contemporary account we have of the conditions and men Clark met in that remote country.[2] A few quotations from the journal will therefore be given here, beginning when Henderson started on his journey:

'March 20, 1775. Having finished my treaty with the Indians at Wataugah, set out for Louisa, [a name sometimes given the Kentucky River.]

'April 7th. ...Five persons killed on this road to Caintuckee by Indians, and Capt. Hart, upon receipt of this news, retreated back with company & determined to settle in the valley to make corn for the Cantuckey people. The same day received word from Dan Boone that his Company was fired uppon by Indians. Killed two of his men, tho he kept the ground & saved the baggage. ...

'18th. Campt...in the eye of the rich land.

[1] The criss-cross of buffalo traces in the American wilderness made 'war-roads' for the Indians long before the invasion of their lands by the whites. The grades were so well chosen by those animals, and their lines of travel so well rid of underbrush, that the traces were not only used by the pioneers for pack-horse trails, but are said to be in some places now used for wagon roads and even railways.

[2] Collins's *History of Kentucky*, II, 498, and *Draper MSS.* (holograph) 1 C.C. 21.

'20th. Arrived at Fort Boone, ...Kentucky River, where we were Saluted by a running fire of about 25 guns, all that was then at fort.

'Saturday 22nd. Finished running off all the lots we could, ... to wit 54. gave notice of our intention of having them drawn for in the evening; but as Mr. Robt. McAfee, his brother, Sam¹, & some more were not satisfied whether they would draw or not, wanting to go down the river about 50 miles near Capt. Harrod's settlement, where they had begun improvements and left them on the late alarm, &c, and being informed by myself, in hearing of all attending, that such settlements should not entitle them to lands from us, and appearing concerned and at a loss what to do, ...the lottery was deferred til next morning, sunrise, thereby giving them time to come to a resolution.

'Sunday 23. draw'd lots &c Spent the day without public worship.

'Monday 24. Imploy'd in viewing the respective lots and endeavoring to satisfie the drawers by exchanging [lots] of my own and those over whom, of our company, I had influence. [For nine days more the Colonel was busy trying to please all the settlers with their lots.]

'May 3d, ...Capt. John Floyd arrived...from a camp on Dick's River, where he had left about 30 men of his company from Virginia, and said he was sent by them to know on what terms they might settle on our lands. ...Was much at a loss on account of this gents arrival and message, as he was surveyor of Fincastle under Col. Preston, a man who has exerted himself against us. ...This man appeared to have a great share of modesty, an honest, open countenance, and no small share of good sense, and, petitioning in behalf of his whole company [including] Mr. Dandridge...of Virg-[inia] and one Mr. Todd, two gents of the law, ...and several other young gents of good families, we thought it most advisable to secure them to our interest if possible and not show the least distrust of the intentions of Capt. Floyd, on whom we intend to keep a very strict watch. Accordingly...promised them land and 1000 acres to the principal gents. ...this we would not have done but for scarcity of men and the doubt with respect to the Virginians coming into our measure, acknowledging [our] title, &c. [Floyd — a most capable and lovable young gentleman — was to be gloriously identified with Kentucky and die, a hero, defending it — a very Bayard of the west.]

'We restrained these men to...make choice of any lands not before marked by...a certain Harrod and his men, who were settled somewhere abt 50 miles west of us, ...and of whom we could form no conjecture; but thought it best to prevent any interruption to him or his men 'til we should [learn] what he intended with respect to us and our titles. [Henderson's troubles were beginning, and he was in mortal dread of the outnumbering Virginians in Harrod's settlement. His Journal account of his interview with Harrod is both amusing and pathetic.]

'Tuesday 9th. ...Our game soon, — nay as soon as we got here if not before — was drove very much. 15 or 20 miles was as short a distance as good hunters thought of getting meat. Nay sometimes they were obliged to go thirty, tho' by chance, once or twice a week, buffalo was killed within 5 or six miles. [Here was a real danger facing all the settlers. Game was their main food and essential to their very existence. When Indians forced them into crowded forts it became almost impossible to kill enough game, and starvation nearly caused Kentucky to be abandoned. Henderson's next entry is suggestive:]

'Saturday 12. No washing here on this day. No scowering of floors, sweeping of yards, or scalding of bedsteads.

'Sunday 14. No divine service, our Church not being finished. About 50 yards from the river behind my camp and a fine spring a little to the west, stands one of the finest elms that perhaps nature has ever produced. The tree is produced on a beautiful plain, surrounded by a turf of fine white clover, forming a green to the very stock. The trunk is about 4 feet through to the first branches, which are about 9 feet from the ground. From thence it regularly extends its large branches on every side at such equal distances as to form the most beautiful tree the imagination can suggest. The diameter of the branches from the extreme ends is 100 feet; and every fair day it describes a semicircle on the heavenly green around it of upwards of 400 feet in circuit. At any time between the hours of 10 and 2, 100 persons may commodiously seat themselves under the branches.

'This Divine tree, or rather one of the many proofs of the Existence from all eternity of its Divine Author, we came in time enough to redeem from destruction. This same tree is to be our Church, State House, Council Chamber. Having many things on our hands have not had time to erect a pulpit, seats, &c., but hope by Sunday to perform divine service for the first time in a public manner, and that to a set of scoundrels who scarcely believe in God or fear a Devil, if we were to judge from most of their looks, words, and actions.'

[When the myriads of fine trees in the wilderness were generally thought mere hindrances to land cultivation and fit only to be burned, every nature-lover will respect the harassed Colonel who could so appreciate this noble specimen. His severe judgment of the other pioneers, however, must be taken with much allowance for prejudice; for he looked on them as enemies of his company. None of them, nor perhaps even the pompous Colonel himself, presented a particularly pleasing personal appearance after weeks of travel and wilderness life; but many of them were venturesome young men of social position at least equal to his own. Probably they had no liking for his assumption of proprietorship, and were not averse to defying his pretensions, or having fun at his expense. Some of them later proved to be men of decided merit and won high repute.]

'Monday 15th. ...arrived here 10 men,...eight from Dunmore [County, Va.] Major Bowman, Capt. Bowman & one Capt Moore were the principal men.' [The two Bowmans were to play prominent parts in the coming war.]

On May 25th, the Transylvania Assembly, or 'Convention,' met, with Colonel Henderson as master of ceremonies, and with great formality elected a chairman and passed abortive laws to establish courts, organize a militia, regulate fees, and protect game. Next day Henderson's diary says: 'Finished Convention — everybody pleased,' [but everybody did not long remain pleased, as his later entries show:]

'June 3d. People arrived from St. Asaph; had wantonly broke up, hid their tools and on their way home.
'6th. Abundance of people going away, selling their lots and will not be detained.' [On the 7th. news arrived of the 'Battle of Boston,' and the Revolution had begun.] '12th. The people going away.' '17th. a muster at the fort. ...32 men appeared under arms — in bad order.'

Henderson soon found that his company could not impose its proprietary government on the Kentucky pioneers, and he returned to North Carolina, a sadly disappointed man. His next efforts were to prevent Virginia from asserting jurisdiction over Kentucky. In this, too, it will be found he was unsuccessful. In pioneer parlance, his great Transylvania land scheme proved a mere 'flash in the pan.' [1]

While Boone was clearing his Wilderness Road, George Rogers Clark, as deputy of Colonel Hancock Lee, Washington's successor as chief surveyor for the Ohio Company, was on his way to central Kentucky. His salary was only eighty

---

[1] In 1775 Governor Dunmore by proclamation declared Henderson & Company's claim to Kentucky void, and prohibited settlement under it. Next year Virginia's new state government also repudiated the claim. Some years later it was induced to grant the company land in western Kentucky to compensate for its outlays.

In a recent work by one of his descendants, Henderson is absurdly represented as the great leader of western development. Aside from founding the valuable outpost of Boonesboro, about all he really accomplished in Kentucky was to arouse Virginia's opposition to the Transylvania scheme and expedite her assertion of jurisdiction.

pounds a year, but he was given the far more valuable privilege of taking what lands he wanted for himself. All that is known of his journey appears in the interesting Journal of Nicholas Cresswell, an intelligent, educated and observant young Englishman.[1] Cresswell and six others, with two servants, were going down the Ohio in two canoes when Clark joined them on his way to meet Colonel Lee in Kentucky. In the party, said Cresswell, were

'Mr James Nourse, an English gentleman going down to the Kentucky River to take up land in the right of his brother who is an officer in the British Navy, Mr. Benjamin Johnston and Captain Taylor who are going to take up land on the Kentucky River...George Rice and Captⁿ Taylor's brother. ...May 4th. ... Fort Fincastle [Wheeling] we took into our company Captain George Clark. [Next day at Grave Creek, where Clark had been living, they visited the Indian mounds — a subject in which he was throughout life interested.] May 7th This morning Captn Clark (who I find is an intelligent man) showed me a root that the Indians call pocoon, good for the bite of a rattle snake. The root is to be mashed and applied to the wound, and a decoction made of the leaves which the patients drink. The roots are exceedingly red; the Indians use it to paint themselves with sometimes.'
[Reports came of Indian hostilities and Cresswell says:] 'May 10th ...held a council whether we should proceed or turn back. After much altercation our company determined to persevere, tho' I believe they are a set of Damned cowards. [They knew much more about the danger from Indians than Cresswell.] May 14th ...Mr Edmund Taylor and I entered into a discourse on politics which ended in high words. Taylor threatened to tar and feather me. Obliged to pocket the offense. Find I shall be torified if I hold any further confab with these red-hot liberty men. (Mem. Taylor's usage to be remembered.) May 24th. ...Captn. Michael Cresop met us, informed us it is 100 Miles to Harwood's Landing the place our company intends to take up land. No danger of the Indians. Captn. Clark left us and went with Captn. Cresop. Clark always behaved well while he stayed with us.'

Soon after this the Lee and Clark party laid out a town called Leesburg, in the outskirts of what is now Frankfort, and there Clark wrote in July a cheery letter to his brother Jonathan, saying: 'We have laid out a town [Leesburg] seventy miles up the Kentucky, where I intend to live and I don't doubt but there will be fifty families living in it by Christmas. ...A richer and more beautiful country than this, I believe

[1] *The Journal of Nicholas Cresswell* (Dial Press, New York, 1924), 71-2, 78.

has never been seen in America yet. Col. Henderson is here and claims all ye country below Kentucky [River]. If his claims should be good, land may be got reasonable enough, and as good as any in the world. My father talked of seeing this land in August. I shall not advise him whether to come or not, but I am convinced that if he once sees ye country, he never will rest satisfied untill he gets in it to live. I am engrossing all ye land I possibly can, expecting him.'[1] The young captain had again become a man of business and, like nearly every one in the western country, was deeply engaged in the 'land trade,' as the taking up, buying, selling, and swapping of lands was commonly called. The French and Pennsylvanians were fur traders; but amongst the Virginians trade largely centered in wild lands. Clark, being an active surveyor, and one of the earliest on the ground, was able to take up many large and choice tracts which seemed likely to become of great value.[2] He was thought to be, and he considered himself, a rich man; but war soon proved that his wealth lay mainly in great expectations.

The doubt which he expressed about the validity of Henderson & Company's claim to a large part of Kentucky suggests that no man really knew who owned any part of it. It seemed a veritable 'no-man's land.' Under her charter Virginia claimed it; the King claimed it;[3] Spain claimed it; the Cherokees claimed it; and, by purchase from them, Henderson & Company claimed about half of it. Nor were these all the claimants. The promoters of two interlocked syndicates of northern land speculators, known as the 'Indiana' and 'Vandalia' Companies, claimed all of West Virginia and eastern Kentucky. Their claims were based on the most audacious

---

[1] *Illinois Historical Collections*, VIII, 9.

[2] One tract of 1400 acres contained a valuable salt 'lick,' where salt was made during the Revolution. (*Certificate Book*, Commission appointed on Kentucky land claims, *Register of Kentucky State Historical Society*, XXI, 52, giving Clark's certificate.) Salt was hardly less essential than game for the settlers' food supply, being necessary to preserve meat for winter use. It was exceedingly scarce, but fortunately the pioneers found several salt licks where men would go in parties, with pans or 'kittles,' and laboriously boil the water for salt.

[3] The claim of George III to personal ownership of the ungranted lands west of the Alleghenies — commonly called 'waste lands' — raised in America the old British issue between royal prerogative and popular rights. The revolting American colonists all denied his personal ownership of such lands and also his authority to deprive them of their territorial or other rights. This denial was the theoretical justification of the Revolution, yet was often forgotten in the angry dispute which arose between the states themselves over the western lands.

and powerfully supported fraud in all American history.[1] At this point it must suffice to say that, some years before the Revolution, the promoters set up a pretended title to West Virginia and eastern Kentucky under deeds from the Six Nation Iroquois Indians of central New York, claiming that those savages had conquered and could lawfully convey the whole region. In truth the Iroquois never owned a foot of the territory they were induced to claim and pretend to convey. Their alleged conquest was a fiction invented over fifty years earlier by British officials to support Great Britain's claim to the Mississippi Valley against France. Alleging that the Iroquois were subjects of their King, London diplomatists and map-makers, royal governors of New York, and others conspired to magnify the domain of those savages in order to claim it as British territory. As Parkman said: 'The English laid claim to every mountain, forest, or prairie where an Iroquois had taken a scalp.'[2] They claimed much more. The British Board of Trade, having charge of colonial affairs, even had the temerity to assert that, in some remote and unspecified past, the Iroquois had conquered all the resident tribes and owned all the lands of a vast region extending from New York to the Gulf of Mexico, to the Pacific, and even to the 'Northwest Passage,' wherever that might be![3]

To carry through their scheme, the promoters bribed the King's Superintendent of Indian Affairs north of the Ohio, Sir William Johnson, by giving him a large interest. In London they employed the most influential political corruptionists of the time, and by gifts of shares in their company bought the support of many of the most eminent officials of the British Government — department secretaries, noblemen, the King's Lord Chamberlain, even a Prime Minister, even the Lord High Chancellor of England![4] The scheme was almost consumated when the outbreak of the Revolution fortunately

[1] Detailed accounts of it will appear in the author's *History of the Revolutionary West in Diplomacy and Politics*, in preparation, and in his *History of Kentucky*, Volume I, to be issued by S. J. Clarke Publishing Company, Chicago.

[2] *Montcalm and Wolfe*, I, 125.

[3] To win the King's approval of their pretended title, the promoters got the Iroquois chiefs to tempt him with a gift (subject to their previous grant to the companies) of all West Virginia, nearly all Kentucky, and the best part of Tennessee. The King accepted the gift, although by doing so he ignored the charter titles of Virginia and North Carolina and broke faith with the Cherokees, whose 'Indian title' to the region and peaceful possession he had just before solemnly guaranteed by treaty with them.

[4] See Alvord's *Mississippi Valley in British Politics.*

ended the King's power over the colonies and made any land grants by him in America worthless.

The promoters then transferred their activities from London to Philadelphia, where they endeavored to get their pretended Indian title confirmed by the Continental Congress. In that body they wielded a sinister influence which nearly disrupted the Confederation. During the first six of the eight years of the Revolution they, and states coöperating with them in disputing Virginia's western claims, prevented the adoption of any Articles of Confederation, and almost caused the loss of the war for independence. Throughout the Revolution the promoters contested Virginia's jurisdiction west of the Alleghenies, and had emissaries there stirring up opposition to her government. More perhaps than all Great Britain's troops and Indian allies, these 'land jobbers,' as Madison called them, hampered our efforts to win the western country.[1] In short, they played a tremendously important part, not only in the history of the Revolutionary West, but in moulding the destiny of our nation. Yet, although their baneful activities in *British* politics have been pretty thoroughly ventilated,[2] their infinitely more important influence in *American* politics, and on the war for independence, has never been more than superficially noticed in Revolutionary history. One popular but uninformed writer even declared it a 'waste of time' to investigate the doings of these land companies![3]

During the Revolution, states north of Virginia disputed her claim to territory west of the Alleghenies. Having themselves no charter claims to the western country, they contended that if the British were driven out it would be only by the 'joint effort, blood and treasure' of all the states, and therefore the whole region should be the common property of all.[4] Legally this contention was untenable, yet strong arguments were made in support of it, based on other than legal grounds. Virginia's charter claim was said to give her only one of those

[1] Clark, who knew, so declared after the war. That he was right will appear later.

[2] *Mississippi Valley in British Politics,* by C. W. Alvord; Carter's *Great Britain and Illinois.*

[3] Roosevelt's *Winning of the West,* II, 172. As Professor Alvord says, Roosevelt, brilliant writer though he was, merely 'dabbled' in western history. In that field he was truly a 'rough rider,' galloping recklessly over rich mines of source materials utterly unconscious of what was in them.

[4] The unsubstantial nature of the claims of Massachusetts and Connecticut will be fully discussed in the author's *Revolutionary West, ante* note I, p 22.

technical rights which, as Edmund Burke said, may become
'the most odious of all wrongs and the most vexatious of all
injustice.' If she were permitted to control so great a country,
people in other states feared she would become a worse op-
pressor than the British King. This, as well as their desire
for shares of the rich lands, led these northern states to com-
bat her western charter claims and urge Congress to appropriate the whole trans-Allegheny region as the common property
of all the states. In this contention they were encouraged and
strongly supported by the land company promoters, who confidently looked to Congress to confirm their fictitious Indian title.

In view of all these conflicting claims to Kentucky, the
Virginians there were uneasy about their land titles, and at
sea about the proper course to secure them. Soon after Henderson left, eighty-four of them petitioned the Revolutionary
Convention, then governing Virginia, to take them under its
protection; but they evidently doubted whether the country
belonged to Virginia, or the King, or the land companies,
or Congress. Their petition said: 'If your honors apprehend
that our case comes more properly before the honorable the
General Congress, . . . in your goodness, recommend the same
to your worthy delegates to espouse it as the cause of the
Colony.' [1] But the convention paid no attention to such
petitions, for it was too deeply immersed in other problems
to consider the state's claim to Kentucky. Clark, convinced
that some way out of the complex of conflicting claims must
be found, set out in the autumn of 1775 for eastern Virginia
to learn the attitude of those in authority concerning the subject. For some months he pursued his inquiries — no doubt
with the aid of his friends Mason and Jefferson and his
brother Jonathan, who were all members of the convention.

Up to this time, although half a year had passed since
the Kentucky settlers learned of the battle of Lexington, their
trading and home building had gone on as usual, for so far
there had been no general war in the west. Both sides still
hoped for reconciliation, and neither inclined to adopt the
bloody methods which afterward prevailed. But the obstinate British King and Ministry were fast driving the colonists to assert their independence, and by the next year the
war broke out everywhere in full fury.

[1] *Virginia State Library*, B 938; cf. *Kentucky Petitions;* Perkins's *Western Annals*,
158; Collins's *Kentucky*, II, 510.

CHAPTER III

THE REVOLUTION BEGINS:
KENTUCKY MADE A COUNTY

A GLANCE at a map of the United States will show that the British had three main ways of attacking the Americans. The first was by landing their troops at Atlantic seaports. The second was to cut off New England from the other states, as Burgoyne tried to do, by seizing the routes from Canada to New York City, along the line of Lake Champlain and the Hudson River. The third way was for the British to lead their western Indian allies to destroy the settlements along the frontiers from Pennsylvania to Georgia. How vulnerable the confederated states were in that direction, British military leaders saw better, perhaps, than many of ours, and certainly much more clearly than the many historians of the war who have seemed to think there was no war worth mentioning save along the Atlantic seaboard and the northern frontiers of New England and New York.

In truth the western frontiers played a vitally important part in the general struggle for independence. As Professor Frederick Turner first clearly pointed out,[1] they furnished Washington with many of his best fighting men. The invaluable services of the frontier riflemen in three of the most decisive battles in the eastern war — Saratoga, King's Mountain, and Cowpens — are well known. Nor were the western frontiers only the breeding ground of fighting men. With their virgin soil and abundant mast and grasses, they made a great stock range during the Revolutionary era. Their droves of cattle, sheep, and swine, and their pack-horse trains of grain sometimes largely fed the eastern armies; for, when roads were few and indescribably bad, those animals could be driven great distances and could find forage on the way. Had the half-starved eastern armies depended on wagon trains for their food supply, they would probably have been forced to disband, as Washington constantly feared, long be-

[1] *Proceedings Wisconsin Historical Society*, Dec. 14, 1893; *The Frontier in American History*. (Holt, 1920.)

fore the war was won. If the western Indians had not been kept engaged in their own country, but left free to ravage the scattered frontiers, Washington's frontier riflemen would inevitably have left him to protect their homes and families, and the flow of frontier supplies been stopped. Remembering how long doubtful was the issue of the eastern conflict, one can realize how disastrous would have been the loss to the eastern armies of those valuable men and supplies.

The British ministry, with the King's express approval, deliberately employed the Indians to destroy those frontiers. The willing agent for conducting this ruthless war was Colonel Henry Hamilton, Lieutenant-Governor of the western British possessions, with headquarters at Detroit. An experienced soldier, he was not only given a free hand in military affairs, but was supplied with what were then considered enormous funds for buying the support of the Indians and carrying on the war.[1] At Detroit were over two thousand people, mainly French, and a varying military force of militia and British regulars, numbering at the most critical time over eight hundred men.[2] Throughout the war Detroit was the western center of British trade and military operations. Its geographical position made it so. (See map facing page 25.) It not only controlled the important lake transportation, but was also convenient to the cross-country trade and war routes from the western end of Lake Erie to the Ohio and Mississippi. By these routes it carried on a thriving trade with Vincennes, the Illinois towns, and New Orleans. To Detroit went thousands of Indians for food, blankets, guns, powder, lead, tomahawks, and scalping knives; and thence Hamilton directed his subordinate commandants at Mackinac, at Vincennes on the Wabash, at Kaskaskia and Cahokia in Illinois, and his white 'Indian agents' at many Indian towns.[3]

Estimates of Indian numbers have varied so widely that it is impossible to say what they were; but the tribes north of the Ohio, which engaged in the war at one time or another,

[1] Sir Guy Carleton, the commander-in-chief in Canada, wrote him in September, 1777: 'The conduct of the [western] war has been taken entirely out of my hands, and the management of it upon your frontier been assigned to you, as you will have seen by a letter from Lord George [Germaine], a copy of which I sent you.' Michigan *Pioneer Collections*, IX, 351.

[2] *Hamilton's Report*, holograph diary, British Museum, Add. 24320 f., 1-6.

[3] Amongst them were the towns of the Miamis (Fort Wayne), the Ouiatenans (Lafayette), the Pottawatomies (St. Joseph, Mich.), and the Hurons (Sandusky).

numbered perhaps eight or ten thousand warriors.[1] The southern Indians were still more numerous; but, being cut off from British support, ill supplied with guns and ammunition, and less pressed upon by white settlements, they were much less active in the war than the tribes north of the Ohio.

In all the states men foresaw the terrible character of the coming storm and tried to prepare for it. Nowhere else perhaps was the need for preparation so great as in the settlements of Kentucky. Set far out 'like an island in the wilderness' — a two hundred mile over-mountain journey from their nearest frontier neighbors on the Holston — they seemed doomed. Many thought the founding of the far-away settlements folly, and predicted their early abandonment; many deserted them. The number that remained is unknown; but whereas in 1775 there was a great inflow of people to Kentucky, the next year there was a much more rapid outflow. Few save sturdy men were left. In this extremity two things were essential to the very existence of the little band of settlers — a recognized government with military organization, and a capable leader. The leader they found in George Rogers Clark.

In view of the greater age and experience of other pioneers — such as Harrod, Boone, Logan, and Kenton — the choice of one so young as Clark has excited wonder; but the explanation does not seem difficult. In a remote community battling for existence, a man's worth is soon known. These older men were noted for bravery and personal exploits, but none of them appears to have possessed the breadth of information, the intelligence, or the elevation of bearing that go far to impress even the commoner class of pioneers and make the accepted leader. Clark, from all accounts, had not only the best qualities of the pioneer, but his person was commanding, his manner engaging, he was an interesting talker, and besides had a natural dignity which commanded respect. Naturally lively and witty, his usual manner, after he be-

---

[1] How impossible is a reliable estimate will be seen by comparing the numbers given by different writers, varying all the way from four or five thousand to over sixty thousand. Winsor's *Western Movement* (88) roughly estimates about 20,000 warriors east of the Mississippi and north of the Ohio. The *Critical and Narrative History* (VI, 650 *et seq.*) gives many estimates, including Bancroft's of 180,000 east of the Mississippi and south of the Great Lakes. Jefferson's *Notes on Virginia* (151–55) gives varying lists based on early reports from George Croghan and others, but they were evidently mere guesses. See also Dalton's list in 1783. (*Pennsylvania Packet*, August 12, 1783, and *Draper MSS.* 32 J 118.)

came burdened with war responsibilities, was calm and reserved. A Kentucky contemporary said: 'His appearance, well calculated to attract attention, was rendered particularly agreeable by the manliness of his deportment and the intelligence of his conversation.' [1]

First among the pioneers, Clark seems to have appreciated the vital need for promptly securing for Kentucky a government with military authority and an organized militia. As things were, concert of action against the enemy was entirely a matter of individual choice. Whether a settler would join a scouting party, or stand guard, or contribute his share of work or provisions, he determined for himself; for, there being no government, no man could be compelled to do his duty. The situation was intolerable; it threatened the loss of the country and the lives of all. To meet it the settlers had choice of four courses: (1), they could declare themselves British subjects and perhaps thus at once win safety, but this course they showed no inclination at any time to consider; (2) they could acknowledge Henderson & Company as proprietors, but this they were no more disposed to do; (3) they could appeal to Virginia to take them under her protection and give them a county government and representation in her assembly, but in view of the adverse claims of other states and the land companies, Virginia feared to assert her ownership of Kentucky; (4) lastly, they could set up an independent state of their own and ask admission to the Confederation.

To these problems Clark devoted much thought. He said:

'It was at this period [1775] that I first had thought of paying some attention to the interest of this country. The proprietors [Henderson & Company] at first took great pains to ingratiate themselves in the favour of the people, but, too soon for their interest, began to raise [the price] on their lands, which caused many to complain. A few gentlemen made some attempts to persuade the people to pay no attention to them. I plainly saw that they would work their own ruin, as the greatest security they had for the country would be that of making it to the interest of the people to support their claim, and that by their conduct this would be the moment to overset them.

'I left the country in the fall, 1775, and returned the spring following. While in Virginia I found there was various opinions re-

[1] Marshall's *Kentucky*, i, 49. As the Reverend Mr. Jones described him, so he evidently was, 'a young gentleman,' courteous and self-respecting. One can- not read his many extant letters and the letters of his contemporaries mentioning him without being impressed with this fact.

specting Henderson's claim. Many thought it good, others doubted whether or not Virginia could, with propriety have any pretensions to the country. This was what I wanted to know. I immediately fixed my plan, — that of assembling the people, get them to elect deputies, and send them to the Assembly of Virginia, and treat with them respecting the country. If valuable conditions was procured, to declare ourselves citizens of the state, — otherwise establish an independent government, and, by giving away a great part of the lands and disposing of the remainder otherwise, we could not only gain great numbers of inhabitants, but in good measure protect them.[1]

'To carry this scheme into effect, I appointed a general meeting at Harrodstown, on the 6th of June, '76, [giving notice] that something would be proposed to the people that very much concerned their interest. The reason I had for not publishing what I wished to be done, before the day, was that the people should not get into parties on the subject; and, as everyone would wish to know what was to be done, there would be a more general meeting. But, unfortunately, it was late in the evening of the day, before I could get to the place. The people had been in some confusion, but at last concluded that the whole design was to send delegates to the assembly of Virginia with a petition praying the assembly to accept of them as such, to establish a new county, &c. The polls were opened and, before I arrived, [they had] far advanced in the election, and had entered with [such spirit] into it that I could not get them to change the principle — that of delegates with petitions, to that of deputies under the authority of the people. In short I did not take much pains. [Clark's reason for wishing to send deputies, rather than delegates, to the Assembly was that deputies would be diplomatic agents of the Kentucky people, empowered to negotiate with Virginia for satisfactory terms before acknowledging her jurisdiction.] Mr. John Gabriel Jones and myself was elected, the papers prepared, and...in a few days we set out for Williamsburgh, in hopes [of] arriving before the [convention] then sitting, should arise.'

The papers which the two young delegates carried to the Assembly were petitions of the settlers denying Henderson & Company's proprietary claims, and praying for a county government and to be taken under Virginia's protection. Before they arrived at the capital, however, they learned that the convention had adjourned and the Assembly would not meet until October.

[1] What might have resulted had the Kentucky settlers failed to procure such terms and had set up an independent government can only be surmised. Quite likely, as he said, 'by giving away a great part of the lands and disposing of the remainder,' they 'could not only gain great numbers of inhabitants, but in good measure protect them.' Such action on their part, however, might well have led Virginia to abandon her claim to Kentucky, and thus changed the whole course of the nation's history.

'We were now' [says Clark] 'at a loss, for some time what [to do],
but concluded that we should wait until the fall session; in the meantime I should go to Williamsburg and attempt to procure some
powder for the Kentuckians and watch their interests. [Upon that
mission hung the existence of the Kentucky settlements, for powder
was then the scarcest essential of war and the Kentuckians had
almost none.[1]] We parted. Mr. Jones returned to Holston to join
the forces that were raising in order to repel the Cherokee Indians,
(as they had lately commenced hostilities) and myself proceeded to
the Governor of Virginia. Mr. Henry, the governor, lay sick at his
seat in Hanover, where I waited upon him. [Clark was then only
twenty-three years of age — Governor Henry much older and perhaps then the most eminent and influential man in Virginia. A
picture of the browned young pioneer stating the case of the Kentucky settlers to the famous apostle of liberty would be interesting.[2]]
He appeared much disposed to favor the Kentuckians and wrote
by me to the Council on the subject. I attended them. My application was for five hundred pounds of powder only, to be conveyed
to Kentucky as an immediate supply. After various questions and
consultations, the Council agreed to furnish the supply; but, as we
were a detached people and not yet united to the state of Virginia,
and it was uncertain, until the sitting of the assembly, whether we
should be or not, they would only lend us the ammunition as friends
in distress, but that I must become answerable for it in case the
assembly should not receive us as citizens of the state.

'I informed them that it was out of my power to pay the expense
of carriage and guards necessary for those supplies; that the British
officers on our frontiers were making use of every effort to engage
the Indians in war; that the people might be destroyed for want of
this small supply; and that I was in hopes they would consider these
matters, and favor us by sending the ammunition at public expense.
They replied that they were really disposed to do everything for
us in their power, consistent with their office, which I believed.
After making use of many arguments to convince me that even what
they proposed was a stretch of power, they informed me they could
go no further. An order was issued to the keeper of the magazine
to deliver me the ammunition.'[3]

Here was the great western land issue raised for Virginia
in a new and concrete form, and it required prompt and definite decision. The demand made by the young delegate upon
the eminent men of the governor's council really involved far

---

[1] After Clark and Jones left Kentucky,
so scarce was powder there that Logan
journeyed afoot some two hundred miles
over mountains to Holston to get what he
could carry back.

[2] The two were hardly strangers, how-

ever, for Mr. Henry had long been the
legal counsellor of Clark's father in an
old inherited land litigation. Jefferson
and John Randolph, the elder, were also
Mr. Clark's counsel in the litigation.

[3] *Illinois Historical Collections*, VIII.

more than five hundred pounds of powder; and both he and they knew this. It was a demand that they should, by overt act, commit Virginia to an assertion of her right to the western country within her charter bounds, against all other claimants — not only against Henderson & Company, but against the Indiana and Vandalia Companies and a northern majority of states in the Continental Congress.

On receiving the Council's *ultimatum*, most men, especially if young like Clark, would have given up further effort to convince them. Indeed, the position in which the council members were placed by his demand was a very delicate one. They probably constituted the proper department of government to determine the political question whether the state should assert her western jurisdiction, but they feared doing so would be considered a 'stretch of power' which would be severely condemned. To order the state's precious powder sent from the public magazine to the far-away settlers, *as Virginia's citizens*, was plainly to assert such jurisdiction over the country they occupied. Furthermore, the council members knew that the recently elected assembly would consider the same question, and naturally they hesitated to anticipate its decision. On the other hand, they must have feared to have Virginia lose the coveted region of Kentucky, and with it probably all the rest of her western charter territory. On that fear Clark promptly determined to play. He had been appointed by the Harrodsburg meeting of settlers only as their delegate to the Assembly; but he now resolved to usurp the character of deputy and in their behalf to treat with the state government for terms of union. How he did this his narrative tells:

'I had, for twelve months past, reflected so much on the various situation of things respecting ourselves [and] continent at large, that my resolution was formed before I left the Council Chamber. I resolved to return the order that I had received and immediately repair to Kentucky, knowing that the people would readily fall into my first plan, as what had passed had almost reduced it to a certainty of success. I wrote to the Council and enclosed the order, informing them that I had weighed the matter and found that it was out of my power to convey these stores, at my own expense, such a distance through an enemy's country; that I was sorry to find that we should have to seek protection elsewhere, which I did not doubt of getting; that if a country was not worth protecting, it was not worth claiming, &c, &c. [Here was his counter ultimatum.] What passed on the reception of this letter I cannot tell. [He says

he supposed it was 'what might be expected' from 'a set of gentlemen zealous in the welfare of their country and fully apprised of
what they might expect to take place at Kentucky.' [1]]
'I was sent for. ... Being a little prejudiced in favor of my mother country I was willing to meet [them] half way. Orders was immediately issued, dated Aug[t] 23[d], 1776, for the conveying those
stores to Pittsburg and there to wait further orders from me.'

Thus was Virginia committed, by overt act of its executive,
to maintaining against all the world its western charter jurisdiction. It was her 'wager-of-battle' with the states north of
her and the land companies for her great western charter
territory.

'Things being amicably settled,' says Clark, 'I wrote to
Kentucky, informing them what had been done, and recommending it to them to send to Pittsburg and convey the
ammunition by water to their own country. (this they never
received) and myself waited until the fall session.' Meantime
he visited his father's home in Caroline, and no doubt conferred with his friends, Mason and Jefferson, and other leaders
likely to influence the Assembly's action about giving Kentucky a county government.

The contest began on the first day of the October session,
and it was a most determined one. On that day the Indiana
Company presented a memorial vigorously protesting against
Virginia's claiming the territory west of the Alleghenies.
Colonel Henderson also was there and active in making a like
protest. Another bitter opponent was an ambitious and unlovable Scot, Colonel Arthur Campbell — sometimes called
'Long Jaw' — who was a chronic malcontent and disturber
of peace along the frontiers. He was county lieutenant and
chief military officer of Virginia's westernmost county of
Fincastle, which had been declared to extend to the utmost
bounds of the colony — and therefore to embrace Kentucky.
He was a member of the Assembly and fought hard against
making the new county; for it would deprive him of authority
over that promising region, and confine him to a comparatively
small mountain county.[2] Here began Campbell's enmity

[1] *Illinois Historical Collections*, VIII,
214.
[2] Clark says: 'We laid our papers before the Assembly. They resolved that
we could not take our seats as members,
but that our business should be attended
to. Col. Henderson, one of the purchasers
of the Cherokees, being present, retarded
our business much. Colonel Arthur
Campbell, one of the members, being

toward Clark, which was found cropping out for years afterward.

At one time during the contest, when the defeat of the bill seemed certain, Clark and Jones were about ready to give up the fight and return to Kentucky. Before doing so, however, they presented a short petition of their own to the Assembly, saying: 'The last service that lies in their power, prior to the return of your petitioners to their constitutents, which will be tomorrow, is to acquaint this honorable House of their defenseless state and implore their immediate protection.' The paper, evidently written by Clark, points out the strategic importance of Kentucky as follows:

'They cannot but observe how much it is to the interest of Virginia to prevent the inhabitants from abandoning that settlement [Kentucky] and how necessary and advantageous it will be to the Public [meaning the United States] in case of an Indian War... with nations of Indians lying west of the River Ohio, as their situation is so contiguous to those nations that the seat of war may be carried thither and thus secure the frontiers effectually, at once. Add to this, that in this service they can save the Public at least one half of what an army must cost to be levied anywhere else on the frontier counties, or any part of America.' [1]

After more than two months of determined opposition, and after a long deadlock between the two houses of the Assembly, a bill was passed (December 7, 1776) separating Kentucky from Fincastle and making it a new county.[2]

also opposed to our having a new county, wished us annexed to the county on the frontiers of which we lay and which he represented.' (*Illinois Historical Collections*, VIII, 214.)

[1] This shows that, even thus early, Clark saw the great importance of the Kentucky settlements and the western warfare in protecting the inner frontiers of the Atlantic States.

[2] October 8th the petitions were presented. On the 11th the House of Delegates, in committee of the whole, "Resolved; that the inhabitants of the western part of Fincastle...ought to be formed into a distinct county.' Five days later, a 'bill for the dividing of Fincastle into two distinct counties' was read a second time and 'committed to Mr. Jefferson and the members for Augusta and Botetourt.' Jefferson was its main champion. Although little noticed by historians, nothing in his life displays to better advantage his fine grasp of great opportunities for his country than his far-seeing coöperation in all Clark's efforts to win the country west of the Alleghenies.

The next action of the House was ominous. The bill had passed two readings, but, on October 24th, the committee to which it had been referred was discharged. Next day the third reading, which was necessary to secure a vote, was denied 'and the said bill directed to be read in the usual course of proceedings!' To any one familiar with legislative procedure, and the importance of having a bill hold its place on the calendar after preliminary readings, the discouraging effect of this action by the House will be apparent. Henderson, the Indiana Company, and Colonel Arthur Campbell, were apparently too strong for the friends of the bill. By October 30th, however, it secured another first

By this action the Kentucky pioneers were assured of support and protection by the mother state. What was still more important, they were given a government empowered to organize militia for defense and compel discipline. The creation of the new county was the political birth of Kentucky, and for his services in bringing it about historians have declared Clark the 'Founder' and 'Father' of the Commonwealth.

[Clark's narrative continues:] 'Mr. Jones and myself parted at Williamsburg; but, learning that the ammunition was yet at Pittsburg, we resolved to go by that post and take it down the river. We agreed to meet there, but the weather proving severe, it was late in the fall before we could set out. . . . However trifling a small quantity of ammunition, or the loss or acquisition of a few men may appear in the scale of affairs among people in general, to the Kentuckians the loss of either, I knew, would be sensibly felt. . . . I felt that the Indians were fully preparing for war in the spring; that those of them that attended at Fort Pitt, under the colour of friendship, were in fact acting as spies; that they had some ideas of our intention of going down the river, and would attempt to intercept us. Sensible that our safety solely depended upon expedition only, without waiting to recruit our party, we set out with seven hands only in a small vessel and by the most indefatigable labour made our way good. We passed the Indians in the night, or by some means or other got ahead of them; for, the day before we landed near Limestone, we plainly discovered that they were in pursuit of us. We hid our stores in four or five different places, at a considerable distance apart, and, running a few miles lower in our vessel, set it adrift and took by land for Harrodstown, in order to get a force sufficient and return to our stores. We passed by the Blue Lick and, the third day, . . . while we were resting ourselves, four men came to us, that had been exploring land in that quarter, and informed us. . . that John Todd was with a party somewhere in that part of the country; that if we could find him we should be strong enough to return to the river, but this was uncertain. As several

reading and this further order: 'committed to Mr. Jefferson, Mr. Simms, Mr. Bullitt, the members of Fincastle [Campbell was one], Augusta, Botetourt. *Ordered* that it be an instruction to the said committee that they receive a clause, or clauses, for laying off Kentucky into one distinct county.' Thus the House again declared its approval of the substance of the Kentucky petition, but the Senate had not expressed itself; and there were still difficulties ahead.

November 19th another of Clark's friends — and a very influential one, George Mason — was added to the committee. On the 23d Mr. Jefferson reported amendments which were agreed to, and it was 'Ordered that the amendments be engrossed and read a third time.' The bill thus amended was passed by the House, and sent (Campbell being the messenger) to the Senate for its concurrence. This the Senate refused. Thereupon a 'deadlock' followed, lasting fourteen days. A series of votes was taken, and messages passed between the two houses, each refusing to yield — until, on December 7th, the Senate finally withdrew its objections and the bill was passed and became a law.

of our party were much fatigued, we agreed that I and two others should proceed to Harrodstown for the proposed party; that Mr. Jones and the rest should remain in that neighborhood until our return. In a short time after I had set out, Todd arrived at the same place, and after some consultation, concluded that they were able to go to the river and bring on the ammunition & other stores, and accordingly set out with ten men, and, ...on the 25th Dec., met the Indians on our trail and got totally routed. Mr. Jones was killed, and three others got killed and taken prisoners. Fortunately for us, the prisoners did not discover our hidden stores to the Indians. The party, sent from Harrods, brought them safe to that place which gave universal joy.'

The foregoing quotations from Clark, and others to follow, are from two of his letters narrating his western career up to the summer of 1779. The first he wrote in the autumn of that year at the request of his friend, Colonel George Mason, and is commonly called the *Mason Letter*. The other was written ten years later, at the request of James Madison and United States Senator John Brown of Kentucky, but was never finished. It was found amongst Clark's papers after his death and is commonly called his *Memoir*.[1] When he wrote it he was unable to assist his recollections by reading the Mason Letter, for Colonel Mason had mislaid it and it was not found until over fifty years later. The two narratives, however, although covering the same period and a great variety of events, are remarkably consistent, being in almost every material detail corroborated by the contemporary writings of others. The

[1] Madison and Brown strongly urged Clark to give them all the facts, saying: 'You cannot be too minute in detail of causes and effects, of views and measures, of occurrences and transactions. ...Circumstances and facts which may appear unimportant to you, will not be thought so by others. ...Treaties with, and speeches to and from the Indians may be inserted with propriety, as 'tis of importance to preserve them.' (*Draper MSS.* 53 J 80, *et seq.*)

To aid the reader more easily to follow the narratives as quoted, the spelling in some instances, and the punctuation in many, will be corrected, and first letters of sentences capitalized. Even these changes are made reluctantly, for the author knows the objection many historians make to them. As the book is not intended, however, for the critical readers only, but also for others who are unpractised in reading old-style writings, and likely to be fatigued and perhaps misled by lawless spelling, punctuation, and capitalizing, it is deemed best to make the limited corrections mentioned, especially when the original text is accessible to all in other publications. It is believed the corrections made in no instance alter the sense of any sentence in the original. The Mason Letter and Memoir will both be found in the *George Rogers Clark Papers, Illinois Historical Collections*, VIII. English gives them with considerable alteration of spelling in his *Conquest of the Northwest*. Quaife's *Conquest of the Illinois* is a recent modernized edition of the Memoir.

In the following pages where one narrative substantially duplicates the other, or one fails to state what is in the other, quotations are made indiscriminately from either or both.

Memoir was not intended for a finished narrative, but merely as a 'collection of facts,' Mr. Madison having said he would 'carefully attend to the arrangement and style so as to usher it into the world in a dress suitable to the importance of the subject.'

Clark was an unpractised and singularly unwilling and careless writer. He had an odd way of using disjointed clauses instead of complete sentences, as if merely jotting down suggestions for his reader, or reminders for himself. Other faults — almost universal in his day — were lawless spelling, capitalizing, and punctuation. Yet it will be found that both his narratives disclose rare directness and force of expression, often exceedingly graphic and sometimes quite eloquent.

CHAPTER IV

CLARK PLANS CAPTURE OF BRITISH POSTS

THE powder Clark had procured arrived at Harrodsburg none too soon, for throughout 1777 band after band of Indians overran Kentucky, slaughtering settlers who ventured to remain on their clearings, and driving the rest into their four small forts. Many fled back east over the mountains; others would have done so, but the danger in flight became even greater than in the forts. Unless the country was to be lost, every man was needed. Fortunately there was now a local government with authority essentially military, and with Clark, as major, in chief command. The following order will illustrate the simplicity of its method:

At a court martial of all the officers of the county: Prest, Geo. R. Clark, Danl Boone, Jas. Harrod, Jn Todd: Ordered that any person called into service by the Invasion Law, as is the case with all now in this county, in case he leaves the service be looked upon as a deserter, & the Commanding Officer is desired to advertise all such throughout the colony, as deserters, in the most public manner.

G. R. CLARK, *Presd*.

Proceedings for punishing deserters were probably neither expensive nor slow; but that offense was rare amongst the men who had the courage to remain in the country, and was almost entirely confined to traders and men of lower grades. Here a persistent error should be corrected. The pioneers of Kentucky are usually described as of one general class — brave Indian fighters, but rude and ignorant. Certainly there were many of that kind, but also many of a very different kind. It should be clearly understood that the rush of settlers to Kentucky in 1775 and early 1776 was very different from ordinary migrations to the borders of civilization. It occurred at a time of great excitement in Virginia and adjoining colonies over the recently explored land of promise; and it drew into its current a great many enterprising young men from well-known families. Few of them, perhaps, represented over-well the culture standards of their own families, for they were evidently fonder of adventure than of books, and more interested in western lands than in eastern society; but they were no boors. The amusingly ill-written letters of some of them may seem to indicate that they were almost wholly uneducated, when, if their spelling, capitalizing, and punctuation be modernized, their vocabulary and composition will be found to be very good, and to indicate that they were much better talkers than scribes. Others wrote excellent English for that period. Despite the rough conditions of life where they were, many of them preserved much of the courtesy of the old eastern colonial society in which they had been reared. Men of this class inevitably furnished the brains and became leaders and mainstays in the western struggle for independence and empire. No inferior class would have visioned the greatness of the American cause, or been willing to make the sacrifices necessary to carry it to success.[1]

On returning to Kentucky Clark kept a brief diary, beginning Christmas Day, 1776, with an entry telling of the attack on the powder party and the killing of Jones and three others. It continued, with occasional breaks, until March 30, 1778, and thus covers an important period. A few quotations from it will give an idea of what the pioneers encountered:

'29th. [Dec., 1776.] A large party of Indians attacked McClellan's Fort and wounded Jno McClellan, Chas. White, Robt Todd, and Edw[d] Worthington, the first two mortally.

'30. Chas. White died of his wound.

'January 1777, 6. Jno. McClellan died of his wounds.

'30. Moved to Harrodsburg from McClellan's Fort. [McClellan's

[1] A surprisingly large proportion, especially those who remained through 1776 and 1777 to battle for the country, were of this class. Such pioneer names as Harrison, Todd, Lee, Rogers, Floyd, Randolph, Clark, Taylor, Hite, Walker, Jouett, Hart, Lewis, Spottswood, Dandridge, Hanson, Bowman, Crittenden, Worthington, Chapline, Shelby, Slaughter, Callaway, and many others had been highly respected ones in the old colonies.

That the higher class pioneers of Kentucky have been thus confused with the common type has been mainly due to the fact that, for over a hundred and fifty years, most of the truth about the west during the Revolution has lain buried in unpublished letters and documents in the chaos of ill-kept state and county offices, or hidden away in the dusty garrets of private houses. Fortunately many of these writings have been preserved and are now being made available for the historic investigator. They will throw much needed light on western events and the men who won the western country and paved the way for later expansion, and will also expose many errors in printed accounts of them.

When western Revolutionary history was being made, it enlisted little interest in the east where the printing presses ran and historians wrote. This, perhaps more than anything else, explains the grossly undue prominence given to eastern events and men in early histories of the Revolutionary War.

was abandoned for lack of men, leaving only three little forts in Kentucky — Harrod's, Boone's, and Logan's.]

'March 5. Militia of the county embodied.

'6. Thomas Shores & Wm. Ray killed at the Shawnee Spring.

'7. The Indians attempted to cut off from the fort a small party of our men. A skirmish ensued. We had 4 men wounded and some cattle killed. We killed and scalped one Indian, and wounded several.

'8. Brought in corn from the diff^t cribs until the 18th day. [Apprehending an Indian siege, they were getting in provisions.]

'9. Express sent to the Settlement.' [That meant dire need of men or supplies, for men were few and not one could be spared. 'The loss of a single man at this time,' said Clark, 'was sensibly felt, and general actions with the enemy ought to be guarded against, without an apparent superiority, as the enemy could easily retrieve their losses, by recruits from various Nations, which was an advantage we could not expect to enjoy for some time.']

'18 A small party of Indians killed and scalped Hugh Wilson about ½ mile from the fort, near night, & escaped.

'19 Archibald McNeal died of his wounds rec^d 7th inst.

'28 A large party of Ind^s attacked the stragglers about the fort; killed and scalped Garret Pendergreet; killed, or took prisoner, Peter Flin. (March 7th Indians killed one man at Boonesborough and wounded one.)

'April 6 Stoner arrived with news from the Settlement.

'19 Jno Todd and Richd Callaway elected Burgesses. Jas. Barry married to widow Wilson.'

Wilson was killed only a month before, yet his widow's early remarriage probably indicated no indifference to her loss; for, in a pioneer community a widow with small children was in great need of a husband's help and protection. Amidst the dangers surrounding all, the burden of caring for their women and children was a heavy one for the men. At Harrodsburg, on May 1, 1777, there were only eighty-four men 'fit for service,' but ninety-four women and children, besides fourteen disabled white men.[1]

[Said Clark:] 'To enumerate all the little actions that happened, it is impossible. They were continual and frequently severe when compared to our small forces. The Forts were often attacked. Policy seemed to have required that the whole should be embodied in one place, but depending on hunting for the greatest part of our provisions forbade it. No people could be in a more alarming situation. Detached at least two hundred miles from the nearest settle-

[1] *Draper MSS.* 48 J 10; Levi Todd's statement, March, 1777, Butler's *History of Kentucky*, pp. 95; Marshall's *History of Kentucky*, I, 55. Cf. McElroy's *Kentucky in the Nation's History*, 147–48.

ment of the States, surrounded by numerous nations of Indians, - each one far superior in number to ourselves and under the influence of the British Government and pointedly directed to destroy us, — ...I was frequently afraid that the people would think of making their peace with Detroit and suffer themselves and their families to be carried off. Their distress may be easily conceived from our situation, but they yet remained firm in hopes of relief. Our conduct was very uniform; the defense of our forts, the procuring of provisions, and, when possible, surprising the Indians (which was frequently done) burying the dead, and dressing the wounded, seemed to be all our business.

'The whole of my time, when not thus employed [was used] in reflecting on things in general, particularly Kentucky — how it accorded with the interest of the United States; whether it was to their interest to support it, or not, &c. This led me to a long train of thinking, the result of which was to lay aside every private view and engage seriously in the war and have the interest and welfare of the public my only view, until the fate...of the continent should be known, divesting myself of prejudice, partiality, &c. in favour of any particular part of the community, but to persue what I conceived to be the interest of the whole. This ...enabled me better to judge of the importance of Kentucky to the Union, situated as it was in the center almost of the Indians, ...as an impediment in their way to the more interior frontiers. As soon as they should accomplish the destruction of [Kentucky] they would bodily let loose on the frontiers, and, instead of the states receiving supplies from thence, they would be obliged to keep large bodies of troops for their defence. It would be almost impossible to move an army at so great a distance to attack their towns, if they could find them.

'By supporting and encouraging the growth of Kentucky, those obstacles would, in a great measure, be removed, for, should the British officers bend their whole force against the interior frontiers, as a certain mode of distressing the states, we might, with a little assistance, at any time march from this country [Kentucky]...to any part of their country we chose. Those ideas caused me to view Kentucky in the most favourable point of view, as a place of the greatest consequence and which ought to meet with every encouragement, and that nothing that I could engage in would be of more general utility than its defense. And as the commandants of the different towns of the Illinois and Wabash, I knew, [were] busily engaged in exciting the Indians, their reduction became my first object, expecting that it might probably open a field for further action.

'I sent two young hunters, S. More & B. Linn, to those places as spies, with proper instructions for their conduct. To prevent suspicion, neither did they, nor any person in Kentucky ever know my design, until it was ripe for execution.' [1]

[1] *Illinois Historical Collections*, VIII, 213.

That design was nothing less than to carry an expedition
against those distant posts, and drive out the British. It was
the beginning of the first act in the military drama in which
Kentucky and the region south of it were to be saved and the
great country north of the Ohio won for the United States.
A more daring offensive is hardly to be found in history.
In view of the remoteness and strength of the enemy and the
distractions of a desperate defensive war, that Clark should
have thought out and prepared this bold plan of distant
conquest has excited wonder. That he did so was mainly due
to his most marked mental characteristic — his realizing
imagination. The geographic vision of most men goes little
beyond their immediate surroundings, and probably few in
the little Harrodsburg fort had more than a hazy notion of the
vast regions north of them across the Ohio. Living amidst a
boundless forest, and engaged in a life-and-death struggle,
few of them gave thought to anything but the pressing work
at hand. But even in the wilderness Clark seems not to have
been bewildered. In both his plans and performances he
showed that his imaginative grasp took in the broad expanse
of the enemy's country — its distances, the distribution and
numbers of its white and Indian populations, its transportation facilities and difficulties, and other details; and it was
this which enabled him to make his calculations with surprising accuracy.[1]

Professor Hart of Harvard, in his latest work, says: 'No
story of the Arabian Nights is more romantic or improbable
than Clark's conception of his plan of conquest and his success in carrying it out.' Wonderful, however, as the story is,
there was nothing haphazard about it. 'Luck is ever infatuated
with the efficient.' The results Clark obtained were the results
of careful forethought and preparation. The usual descriptions of him, as merely a daring and lucky young Indian fighter
who won success by intuition, display a total failure to comprehend the man. In the crowded little Harrodsburg fort,
many a day or night, while his comrades were talking of stirring events near at hand, or were concerned with personal
affairs, he must have sat absorbed in contemplation of the

[1] Jefferson appreciated this. Writing
to his young friend, he said: 'Any observations of your own... in the western
country will come acceptably to me,
because I know you see the works of
Nature in the great & not merely in
detail.' (*Draper MSS. 52 J 58.*)

big problems of the war — of 'the interest of the continent,' or 'things in general,' as he calls them. It is hardly to be wondered, therefore, that his companions often found him reserved, though in time of relaxation all agree that he was affable and lively.

While he awaited the return of his spies from the Illinois, he said ' the bloody war in Kentucky continued.' His diary tells the story:

'April 24. ...40 or 50 Indians attacked Boonesborough, killed and scalped Dan¹ Goodman, wounded Capᵗ Boone, Capᵗ Todd, Mr. Hite & Mr. Stoner. Indians, 'tis thought, sustained much damage.' 'April 29. ...Indians attacked the fort. Killed ensign McConnell.'[1] 'May 18th McGarry & Haggin sent, expresses, to Fort Pitt.' [The continental commander there, General Hand, was trying to make peace with the Shawnees and get them to return captured prisoners and horses, so McGarry and Haggin were sent to recover the horses taken from Kentucky. The loss of them was a serious matter, for horses were needed to carry supplies, to work crops, and to hunt buffalo and other big game. When a fort was besieged by Indians its meat supply could be obtained only by mounted hunters. They would steal out by night, travel many miles to the game, load their horses with meat, return in the night, and again steal or rush by the savages into the fort.[2]]

'May 23 A large party of Indians attacked Boonesborough Fort, kept a warm fire until 11 o'clock at night, began it next morning & kept a warm fire until midnight, attempting several times to burn the fort. 3 of our men were wounded, not mortally. The enemy suffered considerably.

'May 26 A party went out to hunt Indians. One wounded Squire Boone & escaped.

'May 30 Indians attacked Logans Fort, Killed Wm. Hudson, wounded Burr Harrison & Jno Kennedy.

[1] This day a war council was held. The minutes say: 'The President produced a letter, signed by Capt. Benjamin Logan, desiring that the small forces might be speedily collected from the three stations that we might give the enemy a repulse & recover...the plunder, and desired the opinion of the Council concerning it, which was as follows: That as we supposed the enemy's number in the Country was very great, & a battle would be extremely hazardous and probably endanger the loss of the Country, upon which his letter was rejected.' (*Draper MSS.* 18 J 56).

[2] Horses were also needed for 'expresses' to carry important messages, for scouting to learn the movements of the Indians, for rapidly pursuing them, and for long marches to attack their towns. Actual fighting, however, was done afoot, in scattered lines, and, where practicable, from behind trees or other cover.

Some writers have seemed to think that stealthy raids to capture horses from the Indians savored of theft and were for private gain. Simon Kenton, who was distinguished for exploits of this kind, felt deeply aggrieved to find himself thus classed with horse thieves. In fact, such raids were amongst the most essential — as they were amongst the most daring and patriotic — of public services.

'June 5 Harrod & Elliott went to meet Col. Bowman & Co. Glenn & Laird arr^d from Cumberland. Danl Lyons, who parted with them on Green River, we suppose was killed going into Logans Fort. Jn Peters & Elisha Bathy we expect were killed coming home from Cumberland.

'June 13 Burr Harrison died of his wounds, received the 30th of May.[1]

'June 22 Benn Linn & Saml Moore arr^d from Illinois. Barney Stagner sen^r killed & beheaded ½ mile from the fort. A few guns fired at Boon's.'

Linn and Moore were Clark's spies, returned from the Illinois. Following his instructions, they had gone to St. Louis, 'as hunters who had come to dispose of some beaver skins and procure supplies there.' Thence they passed over to Kaskaskia, where they gained desired information; but, becoming suspected of being enemies, they had to flee for their lives. Clark wrote:

'They returned to Harrodstown with all the information I could reasonably have expected. I found from them that...[the enemy] had but little expectation of a visit from us, but that things were kept in good order, the military trained &c that they might, in case of a visit, be prepared; that the greatest pains were taken to inflame the minds of the French inhabitants against the Americans; notwithstanding [which] they discovered traces of affection in some of the inhabitants; that the Indians in that quarter were engaged in the war, &c.'

Thus informed of the situation in the Illinois, Clark, on October 1, 1777, left Kentucky for the Virginia capital to propose to Governor Henry an expedition to reduce the British posts north of the Ohio. Resting but a day at his father's home, he set out for Williamsburg. There he did not at once open his plan to the governor, but says he used his time 'in making remarks of everything I saw, or heard, that could lead me to a knowledge of the disposition of those in power.' He also settled his accounts as major of the Kentucky militia. His diary says: 'Nov. 18th. Settled with the auditors. Drew the money of the treasurer, £726.6s. Bought a piece of cloth for a jackote, price £4.15; buttons and mohair 3/.' No doubt leaving the cloth and buttons with his tailor to make his 'jackote' during his absence, he next day

---

[1] He was a boyhood friend of Clark, whose brother Jonathan's diary mentions frequent visits at the Harrison home.

again went to his father's home in Caroline; but, on December 6th, he reappeared in Williamsburg to put the feasibility of his plan of conquest to the test of Governor Henry's decision. How visionary it must have seemed! Up to this time the Indian warfare had consisted only of sporadic raids by small bands; but there were thousands of Indians north of the Ohio. To carry a war into their own county, as Clark was about to propose, might arouse them all; and the colonies were in no condition to provoke a greater Indian war. At the very time he was proposing his scheme of conquest, Washington at Valley Forge dreaded lest his army 'starve, dissolve, or disperse.' Virginia, too, whose fields and grazing lands had so largely supplied his men, was becoming exhausted; and she had hundreds of miles of border to guard against the Indians. The official and personal letters of that time show how impossible it was for the state to furnish all threatened sections with the troops and supplies needed for defense.

Virginia had also other reasons for hesitating to incur the burden of an offensive war north of the Ohio. It was extremely doubtful whether she would be allowed to retain that region, even if the British were driven out; for, as already seen, most of the states were urging Congress to claim it as the common property of all. Still another danger of her losing the benefit of any such conquest arose from the diplomatic intrigues of France and Spain. Spain feared the Americans would grow strong enough to seize Louisiana, and to protect it was anxious to secure for herself the region west of the Alleghenies; and in this policy France was her secret and powerful ally.[1]

On the other hand, Virginia had strong motives for supporting Clark's project, if he could show a probability of its success. Kentucky contained an extremely fertile country; a few Virginians had settled there; many more owned lands there; many others contemplated going there when peace should come; in West Virginia were millions of acres of promising mineral lands; and the country north of the Ohio was prospectively even more valuable. Unless the British were driven from the posts there, all these regions would most likely be lost to the state forever, and the Indians left free to carry torch and tomahawk along her whole inner frontiers.

[1] As to France's aim to recover the Mississippi Valley for herself, see Professor Frederick's Turner's 'Policy of France, etc.,' in *American Historical Review*, x, 249.

Says Clark's diary: 'December 10, Got to Williamsburgh. Bought 2 shirts and a book, £5.' Presumably the shirts were of the laced or ruffled kind then fashionable, and his 'jackote' finished by his tailor, so that he was attired as became a young gentleman of the period and ready to present himself to the governor and council. On the same day he said:

'I communicated my views to Governor Henry. At first he seemed to be fond of it; but to detach a party at so great a distance, (although the service performed might be of great utility,) appeared daring and hazardous, as nothing but secrecy could give success to the enterprise. ...He had several private councils composed of select gentlemen. [They embraced three of the greatest Virginians in that day of Virginia's great men — Thomas Jefferson, George Mason, and George Wythe.] After making every inquiry into my proposed plan of operation, (and particularly that of Retreat in case of Misfortune, which I intended across into the Spanish Territory), the Expedition was resolved on.' [1]

Fortunately there has been preserved by that wonderful historic collector, Dr. Lyman Draper, an old and worn copy of a most interesting letter in which Clark fully outlined for Governor Henry his plan to capture Kaskaskia. Although published over twenty years ago,[2] it has been unnoticed by nearly all who have since written of his expedition.[3] It shows the facts upon which he based his plan of conquest, the plan itself as he had worked it out, and lastly, the substantial identity of plan and subsequent achievement. In brief terms it discloses every feature of the programme which he later carried out: his taking his men down nearly to the mouth of the Ohio; his overland march thence to Kaskaskia; his arrival there at night, his surprise and capture of the place; his important winning over of the French inhabitants by kind treatment; and lastly and equally important, his overcoming the opposi-

[1] *Illinois Historical Collections*, VIII, 33; Council Order.

[2] By Turner in *American Historical Review*, VIII 491.

[3] It exposes the error of many who have assumed that the plan of conquest was Governor Henry's. Jefferson afterward said: 'Of Clark's expedition I had approved previous to his entering on it. It was an idea of his own, & he came down from his native county to propose to Govr Henry to raise volunteers himself and undertake the reduction of the Illinois posts. Govr Henry approved the design, but considering secrecy as essential to success, could not ask authority from the legislature, but consulted Colo. Mason, R. H. Lee, some others and myself, who not only advised it, but pledged ourselves to Clarke to use our best endeavors in the legislature, if he succeeded, to induce them to remunerate himself and his followers in lands.' (*Jefferson Papers, Library of Congress*, Series 2, vol. 67, no. 99.)

tion of many hostile Indians. His letter said if Kaskaskia 'was in our possession, it would distress the garrison at Detroit for provisions; it would fling the command of the two great rivers into our hands, which would enable us to get supplies of goods from the Spaniards, and to carry on trade with the Indians.' All this proved prophetic.[1]

A serious obstacle to the plan arose, however, for it was thought Governor Henry had no power to send troops across the Ohio without an enabling act of the Assembly. The expedition, said Clark, could therefore only be 'determined on...as soon as a Bill could be passed to enable the governor to order it'; but 'to lay it before the assembly would be dangerous, as it would soon be known throughout the frontiers and probably the first prisoner taken by the Indians would give the alarm, which would end in the certain destruction of the party.' The dilemma was solved by an adroit deception of all save a few of the governor's friends in the Assembly, which was led to pass an act, professedly for the defense of the state, but really authorizing the campaign of conquest, 'though but few in the house knew the real intent of it.'[2]

In his letter to Mason, Clark said:

'After giving the council all the intelligence I possibly could, I resolved to pursue my other plans; but being desired by the governor to stay some time in town, I waited with impatience, he, I suppose, believing that I wanted the command, and was determined to give it to me; but it was far from my inclination at that time. I was summoned to attend the council board; the instructions and necessary papers were ready for putting in the name of the person in command. I believe they expected me to solicit for it, but I resolved not to do so, for reasons I hinted you before. However I accepted it, after being told the command of this little army was intended for me. I then got every request granted, and [was] fully empowered to raise as many men as I could, not exceeding a certain number, [three hundred and fifty.] The governor and coun-

[1] The capture did distress the garrison at Detroit for provisions, and added enormously to the outlays of the British in the western war; it did 'enable us to get supplies from the Spaniards,' of food stuffs, powder, lead, salt, clothing, medicines, and other essentials, without which the western war could hardly have been won; it did open the way for trade with the Indians and the winning over of many hostile tribes. The great importance to the British of the Mississippi route between Canada and the seaport of New Orleans was made painfully evident to them when, in 1776, their only other outlet to the sea, by way of the St. Lawrence, was blocked by the American capture of Montreal. (*Michigan Pioneer Collections*, IX, 371.)

[2] *Illinois Historical Collections*, VIII, 115–61.

cil so warmly engaged in the success of the enterprise, that I had very little trouble in getting matters adjusted; and, on the second day of January 1778, received my instructions, and £1200 for the use of the expedition, with an order on Pittsburg for boats, ammunition, &c. [A paltry sum, certainly — twelve hundred pounds in Virginia paper money — to finance such an undertaking.]

'After being engaged, I was then as determined to prosecute it with vigor, as I was before indifferent about the command. I had, since the beginning of the war, taken pains to make myself acquainted with the true situation of the British posts on the frontiers, and since find that I was not mistaken in my judgment. I was ordered to attack the Illinois — in case of success to carry my arms to any quarter I pleased.[1] I was certain that with five hundred men I could take the Illinois, and, by treating the French inhabitants as fellow citizens and [showing] them I meant to protect rather than treat them as a conquered people, engaging the Indians to our interest, &c, it might probably have so great an effect on their countrymen at Detroit, (they already disliked their master) that it would be an easy prey for me. I should have mentioned my design to his Excellency, but was convinced, or afraid, that it might lessen his esteem for me, as it was a general opinion that it would take several thousand to approach that place. I was happy with the thoughts of fair prospects of undeceiving the public respecting their formidable enemies on our frontiers.'[2]

From Governor Henry, Clark received two sets of written instructions — one public and to be exhibited as occasion might require, the other secret.[3] The public instructions merely authorized him to enlist seven companies, to 'proceed to Kentucky and there obey such orders and directions as you shall give them, for three months after their arrival at that place, but to receive pay &c in case they remain on duty a longer time.' All that the volunteers could know from these public instructions was that they were to be taken to Kentucky, and all of them thought they were only going that far. The Governor's secret instructions followed in all substantial respects the plan Clark had outlined. With this force he was directed to 'attack the British post at Kaskaskia; to take especial care to keep the true destination of your force secret, as its success depends on this'; and to treat British captives humanely. 'If the white inhabitants,' said the Governor, 'will give undoubted evidence of their attachment to this state, (for it is certain they live within its limits), by

---

[1] *Illinois Historical Collections*, VIII, 116, Henry to Clark, January, 1778.   [2] *Id.*, VIII, 116.   [3] *Id.*, VIII, 34, 36.

taking the test prescribed by law,... let them be treated as
fellow citizens & their persons and property duly secured,' but
otherwise 'they must feel the miseries of war, ...under the
directions of humanity.' A few days later, Governor Henry
wrote Colonel Clark saying: 'Colo David Rogers is to go to
New Orleans, on the Business of Trade I mention'd to you,
& I have opened the secret Nature of your Expedition to
him, as it was necessary for his safety. ...Proceed as you
find the Interest of your Country directs, when you get to
the place you are going to. What I have in View is that your
operations should not be confin'd to the Fort & the Settlement at the place mention'd in your secret Instructions [Kas-
kaskia] but that you proceed to the Enemy's Settlements above,
[Detroit] or across, [Vincennes] as you may find it proper.' [1]

For a while Clark seems to have been too much engaged
with his expedition to make his usual diary entries, for none
appear until early January, when he says he advanced Major
Smith £150 'to raise 200 men and meet me at Kentuck last
of March. [When that time came, Smith, through no fault
of his own, failed to keep his engagement.]

'18th. Found my old friend L. Helm at Mr. Floyds. ...
Appointed him to raise a company. Paid him wages for past
service.' Helm became one of Clark's most valuable captains.
He was an interesting, if somewhat rugged, character — outspoken, abounding in wit and fun, fearless, even in the presence of danger that would have appalled most brave men,
intelligent, level-headed, and absolutely trustworthy. His
reputation for courage was unique, even amongst the pioneers.
Five days later the diary says: 'Appointed Joseph Bowman
captain, Isaac Lieu[t], to raise a company for my regiment.'
Joseph Bowman was to be his next in command in the hard
campaigns to follow.

February 1st Clark reached Redstone Fort (now Browns-
ville), the point on the Monongahela River whence travelers
from the east, after crossing the mountains, usually took boats
to Pittsburg. Here he found William Harrod, a seasoned
veteran, and appointed him 'captain to raise a company.'
At Redstone, he says:

'I received information from Captain Helm that several gentlemen in his quarter took pains to counteract his interest in recruit-

[1] *Illinois Historical Collections*, VIII, 38.

ing, as no such service was known by the assembly. Consequently, he had to send to the Governor to get his conduct ratified. I found also opposition to our interest in the Pittsburg country, as the whole was divided into violent parties between the Virginians and Pennsylvanians, respecting territory — each trying to counteract the other. The idea of our men being [enlisted] for the state of Virginia affected the vulgar of one party [the Pennsylvanians] and, (as my real instructions were kept concealed, and only an instrument from the Governor, written designedly for deception, was made public, wherein I was to raise men for the defense of Kentucky), many gentlemen of both parties conceived it to be injurious to the public interest to draw off men, at so critical a moment, for the defense of a few detached inhabitants [of Kentucky] that had better be removed, &c.'[1] 'Not knowing my destination, and through a spirit of obstinacy, they combined and did everything that lay in their power to stop the men that enlisted, and set the whole frontiers in an uproar, — even condescended to harbor and protect those that deserted. I found my case desperate: the longer I remained the worse it was. I plainly saw my principal design [against Detroit] was baffled. I resolved to push to Kentucky with what men I could gather in West Augusta. Being joined by both Captains Bowman and Helm, who had each raised a company for the expedition, (but two thirds of them were stopped by the undesigned enemies to the country that I before mentioned,) in the whole I had about one hundred and fifty men collected and set sail for the Falls [of Ohio.] I had, previous to this, received letters from Captain Smith, on Holston, informing me that he intended to meet me at that place with near two hundred men, which encouraged me much, as I was in hopes of being able by that reënforcement at least to attack the Illinois with a probability of success.' [But for Clark's belief that he could rely on Smith's bringing those two hundred men, he probably would never have left Pittsburg to conquer the Illinois.]

'Meeting several disappointments, it was late in May before I could leave the Redstone settlement with those companies and a considerable number of families and private adventurers [intending to settle at the Falls of the Ohio.] ...Taking in our stores at Pittsburg and Wheeling, we proceeded down the river with caution.'

In his letter to Mason, he said: 'We...had a very pleasant voyage to the Falls of the Ohio.' That 'Beautiful River' — 'la Belle Rivière' of the French — was indeed a noble stream, flowing in meandering lines between densely forested hills,

---

[1] As Clark's Mason and Memoir letters cover the same period, but sometimes one best narrates an event or supplies an omission in the other, quotations from each are here and elsewhere broken to insert supplementary statements from the other — changes from one to the other being indicated simply by separating quotation marks. All the quotations are from the letters as given in volume VIII, *Illinois Historical Collections.*

with here and there broad stretches of fertile bottom lands, covered with an even more luxuriant forest growth down to the water's edge. There great sycamores — 'bare-armed sentinels of the forest' — and other water-loving trees hung far out over the shaded stream. But it took stout hearts to enjoy such scenery then; for on the northern side of the river were Indian enemies, ever alert for opportunities to kill; and rarely did a white man's boat venture upon it that fierce eyes were not peering through dense undergrowth for victims.

On arriving at the mouth of the Kentucky, Clark says he 'sent expresses...for Capt. Smith to join me immediately, as I made no doubt but that he was waiting for me. But you may easily guess at my mortification on being informed that he had not arrived; that all his men had been stopt by the incessant labours of the populace, except part of a company that had arrived under command of one Capt Dillard, — some on their march being threatened to be put in prison if they did not return.' Up to this moment, Clark thought that with Smith's two hundred men he could count on having a total force of about three hundred and fifty. To have the number thus reduced more than half, he said, 'alarmed me, as I was afraid the disappointment would prove fatal to our scheme'; but, he added,

'it made me as desperate as I was before determined. Reflecting on the information that I had, of some of my greatest opponents censuring the Governor for his Conduct, as they thought, in ordering me for the protection of Kentucky only, — that, and some other secret impulses occasioned me, in spite of all counsel...to risque the expedition, to convince them of their error, — until that moment secret to the principal officers I had. I was sensible of the impression it would have on many to be taken near a thousand [miles] from the body of their country to attack a people five times their number, and merciless tribes of Indians, their allies and determined enemies to us. I knew our case was desperate, but the more I reflected on my weakness, the more I was pleased with the enterprise.'

'I moved on to the Falls and viewed the different situations, but reflecting that my secret instructions were yet unknown, even to the party with me, and not knowing what would be the consequence when they should be divulged,...I wished everything secured as much as possible....I observed the little island of about seventy acres ['Corn Island'] opposite to where the town of Louisville now stands, seldom or never was entirely covered by the water. I resolved to take possession and fortify, which I did on the...day of June, dividing the island among the [immigrant] familes for gardens.' 'On this island I first began to discipline my little army, knowing that to be the most essential point towards success.' 'On the arrival of Col. Bowman, part of the [Kentucky] militia, and several of the gentlemen of the country, we found on examination that we were much weaker than expected, and the Indians...more numerous, ... as the British continued to add to their strength by exciting others to join them. [Four months before, Boone and twenty-seven other men, while salt-making, were captured by the Indians, — a serious loss when men were so scarce.] Under these circumstances we could not think of leaving the posts of Kentucky defenceless; [but concluded] that it was better to run a great risk with our party, than to divide our forces in such manner as to hazard the loss of both, of course. We agreed to take but one complete company and part of another from Kentucky, expecting that they would be replaced by troops yet expected from Major Smith. Those were our deliberations.

'After my making known my instructions, almost every gentleman warmly espoused the enterprise and plainly saw the salvation of Kentucky almost in their reach; but [some] repined that we were not strong enough to put it beyond all doubt. The soldiery in general debated on the subject, but determined to follow their officers. Some were alarmed at the thoughts of being taken so great distance into the enemy's country; [thinking] that if they should have success in the first instance, they might be attacked in their posts without a possibility of getting succor, or of making their retreat. (In case of retreat, it was designed to the Spanish government.) Spies were continually among the whole. Some dissatisfaction was discovered in Captain Dillard's company; consequently the boats were well secured and sentinels placed where it was thought there was a possibility of their wading from the island,... but got outgeneraled by their lieutenant, whom I had previously formed a very tolerable opinion of. They had, by swimming in the day, discovered that the channel opposite to their camp might be waded; and, a little before day, himself and the greatest part of the company slipped down the bank and got to the opposite shore before they were discovered by the sentinels.

'Vexed at the idea of their escape in the manner they did, (as one of my principal motives for taking post on the island was to prevent desertion, and intending to set out the next day), I was undetermined for a few moments what to do, as it might take a party several days to overtake [them.] ...Having no distrust of those that remained, the example was not immediately dangerous, but might prove so hereafter. Recollecting that there were a number of horses belonging to gentlemen from Harrodsburg, I ordered a strong party to pursue them, and for the foot and horse to relieve each other regularly, and to put to death every man that was in their power that would not surrender. They overhauled them in about twenty miles The deserters, discovering them at a distance, scattered in the woods. Only seven or eight were taken. The rest made their way to the different posts. Many that were not woodsmen almost perished. The poor lieutenant, and the few that remained with him, after suffering almost all that could be felt from hunger and fatigue, arrived at Harrodstown. Having heard of his conduct [the people there] would not for some time suffer him to come into their houses, nor give him anything to eat. On the return of the party the soldiery hung and burnt his effigy.'

This severe treatment of the deserters was no doubt necessary, but as the lieutenant and his men had been deceived by Governor Henry's public instructions, and had enlisted only to defend Kentucky, it is not surprising that they resented being taken hundreds of miles into the enemy's country. More surprising was the readiness of the remaining men to follow Clark farther. He had brought them a great distance into the wilderness before giving them an inkling of the daring service he was now asking of them. Still more remarkable was his success in preserving the secret of his real objective. After nearly a century and a half of search by many investigators amongst the letters and other papers of his time, not one has been found indicating that any of his officers or men in the expedition suspected its object until he disclosed it to them, as stated in his narrative.

CHAPTER V

BRITISH WESTERN FORCES AND PLANS

LEAVING Clark at Corn Island on his journey down the Ohio, it will be well here to take a survey of the British side of the war in the west. Governor Hamilton's white forces varied much in number from year to year. At Detroit, during the most critical time, he had over eight hundred troops, including Canadian militia and volunteers and eighty British regulars of the 'King's Own Regiment.' [1] Besides a number of pirogues plying the lakes there were six armed vessels on Lake Erie, three being schooners carrying eight or ten guns each. [2] At Mich-i-li-Mackinac (now Mackinaw City), Vincennes, Kaskaskia, and Cahokia were militia garrisons of uncertain numbers. At Vincennes, late in 1778, Hamilton enlisted two hundred and fifty militiamen, and said there were three hundred men there used to fire arms as hunters.' [3] At Kaskaskia, which had about eight hundred inhabitants, [4] the commandant, Philip de Rochblave, was a violent enemy of the Americans. A company of British regulars was stationed there, but had been called to Canada. Cahokia, nearly opposite St. Louis, contained perhaps four hundred people, [5] and was a favorite trading place for the Indians from the upper Mississippi and Missouri.

---

[1] *British Museum*, Add. MSS. 24320, f., 1–6. At the end of September 1778, when about to march against Clark, Hamilton reported his troops as follows:

Garrison, rank and file fit for duty, 188, sick 11, artillery 18, total	217
Militia, captains 5, lieutenants 20, privates 540, total	565
Volunteers Company: fit for duty 36, sick 3, imprisoned 1, absent 2, total	42
Grand total	824

Soon afterwards eighty British regulars of the 'King's Own Regiment' from Niagara seems to have increased this total to 904 men. (*Id.*)

[2] See Quaife's interesting *Royal Navy on the Upper Lakes*, Burton's *Historical Collection Leaflets* vol. 2, no. 5. For census of upper lake government boats 1759–1778 see *Wisconsin Historical Collection*, XI, 198, *et seq.*

[3] Hamilton to Haldemand, Dec. 18, 1778. *Illinois Historical Collections*, I, 227–36.

[4] "250 families," Maj. Bournan's letter to Hite: *Author's MSS.* and *Illinois Historical Collections*, VIII, 615.

[5] The population of these towns varied greatly from time to time and was differently reported in different years, so that no definite figures can be given with confidence. The census of Detroit April 26, 1778, showed 2144. (*Michigan Pioneer Collection*, IX, 469) on March 31, 1779, it was 2651, including 400 prisoners. (*Id.*, X, 312–26.)

There can be no question that King George III and his ministers deliberately planned a cruel savage war against his American subjects — for his subjects he still claimed they were. His war minister, Lord Germaine, wrote Sir Guy Carleton, the British commander in Canada: 'As it is His Majesty's resolution that the most vigorous efforts should be made, and every means employed that Providence has put into His Majesty's Hands, for crushing the Rebellion and restoring the Constitution, it is the Kings command that you should direct Lieut. Governor Hamilton to assemble as many of the Indians to his district, as he conveniently can, and... employ them in making a diversion and exciting an alarm upon the frontiers of Virginia and Pennsylvania.'[1] George III himself wrote: 'Every means of distressing America must meet with my concurrence.'[2] With mock humanity he directed that the Indians be 'restrained from committing violence upon the *well affected and inoffensive*.' The savages were only to be turned loose upon his own rebelling subjects. His minister declared that to 'bring the war to a more speedy issue, and restore those deluded people to their former state of happiness and prosperity, are the favorite wishes of the Royal Breast and the great object of all His Majesty's measures,' but in the next sentence added: 'A supply of presents for the Indians and other necessaries will be wanted for this service, and you will of course send Lieut. Gov. Hamilton what is proper and sufficient.'[3] Amongst such 'necessaries' sent were 'red handled scalping knives' by the gross — sixteen gross, or 1504 knives, in one consignment.[4]

Hamilton's agency in the savage warfare, despite his later denial, is shown over his own hand.[5] January 15, 1778, he wrote Carleton: 'The alarm on the Ohio, and the rivers which fall into it from the eastward, has been very general and a large tract of country is deserted by the inhabitants. ...The parties sent out from hence have been in general successful, tho' the Indians have lost men enough to sharpen their resentment. They have brought in seventy three prisoners

[1] *Michigan Pioneer Collections*, IX, 347.
[2] *Formation of the Union*, by Albert Bushnell Hart, pp. 70.
[3] See *Michigan Pioneer Collections*, IX, 347–48.
[4] *Farmer's Detroit*, 246.
[5] March 26, 1777, Lord Germaine wrote Carleton: 'Making a diversion on the frontiers of Virginia and Pennsylvania, by parties of Indians conducted by proper leaders, as proposed by Lt. Gov. Hamilton, has been maturely weighed' and approved. (*Michigan Pioneer Collections*, IX, 346–47.)

alive, twenty of which they presented to me, and one hundred and twenty nine scalps.' [1] Of the fifty-three unfortunates who were not 'presented' to Hamilton, some were probably made slaves, some few adopted into the tribes, and the rest tomahawked, or tortured to death. The favorite mode of torture was by slow burning at the stake, accompanied with merciless beating and demoniacal shouting and dancing.

In the British House of Lords, a minister of the King, Lord Suffolk, defended the savage war and declared: 'there were no means which God and nature might have placed at the disposal of governing powers to which they would not be justified in having recourse.' This declaration brought from Lord Chatham an outburst of indignant eloquence rarely equalled. Chatham's just indignation, however, was mild compared with the fury of the American borderers and pioneers whose wives, children, and friends had been subjected to fiendish Indian barbarities. These men of the west deemed the savage far worse — as he certainly was far more dangerous and cruel — than any wild beast of the forest, and thought that to kill an Indian enemy, without regard to rules of civilized warfare, was an act of undeniable virtue. This attitude toward the Indians had prevailed in the colonies for generations. In Massachusetts the Reverend Solomon Stoddard urged using fierce dogs 'to hunt Indians as they do bears,' and tear them limb from limb; for, said he, they 'act like wolves and are to be dealt with as wolves.' [2] Rewards were paid for their scalps much as bounties are now given for wolf scalps. The truth is that when civilized and barbarous peoples are at war, the methods of the barbarous are nearly always imitated by the civilized; as, for example, in the World War when the use of poison gas was deliberately adopted by the Allies, including the Americans.

Dark, however, as any truthful picture of the British side of the savage war must be, justice demands the statement that the Americans did not employ Indians more freely only because they lacked the means to buy their support. [3] Again,

[1] *Michigan Pioneer Collections,* IX, 430; cf. 399.

[2] Winsor's *Critical and Narrative History,* VI, 613–14, 673.

[3] On May 14, 1774, Dr. Joseph Warren wrote Samuel Adams suggesting that the colonies employ the Indians. General Schuyler of New York wrote that he 'would not hesitate a moment to employ any Indians that might be willing to join us.' John Adams said: 'We need not be so delicate as to refuse the assistance of the Indians, provided we cannot keep them neutral.' April 1, 1775,

the charge that the British were guilty of inhumanity in rewarding the savages for American scalps suggests that a like practice had been common in the French and Indian War, when both sides offered such rewards. During the Revolution, however, the Americans never offered them for the scalps of their British kinsmen, although even this was suggested.[1]

While Clark was on his way to Kaskaskia, Hamilton was planning, with white troops and a great body of northern and southern Indians, to sweep Kentucky and the Allegheny frontiers and take Pittsburg. The campaign, he said, would 'have the effect of destroying the crops and habitations of all the advanced settlers,' and 'driving these settlers back upon their brethren of the Atlantic states, whom they would greatly distress by an additional consumption of goods and provisions.' In preparation for this grand attack, he secured plans of the Pittsburg fort, carried on an active correspondence to secure the coöperation of the southern Indians, and sent numerous bands of savages against the Kentucky settlements. It was one of these bands which captured Boone and his salt-boiling party.

On June 14th, Hamilton held a grand war council at Detroit with chiefs and head warriors of all the main Indian nations north of the Ohio. Over sixteen hundred savages were present.[2] The council lasted many days. Amongst the white

Massachusetts, by its regulating committee, recited the employment of Indians as enlisted minute men, urging them to 'join us in defense of our rights,' and next month sought recruits amongst the Nova Scotia Indians. July 1, 1775, Congress resolved to use them, if the British did so. Twenty days later, Franklin proposed a perpetual alliance with the Six Nations, 'offensive and defensive.' December 2d. following, Congress resolved 'in case of necessity,' to call for the help of certain tribes. April 19, 1776, Washington wrote: 'I submit to Congress whether it would not be better immediately to engage them on our side,' for, said he, 'they will either be for, or against us.' A month later Congress resolved that 'it is highly expedient to engage the Indians in the service of the United Colonies,' and, June 3d, authorized him to employ 2000 Indians in Canada. Two weeks later it removed this restriction, and authorized him to employ the savages anywhere. Yet only

three weeks after this, in the Declaration of Independence, Congress denounced the King's employment of them as inhumane, and then, four days later, expressly gave Washington general authority to employ them! See Winsor's *Critical and Narrative History,* vi., 613–14, 673 cf.

[1] The continental commander at Pittsburg wrote (January, 1779): 'I have the pleasure to inform you that I have now a party out to take a scalp, or prisoner, and another party is preparing for a tour. ...I would readily agree for a premium on Indian scalps, but I should not choose to offer a reward for the scalps of the British until I get some distance into the Indian country, so as to prevent a perversion of the real design of government.' (Brodhead to President Reed, January 5, 1779. *Pennsylvania Archives,* vii, 456.)

[2] Mohawks and Senecas from western New York, Shawnees and Delawares from Ohio, Hurons or Miamis from both sides of Lake Erie, Ouiatenans from the

men present were Major Hay, chief Indian agent, and Captain McKee (both of whom were later to take interesting parts in the war), Captain Lernault (who afterwards became Hamilton's successor at Detroit), Lieutenant Caldwell of 'the King's Own Regiment' of British regulars, and Simon Girty, a renegade Pennsylvanian who was more cordially hated by the western Americans than any other man, and the bug-a-boo of pioneer children.

Hamilton opened the council with a speech to the painted savages, saying:

'Children! — Ottawas, Chippewas, Hurons, Pottawatomies, Shawnees, Delawares, &c. — Let us, before all things, return thanks to the Great Spirit above, who has permitted us to meet together this day. ... With these strings of wampum I open your eyes, that you may see clear and your ears may listen to my words; since I speak by order of the Great King, who is the Father of us all, whether white or brown skins. For myself, I shall never forget the manner in which you have acted since I have resided among you, nor the good will with which you took up your Father's axe, striking as one man his enemies and yours, the Rebels. ... You may remember, when you received a large belt of alliance here last year, the number of nations who took hold of it. You know the consequences have been good, as you have succeeded in almost all your enterprises, having taken a number of prisoners and a far greater number of scalps. [The excess of scalps seemed not unpleasing to the Lieutenant Governor.] You have forced them from the frontiers to the coast. ... Some Delawares are this day arrived, who are desirous of showing their intention of joining their brethren, and have presented me with two pieces of dried meat [scalps], one of which I have given the Chippewas, another to the Miamis, that they may show in their villages the disposition of the Delawares.' [An Ottawa chief, replying to him, said:] 'You know my business at this place is to bring you some prisoners and scalps. I had no thought of a council.'

It may be said here that the Indians were ever fond of impressive ceremony. In all important meetings they observed rituals hardly less perplexing to the uninitiated than the religious rites of the ancients, or of some modern churches. On these occasions, the use of belts of wampum (strung shells,) medals, tobacco pipes, and sundry other symbols, expressed to the Indian mind a great variety of ideas. They greatly

upper Wabash, Saginaws of northwestern Michigan, Ottawas of the Mackinac region, Pottawatomies from the eastern side of Lake Michigan, and Chippewas from south of Lake Superior.

admired oratory abounding in figurative language, which, although often overstrained, was sometimes highly poetic and moving. Their speeches abounded in references to the Great Spirit, to the personified powers of earth, heaven, winds, and sea — to 'honest hearts,' 'false tongues,' 'bad birds' (false rumors), and they also often made extravagant assertions about the virtues and prowess of the orator or his nation. In all formal councils with them, the white men deferred to their taste and endeavored to conform to their ritual and use their symbolic language; but the inflated addresses of white men nearly always seem ridiculous. Few of them reached the average of Indian eloquence.

While Hamilton was planning destruction for the western Americans, Congress was laying plans to capture Detroit, and only four days before his council with the Indians there,

'Resolved, That an expedition be immediately undertaken, the object of which shall be to reduce, if practicable, the garrison of Detroit, and to compel to terms of peace such of the Indian nations, now in arms against these states, as lie on, or contiguous to, the route between Fort Pitt and Detroit;...That three thousand men be engaged in the service; ...That the governor and council of the state of Virginia be requested, on the application of the Board of War, or of brigadier McIntosh, [the continental commander at Pittsburg] to call forth such a body of militia, not exceeding twenty five hundred men, as shall be judged necessary to compleat the number of men appropriated for this service.' [1]

Governor Henry at once set about raising the twenty-five hundred men Congress asked from Virginia; for, although he had authorized Colonel Clark to proceed against Detroit after taking Kaskaskia,[2] he probably had little idea that the young colonel could do more than effect a foothold in the Illinois town. Meantime, plans for McIntosh's expedition and estimates of the men, money, and supplies necessary for it were prepared for Congress by Colonel George Morgan, its Indian agent at Pittsburg.[3] Only half of the troops — fifteen hundred men — were to assemble at Pittsburg, and the cost of marching them only twenty days into the enemy's country was estimated at one hundred and eighty-two

[1] *Journal of Congress* (Claypoole, Philadelphia), IV, 343.
[2] *Illinois Historical Collections*, VIII, 38.
[3] Morgan was also a leading shareholder and active agent of the Indiana Company promoters.

thousand pounds, Virginia money. The supplies and transportation required were stated as follows: 'Flour 609,937 lbs; 600 pack-horsemen; . . . 120 bullock drivers; cattle, 2440 head, at 300 lbs. net.' Morgan's report concluded with the remark that 'in the foregoing calculations no regard is had to the carriage of ammunition, tents, tools, hospital stores, artillery, nor officers baggage.'[1] Nothing, however, came of this expedition. Because of the expense, Congress 'Resolved, that the expedition against the fortress of Detroit be for the present deferred.'[2]

[1] What the total outlay would have been, had it included these omitted items, Morgan does not state; but even without them it was one hundred and fifty times what Clark had received, aside from a few cheap boats and provisions furnished him at Pittsburg. For the estimate above, see *George Morgan's Letter Book*, Carnegie Library, Pittsburg.

[2] *Journal of Congress* (Claypoole, Philadelphia), IV, 427.

CHAPTER VI

CAPTURE OF KASKASKIA

COLONEL CLARK, after a month's stay on Corn Island drilling his men and awaiting a rise in the Ohio which would permit his little boats to pass over the Falls, was ready to embark for his venture into the enemy's country. The Ohio is here about a mile wide. The main current, which passes north of the island and is very swift and tortuous, is impossible to navigate except at flood stage, and even then the passage is perilous. 'Every preparation,' said Clark, 'was now made for our departure. After spending a day of amusement, in pastime with our friends of Kentucky, — they to return to the defense of their country and we in search of new adventures, — on the 24th of June 1778 we left our little island and ran about a mile up the river, in order to gain the main channel, and shot the falls at the very moment of the Sun's being in a great eclipse, which caused various conjectures among the superstitious.' Of the one hundred and seventy or eighty men who made the little army, many, in their buckskin clothes and coonskin caps, no doubt made a rough looking lot; but history hardly records a braver. As they entered the boiling rapids, the sun's eclipse — certainly one of nature's most appalling events — darkened the world like an omen of evil; yet on they went — how absurd it seems — to conquer an empire!

'As I knew [said Clark] that spies were kept on the river below the towns of the Illinois, I had resolved to march part of the way by land, and of course left the whole of our baggage, except such as would equip us in the Indian mode. The whole of our force, after leaving such as were judged not competent to the expected fatigue, consisted only of four companies — captains Jno. Montgomery, Jos. Bowman, Leonard Helm, and Wm. Harrod.' 'We double-manned our oars and proceeded, day and night, until we ran into the mouth of the Tennesee River.'

'I had fully acquainted myself that the French inhabitants in those western settlements had great influence among the Indians in general, and [were] more beloved by them...than any other Europeans; that their commercial intercourse was universal throughout the west and northwest country: and [that] the governing interests on the lakes was mostly in the hands of the English, not much beloved by them. Those, and many other ideas similar thereto, caused me to resolve, if possible, to strengthen myself by such train of conduct as might probably attach the whole [French population] to our interest, and give us influence at a greater distance than the limits of the country we were aiming for. These were the principles that influenced my future conduct; and fortunately I had just received a letter from Col. John Campbell, dated Pittsburg, informing me of the contents of the treaty between France and America.

'As I intended to leave the Ohio at Fort Massac, [an abandoned French post] three leagues below the Tennessee, I landed on Baritaria, a small island in the mouth of that river, in order to prepare for the march.'

[A contemporary who lived in Illinois [1] said: 'The country between Fort Massac and Kaskaskia, at that day, in 1778 — was a wilderness of one hundred and twenty miles and contained, much of it a swampy and difficult road. Clark's warriors had no wagons, pack-horses, or other means of conveyance of their munitions of war, or baggage, other than their own robust and hardy selves. Col. Clark himself was nature's favorite, in his person as well as mind. He was large and athletic, capable of enduring much, yet formed with such noble symmetry and manly beauty that he combined much grace and elegance together with great firmness of character. He was grave and dignified in his deportment, agreeable and affable with his soldiers when relaxed from duty; but in a crisis, when the fate of a campaign was at stake or the lives of his brave warriors were in danger, his deportment became stern and severe. His appearance in these perils indicated, without language to his men, that every soldier must do his duty.']

'In a few hours after [landing],' continues Clark, 'one John Duff and a party of hunters coming down the river were brought to by our boats. They were men formerly from the states.' 'They were eight days from Kaskaskia. Before I would suffer them to answer any person a question, after their taking the oath of allegiance, I examined them particularly. They... appeared to be in our interest. Their intelligence was not favorable.' 'They said that... Mr. Rocheblave commanded at Kaskaskia &c. that the militia was kept in good order and spies on the Mississippi, and that all hunters, both Indians and others, were ordered to keep a good lookout for the rebels; that the fort was kept in good order as an asylum &c; but they believed the whole to proceed more from the fondness for parade than the expectation of a visit; that they were convinced that, if they were to get timely notice of us, they would collect and give us a warm reception, as they were taught to harbour a most horrid idea of the barbarity of the rebels, especially the Virginians; but that if we could surprise the place, which they were in hopes we might, they made no doubt of our being able to do as we pleased.' 'They asked leave to go on the expedition. I granted it and ordered

[1] Governor Reynolds, who is said to have known Clark well.

them what to relate, particularly, on pain of suffering. They observed my instructions, which put the whole in the greatest spirits, sure, by what they heard, of success.' 'They proved valuable men. The acquisition to us was great, as I had had no intelligence from those posts since [the report] of the spies I sent twelve months past.

'But no part of their information pleased me more than that of the inhabitants viewing us as more savage than their neighbors, the Indians. I was determined to improve this, if I was fortunate enough to get them in my possession, as I conceived the greater the shock I could give them at first, the more sensibly they would feel my lenity, and become more valuable friends. This I conceived to be agreeable to human nature as I observed it in many instances.'

Although the Illinois towns contained some people of considerable wealth, intelligence, and refinement, the inhabitants generally were simple, credulous people, who had been plied by their British rulers with stories well calculated to make them dread the barbarity of the rebels. This dread had been much intensified by recent news of a raid against the British settlements on the lower Mississippi by a party of forty Americans under Captain James Willing of Philadelphia. With the connivance of the Spanish governor, Willing secured a vessel and supplies at New Orleans and surprised and captured several British vessels, including a brig of fourteen guns manned by forty men. Proceeding up the Mississippi, he played havoc amongst the British settlements on the east side of the river, plundering and burning, 'more like an Indian warrior than a civilized enemy,' wrote a Spanish resident at the time. Rochblave, commanding at Kaskaskia, soon afterward wrote: 'The majority of the inhabitants, knowing the maneuvers which had occurred in the lower part of the Mississippi, were resolved to defend themselves.' [1]

Of the overland march to Kaskaskia Clark said: 'Nothing extraordinary happened during our route, excepting my guide losing himself and not being able, as we judged by his confusion, of giving a just account of himself. It put the whole troops in the greatest confusion. I never in my life felt such a flow of rage, — to be wandering in a country where every nation of Indians could raise three or four times our number and a certain loss of our enterprise by the enemies getting timely notice [of our presence.] I could not bear the thought of returning; in Short every idea of the sort put me in that passion that I did not master for some time.' 'We soon discovered that he was totally lost, without there was some other

---

[1] Rochblave to Carleton, *Illinois Historical Collections*, ii, xli, note.

cause for his present conduct. I asked him various questions, and from his answers could scarcely determine what to think of him, whether or not he...was lost. The thought...that he wished to deceive us made the cry of the whole detachment that he was a traitor. He begged that he might be suffered to go some distance into a plain, that was in full view, to try to make some discovery, whether or not he was right. I told him he might, but that I was suspicious of him;...that from the first of his being employed [he] always said that he knew the way well; that there was now a different appearance; that I saw the nature of the country was such that a person once acquainted with it could not, in a short time, forget his way; that a few men should go with him to prevent his escape; and that, if he did not discover and take us into the Hunters Road, that led from the east into Kaskaskia, that he had frequently described,...I would have him immediately put to death, which I was determined to have done. But, after an hour or twos search, he came to a place that he perfectly knew, and we discovered that the poor fellow had been, as they call it, bewildered.[1]

'In the evening of the fourth of July we got within a few miles of the town, where we lay until near dark, keeping spies ahead; after which we continued our march and took possession of a house, wherein a large family lived, on the bank of the Kaskaskia river, about three quarters of a mile above the town. There we were informed that a few days before the people were under arms, but had concluded that the cause of the alarm was without foundation, and that at present all was quiet; that there was a great number of men in town, but that the Indians had generally left it. We soon procured a sufficiency of vessels, the more in ease to convey us across the river. ...I was now convinced that it was impossible that the inhabitants could make any resistance, as they could not now possibly get notice of us time enough to make such resistance. My object was now to conduct matters so as to get possession of the place with as little confusion as possible, but to have it even at the loss of the whole town.

'Not perfectly relying on the information we got at the house, (as [our informant there] seemed to vary in his information, and [a noise] was just heard in town, which he informed us he supposed was the negroes at a dance &c), with one of the divisions I march[ed] off to the fort and ordered the other two into different quarters of the town. If I met with no resistance, at a certain signal a general shout was to be given, certain part[s] were to be immediately possessed, and men of each detachment, that could speak the French language, [were] to run through every street and proclaim what had

---

[1] Captain Bowman, a few weeks after the march, wrote his uncle in Virginia: 'We started with about four days provisions and steered a north-west course for the Illinois and in six days time we arrived there in the night. We traveled two days without any provisions, being very hungry. Our men were all determined to take the town, or die in the attempt.' Holograph, *Author's MSS.*; *Illinois Historical Collections*, VIII, 614.

happened, and inform the inhabitants that every person that appeared in the streets would be shot down. This disposition had its desired effect. [Clark with the main division marched silently against the fort, effected an entrance, captured the commandant, Rochblave, in bed, gave the agreed signal, and 'a general shout' of all the troops of the three divisions told the amazed inhabitants of the presence of their dreaded enemies.]

'In a very little time we had complete possession, and every avenue guarded to prevent any escape to give the alarm to the other villages. Various orders had been issued not worth mentioning. I don't suppose greater silence ever reigned among the inhabitants of a place than did at this, — not a person to be seen, not a word to be heard by them for some time, but, designedly, the greatest noise [kept up by the troops] continually the whole night. [They went] round it intercepting any information, [ever] a capital object. ...In about two hours the whole of the inhabitants were disarmed and informed that if anyone was taken attempting to make his escape, he should be immediately put to death. Mr. Rocheblave was secured, but as it had been sometime before he would be got out of his room, I suppose [his delay] was to inform his lady what to do, ...to secure his public letters &c, as but few were got. His chamber not being visited for the night, she had full opportunity of doing [that], but by what means we could never learn. I dont suppose [the letters were hid] among her trunks, although they never were examined. She must have expected the loss of even her clothes, from the idea she entertained of us.' [Such consideration for the privacy of the lady's chamber on the part of the dreaded 'Big Knives' illustrates a Quixotic chivalry by no means rare amongst the pioneers.]

In his *Winning of the West*, Roosevelt gives a romantic account of the capture which has been much quoted. He says:

'Inside the fort the lights were lit, and through the windows came the sounds of violins. The officers of the post had given a ball, and the mirth-loving creoles, young men and girls, were dancing and revelling within, while the sentinels had left their posts. One of his captives showed Clark a postern-gate by the river-side, and through this he entered the fort, having placed his men round about at the entrance. Advancing to the great hall where the revel was held, he leaned silently with folded arms against the door-post, looking at the dancers. An Indian, lying on the floor of the entry, gazed intently on the stranger's face as the light from the torches within flickered across it, and suddenly sprang to his feet uttering the unearthly war-whoop. Instantly the dancing ceased; the women screamed, while the men ran towards the door. But Clark, standing unmoved and with unchanged face, grimly bade them continue their dancing, but to remember that they now danced under Virginia and not Great Britain. At the same time his men burst into the fort, and seized the French officers.' [This whole story is mere romantic invention.[1]]

Continuing, Clark says: 'Several particular persons, were sent for, in the course of the night, for information, &c; but we got very little, ...except from the conduct of several persons then in town, there was reason to suppose that they were inclined to the American interest; that a great number of Indians had been and were then in the neighborhood of Cahokia, 60 miles from this place; that Mr. Cerré, a principal merchant, — one of the most inveterate enemies we had, — left this place a few days past with a large quantity of fur for Michilimackinac and from thence to Quebec, from which place he had lately arrived; that he was then in St. Louis, the Spanish capital; that his lady and family were then in town, with a very considerable quantity of goods. ...I immediately suspected what these informers aimed at, — making their peace with me, at the expense of their neighbors. My situation required too much caution to give them much satisfaction. I found that Mr. Cerré was one of the most eminent men in the country, of great influence among the people. I had some suspicion [that] his accusers were probably in debt [to him] and wished to ruin him; but, ...from what I had heard of him, he became an object of consequence to me. [I thought] that perhaps he might be wavering in his opinion respecting the contest; that, if he should take a decisive part in our favor, he might be a valuable acquisition. In short, his enemies caused me much to wish to see [him]; and as he was then out of my power, I made no doubt of bringing it about through the means of his family. Having them in my power, I had a guard immediately placed at his house, his stores sealed, &c, ...making no doubt that when he heard of this he would be extremely anxious to get an interview.

'Messrs. R[d] Winston and Danl Murry, who proved to have been in the American interest, by the morning of the 5th, had plenty of provisions prepared. After the troops had regaled themselves, they were withdrawn from within the town and posted in different positions on the borders of it. Every [soldier] had been expressly forbid holding any conversation with the inhabitants; all were distant, their town in complete possession of an enemy whom they entertained the most horrid idea of, and [they] not yet being able to have

---

[1] vol. II, 187. The location of the fort by the river, the 'postern gate' episode, the 'great ball,' the lighted fort, violins, dance and revel, Clark's entrance and arm-folded pose, the sleeping Indian and his unearthly warwhoop, Clark's melodramatic command for the dance to continue are all pure fiction.

Roosevelt cites *Major Denny's Journal* and says: 'The story was told to Major Denny by Clark himself some time in '87 or '88.' This statement is wholly erroneous. Major Denny's *Journal* makes no mention whatever of any such story and says nothing of Clark having told it to him. The plainly romancing *editor* of the book does, indeed, in his introduction, concoct a story which Roosevelt adopts and improves upon with free fancy for dramatic effect. His charming but superficial and often reckless and blundering work has done much to pervert western Revolutionary history.

Denny's diary is published with the title '*Record of Upland. ...Denny's Diary.* (Lippincott, Philadelphia, 1860.)

any conversation with one of our people. Even those that I had conversation with were ordered not to speak to the rest. [The young commander evidently knew the awful power of silence.]

'After some time they were informed that they might walk freely about the town. After finding they were busy in conversation, I had a few of the principal militia officers put in irons, without hinting a reason for it, or hearing anything they had to say in their own defense. The worst was now expected by the whole. I saw the consternation the inhabitants were in, and, I suppose, in imagination felt all they experienced in reality; and felt myself disposed to act as an arbiter between them and my duty. ['My principle would not suffer me to distress such a number of people, except, through policy, it was necessary.'] A little reflection convinced me that it was [my] interest to attach them to me, ...for the town of Cohos [Cahokia] and St. Vincents [Vincennes] and numerous tribes of Indians, attached to the French, were yet to influence. I was too weak to treat them any other way.' [His position certainly was weak, for the French were much more numerous than his little army; and he was yet uncertain whether they would become friends or remain foes. The temptation was great to secure his own safety by keeping them under subjection and taking by force whatever he required for his troops. A commander of dull imagination would likely have done that, with the result that the French would have furnished him necessary supplies only reluctantly, and scantily, would have spread injurious reports amongst the French at other British posts and their Indian friends, and, in the end, would probably have made Kaskaskia a fatal trap for him and his men. But Clark's plan, as he said, was 'to attach them to me,' and this he proceeded to do by leaving them in dreadful suspense and intensifying their fear of him!]

'After some time the priest got permission to wait on me. He came, with five or six elderly gentlemen with him. However shocked they already were from their situation, the addition was obvious and great when they entered the room where I was sitting with other officers [all making] a dirty, savage appearance. As we had left our clothes at the river, we were almost naked, and torn by the bushes and briars. They were shocked, and it was some time before they could venture to take seats, and longer before they would speak. [An interesting scene for the painter!] They at last were asked what they wanted. The priest informed me (after asking which was the principal) that as the inhabitants expected to be separated, never perhaps to meet again, they begged through him that they might be permitted to spend some time in the church to take their leave of each other. (I knew they expected their very religion was obnoxious to us.) I carelessly told him I had nothing to say to his church; that he might go there if he would; if he did, to inform the people not to venture out of town. They attempted some other conversation, but were informed that we were not at leisure. They went off, after answering me a few questions that I asked them with a very faint degree [of seeming interest] that they might not be totally discouraged from petitioning again, as they had not yet come to the point I wanted. The whole town seemed to have collected to the church. Infants were carried, and the houses generally left without a person in them. ...Orders were given to prevent the soldiers from entering a house.

'They remained a considerable time in the church, after which the priest and many of the principal men came to me to return thanks for the indulgence shown them, and begged permission to address me further on a subject that was more dear to them than anything else; that their present situation was the fate of war; that the loss of their property they could reconcile [themselves to], but were in hopes that I would not part them from their families and that the women and children might be allowed to keep some of their clothes and a small quantity of provisions; that they were in hopes by industry that they might support them; that their whole conduct had been influenced by their commandants, whom they looked upon themselves [as] bound to obey; that they were not certain of being acquainted with the nature of the American war, as they had but little opportunity to inform themselves; that many of [them] frequently expressed themselves as much in favor of the Americans as they dared do. In short they said everything that could be supposed that sensible men in their alarming situation would advance. All they appeared to aim at was some lenity shown their women and families, supposing that their goods would appease us.

'I had sufficient reason to believe there was no finesse in all this, but that they really spoke their sentiments and the height of their expectations. This was the point I wished to bring them to. I asked them, very abruptly, whether or not they thought they were speaking to savages, and said that it was certain they did, from the tenor of their conversation. Did they suppose that we meant to strip the women and children, and take the bread out of their mouths? or that we would condescend to make war on the women and children, or the church? [I told them] that it was to prevent the effusion of innocent blood by the Indians, through the instigation of their commandants and emissaries, that caused us to visit them, and not the prospect of plunder; that, as soon as that object was attained, we should be perfectly satisfied; that as the King of France had joined the Americans, there was a probability of there shortly being an end to the war, (this information very apparently affected them); that they were at liberty to take which side they pleased, without any dread of losing their property, or having their families destroyed. As for their church, all religions would be tolerated in America, and — so far from our meddling with it — any insult offered to it should be punished; and, to convince them that we were not savages and plunderers as they conceived, that they might return to their families and inform them that they might conduct themselves as usual with all freedom and without apprehension of any danger; that ...the information I had got, since my arrival, so fully convinced me of their being influenced by false information from their leaders, that I was willing to forget everything past; that their friends in confinement should [be] immediately released, &c, and the guards withdrawn from every part of the town, except Cerré's; and that I only required a compliance to a proclamation I should immediately issue.

'This was the substance of my reply to them. They wished to soften the idea of my conceiving that they supposed us to be savages and plunderers, [and explained] that they had conceived that the property in all towns belonged to those that reduced [them] &c, &c. I informed them I knew that they were taught to believe that we were little better than barbarians, but that we would say no more on the subject; that I wished them to go and relieve the anxiety of the inhabitants. Their feelings must be more easily guessed than expressed. They retired, and in a few minutes the scene was changed from an almost mortal dejection to that of joy in the extreme,— the bells ringing, the church crowded, returning thanks, in short every appearance of extravagant joy that could fill a place with utmost confusion. I immediately set about preparing a proclamation to be presented to them before they left the church; but, wishing to prove the people further, I omitted it for a few days.'

CHAPTER VII

ENEMIES MADE FRIENDS: VINCENNES WON OVER

DURING the busy night of the capture and the following day, Clark was occupied with much more than his policy of terrorizing and then winning over the French inhabitants of Kaskaskia. Hardly had the town been secured, before he sent Simon Kenton and two others to Vincennes, as spies, to learn the military situation there; for in case he should gain complete control of the Illinois, Vincennes would naturally be his next objective. The same day, too, he called on Captain Bowman and thirty of his men to take horses and hasten to surprise and capture Cahokia.

'As I made no doubt' [said he] but that any report that would be now made of us through the country would be favorable, I was more careless who went or came into the town; but, not knowing what might happen, I [was] yet uneasy as [to] Cahokia, and was determined to make a lodgement there, as soon as possible, and gain the place by something similar to what had been done, at [Kaskaskia.] Ordered Maj' Bowman to mount his company and part of another, (and a few inhabitants to inform their friends what had happened,) on horses to be procured from the town, and to proceed without delay, and if possible get possession of Cahokia before the ensueing morning; that I should give him no further instructions on the subject, but for him to make use of his own prudence. [The men responded with alacrity, and when one remembers that they had just been through a six days forced march — the last two without food — and through a sleepless night of intense excitement, their zeal and the test of endurance before them will be appreciated.] He [Bowman] gave orders for collecting the horses, on which numbers of gentlemen came and informed me that they was sensible of the design; that the troops were much fatigued; that they hoped I would not take it amiss at their offering themselves to execute whatever I should wish to be done at Cahokia; that the people [at Cahokia] were their friends and relations, and would follow their example; at least they hoped that they might be permitted to accompany the detachment. Conceiving that it might be good policy to show them that we put confidence in them, . . . I informed them that I made no doubt that Major Bowman would be fond of their company and that as many as chose it might go.

'. . . It was late in the morning of the 6th before they reach [ed] Cahokia. Detaining every person they met with, they got into the

borders of the town before they were discovered. The inhabitants
were at first much alarmed at being thus suddenly visited and
ordered to surrender the town, even by their friends and relations,
but [the Frenchman] gave the people a detail of what had happened
at Kaskaskia. The Major informed them not to be alarmed; that
although resistance at present was out of the question, . . . they were
at liberty to become free Americans, as their friends at Kaskaskia
had, or that [any] . . . might move out of the country, except [those]
that had been engaged in inciting the Indians to war. Liberty and
Freedom and huzzahing for the Americans rang through the whole
town. The Kaskaskia gentlemen dispersed among their friends.
In a few hours the whole was amicably settled and Major Bowman
snugly quartered in the old British fort. Some individuals said
that the town was given up too tamely, but little attention was paid
to them. A considerable number of Indians that were then encamped
in the neighborhood (as this was a principal post of trade,) immediately fled. . . . The intermediate villages followed the example of the
others, and as a strict examination was not made as to those who
had a hand in encouraging the Indians to war, in a few days the
country appeared to be in a perfect state of harmony.[1] . . .

'Mr. Cerré, formerly mentioned, . . . was yet in St. Louis and preparing to prosecute his journey to Canada, but was stopped in consequence of the information [he received of the guard over his stores
and family in Kaskaskia.] After learning the situation of things,
agreeable to my expectations he resolved to return; but, learning
that there was a guard kept at his house, and at no other, and that
several had attempted to ruin him by their information to me, was
advised not to venture over without a safe conduct. He applied to
the Spanish governor for a letter for that purpose and came to St.
Genevieve, opposite to Kaskaskia, and got another from the commandant of that post to the same purpose, and sent them to me.
But all the interest he could make through the Spanish officers,
and the solicitation of his particular friends, [whom] I found to be a
great majority of the people, could not procure him a safe conduct.
I absolutely denied it and hinted that I wished to hear no more on
the subject. Neither would I hear any persons that had anything to
say in vindication of him, informing [them] that I understood that
Mr. Cerré was a sensible man; that, if he was innocent of the allega-
tions against him, he would not be afraid of delivering himself up;
that his backwardness seem[ed] to prove his guilt; that I cared very
little about him. I suppose a runner immediately gave him this
information. In a few hours, he came over, and before visiting his
family, presented himself before me.[2]

---

[1] See Bowman's letters describing the
capture, *Illinois Historical Collections*,
VIII, 612–13.

[2] Cerré wrote Clark the following letter
begging the passport:

SIR: I was extremely chagrinned that

I was not at home at the time of your
arrival at Kaskaskia. I would have had
the honour of giving you proofs of my
entire submission to my superiors. But,
since my profession is that of a merchant
and I am, consequently, obliged to travel

'I told him that I supposed that he was fully sensible of the charges that were exhibited against him, particularly that of inciting the Indians to murder &c — a crime that ought to be punished by all people that should be so fortunate as to get such persons in their power; that his late backwardness almost confirmed me [of] his guilt. He replied that he was a mere merchant; that he never concerned himself about state affairs, further than the interest of his trade required; that he had [not] as yet an opportunity to fully acquaint himself with the principles of the present contest, [so] as to enable [him] finally to settle his own opinion to his satisfaction; that being generally so far detached from the seat of affairs,...he was always doubtful of his only [hearing] one side of the question; that he had learned more in a few days past than he ever before knew; that it only confirmed his former suspicion. I read him part of a letter from Governor Hamilton of Detroit to Mr. Rochblave, wherein he was alluded with much affection. He said that when he was there he behaved himself as became a subject; that he defied any man to prove that he ever encouraged an Indian to war; that many had often heard him disapprove of the cruelty of such proceedings; that there were...a number in town that were much in debt to him; perhaps the object of some of them was to get clear of it by ruining...him; that it would be inconsistent for him, in his present situation, to offer to declare his present sentiments respecting the war; but wished to stand every test; [as]...encouraging the Indians is what he ever detested. He excused his fear in coming over the Mississippi as soon as he could have wished. I told him to retire to another room, without making him any further reply.

'The whole town was anxious to know the fate of Mr. Cerré. I sent for his accusers, a great number following them, and had Mr. Cerré called. I plainly saw the confusion his appearance made amongst them. I opened the case to the whole; told them that I never chose to condemn a man untried; that Cerré was now present; that I was ready to do justice to the world in general by the punishment of Mr. Cerré, if he was found guilty of encouraging murder,

to the different posts of this country to make a living for my family, my unlucky star, or to speak more correctly, the annual habit I have of commencing my journeys at this time, cause my misfortune. According to public rumor, my enemies, jealous of the efforts I make to obtain a comfortable mediocraty, have profited by my absence to blacken me and destroy me in the opinion of persons to whom I have not the pleasure of being known. I am well persuaded that, when my past and future conduct are once known to you, you will render me the justice that is due to every good and submissive subject. I fear that in the first moment the false reports of my enemies may cause injury to my fortune, the only object of their hatred. Besides I have in my hands the affairs of the deceased M. Viviat to arrange with several persons at Kaskaskia, who require my presence. I venture to solicit you, sir, to have the goodness to grant me a passport to return home, so that I may clear myself of the accusations that have been made against me and attend to the affairs that calls me there. This is the favour that the most submissive subject desires from you, sir,

 your very humble and
  very obedient servant
        Cerré

or acquit him, if innocent of the charge; that they would give in their information. Cerré began to speak to them, but was ordered to desist. His accusers began to whisper to each other and retire for private conversation. At length but one, of six or seven, was left in the room. I asked him what he had to say to the point in question. In fact I found that none of them had anything to say to the purpose. I gave them a suitable reprimand, and, after some general conversation, I informed Mr. Cerré that I was happy to find that he had so honorably acquitted himself of so black a charge; that he was now at liberty to dispose of himself and property as he pleased; if he chose to become a citizen of the Union, it would give us pleasure; if not, he was at full liberty to dispose of himself. He made many acknowledgements and concluded by saying that the many doubts that he had were now cleared up to his satisfaction, and that he wished to take the oath immediately. In short he became a most valuable man to us. As simple as this may appear, it had great weight with the people and was of infinite service to us.'

Simple, too, as Clark's narrative of all this is, it is extremely well done and discloses a native talent for graphic description rarely equaled by one so little tutored or practised in the art of composition, and so careless about it. This literary excellence in his writings has been generally overlooked — no doubt because obscured by his incomplete and disjointed sentences, misspelling, and confusing punctuation and capitalizing. True, the actual situations and doings he describes were themselves so dramatic that they could hardly be truly told without making a dramatic narrative; but allowing for that, his diction has rare merits of its own and he also discloses an excellent vocabulary.

Amongst new-made and untried French friends, whether Clark could hold the towns he had already taken seemed extremely doubtful. He was nearly a thousand miles from his base, with less than two hundred men whose term of enlistment was about to expire, with no prospect of reinforcements, with Vincennes in British possession and Hamilton at Detroit, and with hostile Indian tribes surrounding him, any one of which was an over-match for his whole force. His immediate danger was from the savages. Fatal collision with them could only be avoided by putting on a bold front to mask his weakness, and by audacious acting to give them an exaggerated idea of his power. Daring theatricals had to supply his want of men.

'I determined to send no message to the Indians for some time, but wished interviews to happen between us through the means of the French gentlemen, and appear careless myself. ... I had been always convinced our general conduct with the Indians was wrong; that inviting them to treaties was...construed by them in a different manner from what we expected, and imputed by them to fear, and that giving them great presents confessed it. I resolved to guard against this. ... I took great pains to make myself acquainted with the French and Spanish methods of treating Indians, and of the manner and disposition of the Indians in general; and, as the Indians in this quarter had not yet been spoiled by us, I was resolved that they should not [be.]'

'As I could now get every piece of information I wished for, I was astonished at the pains and expense the British were at in engaging the Indians; and [found] that they had emissaries in every nation throughout these extensive countries, and with great [outlay, were] even bringing the [Indian] inhabitants about Lake Superior by water to Detroit, and fitting them out from thence, that the sound of war was universal among them, — scarcely a nation but what had declared it and received the Bloody Belt and Hatchet. ...

'I inquired particularly into the manner the people had been governed formerly, and, much to my satisfaction, [found] it had been as severe as under military law. I was determined to make an advantage of it, and took every step in my power to cause the people enjoyment by [becoming] American citizens, which I soon discovered enabled me to support, from their own choice, almost a supreme authority over them. I caused a court of civil judicature to be established at Cahokia, elected by the people. Major Bowman, to the surprise of the people, held a poll for [electing] a magistracy and was elected and acted as judge of the court. The idea of Mr. Bowman holding a poll is easily perceived. ... There was an appeal to myself in certain cases, and I believe that no people ever had their business done more to their satisfaction [than] they had through the means of these regulations for a considerable time.'

'A friendly correspondence which immediately commenced between the Spanish officers and ourselves added much to the general tranquillity and happiness. But as to myself, enjoyments of this nature was not my fortune. I found myself launched into a field that would require great attention, and all the address I was master of to extricate myself from, in doing that service to my country which appeared now in full view, with honor to them and credit to myself.'

'Post Vincennes...was the next object in my view. ...More fully to know the sentiments of the inhabitants, ...and to execute my plans, I pretended that I was about to send an express to the Falls of Ohio for a body of troops to join me at a certain place in order to attack it. It soon had the desired effect; advocates appeared among the people in their behalf.'

'From some things that I had learned, I had some reason to suspect that Mr. Gibault, the priest, was inclined to the American interest previous to our arrival in the country. . . . I made no doubt of his integrity. I sent for him and had [a] long conference with him on the subject of Vincennes. In answer to all my queries, he informed me that he did not think it was worth my while to cause any military preparation to be made at the Falls for [an] attack on Vincennes, although the place was strong and a great number of Indians in [its] neighborhood, who to his knowledge were generally at war; that Gov. Abbott had a few weeks [before] left the place on some business at Detroit; that he expected that when the inhabitants were fully acquainted with what had passed at the Illinois towns and the present happiness of their friends, and made fully acquainted with the nature of the war, . . . their sentiments would greatly change; that he knew that his appearance there would have great weight, even amongst the savages; that, if it was agreeable to me, he would take this business on himself, and had no doubt of his being able to bring that place over to the American interest, without my being at the trouble of marching troops against it; that, his business being altogether spiritual, he wished that another person might be charged with the temporal part of the embassy, but that he would privately direct the whole &c. He named Dr. Laffont as his associate.

'This was perfectly agreeable to what I had been secretly aiming at for some days. The plan was immediately settled, and the two doctors, with their intended retinue, among whom I had a spy, set about preparing for their journey, and set out on the 14th. of July with . . . great numbers of letters from their friends to the inhabitants. . . . Mr. Gibault [had] verbal instructions how to act in certain cases. . . . [He and his] party arrived safe, and, after their spending a day or two in explaining matters to the people, they universally acceded to the proposal, (except a few emissaries that were left by Mr. Abbott, that immediately left the country), and went in a body to the church, where the oath of allegiance was administered to them in the most solemn manner. An officer, [Captain Bosseron] was elected, and the fort immediately [garrisoned], and the American flag displayed, to the astonishment of the Indians, and everything settled far beyond our most sanguine hopes.

'The people there immediately began to put on a new face and to talk in a different style and to act as perfect freemen, with a garrison their own, with the United States at their elbows. Their language to the Indians was immediately altered. They began as citizens of the state, and informed the Indians that their old Father, the King of France, was come to life again and had joined the Big Knife, and was mad at them for fighting for the English; that they would advise them to make peace with the Americans as soon as they could, otherwise they might expect the land to be very bloody, &c. [The Indians] began to think seriously throughout those countries. This was now the kind of language they generally got from their ancient friends of the Wabash and Illinois, through the means of their correspondence breeding among the nations. Our batteries began now to play in a proper channel.

...'Mr. Gibault and party accompanied by several gentlemen of Vincennes, returned about the first of August with the joyful news. During his absence on this business, which caused great anxiety in me, (for without the possession of this post all our views would have been blasted), I was exceedingly engaged in regulating of things in the Illinois.' 'I now found myself in possession of the whole of a country where I found I could do more real service than I expected; which occasioned my situation to be the more disagreeable, as I wanted men.' 'I was at great loss to determine how to act, and how far I might venture to strain my authority. ...My instructions were silent on many [such points], as it was impossible [for the Governor] to foresee the events that would take place. To abandon the country, and all the prospects that opened to our view in the Indian department at this time, for the want of instruction in certain case, [I] thought would amount to a reflection on government as having no confidence in me. I resolved to usurp the authority necessary to carry my points.' 'By great presents and promises I got about one hundred of my detachment enlisted for eight months.' '[I] appointed French officers in the country to complete a company of the young inhabitants, established a garrison at Cahokia, commanded by Captain Bowman, another at Kaskaskia [under] Captain Williams, late lieutenant. Post Vincennes remained in the situation as mentioned.'

'Surrounded by numerous nations of savages, whose minds had been long poisoned by the English, it was with difficulty that I could support that dignity that was necessary to give my orders that force that was necessary.' 'In all the titles I gave myself in necessary writings, &c. the Falls of Ohio was mentioned [perhaps thus: 'Headquarters Western American Army, Falls of Ohio, Illinois Detachment.'] in order that the troops we had [should seem] only a detachment from that place, though sufficient to answer our present purpose; that the body of our forces were there fortifying; that great numbers more were daily expected to arrive. ... Every man we had was taught to speak in this strain. From many hints and feigned information of mine before I left that place, the greatest part of them believed the most of this to be true. In short an excuse for our marching into the Illinois with so small a force was really necessary.' 'To color my staying with so few troops, I made a feint of returning to the Falls, as though I had sufficient confidence in the people, hoping [however] that the inhabitants would remonstrate against my leaving them, which they did in the warmest terms, proving the necessity of the troops at that place. They were afraid, if I returned, the English would again possess the country. Then, seemingly by their request, I agreed to stay with the two companies of troops and [intimated] that I hardly thought, as they alleged, that so many were necessary, but, if more were wanted, I could get them at any time from the Falls, where, they were made to believe, was a considerable garrison.'

'Being apprehensive that the British party at Detroit, finding it hard to regain their lost interest among the savages, would probably make a descent on the Illinois, . . . for fear of their finding out our numbers, (parties of men [were] coming and going from Kentucky and other places, recruits, &c), I suffered no parade, except of the guards, for a considerable time, and took every other precaution to keep every person ignorant of our number, which was generally thought to be nearly double what we really had.'

'As soon as possible I sent off those soldiers that could not be got to stay, with Mr. Rochblave and letters to his Excellency, letting him know my situation and the necessity of troops in the country. . . . 'Coln. Wm. Lynn, that had accompanied me as a volunteer, took charge of the party, that was to be discharged on their arrival at the Falls, and orders were sent for the moval of that post to the main land. Captain Montgomery was dispatched to government with letters, and also conducted Mr. Rochblave thither. . . . I informed the governor, by Col. Montgomery, of the whole of our proceedings and present prospects, pointing out the necessity of an immediate augmentation of troops, and that some person should be sent as head of the civil department [in the Illinois.]

'I again turned my attention to Vincennes. I plainly saw that it would be highly necessary to have an American officer at that post. Captain L. Helm appeared calculated to answer my purpose. He was past the meridan of life and a good deal acquainted with Indian business. I sent him to command at that post, and also appointed him agent for Indian affairs in the Department of the Wabash, . . . expecting by the fall to receive reinforcements from the governor, when a strong garrison should be sent to him. He was fully possessed. . . of my ideas and the plans I proposed to pursue, and about the middle of August he set out to take possession of his new command. [By Helm Clark sent speeches to the Wabash tribes. In striking contrast with the persuasive methods then almost universal in dealing with the Indians — in which tempting presents, cajolery, and rum were relied on — is the following defiant address:

'You Indians living on the Wabash! We are not come with design to take your lands from you. . . . We only desire to pass through your country to Detroit, to turn out your Father who is there; for your late Father, the King of France, is come to life, and will recover the country he lost to the English. Here are several belts for you to consider: a white one for the French, a red one for the Spanish, a blue one in the name of the Colonies, a green one offering peaceable terms from the Americans, and lastly, a red one offering you war, if you prefer that. We desire you to leave a very wide road for us, as we are many in number and love to have room enough for our march; for, in swinging our arms as we walk, we may chance to hurt some of your young people with our swords.' [1]]

'[An] Indian chief called 'Tobacco's Son,' a Piankeshaw, at this [time] resided in a village adjoining Vincennes. This man was called

[1] *Michigan Pioneer Collections*, IX, 486; *id.*, X, 301.

by the Indians 'The Grand Door to the Wabash,' ...as nothing of importance was [to] be undertaken by the league [on] the Wabash without his assent. I discovered that to win him was an object of great importance. I sent him...spirited compliments by Mr. Gibault. [That the 'spirited compliments' delivered to the 'Grand Door' were not 'fire-water' is persuasively shown by the next sentence.] He returned them. I now, by Captain Helm, touched him on the same spring that I had done the inhabitants,...directing Captain Helm how to manage, if he was pacifically inclined, or otherwise.

'The Captain arrived safe at Vincennes, and was received with acclamation by the people; and, after the usual ceremony was over, he sent for the Grand Door and delivered my letter to him. After having read it he informed the Captain that he was happy to see one of the Big Knife chiefs; that, it was true he had joined the English, but confessed that he always thought the sky looked gloomy and as the contents of the letter was a matter of great moment, he could not give an answer for some time; that he must collect his councillors. ...In short, he put on all the courtly dignity he was master of, and Captain Helm following his example, it was several days before this business was finished, as the whole proceeding was very ceremonious.

'At length the Captain was invited to the Indian council, and informed by the Tobacco that they had maturely considered, ... and had got the nature of the war between the English and us explained to their satisfaction; that he found that the Big Knive was in the right;...that perhaps, if the English conquered, they would serve them in the same manner they intended to serve us &c; in short...that he [would] tell all the red people on the Wabash to bloody the land no more for the English, and jumped up, struck his breast, called himself a man and a warrior, and said that he was now a Big Knife, and took Captain Helm by the hand. ...

'Thus ended this valuable negotiation and the saving of much blood. This man proved a zealous friend to the day of his death, which happened two years after. ...He desired to be buried [with] the Americans. His body was conveyed to the garrison of Cahokia and buried with the honours of war. ...He appeared in all his conduct as if he had the American interest much at heart. [His nation, too, remained valuable friends for years after his death.] In a short time almost the whole of the various tribes of the different nations on the Wabash, as high as the Ouiatenon, came to Vincennes and followed the example of their grand chief. As expresses were continually passing between Captain Helm and myself the whole time of the treaties, the business was settled perfectly to my satisfaction, and greatly to the advantage of the public. The British interest daily lost ground in this quarter, and in a short time our influence reached the Indians at the river St. Joseph and the border of Lake Michigan.'

'St. Vincents being a post of great importance, and not being able

to spare many men to garrison it, I took uncommon pains entirely to
attach [the people] to our interest. ...[They] knowing no other kind
of government than what might be expected from the lust of power,
pride, and avarice of the [British] officers commanding in that
country, — (whose will was law to the whole and certain destruction
to disobey the most trifling command), — nothing could have been
more to my advantage, as I could temper the government as I
pleased, and every new privilege appeared to them as fresh laurels
for the American cause. I by degrees...laid aside every unnecessary
restriction they labored under.' 'Every method was pursued to
convince the French inhabitants that their interest...was studied;
every restriction that [they] were under that was disagreeable to
them, was done away; their business with the commanding officers
was done without fees, neither any to the courts that weekly sat on
their business; and many other little things [were ordered] that [had]
good effects.' 'I made it a point to guard the happiness and tranquillity of the inhabitants, ...supposing that their happy change,
reaching the ears of their brothers and countrymen on the lakes and
about Detroit, would be paving my way to that place. ...It had
the desired effect. ...Many letters of congratulation [were] sent
from Detroit to the gentlemen of the Illinois, which gave much
pleasure.' 'Many traders and others, watching their opportunities,
...came across with their goods and settled in the Illinois and Vincennes. This also had a good effect among the Indians. The
friendly correspondence between the Spaniards and ourselves was
much to our advantage, as everything the Indians heard from them
was to our interest.'

Two weeks after taking Kaskaskia, Clark opened correspondence with a man to whom Americans should be forever grateful. This was Oliver Pollock, the financial agent in
New Orleans for both Virginia and Congress. An Irish Catholic, he was one of those big-minded and big-hearted men who
realized the transcendent importance of the American struggle
for liberty and national greatness, and was animated by an
ardent patriotism which, reckless of self-interest, gladly
made any personal sacrifice demanded for his country. His
services in upholding the Revolution in the west were invaluable. That such a man should be almost wholly unknown
to the nation he served so well is hardly creditable to American history.

To procure necessary supplies for his troops Clark drew bills
on the state and sent them to Pollock for acceptance. At first
Pollock did accept and pay them, but he wrote Clark that,
owing to his previous advances for Virginia, it 'is exceedingly
inconvenient for me to pay your bills. But the cause in which

we are embarked urges me to strain every nerve, and luckily
having a number of good friends hitherto enabled me to serve
my country. In consequence of this I have accepted your Bills
and the holder of two of them happens to be one of my friends
and says he will not call on me before January, by which time
I hope to be provided with flour by the states, or you, to pay
them. The others I must pay when due.' [1]

Clark having been compelled to draw other bills, Pollock
again wrote him, saying: 'You draw on me sundry bills for the
account of Virginia which, with those already come to hand,
amount to $8,550.4. I am in great distress with respect to the
payment of those bills. Notwithstanding this, I have accepted all your Bills in full expectation of the states supplying me with funds by the latter end of this year, a disappointment in which will effectually ruin me, and in consequence of
which I hope you'll urge the State of Virginia... to be speedy
in forwarding down flour to pay for those bills and lodge
funds here for any future demands.'[2] No flour or funds were
sent him, however, and Pollock had to let bills he had accepted go to protest. Learning of this, Clark wrote him:
'I am sorry to learn you have not been supplyed with funds as
Expected. Your protesting my late Bills has not surprised me,
as I Expected it. Being surrounded by Enemies (M^r. Hamilton
& his Savages) [and] being obligated for my own safety to lay
in Considerable Stores, I was oblidged to take every step I
possibly could to procure them, [being] unwilling to use force
&c.' [3]

Soon after Pollock learned of the capture of Kaskaskia he
wrote to Clark urging him to drive the British from the lower
Mississippi. No man knew better than Clark the importance
of clearing the lower Mississippi of enemies, but he knew also
that the British sea-power might at any time close it, and
furthermore he had before him another and far more important

[1] Several historians have magnified
many times the total of money and supplies received by Clark from Pollock,
being misled by a failure to distinguish
those furnished Clark from those furnished to the state of Virginia, Congress,
or others, as shown in the numerous and
conflicting reports of various commissions
appointed after the Revolution to settle
western military accounts. Some of
these writers also assume that Clark's

bills on Pollock were all accepted and
paid, whereas most of them were protested because Pollock was without funds.
See 'Financing of Clark's Conquest, etc.'
(James) in *Mississippi Valley Historical
Review*, IV, 96, 330. In the list of Clark's
bills is one for 1237 piastres to Cerré,
already become an active supporter of
the American cause.

[2] *Draper MSS.* 48 J 37; cf. *id.*, 33, 41.

[3] *Illinois Historical Collections*, VIII, 330.

object, namely, securing his conquest north of the Ohio and extending it to Detroit. From this last object he never allowed anything surmountable to swerve him. As Detroit was the British key to the west, so it was the key to Clark's plans throughout the war.

CHAPTER VIII

STRATEGIC DEALINGS WITH INDIANS

'Domestic affairs [says Clark] being partly well settled, the Indian department became next the object of my attention and of the greatest importance. My sudden appearance in their country put them under the greatest consternation. They were generally at war against us, but the French and Spaniards appearing so fond of us, confused them. They counselled with the French traders to know what was best to be done, and of course were advised to come and solicit for peace.' 'The French gentlemen at the different posts that we now had possession [of] engaged warmly in our interest. They appeared to vie with each other in promoting the business,... through the means of their correspondents, trading among the Indians, and other ways. In a short time the Indians of various tribes inhabiting this region [of] Illinois, in great numbers came to Cahokia in order to make peace with us. From the information they generally got from the French gentlemen (whom they implicitly believed)...they were truly alarmed; and, of course, we were visited by the greatest part of them without any invitation from us.' 'Those treaties, ...continued between three and four weeks, [and were] probably conducted in a [manner] different from any other known in America at that time. They commenced about the last of August.'

'It was with astonishment that we viewed the amazing number of savages that soon flocked into the town of Cahokia to treat for peace and to hear what the Big Knives had to say, — many of them 500 miles distant, — Chippewas, Ottoways, Pottawatomies, Missessogies, Puans, Sacs, Foxes, Sayges, Tauways, Maumees, and a number of other nations, all living east of the Mississippi and many of them then at war against us. I must confess that I was under some apprehension among such a lot of devils; and it proved to be just, for, the second or third night, a party of Puans and others endeavored to force by the guards into my lodging to bear me off, but were luckily detected and made prisoners by the alacrity of the serjeant.'

'They came down, as others had done, pretending to treat for peace. They were lodged in the yard of Mr. Bradies, ...about one hundred yards from my quarters and nearly the same distance from the fort. The little river, Cahokia, ...on the opposite side of the...street...was then about knee-deep. [We] having business at the time with other Indians, they listened to what was passing, loitered about, and got pretty well acquainted with our people. Having received but a bad report of them, I took apparently but little notice of them. They had observed the house I lodged in very quiet

of nights, and had supposed the guards to be but few. [They] formed
their plan in the following manner: Some of them were to cross the
river, fire off their guns opposite to their quarters, on which they
[and the others] were to attempt to get in [my quarters] under the
protection of the quarter-guard, as flying from other Indians, their
enemies, that had fired on them [from] across the river. If they succeeded [they] were to butcher the guard and carry myself off. A few
nights after their arrival they made the attempt, about one oclock.
Having too much to think of to sleep much, I happened to be awake
at the time the alarm was given. They were...at the yard gate
when the sentinel presented his piece. Being a light night they saw
the guard parading in front of the door was more numerous, perhaps,
than they expected. They took a by-way and got into their quarters.' 'The town took the alarm and was immediately under arms,
which convinced the savages the French were in our interest.'

'The guard was positive it was those [Puan] Indians. They were
immediately examined. [They] said it was their enemies that had
fired on them across the creek; that they wanted to get under the
protection of the guard, but were not permitted and made the best
of their way back to defend themselves. But some of the French
gentlemen, being better acquainted with them than the rest, insisted that it was they,...sent for a candle and discovered that the
leggins and moccasins of the fellows that had crossed the river
[were] quite wet and muddy. They were quite confounded [and]
wanted to make various excuses, but [were] not suffered to speak.
Their design was easily seen through. I said little to them, and (as
there were a good many of other nations in town and, to convince
the whole of the strict union of the French and us) I told them, as
they had disturbed the town, the people might do as they pleased
with them and went away; but whispered that the chiefs should
be sent to the guard-house and put in irons, which was immediately
done by the inhabitants. They, in that situation, were every day
brought into the council, but not suffered to speak.' 'I was determined to follow the principle of treatment that I had set out upon,
let the consequence be what it would. ...They insisted that it was
only to see whether the French would take part with the Americans
or not; that they had no ill design. This treatment of some of the
greatest chiefs among them, occasioned great confusion among the
rest of the savages.

'The prisoners, with great submission, solicited to speak to me,
but were refused. They then made all the interest they possibly
could amongst the other Indians, (who were much at a loss what to
do, as there were strong guards through every quarter of the town),
to get to speak to me; but I told the whole that I believed they
were a set of villians; that they had joined the English and they
were welcome to continue in the cause they had espoused; that I
was a man and a warrior; that I did not care who were my friends or
foes, and had no more to say to them. Such conduct alarmed the
whole town, but I was sensible that it would gain us no more ene-

mies than we had already; and, if they afterwards solicited terms, that they would be more sincere and probably [my course would have] a lasting good effect on the Indian nations.

'Distrust was visible in the countenance of almost every person during the latter part of the day. To show the Indians that I disregarded them, I remained in my lodging in the town, about one hundred yards from the fort, seemingly without a guard, but kept about fifty men concealed in a parlour adjoining and the garrison under arms. ... There was great counselling among the savages during the night; but, to make them have a greater idea of my indifference about them, I assembled a number of gentlemen and ladies and danced nearly the whole night. [Think of it! Amidst this 'amazing number of savages,' angered by the arrest of the offending ones, and no doubt contemplating the massacre of Clark and his little band, the young commander orders a dance!]

'In the morning I summoned the different nations to a grand council, and had the chiefs under guard released and invited to the council that I might speak to them in presence of the whole.' 'I began this business fully prepared, having copies of the British treaties. After the great ceremonies commonly made use of at the commencement of Indian treaties, they as the solicitors, opening ... after laying the whole blame of their taking up the bloody hatchet to the delusions of the English, acknowledging their error, and [with] many protestations of guarding in future against those bad birds flying through the land, (alluding to the British emissaries sent among them), concluded, hoping that as the Great Spirit had brought us together for good, ... they might be received as our friends, and that the peace might take place of the bloody belt, — throwing down and stamping on those emblems of war that they had received from the British, such as red belts of wampum, flags, &c, &c.

'I informed them that I had paid attention to what they had said and that the next day I would give them an answer, when I hoped that the hearts and ears of all people would be open to receive the truth, which should be pure without deception; that I recommended [them] to keep themselves prepared for the result of this day, on which perhaps their very existence as nations depended &c, and dismissed them, — not suffering any of our people to shake hands with them, as peace was not yet concluded, — telling them it was time enough to give the hand when the heart could be given also. They replied that such sentiments were like [those of] men who had one heart and that did not speak with a double tongue, &c.

'The next day I delivered them the following speech:

'"Men and Warriors! Pay attention! You informed me yesterday that the Great Spirit had brought us together, which you hoped was good, as He is good. I also have the same hope, and whatever may be agreed to by us, ... I expect that each party will strictly adhere to, whether for peace or war, and henceforward prove ourselves worthy of the attention of the Great Spirit. I am a man and a warrior, and not a councillor. [I] carry in my right hand war and peace in my left. ...I was sent by the great Council Fire of the Big Knife and their friends to take possession of all the towns that the English possess in this country, and to remain here watching the motions of the red people; to bloody the paths of those that continued the attempt of stopping the course of the river, but to clear the roads that lead from us to those that wish...to be in friendship with us, that the women and children might walk without anything being in the way for them to strike their feet against; but to continue to call on the Great Fire for a sufficient number of warriors to darken the land of the [enemy], so that the inhabitants should hear no sound in it but that of birds that live on blood. I know that a mist is yet before your eyes. I will dispel the clouds that you may clearly see the cause of the...war between the Big Knife and the English, — that you may judge yourselves which is in the right; and then, if you are men and warriors, as you profess yourselves to be, prove it by strictly adhering to what you may now declare, without deceiving...and prov[ing] yourselves only old women!

' "The Big Knives are very much like the Red People; they dont know well how to make blankets, powder, and cloth. ...They buy from the English, ...and live chiefly by making corn, hunting, and trade, as you and the French, your neighbors, do. But the Big Knives daily are getting more numerous, like the trees in the woods, so that the land got poor and hunting scarce, having but little to trade with, the women began to cry, to see their children naked, and tried to learn to make clothes for themselves, and soon gave the husbands blankets of their own making; and the men learned to make guns and powder, so that they did not have to buy so much from the English. They, the English, got mad and put a strong garrison through all the country, (as you see they have done among you, on the lakes, and among the French,) and would not let our women spin, nor the men make powder, nor let us trade with anybody else, but said that we should buy all from them, and, since we have got saucy, they would make us give them two bucks for a blanket that we used to get for one, and that we should do as they please, [and] killed some of us to make the rest fear. This is the truth and the cause of the war between us, which did not take place for some time after they had served us in this manner. The women and children were cold and hungry and continued to cry. The young men were lost and had no councillor to put them in the right path. The whole land was dark, and the old men hung their heads for shame, as they could not see the sun; and thus there was mourning for many years.

' "At last the Great Spirit took pity on us and kindled a great council fire that never gave out, at a place called Philadelphia, stuck down a post, and left a tomahawk by it, and went away. The sun immediately broke and the sky was blue. The old men held up their heads and assembled at the fire, took up the hatchet, sharpened it, and put it into [the] hands of the young men, and told [them] to strike the English as long as they could find one on this side of the Great Water. The young men immediately struck the war-post and blood issued. Thus the war began, and the English were driven from one place to another until they got weak and hired you Red People to fight for them and help them. The Great Spirit, getting angry at this, he caused your old Father the French King and other nations to join the Big Knife and fight with them all their enemies, so that the English is become like a deer in the woods.

'"From this you may see that it is the Great Spirit that caused your waters to be troubled, because you fought for the people he was mad with; and if your women and children should cry, you must blame yourselves for it and not the Big Knife.

'"You can now judge who is in the right.

'"I have already told you who I am. Here is a bloody belt and a white one. Take which you please. Behave like men and dont let your pres[ent] situation, — being surrounded by the Big Knife, — cause you to take up the one belt with your hands, when your hearts drink up the other. If you take the bloody path, you shall go from this town in safety and join your friends the English; and we will try like warriors who can put the most stumbling blocks in the roads and keep our clothes the longest perfumed with blood.

'"If you should take the path of peace, and now be received as brothers to the Big Knife, French, &c, and should hereafter listen to bad birds that will be flying through your land, you will then be counted, — not men but, having two tongues, ought to be destroyed without listening to what you say, as nobody can understand you.

'"As I am convinced you never before heard the truth, I would not wish you to give me an answer before you have time to counsel, if you wish it. We will part this evening, and when you are ready, if the Great Spirit will bring us together again, let us prove ourselves worthy by speaking and thinking with but one heart and one tongue &c."

'Whatever their private consultations on this speech might be, I never could learn, but on their return the next day business commenced with more than usual ceremony. A new fire was kindled and all the gentlemen in town were collected, and after all their preparatory ceremony was gone through, the chief that was to speak advanced, near to the table where I sat with a belt of peace in his hand, another [chief] with the sacred pipe, and a third with the fire to kindle it, which was first presented to the heavens, then to the earth, and, completing a circle, was presented to all the spirits, invoking them to witness what was about to be concluded on, [then] to myself and, descending down, to every person present. The speaker then addressed himself to the Indians, the substance of which was that they ought to be thankful that the Great Spirit had taken pity on them and had cleared the sky and opened their ears and hearts, so that they could hear and receive the truth &c, and — addressing himself to me, — said that they had paid grave attention to what the Great Spirit had put into my heart to say to them; that they believed the whole to be the truth, as the Big Knife did not speak like any other people that they had ever heard; that they now plainly saw that they had been deceived; that the English had told them lies and never told them the truth, which some of their old men had always said, which they now believed; that we were in the right, and as the English had forts in their country, they might, if they got strong, want to serve the red people as they did the Big Knife; that they, the red people, ought to help us; ...that they had, with a sincere heart taken up the belt of peace (and spurned the other away); that they were determined to hold it fast and would have no doubt of our friendship, as judging from the manner of our speaking, there was no room for suspicion; that they would call in all their warriors and cast the tomahawk into the river, where it could never be found again, and suffer no more emissaries (or bad birds) to pass through their land to disquiet their women and children, that they might always be cheerful to smooth the roads for their brothers, the Big Knives, whenever they came to see them; that they would send to all their friends and let them know the good talk they had heard and what was done, and advise them to listen to the same; that they hoped that I would send men among them with eyes to see...they were men and strictly adhered to all that had been said at this great fire that the Great Spirit had kindled...at Cahokia, for the good of all people that would listen to it, &c.

'That is the substance of their answer to me. The pipe was again kindled and presented to all the spirits to be witnesses, smoking of which and shaking of hands concluded this grand piece of business, I suppose with as much dignity and importance in their eyes as the treaty between France and America was to ours. They put on a different appearance. The greatest harmony now reigned, without the appearance of any distrust on their side, but we were not quite so [trustful.]'

[The general gladness did not extend, however, to the captive Puan chiefs. Clark continues:] 'On finishing with the others, I had their irons taken off, and told them that their design was obvious to me, as a bird from their country had whispered me in the ear; that all people said that they ought to die, which they must think themselves that they deserved, and was what I intended; but, on considering the matter, and the meanness of their attempt to watch and catch a bear sleeping, I found that [they were] only old women and too mean to be killed by a Big Knife; but, as they ought to be punished for putting on breech-cloths like men, th[ose] should be taken from them and plenty of provisions given to [take them] home, as women dont know how to hunt; and, as long as [they] staid here [they] should be treated as all squaws ought to be; and, without any further notice of them, [I] conversed indifferently with others present on very trifling subjects.

'They appeared to be much agitated. After some time, they rose and advanced with a belt and pipe of peace, which [they offered] to me, and made a speech which I would not suffer to be interpreted at that time; [but with] a sword lying on the table broke their pipe and told them that the Big Knives never treated with women, and for them to sit down and enjoy themselves as other [women] did, and not be afraid.

'(What they said, was an acknowledgement of their design, excusing themselves by saying that it was owing to bad men amongst them from Michilimackinac, [who] put it into their heads; that they were in hopes we would take pity on their women and children; and, as their lives were spared, when they deserved to lose [them], they were in hopes that peace would be granted them, as it was to others, &c.) [As Clark had refused to treat with them, they feared he would soon destroy their nations; hence their continued dejection.]

'Several chiefs, of other nations present, spoke in their favor, condemning their attempt. As they saw the Big Knife was above little things, they were [hopeful] I should take pity on the families of these men and grant them peace. ... I told them that I had never made war upon them; that if the Big Knife came across such people in the woods, they commonly shot them down as they did wolves, to prevent their eating the deer, but never talked about it; and the conversation dropped for some time.

'These fellows continued busy in private conversation. At last two young men advanced to the middle of the floor, sat down, and flung their blankets over their heads. This, at first, I did not know what to make of. Two of the chiefs, with a pipe, stood by them and spoke nearly in the same manner they had done before, and concluded by saying that they offered those two young men as an atonement for their guilt, and were in hopes that the Big Knife would be reconciled after this sacrifice of them, and again offered the pipe, which I refused and told them to go and sit down, that I would have nothing to say to them, but in a milder tone than I had before spoken to them. It appeared that those people had got so completely alarmed...that they supposed a tomahawk hanging over the heads of every one of their nation; that nothing would save them but to get peace before they left the place and expecting that by our putting to death, or keeping, those two young men as slaves, we should be reconciled.' 'It would have surprised you to have seen how submissively those two young men presented themselves for death. ...This stroke prejudiced me in their favor and, for a few moments, [I] was so agitated that I dont doubt but that I should, without reflection, [have] killed the first man that would have offered...to hurt them.' 'The young men kept their position and frequently would push the blankets aside, as if impatient to know their fate.

'I could have had no expectation of their business ending in this manner. I always intended at last to be persuaded to grant these people peace, but this astonished me. I hardly knew whether it was sincere or not, but everything proved it. Every person present, (which was a great number), seemed anxious to know what would be done; and a general silence took...place. For some time all [was] suspense. I viewed those persons with pleasure. You may easily guess my feelings on the occasion. I had read something similar, but did not know whether to believe it, or not; and never before, nor since, felt myself so capable of speaking. I ordered the young men to rise and uncover themselves. I found there was a very visible alteration in their countenance, which they appeared to try to conceal. I suitably harangued the whole assembly on the subject, and concluded by telling them that I was happy to find that there were men amongst all nations, as we were now witnesses there were at least two among these people. I then spoke to the young men; said a great deal in their praise, & concluded by saying that it was only such men as them that [should be] chiefs of a nation; that it was such that I liked to treat with; that, through them, the Big Knives granted peace and friendship to their people; that I took them by the hand, as my brothers and chiefs of their nation, and I expected all persons would acknowledge them as such. I first presented them to my officers, to the French and Spanish gentlemen present, and, lastly, to the Indians, — the whole greeting them as chiefs, — and ended the business by having them saluted by the garrison.

'I wish I had a copy, or could remember the whole I said on this business, but you may easily conceive from the nature of it. It appeared to give much satisfaction, but I thought the old chiefs appeared much cowed. Our new Nabobs were now treated with respect on all occasions. A council was called to do some business with them, and great ceremony made use of, &c. In order more firmly to rivet what had been done, some presents were given them to distribute among their friends at home, by whom I understood they were acknowledged and held in great esteem, and the Americans much spoke of among them.'

'I had set a resolution never to give [the Indians] anything that should have the appearance of courting them, but generally made some excuse for the little I presented, (such as their coming a long way to see me, [their having] expended their ammunition, worn out their leggins, or met with some misfortune or other); but they were generally alarmed and [the] conclusion of peace satisfied them, and [they] parted with [us] in all appearance well satisfied. I always made it a point to keep spies among them and was pleased to find that the greatest body of those that treated with us strictly adhered to [their treaty promises.]'

'Our influence now began to spread among the nations even to the border of the lakes. I sent agents into every quarter.' 'It is not [worth] while to [give] the particulars of every treaty, as the one already mentioned conveys an idea of the plan we went on. ... Their replies were nearly always the same, ... and a boundary seemed now to be fixed between the British emissaries and our own at the headwaters of the lakes and those of the Mississippi, neither party caring much to venture so far. Some of the nations got divided among themselves, part for us, others for the English.' 'I continued about five weeks in the town of Cahokia, in which time I had settled a peace with ten or twelve nations.' 'Such a sudden change among the Indians in this region in our favor required great attention to keep up the flame from cooling too soon, as the appearance of a reenforcement, which we had reason to expect in the fall, would renew our influence.'

Just across the Mississippi from Cahokia was St. Louis, where the Spanish lieutenant-governor of upper Louisiana, Don Fernando de Leyba, had his headquarters. Writing Governor Henry, Clark said: 'This gentleman interests himself much in favor of the States — more so than I could have expected. He has offered me all the force he could raise in case of attack by Indians from Detroit.' [1] Afterward, writing to Colonel Mason, he described more fully his treatment by the Spaniard, saying: 'An intimacy had commenced between Don Leyba Leut Governor of western Illinois and myself. He omitted nothing in his power to prove his attachment to the Americans, with such openness as left no room to doubt. As I was never before in company of any spanish gen^t, I was much surprised in my expectations; for instead of finding that reserve, thought peculiar to that nation, I here saw not the least symptoms of it. Freedom, almost to excess, gave the greatest pleasure.' [2]

As Spain was on the verge of war with Great Britain, De Leyba doubtless wished to cultivate friendly relations with the dominant young American; and — practised in the urbane and winning ways of old world social circles — knew well how to do it. Clark, on the other hand, relieved for the first time from his most pressing public cares, must gladly have welcomed a change from the rough life he had been so long leading, and have found a delightful contrast in the more refined company of the governor's family and friends.' [3] It was at this time that the one romance of his life is said to have begun. A well-supported tradition says he met, loved, and became betrothed to Terese, the beautiful young sister of the Spanish lieutenant governor. In the full vigor of his young manhood — flushed with success, handsome, affable, and admired by all, — we may imagine how kindly she looked upon him; and, from what was said of her charms, that he became her willing captive.

[1] *Illinois Historical Collections*, VIII, 69.
[2] *Id.* 129.
[3] De Leyba's wife, 'Lady Marie de la Conception y Zerar,' died and was buried at St. Louis September 7, 1778. (*Draper MSS. 22 S. 158.*)

After his five weeks of treaty-making at Cahokia, Clark returned to Kaskaskia, where he said:

'Having so far fixed matters as to have a moment's leisure, which was taken up with deeper reflections than I ever before was acquainted with, my situation and weakness convinced me that more depended on my own behaviour and conduct than all the troops that I had. Far removed from the body of my country, situated among French, Spaniards, and numerous bands of savages in every quarter watching my actions, ready to receive impressions favorable or not so to us,...it was now I saw my work was only begun. ...

'Strict subordination among the troops was my first object, and soon effected it, it being a matter of the greatest consequence to persons in our situation. Our troops being all raw and undisciplined, you must be sensible of the pleasure I felt, (when haranguing them on parade, telling them my resolutions and the necessity of strict duty for our own preservation, &c), for them to return me for answer that it was their zeal for their country that induced them to engage in the service; that they were sensible of their situation and danger; that nothing could conduce more to their safety and happiness than good order, which they would try to adhere to; and hoped that no favour would be shown those that would neglect it. In a short time perhaps no garrison could boast of better order, or a more valuable set of men.'

It is interesting to note that in his addresses and instructions to his men, Clark invariably appealed to their higher motives — their patriotism and sense of duty — and emphasized the service they could render their country.

CHAPTER IX

HAMILTON MARCHES AGAINST CLARK: TAKES VINCENNES

WHILE the Americans were busy fastening their hold on the Illinois, what of Hamilton at Detroit, and his great gathering of Indians to sweep the frontiers and take Pittsburg?

Kaskaskia had been captured the night of July 4th. It is a remarkable proof of the effectiveness of Clark's prompt precautions to prevent news of that event from getting to the enemy, that five weeks elapsed before Hamilton learned there was an enemy in the Illinois! Even then he supposed this enemy was Willing, from the lower Mississippi. August 11th, he wrote Carleton: 'An express arrived here on the 8th. inst. from Cahokia with the news of a party of rebels having surprised Kaskaskia and seized Mr. de Rochblave, the commandant, whom they have laid in irons. The party is reported to amount to three hundred men, but I cannot think they are so numerous, since, by what the express has related, it seems they are but part of those marauders who left Fort Pitt last January, under one Willan, a man who is of one of the best families in Philadelphia, but of infamous character and debauched morals, a proper head for the band of robbers he has conducted down the Mississippi. . . . Reports are industriously propagated among the Indians of a war having broke out with France and Spain.' [1] As already seen, Clark had learned of the French treaty of alliance three months earlier. It was not until full eight weeks after the fall of Kaskaskia that the fact was learned by the British commandant at Michili-mackinac, Major de Peyster, of the New York royalist family of that name. By that time, Clark had possession of Vincennes also, and had treated with the chiefs of many Indian nations in the great council at Cahokia. De Peyster wrote the new commander-in-chief of Canada, General Haldemand: 'I have this moment received a letter from Mons' Chevailier, of St. Josephs, informing [me] that the rebels are in possession of all the Illinois; that the party at the Kaskaskias, consisting of two

[1] *Michigan Pioneer Collections,* IX, 460.

hundred and fifty commanded by one Willing, is a part
of the 700 on their way to that country. Willing has put Mr.
de Rochblave, the commandant, and one Mr. Crie [Cerré]
in irons for having refused the oaths of allegiance to the King
of Spain, the French King, and the Congress. The traders in
that country, and many from this post, are plundered and the
whole country in the greatest confusion, being at a loss to
know which route the rebels will take next.' [1]

At the very time Hamilton learned of his loss of the Illinois,
General Haldemand was writing to him, approving his plan
to attack Pittsburg and the frontiers, and saying: 'It is not
my intention . . . to limit you in anything which shall be re-
quisite for the good and advantage of His Majesty's service,
the exigencies of which, in the department entrusted to your
management at that distance from me, can only be judged of
by you, and therefore must be left to your discretion, in which
I have full confidence.'

With Hamilton and Clark both exercising discretionary
powers, the conduct of the war was likely to depend upon the
generalship of the two men. Their forces were grossly unequal, however, for Hamilton had about four times as many
troops as Clark, besides the support of nearly all the lake
Indians. His greatest advantage, however, was a liberal
supply of good money. Clark had, indeed, won the Illinois
and Wabash French and had won or neutralized many Indians; but he was hundreds of miles from his base, and entirely
dependent for supplies upon his new-made and untried
friends. The advantages, however, were not all with Hamilton. Clark's men, although few, were unrivaled for the kind
of warfare in which they were engaged, and had unbounded
confidence in their young leader. Hamilton's Canadian French
troops were much less dependable, and his British regulars,
while highly disciplined and brave, were much less experienced
than the Virginians in wilderness warfare. The very number
of his Indian allies, too, and the great territory over which
they were scattered, made it difficult to handle them. He had
not enough qualified white men to send among them to keep
them 'firm in the King's interest,' or to accompany the bands
going to war; and both kinds of service were very important. [2]

---

[1] *Michigan Pioneer Collections*, IX, 369.
[2] The Indians, if left to themselves,   were apt to feel neglected and would become lukewarm. If led on their forays

On learning of Clark's irruption, Hamilton promptly planned to recapture Vincennes and the Illinois, and then gather his full strength of Indian allies to sweep Kentucky and the frontiers. His successive reports to Haldemand give a tolerably full account of his plans and activities. After learning of Clark's presence in the Illinois he said:

'There are at least 400 Indians assembled to attack the fort of Kentucky, where Captain Boone was taken last year, and several large parties of Indians range the banks of the Ohio. I have taken every step in my power to intercept the batteaus from the Mississippi on their return, parties having been sent six weeks ago for that purpose. I am in hopes to have a good account of them.'[1] [The bloody execution of their mission will soon appear.]

'25th August a party of 15 Miamis went to war towards the Ohio; Sept. 5, another, of a chief and 30 men; the 6th Baubin himself, with five Chippewas and 15 Miamis for Post Vincennes.'[2] [This day, Hamilton said, one of his Delaware parties] 'brought in fifteen scalps to this place. Many of the war parties bring in prisoners and have shown a humanity hitherto unpracticed among them. They never fail of a gratuity on every proof of obedience they show in sparing the lives of such as are incapable of defending themselves. A prisoner, brought in here by the Shawanese lately, who was taken near one of the forts on the river Kentucke, tells me the Rebels were lately reinforced with three companies, each of 70 men.'[3] 'Sep 16. ...Since last May the Indians in this district have taken 34 prisoners, 17 of which they delivered up and 81 scalps — several prisoners taken and adopted not reckoned in this number.'[4]

'Sept 22nd. ...Preparations for our little enterprise [the recapture of Vincennes and the Illinois] are forwarding with alacrity. This day 15 large pirogues, capable of transporting from 1800 to 3000 lbs each, having had a thorough repair, set off for Wold Rapid. ...I purpose taking presents, not only for the Ouibash [Wabash] and more western Indians, but to encourage the Delawares, Mingoes, and Shawanese to keep good watch towards the banks of the Ohio during the winter season when the savages are usually dispersed for hunting. The Spaniards are feeble and hated by the French; the French are fickle and have no man of capacity to advise, or lead them, [Hamilton was soon to learn the error of this assumption]; the rebels are enterprising and brave, but want resources; and the Indians can have their resources but from the English, if we act without loss of time in the present favorable conjuncture. This may appear a picture with strong lights, and little or no shade, but, as the

and encouraged by competent white men, they would go great distances and do deadly work, but otherwise were prone to scatter in plundering adventures, or else turn about and go home.

[1] *Michigan Pioneer Collections*, IX, 465–75.
[2] *Id.*, 475.
[3] *Id.*, 465.
[4] *Id.*, 476–77.

effects of pushing a force, supported by the zeal of the Indians, (who have hitherto acted with perfect compliance), have not yet been tried, I hope to be excused if perhaps too sanguine. The most considerable of the French in this settlement have shown a very good example, & 'tis better followed than I had expected.

'Sept 23rd 1778. This day I met the Ottawas, the Chippewas, and Pouttouattamies in council, by their own appointment....

'Sept 24th. The oath of allegiance was tendered to the volunteers from the different companies, who appeared to the number of 76, to the officers of militia, & the newly formed companies, &c.

'26th. I gave Capt McKee a message & present of ammunition for the Shawanese, who are under Mr De Quindre, and have not yet broke up their little seige [of Boonesboro. Boone had escaped in time to warn the settlers and the Indians were repulsed.] This evening Mr. Charles Baubin came in from the Miamis. Letters which he brought mention one Clarke with 80 men at St. Vincennes, where the French receive them well. [This is Hamilton's first mention of Clark by name.] The Indians at Ouiattanon as yet undecided and timorous. I shall lose no time to encourage them. Should I arrive time enough... to speak to the chiefs before they take a decisive part, I dont doubt the sight of the chiefs from the Lakes will determine them as I could wish. Gibault the priest, has been active for the rebels. I shall reward him if possible. [The enthusiasm for the campaign of Hamilton's lake Indians, who had not come under Clark's influence, appears from his next entry:]

'Oct. 2nd, We have found it a difficult matter to find two savages to go express with letters for Niagara, they are so desirous of going towards the Ouiabash [Wabash.] I hope however to procure them by tomorrow.

'Octr. 3rd 1778. Last night the savages were assembled, when I sung the war song, and was followed by Captain Lernault, and several officers &c, and warriors going on the enterprise. The best disposition and alacrity shown by all.' [1]

One who has ever seen an Indian war dance and heard the Indian war song can imagine the lurid and horrible scene, and no less horrible sounds, on the commons of Detroit that night. Half naked, fiercely-bedecked and painted warriors, in a great circle about their bloody war-post, dancing their wild, swaying, grunting, leaping, yelling war dance — each brandishing a tomahawk with one hand and a gory scalping knife with the other; and in the midst of this scene is the pleased lieutenant-governor, who joins these 'savage hell-hounds of war' and sings their fierce war song to stimulate them for their bloody work!

[1] *British Museum*, Add. MSS. 24320 ff. 1–6.

At the end of September, Hamilton's diary gives a report of his troops at Detroit, consisting of his garrison, a company of volunteers for his expedition and the militia of the town. It shows the garrison 217, militia 565, and volunteers 42 — a total of 824 men.[1] 'October 7th, a reinforcement of British troops, [from 'The King's Own Regiment'], 80 in number, arrived from Niagara.'[2] This made a grand total of 904 men, not counting Indians. October 2nd, he enters a return of batteaus, pirogues, and canoes for the expedition, as follows: '13 batteaus...capable of carrying 39,300 lbs. 17 pirogues and canoes 33,700 lbs.' '6th. Tents struck before day; embarked our cannon & part of stores.'

Next day (7th) Hamilton marched against Vincennes with five hundred men including Indians. His lieutenant, Scheffelin, said: 'On the 7th October 1778 Lieut Governor Hamilton took his departure from Detroit with a detachment of the Kings VIIIth Regiment, the Detroit volunteers, a detachment of Artillery, two companies of militia, and a number of savages under his command, to retake the posts the Rebels had taken possession of in the Illinois.'[3] Hamilton's report continues: 'At 7 in the morning 3 Hurons arrived with accounts that they said might be depended on, that the Rebels in several bands of 400 men each and by different routes were advancing to Detroit; that the advanced guard of the main body was 800 men &c. Gave little credit to it; called a council, told them my mind, found them well disposed. Vessels arrived in the evening with the re-enforcement from Niagara.'

The daily history of the march is told in Hamilton's letters to Haldemand, and also more briefly in his diary. He says:

'Nothing very material happened till the 15th of December, when a reconnoitering party from our camp seized a lieutenant and three men sent up by the commandant at St. Vincennes [Captain Helm] with written instructions to watch for the English and to hasten back with his intelligence. ...From these men I learned that the commandant had permitted almost all his people to return to their homes, and depended on the French militia, who had all taken an oath of fidelity to the states.

'The 16th. I sent off two parties of Indians, each with an Indian

---

[1] See also Hamilton to Haldemand (*Michigan Pioneer Collections*, IX, 473, et seq.) and his 'Return of the garrison of Detroit,' *Draper MSS*, and *Illinois Historical Collections*, I, 227–36.

[2] *Michigan Pioneer Collections*, X, 301.

[3] *Magazine of American History*, I, 186–93.

officer, to intercept any intelligence of our arrival that might be sent to the Illinois, or the Falls of Ohio. [Evidently Hamilton thought there was an American force at the Falls.] They had orders to keep their stations till they should discover the English flag flying on the fort. At the same time Mr. Hay — appointed to act as major to the Detroit militia, — was detached with Captain La Mothe's Company of Volunteers, Lieut. Du Vernet of the Royal Artillery with the six pounder, and the detachment of the King's Regiment. He [Hay] had with him the interpreters and some chiefs of the different nations. Had our whole force moved forward together, it would probably have been impossible to have restrained the savages from destroying the settlement. As it was, the young men took alarm, that they should have no share in the business, and threw themselves hastily into the canoes, to follow. They were however prevailed on to return.

'A placart was sent to the inhabitants cautioning them to avoid acting on the offensive, as the consequence must be fatal to them, [meaning an Indian massacre.] Major Hay had orders to secure if possible the craft lying before the place, by sending a party in the night in boats to pass the town, and stop any people who should attempt to escape by water. If (as I expected) there was not any resistance made, and if he found the report of the prisoners to be true, he was to order the St. George's Ensign to be hoisted at the fort, as a signal for our out parties to join. Should he find that re-inforcements has joined the Rebels, he was to take post to the best advantage, send off express to me, and await my arrival.

'Having taken these precautions, on the 17th I fell down the river, from the distance of seven leagues. It snowed and blew fresh from day-break till one o'clock, when, to my surprise I perceived the Rebel flag still flying at the fort. I concluded they had been re-inforced, and was confirmed in that belief when I found Lieutenant Scheffelin, with all our boats, lying in a little cove about a mile above the town. The men (however half frozen) were in good spirits. I ordered Captains Maisonville and McLeon to land their men, and, leaving one man to each boat as a guard, marched slowly towards the place, ordering a flanking party, as the brushwood was thick on our left. When we came in sight of the town, I posted sentries and halted the men. A messenger now came from Major Hay, desiring I might send him the St. George's flag, that his men were advantageously posted, and the gun mounted. I ordered the flag to be carried, and went to join him, where I found his men drawn up, and the French militia bringing in their arms. Major Hay told me the Commandant [Helm] was deserted by those he had reposed confidence in, and did not mean to hold out, but that he would not strike his colors till he knew what terms he was to have. [Here was Captain Helm, deserted by almost every man of the Vincennes militia, defying an army of five hundred men — about half of them bloodthirsty savages — and refusing 'to strike his colors till he knew what terms he was to have!'] The six pounder being ready,

I ordered Lieut Du Vernet to proceed with it towards the fort —
six men, with a sergeant of the King's Regiment, marching before
with fixed bayonets, followed by the remainder of the Detachment
of the Volunteers, and Militia under Major Hay.

'As I approached the gate of the fort, I sent a person forward to
summon the commanding officer to deliver his fort up. He desired,
by a written paper, to know who made the demand. I sent for answer
verbally, "the King's Lieutenant Governor, from Detroit!" and
advanced to the wicket.' [1]

To this report of Hamilton, Captain Helm added a most
interesting supplement. This was his intercepted letter to
Colonel Clark, written at the very time Hamilton's army —
regulars, volunteers, militia, and Indian warriors — was
bearing down on him, with bayonets fixed and cannon
mounted.

Dec. 17, 1778 (?)

DR SIR:

At this time theer is an army within three miles of this place. I
heard of their comin several days before hand. I sent spies to find
the certainty. The spies being taken prisoners, I never got intelligence till they got within 3 miles of the town. As I had called the
militia, and had all assurance of their integrity, I ordered, at the
firing of a cannon, every man to appear; but I saw but few. Capt.
Burron [Bosseron] behaved much to his honor and credit; but I
doubt the certaint[y] of a certain gent. Excuse hast[e] as the army
is in sight. My determination is to defend the Garrison, though I
have but 21 men but what has left me. I refer you to the [bearer]
Mr. Wms, for the rest. The army is in three hundred yd of the
village. You must think how I feel; not four men that I can really
depend on, but am determined to act brave. Think of my condition. I know it is out of my power to defend the town, as not one of
the militia will take arms, thoug[h], before sight of the army, no
braver men.

Their flag is at a small distance. I must conclude.

Yr Humble servt

LEOd HELMS [2]

In the long annals of American courage, hardly a parallel
can be found to this performance of Leonard Helm. Compared with it, many famous stories of heroism along the Atlantic Seaboard during the Revolution — however overdrawn
— seem colorless indeed.

Hamilton himself tells the rest of the story, saying that

---

[1] *British Museum, supra.*   *Canadian Archives,* Series B, vol. 122, 250.
[2] *Illinois Historical Collections,* VIII, 89;   English's *Conquest of the Northwest,* 233.

when he advanced to the fort gate to demand surrender, Captain Helm

'came himself, (for indeed he was almost alone), and asked what terms he should have. He was answered humane treatment, that no other terms would be mentioned. He then admitted me, and I instantly posted sentries at the gate to keep out the savages; but while I attended to this, some of them got in at two gun ports which had not been secured. I called to the interpreters and used my best entreaties with the chiefs, who really did all in their power, but the torrent was too strong for such feeble barriers. They bore down the sentries, and, seeing that I had posted another at the door of the commandants quarters, they went to the window which they broke and fell to plundering.

' The soldiers in the meantime drew up in the fort and were quiet spectators of the disorder, which lasted till the curiosity (I cannot say avarice) of the savages was gratified. They had generously restored to Captain Helm whatever was required of his private property. Some stout horses, — 32 lately purchased on the account of the Congress, — they found in the fort, which I would not deprive them of, as they have not committed a single act of cruelty and treated the inhabitants with the humanity which was recommended to them. Had a single shot been fired, probably the settlement would have been destroyed in an hours time.' [1]

Hamilton here, perhaps unconsciously, makes plain the impotence of his general orders to the Indians to act with 'humanity' and spare 'women and children or innocent men.' In the British Parliament, America's great friend, Edmund Burke, denouncing the employment of the Indians, ironically said: 'Suppose there was a riot on Tower Hill. What would the keeper of his Majesty's lions do? Would he not fling open the dens of the wild beasts and then address them thus: 'My gentle lions! my humane bears! My tender-hearted hyenas! go forth; but I exhort you, as you are Christians and members of civil society, to take care not to hurt any man, woman, or child.'

' For some time [Hamiliton continues] the commandant hesitated to take down the Continental flag [Helm must have felt this an indignity to his country that no loyal American should be asked to commit, and it is not said that he took down the flag himself], but at length finding it was left to themselves to do, he had it taken down and we hoisted the St. George's, — which signal drew in our parties, who had taken two prisoners, an American and a Frenchman, who had Capt. Helm's letter to Colonel Clark, commandant

[1] *Illinois Historical Collections*, I, 227–36.

...of the eastern Illinois, acquainting him of the arrival of the English at this place and of his situation. I send your Excellency a copy,[1] as it shows what confidence is to be placed in men [the Vincennes militia] who have once violated a sacred engagement. [Possessed of power and military excuse for hanging every man of the disloyal militia, here was Hamilton's opportunity — far plainer than Clark's at Kaskaskia — to play upon their fear and later win their gratitude by kindness. What he did will now appear.]

'The 18th I convened the inhabitants in the church and in pretty strong terms painted their poltroonery, ingratitude, and perfidy; I read them an oath, to be subscribed only by those who, being sensible of their fault, should publicly acknowledge it and thereby have some claim to the protection of Government. The chief people of the place have, either in an under-hand manner, or openly, imbraced the rebel party; some have been in pay, others registered for service in case of need. ...The oath, which I read in the church aloud and explained to them, I told [them] was not forced upon them, but offered for the consideration of sober people, convinced of their fault and who on their repentence might be once again received under the protection of their king. Humiliating as it is, 158 had signed it in a few days, I, on my part, swore conditionally.'

Instead of trying to win the hearts of his captives, he simply humiliated them and virtually forced them to swear a false and futile oath. Nine days later, he wrote:

'Two hundred and fifty of the militia of this place appeared this day under arms with their officers. ...As to courage, honor, or gratitude, if they were of the growth of this soil they would have showed themselves on the occasion of a handful of Rebels coming to take away the possessions of three hundred men, used to arms as hunters, and used to the mildest government under heaven. I must say, to the praise of the officers and men, they supported the fatigues and hardships of their tedious journey with the utmost cheerfulness. As to the poor savages, [Hamilton is ever sympathetic towards the 'poor savages'] their not firing a single shot on the day of taking possession of the place, nor injuring, nor even insulting a single soul, — (excepting a poor miller, whose house they plundered, being half a league from the fort), — their conduct surely reflects disgrace on some well-instructed Christian regulars who have not held Hospitals as asylums from their fury.'

On Christmas day, Hamilton received intelligence from his 'scouts toward Kaskaskia, who brought in two prisoners, ... that no boats are yet arrived at the Illinois; that the rebels do not exceed four score at Kaskaskia, and 30 at Cahokia, ... that there is no discipline observed by the rebels.' This report

[1] It is now in the British Museum.

was substantially correct, except as to discipline.[1] Here again was Hamilton's opportunity. With his Detroit troops, Indians, and two hundred and fifty Vincennes militia, he had seven hundred and fifty men. Like Clark at Kaskaskia, and Helm at Vincennes, he had found how unreliable the French militia could be, but, unlike Clark, he did not realize that these same Frenchmen, mixed with more trusty troops and skillfully encouraged by a resourceful and intrepid leader, could be made enthusiastic, daring, and efficient soldiers. The fact is that experienced and brave soldier though he was, Hamilton lacked imagination, which has distinguished all great captains, from Alexander to Napoleon, for it is the mind's eye which enables the strategist to see the whole and every part of his field of action, to penetrate the motives of others, to construct skillfully his plans of attack or defense, and to adjust quickly his action to rapidly changing situations and means.

Cold winter rains now flooded the flat Illinois country between Hamilton at Vincennes and Clark at Kaskaskia. The Great Wabash, in front of Vincennes, had broken its banks and become a long and broad lake, five miles wide. Further west, its tributaries, the Embarass, the two Little Wabash Rivers, and many smaller streams were likewise swollen, and even much of the higher flat country was deep in mire, or submerged. Hamilton, thinking his further progress impossible, sent home a part of his militia and determined to go into winter quarters at Vincennes. He strengthened his fort by building 'two large block-houses, musket proof, with loop-holes below, and embrasures above for five pieces of cannon each.' The fort, he said, was 'on the 22nd of February in a tolerable state of defense, the work proposed being finished.' Confident of his security, he sent out parties of Indians during the winter to harass the Kentucky settlers and cut off any reinforcements and supplies for Clark by way of the Ohio, intending in the spring to proceed to the Illinois and take him. Clark did not wait for him!

---

[1] Clark allowed no parade of his troops lest the smallness of their number should become known.

CHAPTER X

CLARK PLANS TO TAKE HAMILTON

[SAYS Clark's Mason Letter:] 'I found my ideas respecting the movement of the English just, having certain accounts by our spies that Governor Hamilton was on his march from Detroit with a considerable party, taking his route up the [Maumee] river. In a few days, receiving certain intelligence that General McIntosh [the Continental commander] had left Pittsburg for Detroit with a considerable army, and knowing the weakness of the fortification of that post at that time, their numbers, &c. I made no doubt of its being shortly in our possession, and that Governor Hamilton, sensible that there was no probability of his defending the fort, had marched with his whole force to encourage the Indians to harass the general on his march, as the only probable plan to stop him, little thinking, that he [McIntosh] had returned [to Pittsburg] and Mr. Hamilton had the same design on me.' [He had good reason for believing Detroit must have fallen, for he knew Congress had ordered McIntosh to march against it with three thousand men, but he did not know that the design had been dropped.]

'It being near Christmas, we feasted ourselves with the hope of immediately hearing from Detroit, and began to think we had been neglected in an express not being sent with the important news of its being ours. But a circumstance soon happened that convinced us that our hope was vain. A young man at the town of Cahokia, holding a correspondence and sending intelligence to Governor Hamilton's party ['giving dangerous information'] was detected and punished accordingly. By [his letter] we learned the return of General McIntosh and Governor Hamilton's intentions on the Illinois, but not so fully expressed in the letter as to reduce it to a certainty. Supposing...they would make their first descent on Kaskaskia, it being the strongest garrison and headquarters, I kept spies on all the roads, but to no purpose. Mr. Hamilton, having the advantage of descending the Wabash, with eight hundred men, — French, Indians and regulars,[1] — took possession of Vincennes on the 17th day of December. He had parties on the road that took some of our spies. Hard weather immediately setting in, I was at a loss to know what to do. Many supposed that he had quit his design and come no further than Ouia, but no intelligence [coming] from Vincennes, I was still under some doubt of his being there, [unless] the commandant [Captain Helm] had kept back the express on account of the high waters.

'In this situation we remained for many days. I intend[ed] to

[1] Major Joseph Bowman, writing some time afterward to his uncle, gave the same number. (*Author's MSS.*)

evacuate the garrison of Cahokia, in case of a siege, but was anxious to have a conference with the principal inhabitants that I knew to be zealous in our interest, to fix on certain plans for their conduct when in possession of the English, if it should be, . . . and set out on the [blank] day of January 1779 for that town, with the intention of staying but a few days. . . . We arrived safe at the town of Prairie du Rocher, about twelve miles above Kaskaskia. The gentlemen and ladies immediately assembled at a ball for our entertainment. We spent the fore part of the night very agreeably, but about 12 o'clock, there was a very sudden change, by an express arriving informing us that Governor Hamilton was within three miles of Kaskaskia, with eight hundred men and was determined to attack the fort that night, which was expected would be before the express got to me. . .

'I never saw greater confusion among a small assembly than. . . at that time, — every person having their eyes on me, as if my word was to determine their good or evil fate. It required but a moments hesitation in me to form my resolutions. I communicated them to two of my officers. . . . I ordered our horses saddled, in order if possible to get into the fort [at Kaskaskia] before the attack could be made. Those of the company that had recovered their surprise, so far as to enable them to speak, begged me not to attempt to return, saying that the town was certainly in possession of the enemy and the fort warmly attacked. Some proposed conveying me to the Spanish shore, — some one thing and some another. I thanked them for their care. . .of my person and told them it was the fate of war; that a good soldier never ought to be afraid of his life where there was a probability of his doing service by venturing it, which was my case; that I hoped that they would not let the news spoil our diversion sooner than was necessary; that we would divert ourselves until our horses were ready; forced them to dance, and endeavored to appear as unconcerned as if no such thing was in agitation.

'This conduct inspired the young men in such a manner that many of them were getting their horses to share fate with me. But, choosing to lose no time, as soon as I could write a few lines on the back of my letter to Captain Bowman at Cahokia, I set out for Kaskaskia. Each man [had] a blanket [so] that in case the fort was attacked we were to wrap ourselves in them [and] fall in with the enemies . . . at the fort, until we had an opportunity of getting so near as to give the proper signal, knowing that we should be let in. [This was a common ruse when endeavoring to get into a besieged fort.] But on our arrival, we found everything as calm as we could expect. The weather being bad, it was then thought the attack could not commence until it cleared up; but no person seemed to doubt of the enemys being at hand. . . . From many circumstances I could not but suppose it was the case, [and] that they deferred the attack for some time in order to give us time to retreat, which I supposed they would rather choose, [judging] by their proceedings. But I was determined that they should be disappointed if that was their wish. There was no time lost during the night putting everything in as good order as possible. ...

'I spent many serious reflections during the night. The inhabitants had always appeared to be attached to us, but I was convinced that I should in the morning have a sufficient trial of their fidelity. (Several of their young men had turned into the fort, in order to defend it.) But, sensible at the same time that in case they took arms to defend the town...the whole would probably be lost, (as I should be obliged to give the enemy battle in the commons), I would have chosen to have had those without families to reinforce the garrison and the rest to have lain neuter.[1]

'I resolved to burn part of the town that was near the fort and guard it, as I knew the greatest service we possibly could do was to sell the fort as dear as possible, there being no probability of escaping after attack or expectation of reinforcements as we were so far detached from the body of our country. The only probable chance of safety was Captain Bowman joining me, (which I expected the next evening down the Mississippi), to defend ourselves until Mr. Hamilton's Indians got tired and returned in four or five weeks, which I expected the greatest part would do if they had not the success that they expected. I had no occasion to consult the garrison on any resolution I should fix upon, as I knew they were all as spirited as I could wish them to be, and I took pains to make them as desperate as possible. ...You must conceive it to be desperate.

'In the morning, the first thing I did was to assemble all the inhabitants, in order to know their resolutions, as they had been the night counselling with each other. They expected some orders issued, which I did not choose to do. At the assembly I asked them what they thought of doing, whether they would endeavor to defend the town, or not. If they did, I would quit the fort, — leaving a small guard, — and head them with the troops; and, if the enemy lay [inactive] until the weather broke, we might...discover their camp and get some advantage of them. They appeared to be in great confusion, and all my fear was that they would agree to defend themselves and, if the enemy was as numerous as...expected, the whole would be lost. But I need not have been uneasy about that, for they had too maturely considered their own interest to think [of] fighting, which they certainly would have done [had] I had only as many troops as would have given any probability of success. They displayed their situation in such a manner as was really moving, and with great truth, but [declined] to act either on one side or the other. ...[They] begged that I would believe them to be in the American interest, but [said] my whole force, joined with them, would make but a poor figure against so considerable [an enemy], and gave hints that they could wish us to take Spanish protection, as they could not conceive we could keep possession a single day, as

[1] The buildings and yard fences, made of strong pickets, would have protected the attacking enemy.

the enemy would immediately set the adjacent houses on fire, which would fire the fort, (not knowing that I intended to burn them myself as soon as the wind shifted.)

'I very seldom found but I could govern my temper at pleasure, but this declaration of theirs and some other circumstances put me in a most violent rage; and, as soon as I could curb my passion, [I gave] them a lecture suitable for a set of traitors, although I could not conceive the whole of them to be such. I ordered them out of the garrison, and told them that I no longer thought they deserved favor from me; that I consequently must conceive them to be my secret enemies and should treat them as such. They endeavored to soothe me into pity, but to have listened to them would have destroyed my intention. I determined to make myself appear to them as desperate as possible, that it might have a greater effect on the enemy. They asked me to issue an order for all the provision in the town, to be brought into the fort immediately, by which I was convinced that it was their desire that I should be able to stand the siege as long as possible, and [that they] only wanted an excuse, (to the person they expected every moment to be their master), for making the supplies. I told them that I would have all the provisions, and then burn the town to the enemies' hand; that they might send the provisions if they chose it; and sent them out of the fort, and immediately had fire set to some out houses.

'Never was a set of people in more distress, — their town set on fire by those that they wished to be in friendship with, at the same time surrounded by the savages, as they expected, from whom they had but little else but destruction to expect. The houses, being covered with snow, the fire had no effect, only on those it was set to. The inhabitants looking on without daring to say a word, I told them that I intended to set fire to all those [houses] that had much provision, for fear of the enemies getting it. They were not in so great a lethargy but they took the hint, and before night they had brought in six months provision of all sorts, by which they were in hopes to come on better terms. [A masterly stroke this, both quickly provisioning the fort and making the townsmen the more interested in his successful defense.]...

'The weather clearing away, Captain Bowman arrived the following day, with his own company and a company of volunteers from Cahokia. We now began to make a tolerable appearance and seemed to defy the enemy. ...Sent out spies, on every quarter to make discovery of them, choosing for many important reasons to attack them two to one in the field, rather than suffer them to take possession of the town. [The form and manner of picketing the yards and gardens made it strong for shielding an attacking enemy.]

'I was convinced that the inhabitants now wished that they had behaved in another manner. I took...advantage of the favorable opportunity to attach them entirely to my interest. ...Instead of treating them more severely, as they expected, on my being reinforced I altered my conduct towards them and treated them with the greatest kindness, granting them every request. My influence among them in a few hours was greater than ever; they condemning themselves, and thought that I had treated them as they deserved; and I believe had Mr. Hamilton appeared we should have defeated him with a good deal of ease, — not so numerous, but the men being much better. Our spies...found the great army that gave the alarm consisted of only about forty whites and Indians, making their retreat as fast as possible to Vincennes, — sent for no other purpose, as we found after, but to take me.' [1]

While Hamilton, confident of his ability to recapture the Illinois in the spring, was making his winter quarters comfortable, Clark said:

'No information from Vincennes for some time past. As once a fortnight was the fixed time for the post, we began to suspect something was wrong. We sent spies that did not return and we remained in a state of suspense.' 'It was concluded to send other spies to Vincennes, and in the meantime prepare ourselves to act. ...Being fully confident that a revolution would shortly take place, either for or against us, we wished to strengthen ourselves as much as possible. The volunteers that accompanied Major Bowman from Cahokia were sent home and an elegant set of colors presented them. Those that were but badly armed, were completed out of the stores, and presents made to the others, &c, as an acknowledgement for the willingness they had shown on the present occasion. They paraded about town, with their new flag and equipments, and viewed themselves as superior to the young fellows of Kaskaskia; which caused so much animosity between the two parties that it did not subside until I interfered, some time after, by a little piece of policy that re-united them, when it suited my convenience.

'After making every arrangement that we thought most conducive to our safety, Major Bowman returned to his quarters [at Cahokia] and we remained in suspense, waiting the return of our spies. But, on the 29th of January 1779, Mr. Vigo, ...a Spanish

[1] From the British archives we now have the other side of this story. Hamilton's report shows that he sent the party from Vincennes to take Clark and that but for the violation of orders by a Canadian, the Ottawa chief who led the party would 'have taken prisoners Col. Clarke with several officers who were going to Cahokia. This Canadian, ... contrary to my positive orders, took away their horses from some of the French hunters, and further threatened that the Indians were to be brought down to the Illinois and put everything to fire and sword.' (*Michigan Pioneer Collections*, IX, 498.) Clark says that during his journey to Cahokia, 'this party lay concealed, keeping a small party near the road to see who passed. They lay by a small branch about three miles from Kaskaskia, there being snow on the ground. I had a guard of about six or seven men, and a few gentlemen in chairs. One of them swamped, within a hundred yards of the place where those fellows lay hid, where we had to delay upwards of an hour. I believe nothing here saved me but the instructions they had, not to kill me, or the fear of being overpowered, — not having an opportunity to alarm the main body, which lay half a mile off, without being discovered themselves.'

merchant who had been at Vincennes, arrived and gave information
that Govr Hamilton, with thirty regulars, fifty French volunteers,
Indian-agents, interpreters, boatmen &c that amounted to a considerable number, and about four hundred Indians had, in December last taken that post and, as the season was so far advanced
that it was thought impossible to reach the Illinois, he sent some of
his Indians to watch the Ohio, disbanding others &c, — the whole
to meet again in the spring to drive us out of the Illinois and attack
Kentucky in a body, joined by their Southern friends; that all the
goods were taken from the merchants of Vincennes for the King's
use; that they were repairing the fort and expected a re-enforcement
from Detroit in the spring; that they appear to have plenty of all
kinds of stores; that they were strict in their discipline, but that he
did not believe they were under much apprehension of a visit, and
believed that, if we could get there undiscovered, that we might take
the place. In short, we got every information from this gentleman
that we could wish for, as he had had good opportunity and had
taken great pains to inform himself, with a design to give intelligence.' [Vigo himself afterwards said that Col. Clark sent him to
Vincennes to report the situation there; that when nearing that
place he was arrested and imprisoned; that later Gov. Hamilton
released him on condition 'that he would do nothing to injure the
British cause *during his journey* home [St. Louis]; that he agreed to
this and departed; that during his stay at Vincennes, he ascertained
the situation of the garrison and *after his return* home to St. Louis,
immediately went to Kaskaskia and gave Clark the information.']
'We now viewed ourselves [as] in a very critical situation, in a
manner cut off from any intercourse between us and the continent;
that Gov. Hamilton, in the spring, by a junction of his northward
and southern Indians, which he had prepared for, would be at the
head of such a force that nothing in this quarter could withstand
his arms; the Kentucky must immediately fall, and well if the de-
solation would end there. [He afterward wrote: 'It was at this
moment I would have bound myself for seven years a slave to have
had five hundred troops.'] If we could immediately make our way
good to Kentucky, we were convinced that before we could raise a
force, even sufficient to save that country, it would be too late, as all
the men in it, joined by the troops we had, would not be sufficient;
and, to get timely succors from the interior frontiers was out of the
question. We saw but one alternative, which was to attack the enemy
in their quarters. If we were fortunate, it would save the whole; if
otherwise, it would be nothing more than what would certainly be
the consequence if we should not make the attempt. Encouraged
by the idea of the greatness of the consequences that would attend
our success, (the season of the year being also favorable, as the
enemy could not suppose that we should be so mad as to attempt
to march 80 leagues, [240 miles] through a drowned country in the
depth of winter,...would be off their guard, and probably would
not think it worth their while to keep out spies), [we thought] that

probably...if we could make our way good, we might surprise them; and we, pulling through the country, would not be in a worse situation than if we had not made the attempt, — those and many other similar reasons induced us to resolve to attempt the enterprise, which met the approval of every individual belonging to us.' Writing Governor Henry soon after this, Clark said: 'I was sensible the resolution was as desperate as my situation; but I saw no other probability of securing the country.'[1]

'Orders were immediately issued for preparations. The whole country took fire at the alarm and every order was executed with cheerfulness by every description of the inhabitants, preparing provisions, encouraging volunteers &c, &c, and, as we had plenty of stores, every man was completely rigged...to withstand the coldest weather.

'Knowing that the Wabash, at this season of the year, in all probability would be [over]flowed for five or six miles in the neighborhood of the enemy, [and] would be dangerous, to navigate this and to convey our artillery and stores, it was concluded to send a vessel round by water, so strong that she might force her way. ...A large Mississippi boat was immediately purchased and completely fitted as a galley, mounting two four-pounders and four swivels and 46 men, commanded by Captain John Rogers. He set sail the 4th. of February, with orders to force his way up the Wabash, as high as the mouth of White River, and to secrete himself until further orders; but if he found himself discovered, to do the enemy all the damage he could, without running too great a risk of losing his vessel, and not to leave the river until he was out of hope of [our] arrival by land. We had great dependence on this vessel. She was far superior to anything the enemy could fit out, without building a new one. ...

'The inhabitants of Kaskaskia, being a little cowed since the affair of the supposed intended siege, nothing was said to them on the subject of volunteers until the arrival of those [from] Cahokia, to whom [was given] an expensive entertainment, to which they invited all their acquaintance of Kaskaskia. All little differences [were] made up, and by twelve o'clock next day application was made to raise a company at Kaskaskia, which was granted and [the company] completed before night, the whole of the inhabitants exerting themselves in order to wipe off past coolness.'

'I conducted myself as though I was sure of taking Mr. Hamilton, [and] instructed my officers to observe the same rule. In a day or two the country seemed to believe it; many, anxious to retrieve their characters, turned out. The ladies began also to be spirited and [to] interest themselves in the expedition, which had a great effect on the young men. On the 4th of [February] I got everything complete, and on the 5th I marched. ...' In all he had one hundred and thirty men, sixty of them French volunteers in the two companies.

---

[1] *Illinois Historical Collections*, VIII, **169.**

With all his feigned display of confidence, as though 'sure of taking Mr. Hamilton,' that the young leader was painfully aware of the desperate chances he was taking appears in his letter to Governor Henry, as follows:

KASKASKIA, ILLINOIS, Feb. 3, 1779

D^r S^r:

As it is now near twelve months since I have had the least intelligence from you, I almost despair of any relief sent to me. I have, for many months past, had reports of an army marching against Detroit, but no certainty.

A late maneuver of the famous Hair-Buyer general, Henry Hamilton, Esqr., Lieut. Governor of Detroit, hath alarmed us much. On the 16th of December last, he, with a body of six hundred men, composed of Regulars, French volunteers and Indians, took possession of St. Vincennes on the Wabash, what few men that composed the garrison not being able to make the least defense. He is influencing all the Indians he possibly can, to join him. I learn that those that have treated with me as yet refused his offers. I have for some time expected an attack from him. He has blocked up the Ohio R[iver] with a party [of] French and Indians.

Yesterday I fortunately got every piece of intelligence that I could wish for, by a Spanish gentlemen [M. Francis Vigo] that made his escape from Mr. Hamilton. No attack [is] to be made on the garrison at Kaskaskia until the spring; passage is too difficult at present. [His Indians he] [1] has sent to war against different parts of [the country] especially Kentucky. Both presents and speeches [are] sent to all the nations south of the Ohio immediately to meet at a great council at the mouth of the Tennessee r[iver] to lay the best plans for cutting off the Rebels, at Illinois and Kentucky [but] the Grand Kite and his nation living at post St. Vincennes told Mr. Hamilton that he and his people were Big Knives and would not give their hands any more to the English, for he would shortly see his Father that was at Kaskaskia. Ninety regulars in garrison [at Vincennes] and about fifty Tawaway Indians, that are shortly to go to war. They are very busy in repairing the fort, which will shortly be very strong: one brass six-pounder, two iron four-pounders and two swivels, mounted in the bastions, plenty of ammunition and provisions and all kinds of warlike stores; making preparations for the reduction of the Illinois and has no suspicion of a visit from the Americans. This was Mr. Hamiltons circumstance when Mr. Vigo left him.

Being sensible that without a reinforcement, which at present I have hardly a right to expect, that I shall be obliged to give up this country to Mr. Hamilton without a turn of fortune in my favor, I am resolved to take the advantage of his present situation and risk the whole on a single battle. I shall set out in a few days with

[1] MSS. torn.

all the force I can raise of my own troops and a few militia that I can depend on, whole [amounting] to only one hundred — of which — goes on board a small G[alley sent [1]] out some time ago, mounting two four-pounders and four large swivels; one nine pounder on board. This boat is to make her way good, if possible, and take her station ten leagues below St. Vincennes until further orders. If I am defeated, she is to join Col. Rogers on the Mississippi. She has great stores of ammunition on board; com[manded] by Lieut. John Rogers. I shall march across by land myself with the rest of my boys. The principal persons that follow me on this forlorn hope are Captain[s] Joseph Bowman, John Williams, Edward Worthington, Richard M[c]Carty and Fran[cis] Charleville; lieutenants: Rich[d] Brashears, Ab[m] Kellar, Ab[m] Chaplin, Jn[o] Baily and several other brave subalterns.

You must be sensible of the feeling that I have for those brave officers and soldiers that are determined to share my fate, let it be what it will. I know the case is desperate, but Sr, we must either quit the country or attack Mr. Hamilton. No time is to be lost. Was I sure of a reinforcement, I should not attempt it. Who knows what fortune will do for us? Great things have been effected by a few men well conducted. Perhaps we may be fortunate. We have this consolation; that our cause is just and that our country will be grateful and not con[demn] our conduct in case we fail, though, if so, this coun[try] as well as Kentucky, I believe, is lost.

I have wrote to Col. Rogers desiring of him not to enter the Ohio River until further intelligence from me. I learn that, by a noble stroke, . . . he has got his cargo above the British posts in Florida. If I have success, I shall immediately send dispatches to him.[2] The expresses that you have sent I expect ha[ve] fallen into the hands of Governor Hamilton.

I have the honor to be S[r] your very humble Serv[t]

G. R. CLARK [3]

---

[1] MSS. torn.

[2] Unfortunately, Rogers went on up the Ohio and, with some of his men, was killed by the Indians. (*Michigan Pioneer Collec-*tions, x, 368; *Draper MSS.* 5 D 24-30.)

[3] Archives, Virginia State Library, Richmond; *Illinois Historical Collections,* VIII, 97.

CHAPTER XI

THE WONDERFUL MARCH TO VINCENNES

We have three main accounts of Clark's march against Vincennes. These are (1) his brief letter to Mason, written in November following; (2) the Journal of Major Joseph Bowman, giving a condensed statement of the main incidents day by day, and (3) Clark's roughly written and unfinished Memoir letter, which, as we have seen, he wrote some ten years later, and which at the request of Mr. Madison and Mr. Brown, stated in detail his objects and strategies. Each of the three accounts supplements the other, and they are remarkably consistent. As the Memoir letter best explains Clark's aims and methods, it will be mainly quoted here, with some parallel accounts from Bowman's Journal and occasional extracts from the Mason letter.

'On the 5th I marched, being joined by two volunteer companies, [the one from Cahokia] commanded by Captain McCarty, and [the other, from Kaskaskia, by] Capt. Francis Charleville. ...We were conducted out of the town by the inhabitants and Mr. Gibault, the priest, who after a very suitable discourse to the purpose gave us all absolution. ['I marched across the country with one hundred and thirty men,' forty others going by boat.[1]]...I cannot account for it, but I still had inward assurance of success and never could, weighing every circumstance, doubt it; but I had some secret check. We now had a route before us of two hundred and forty miles in length, through I suppose one of the most beautiful countries in the world, but at this time in many parts flowing with water, and exceeding bad marching. My greatest care was to divert the men as much as possible, in order to keep up their spirits.'

The officers were mounted (Clark himself, he said, on 'the

---

[1] This was the number Clark gave in his letter to Governor Henry, April 29, 1779 (*Illinois Historical Collections,* VIII, 169), and seems correct; but the number marching by land is variously stated. *Bowman's Journal* says: '170, including [those] on the galley' who were said to be '40' and '46.' His letter to Hite (*id.,* 332; *Author's MSS.*) said 'about 130.' Lieutenant Rogers said: 'our party was 130 strong...about 60 of which were French volunteers.' (*Draper MSS.* 1 L 54.) Clark's letter to Mason (Nov., 1779) says 'our whole party with the boats crew, consisted of only a little upwards of two hundred.' His Memoir letter (he evidently had Bowman's Journal before him) says: '170 men,' of whom 130 went by land and 40 in the galley. Marshall's *Kentucky,* I, 72, says 130 men.

finest stallion by far that is in the [western] country'), but when
the deeply flooded Wabash Bottoms were reached, the horses
had to be left behind. Even before that they were probably
used chiefly as pack-horses and to carry the fatigued, for the
officers themselves are soon found afoot, working in the mire
and water with their men. The cannon and heavy stores having been sent forward by water, the land force was unencumbered with baggage. Despite freezing and thawing winter
weather, chilling rains, and flooded country, there were no
tents, but throughout the march the men were without shelter,
day or night, save perhaps here and there a hollow tree.

Bowman's Journal gives the daily incidents at Kaskaskia
and on the march and says:

'Jany 30th, Col. Clark called a council with his officers and it was
concluded to go and attack Gov. Hamilton at all events, for fear,
if it was let alone till spring, that he with his Indians would undoubtedly cut us all off.

'31 — Sent an express to...Cahokia for the volunteers. Nothing
extraordinary this day.

'Feby 1st. Orders given for a large batteau to be repaired, and
provisions got ready for the expedition concluded on.

'2nd. A pack-horse master appointed and orders to prepare
pack-saddles, etc.

'3rd. The galley, or batteau, finished. Called her the Willing.
Put the loading on board, together with two four-pounders and
four swivels, ammunition, &c....

'4th. About ten o'clock Capt. McCarthy arriv'd with a company
of volunteers from Cahokia, and about two o'clock in the afternoon
the Batteau set off, under the command of Lieut Rogers, with 46 men,
with orders to proceed to a certain station near St. Vincent till
further orders.

'5th. Raised another comp'y of volunteers, under the command
of Capt. Francois Charleville, which added to our force and increased our number to 170, including the artillery [on the galley]
pack-horsemen, &c. About three o'clock crossed the Kaskaskias
River with our baggage and marched about a league from the town.
Rainy and drisly weather.

'7th. Began our march early. Made a good days march for
about 9 leagues. The roads very bad with mud and water. [When a
pioneer says a road is 'very bad' it is difficult for us to realize how
bad it was. '9 leagues' (27 miles) in one day, on such roads — with
a network of small but swollen streams to cross and many detours
to keep out of deep water — was tremendous marching.] Pitched
our camp in a square, baggage in the middle, every company to guard
their own square.

'8th. Marched early through water, which we now began to

meet in those large and level plains where, (from the flatness of the country), the water rests a considerable time before it drains off; notwithstanding, our men were in great spirits, tho much fatigued.

'9th. Made a moderate days march. Rained most of the day.

'10th. Crossed the River of the Petit Ford, upon trees that we felled for that purpose, the water being so high there was no fording it; still raining, and no tents. Encamped near the River, Stormy, &c.

'11th. Crossed the Saline River. Nothing extraordinary this day.

'12th. Marched across bad plain; saw and killed numbers of Buffaloe; the roads very bad from the immense quantity of rain that had fallen; the men much fatigued; encamped at the edge of the Wood. This plain, or meadow, being fifteen or more miles across, it was late in the night before the troops and baggage got together. Now 21 leagues from St. Vincent.'

In six days they had marched one hundred and seventy-four miles, an average of over twenty-eight miles a day. Considering weather, the muddy condition of the so-called 'roads' (in reality not roads at all, but mere wilderness 'traces'), many long detours to escape deep water, and unavoidable delays in crossing many small but swollen streams and several large ones, this was certainly a record of endurance and speed.[1]

The Memoir describes these first six days of the march very briefly, thus:

'Set out, the weather wet (but fortunately not cold for the season), and great part of the plains [being] under water for several inches, it was difficult marching. My object now was to keep the men in spirits. I suffered them to shoot game on all occasions, and feast on [it] like Indians [at] war dances, each company by turns inviting the other to their feasts, which was the case every night, as the company that was to give [the feast] was always supplied with horses to lay up sufficient store of...meat in the course of the day, myself and principal officers hailing the woodsmen, shouting now and then and running as much through the mud as any of them. Thus insensibly, without a murmur, were those men led on to the banks of the Little Wabash, which we reached the 13th, through incredible difficulties, far surpassing anything any of us had ever experienced, (but nothing to what we had [yet] to go through.) Frequently...

---

[1] The direct distance was of course much less. Hamilton said it was '240 miles' from Kaskaskia to Vincennes (*Illinois Historical Collections*, VIII, 182), and in another place '80 leagues' (*id.*, I, 227), evidently allowing three miles to the league. The Mason Letter says '240 miles.' Joseph Bowman to I. Hite, June 14, 1779 (*Author's MSS.*) said the march from February 6th to 'the place' (somewhat indefinite) was 'about 180 miles.' Cf. English's *Conquest of the North-west*, p. 288.

the pleasantries of a day and the diversions of the night wore off the thought of the [hardships of the] preceding day.'

In the remaining twenty-one leagues (sixty-three miles) of the march, there were four rivers to cross — all of them now swollen by flood — first the two Little Wabash rivers, then the Embarass, and finally the Great Wabash, on the east bank of which, some nine miles above its junction with the Embarass, lay Vincennes. This part of the march Clark briefly described in his letter to Mason, thus: 'On the 13th arriving at the two Little Wabash rivers, although three miles asunder they now make but one, the flowed water between them being at least three feet deep and in many places four, being near five miles to the opposite hills. The shallowest place, except about one hundred yards, was three feet. This would have been enough to have stopped any set of men that were not in the same temper we were, but in three days we contrived to cross.'

The descriptions about to be given, from Clark's Memoir letter, of the passage, first of the two Little Wabash rivers, then the Embarass, and lastly the Great Wabash, agree in all substantial respects with Bowman's Journal, parts of which will also be quoted. Bowman brings out better the suffering and feelings of the men, while Clark (being the commander responsible for the success of the campaign, and endeavoring to comply with Madison and Brown's request,) gives more of his own aims and the methods he devised to attain them. His narrative, from day to day, will here follow:

'13th. The [little Wabash rivers] are three miles apart and from the heights of the one, to those of the other, on the opposite shore, is five miles, — the whole under water, generally about three feet deep, never under two, and frequently four. We formed a camp on a height we found on the bank of the river, and suffered our troops to amuse themselves. I viewed this sheet of water for some time with distrust, but accusing myself of doubting, I immediately set to work [and], without any consultation about it, or suffering anybody else to do so in my presence, ordering a pirogue [dug out canoe] immediately built, and acted as though crossing the water would be only a piece of diversion; and, as but few could work at a time, pains were taken to find diversion for the rest, to keep them in high spirits. But the men were well prepared for this attempt, as they had frequently waded further in water, but perhaps seldom about a half-leg deep. My anxiety to cross this place continually increased, as I saw that it would at once fling us into a situation of a forlorn hope, [when] all idea of a retreat would be, in some measure, done away. If the men began, after this was accomplished, to think seriously of what they had really suffered,...they [would] prefer risking any seeming difficulty, that might turn out favorably, rather than to attempt a retreat, when they would be certain of experiencing what they had already felt; and, if the weather should be freezing, [retreat would be] altogether impracticable, except the ice would bear them.

'In the evening of the 14th our vessel was finished and sent to explore the drowned lands, with private instructions what report to make, and if possible, to find some spot of dry land on the bank of the opposite small river; which they did and marked the trees back from thence to camp, and made a very favorable report.' [Bowman says: 'Still raining — Orders given to fire no guns in future, except in case of necessity.']

'Fortunately the 15th happened to be a warm moist day for the season, and the channel of the river where we lay about thirty yards wide. A scaffold was built on the opposite shore, that was about three feet under water, our baggage ferried across and put on it. Our horses swam across, and we began our march, our vessel loaded with those that were sickly &c. We moved on cheerfully, every moment expecting to see dry land which was not discovered until [we came] to the spot mentioned. This being a smaller branch than the other, the troops immediately crossed and marched on, in the water as usual, to gain and take possession of the nearest height they could discover. Our horses and baggage crossed, as they had done at the former river, and proceeded on, following the marked trail of the troops. (As tracks could not be seen in the water, the trees were marked.)

[Bowman says: '16th. Marched all day thro rain and water. Crossed the second river. Our provisions began to grow short.' Clark's Memoir continues]: 'By evening we found ourselves encamped on a pretty height, in high spirits, each laughing at the other in consequence of something that had happened in the course of this ferrying business, as they called it, and the whole at the exploit. ...they thought that they had accomplished. In this, a little antic drummer afforded them great diversion by floating on his drum, &c. All this was greatly encouraged, and they really began to think themselves superior to other men, and that neither the rivers or seasons could stop their progress. Their whole conversation now was what they would do when they got about the enemy, and [they] now began to view the main Wabash as a creek, and made no doubt but such men as they were could find a way to cross it. They wound themselves up to such a pitch that they soon took Vincennes, divided the spoil, and before bed-time were far advanced on their route to Detroit! [The enthusiasm of the effervescent French was here a valuable asset, for in war it is a great motive power. Without it, perhaps no troops could have been either persuaded or forced to undertake what was still before them.]

This, no doubt, was pleasing to those of us that had more serious thought. We were now, as it were, in the enemy's country; no possibility of escape if our enemy should discover and overpower us, (except by the means of our galley, if we should fall in with her.)

'We were now convinced that the whole of the low country on the Wabash was drowned; that the enemy could easily get to us, if they discovered us and wished to risk an action. If they did not, we made no doubt of crossing the river by some means or other. Supposing Captain Rogers had not got to his station, agreeable to his appointment, [we determined] that we would [send] and, if possible, steal some vessels from houses opposite to the town &c. We flattered ourselves that all would be well, and marched on in high spirits.

'On the 17th dispatched Mr. Kennedy and three men off to cross the River Embarass, (this river is six miles from Vincennes), and if possible get some vessels in the vicinity of the town, but principally, if he could do it in safety, get some intelligence. He proceeded on, and getting to the river found...the country between that and the Wabash overflowed. We marched down below the mouth of the Embarass, attempting in vain to get to the banks of the Wabash. Late in the night, finding a dry spot, we encamped and were much amused, for the first time, by hearing the morning gun from the British garrison.'

[Bowman in his account of this day's march says:] '17. Marched early. Crossed several rivers, very deep. About one hour before sunset we got near the River Embarass; found the country all over flown. We strove to find the Wabash, [that is, hunting for miles to find a river in a lake!] Traveled, till 8 o'clock, in mud and water; but, after some time, Mr. Kennedy and his party return'd, — found it impossible to cross the Embarass River. We found the Water falled from a small spot of ground; staid there the remainder of the night. Drisly and dark weather.' [From daybreak till far into the dark winter's night, they had been marching on their way — into what immediate dangers no man knew — to get at an out numbering and fortified enemy.]

[Clark's letter to Mason describes the march on the 17th, thus:] 'On the evening of the 17th we got to the low lands of the river Embarass, which we found deep in water, it being nine miles to Vincennes, which stood on the east side of the Wabash, and every foot of the way covered with deep water. We marched down the [Embarass], in order to gain the banks of the [Wabash], which we did in about three leagues [nine miles.] Made a small canoe and sent an express to meet the boat and hurry it up. From the spot we now lay on [it] was about ten miles to town, and every foot of the way put together, that was not three feet and upwards under water, would not have made the length of two miles and a half; and not a mouthful of provisions. To have waited for our boat, if possible to avoid it, would have been impolitic.

'If I were sensible that you would let no person see this relation,

I would give you a detail of our suffering for four days in crossing those waters and the manner it was done; as I am sure that you would credit it. But it is too incredible for any person to believe, except those that are well acquainted with me as you are, or had experienced something similar to it. I hope you will excuse me until I have the pleasure of seeing you personally.'

[Bowman graphically describes the next two days of the march, thus:] '18th. At the break of day heard Gov. Hamilton's morning gun. Set off and marched down the river. Saw some fine land. About 2 o'clock came to the bank of the Wabash, ['three leagues below the town,' says Clark.] Made rafts for four men to cross and go up to town and steal boats, but they spent the day and the night in the water to no purpose, for there was not one foot of dry land to be found.

'19th. Capt. McCarty's Comp'y set to making a canoe, and at three o'clock the four men [sent to steal boats] returned, after spending the night on some old logs in the water. The canoe finished. Capt. McCarthy with three of his men embarked in the canoe and made the next attempt to steal boats, but he soon returned, having discovered four large fires about a league distant from our camp, and seemed to him to be fires of Whites and Indians. [If they discovered the tired, foodless little army, its doom seemed certain, for it is difficult to see how it could defend itself if attacked by even a very small force of the enemy in boats.] Immediately Col. Clark sent two men in the said canoe down to meet the Batteau [Rogers' galley] with orders to come on, day and night, that being our last hope. Starving. Many of the men much cast down, particularly the volunteers. No provisions of any sort now two days. Hard fortune!'

[Referring to this day, Clark says:] 'To have every string to my bow, . . . I ordered canoes to be built, in a private place. Not yet out of hopes of our boat arriving. If she did, those canoes would augment our fleet. If she did not, . . . they would answer our purpose without her. Many of our volunteers began for the first time, to despair. Some talked of returning. But my situation now was such that I was past all uneasiness. I laughed at them, without persuading or ordering them to desist from any such attempt, but told them I should be glad they would go out and kill some deer. They went, confused with such conduct. My own troops I knew had no idea of abandoning an enterprise for want of provision while there were plenty of good horses in their possession, and I knew that, without violence, the volunteers could be detained for a few days, in the course of which our fate would be known. I conducted myself in such a manner that caused the whole to believe that I had no doubt of success, which kept [up] their spirits, and hunters being out, they every moment had hopes of getting a supply from them, as well as. . .of the galley heaving in sight. (The reason why provisions were now so scarce was the whole of ours being damaged on the march, and game being very scarce in the vicinity of Vincennes.) I was sensible that, if we should not be discovered, in two days, we should effect a passage of the river.'

[Bowman] '20. Camp very quiet, but hungry; some almost in despair. Many of the Creole Volunteers talking of returning. Fell to making more canoes when, about 12 o'clock our centry on the river brought to a boat with five Frenchmen, from the Post, who told us we were not yet discovered; that the Inhabitants were well disposed towards us, &c; [that] Capt. Williams' Brother (who was taken in the Fort) had made his escape. Also told us that Maisonville, with a party of Indians, were 7 days in pursuit of him, with much news more...such as the repairs done the fort, the strength, &c. [We shall soon see the terrible retribution Captain Williams was to visit upon these Indians, who were pursuing his brother to recapture and perhaps tomahawk him.] They informed us of two canoes they had seen adrift at some distance about us. Order'd Capt. Worthington with a party to go in search of the canoes; returned late with one only. One of our men killed a deer, which was distributed in camp. Very acceptable.

'21st. At break of day began to ferry our men over in our two canoes to a small little hill called the lower Mamell, (or Bubbie). Capt. Williams with two men went to look for a passage, but were discover'd by two men in a canoe, but could not fetch them to. The whole army being over, we thought to get to town that night, so plunged into the water, sometimes to the neck, for more than one league, [three miles] when we stop'd on the second hill of the same name, there being no dry land near us on one side for many leagues. Our pilots say we cannot get along, that it was impossible. The whole of the army being over, we encamped. Rain all this day; no provisions.'

[Clark's Memoir said:] 'The men that we had taken said it was impossible that we could make the town that night, or at all with our vessels; but, recollecting what we had done, we thought otherwise, pushed into the water and marched a league, ... being frequently to the arm-pits in water. Here we encamped, our men yet in spirits from the hopes of their fatigues soon being at an end and their wishes accomplished in getting in contact with the enemy.' Was there ever a braver band?

[Bowman's Diary] '22. Col. Clark encourages his men, which gave them great spirits. Marched on in the water, those that were weak and faintish from so much fatigue went in the canoes. We came, one league further, to some sugar camps, where we staid all night. Heard the evening and morning guns from the Fort. No provisions yet. Lord help us!'

[Clark's Memoir describing the events of this day says:] 'This last [day's] march through the water was so far superior to anything the Frenchmen had any idea of that they were backwards in speaking. [They] said that the nearest land to us was a small league, called the Sugar Camp, on the bank of the river. A canoe was dispatched off and returned without finding that we could pass. I went myself and sounded the water [running, muddy, and ice-cold], found [it] as deep as to my neck. I returned with the design to have the men transported on board the canoes to the Sugar Camp, which I knew would spend the whole day and ensuing night, as the vessels would pass but slowly through the bushes. The loss of so much time, to men half starved, was a matter of consequence. I would have given a good deal for a days provision, or for one of our horses.

'I returned but slowly to the troops, giving myself time to think. On our arrival, all ran to hear what was the report. Every eye was fixd on me. I unfortunately spoke seriously to one of the officers. The whole was alarmed without knowing what I said. They ran from one to another bewailing their situation. I viewed their confusion for about one minute, whispered to those near me to do as I did, immediately took some water in my hand, poured on some powder, blacked my face, gave a warwhoop, and marched into the water, without saying a word. The party gazed and fell in, one after another, without saying a word, like a flock of sheep. I ordered those that were near me to begin a favorite song of theirs. It soon passed through the line and the whole went on cheerfully. I now intended to have them transported across the deepest part of the water, but, when getting about waist deep, one of the men informed me that he thought he felt a path. (A path is very easily discovered under water, by the feet.) We examined and found it so, and concluded that it kept on the highest ground, (which it did); and by [taking] pains to follow it we got to the Sugar Camp without the least difficulty...where there was about half an acre of dry ground, (at least not under water), where we took up our lodgings. [Crowded and comfortless lodgings for one hundred and thirty hungry men, this half acre of mud, barely raised above miles of running waters!]

'The Frenchmen that we had taken on the river, appeared to be uneasy at our situation. They begged that they might be permitted to go in the two canoes to town, in the night; that they would bring from their own houses provisions, without a possibility of any person's knowing it; that some of our men should go with them, as a surety of their good conduct; that it was impossible we could march from that place until the water fell,...for the plain before [us] for upwards of three miles was too deep to march. Some of the [troops] solicited that it might be done. I would not suffer it, by no means. I never could well account for this piece [of] obstinacy, and give satisfactory reasons to myself or anybody else why I denied a proposition apparently so easy to execute and so much [to our] advantage; but something seemed to tell me that it should not be done, and it was not.'

[Bowman's Journal:] '23. — Set off to cross a plain, called Horse Shoe plain, about 4 miles long, cover'd with water breast high. Here we expected some of our brave men must certainly perish, having frose in the night, and so long fasting, and no other resource but wading this plain, or rather Leak [lake] of water. We pushed in with courage, Col. Clark being the first, taking care to have the boats close by, to take those that was weak and benumbed (with cold) into them. Never was men so animated with the thoughts of revenging the wrongs done their back settlements as this small Army was. — [Think of it! These men were not fleeing from an enemy, or fear of death. All through history we have record of almost incredible hardships suffered in disastrous retreats, for with their last gasp men fight to save their lives, but Clark's men were on an offensive march, encountering their sufferings and dangers to get at the enemy and win a great country, not to save their lives, but to risk them further!] About one o'clock we came in sight of the town. We halted on a small Nole of dry land, called Warrior's Island, where we took a prisoner that was hunting ducks, — who informed us that no person suspected our coming in that season of the year.'

[Colonel Clark's parallel description of this last day's march is as follows:] 'The most of the weather that we had on this march was moist and warm for the season. This was the coldest night we had. The ice in the morning was from $\frac{1}{2}$ to $\frac{3}{4}$ inch thick, near the shores and in still water. The morning was the finest we had had on our march.

'A little after sun-rise I lectured the whole. What I said to them I forget, but it may be easily imagined by a person that could possess my affections for them at that time. Concluding by informing them that surmounting the plain, that was then in full view, and reaching the opposite woods would put an end to their fatigue; that in a few hours they would have a sight of their long-wished-for object, and immediately stepped into the water, without waiting for any reply. A huzzah took place. As we generally marched through the water in a line, as it was much easier, before a third entered I halted, and, further to prove the men and having some suspicion of three or four, holoed to Major Bowman, ordering him to fall to the rear, with twenty five men, and put to death any man that refused to march; that we wished no such person among us. The whole gave a cry of approbation, — that it was right, — and on we went.

'This was the most trying of all the difficulties we had experienced. I generally kept fifteen or twenty of the strongest men next myself, and judging from my own feelings what must be that of others, getting about the middle of the plain, the water about knee deep, I found myself sensibly failing. As there were here no trees, or bushes, for the men to support themselves by, I doubted that many of the most weak would be drowned. I ordered the canoes to make the land, discharge their loading, and ply backwards and forwards with all diligence, and pick up the men; and, to encourage the party, sent some of the strongest men forward with orders, when they got to a certain distance, to pass the word back that the water was getting [shallow], and, when getting to the woods, to cry out "Land!" This stratagem had its desired effect. The men, encouraged by [it], exerted themselves beyond their abilities, — the weak holding by the stronger, and frequently one with two others holding. This was of infinite advantage to the weak. But the water never got shallower, but continued deepening. Getting to the woods, where they expected land, the water was up to my shoulders. [He was a tall man.] But gaining those woods was of great consequence. All the low men, and weakly, hung to the trees and floated on the old logs until they were taken off by the canoes. The strong and tall got ashore and built fires. Many would reach the shore and fall with their bodies half in the water, not being able to support themselves without it.

'This was a delightful dry spot of ground of about ten acres. We soon found that the fires answered no purpose, but that two strong men, taking a weaker one by the arms, was the only way to recover him; and, it being a delightful day, it soon did.

'But, fortunately, as if designed by Providence, a canoe of Indian squaws and children was coming up to town and took through part of this plain as a nigh way, [and] was discovered by our canoes as they were out after the men. They gave chase and took them. On board...was nearly half quarter of buffalo, some corn, tallow, kettles &c. This was a grand prize and was invaluable. Broth was immediately made and served out to the most weak, with great care. Most of the whole got a little, but a great many would not taste it but gave their part to the weakly, jocosely saying something cheery to their comrades. This little refreshment, and fine weather by the afternoon, gave new life to the whole.

'Crossing a narrow, deep lake, in the canoes, and marching some distance, we came to a copse of timber called the Warriors Island. We were now in full view of the fort and town, — not a shrub between us, — at about two miles distance. Every man now feasted his eyes and forgot that he had suffered anything, agreeing that all that had passed was owing to good policy and nothing but what a man could bear, and that a soldier had no right to think &c, — passing from one extreme to another, which is common in such cases.'[1]

[1] Mason Letter: 'But to our inexpressable joy, in the evening of the 23d, we got safe on *terra firma* within half a league of the fort, covered by a small grove of trees.' (*Illinois Historical Collections*, VIII, 114, 154.)

CHAPTER XII

VINCENNES SURRENDERS

IN the thrilling game of war one of the most extraordinary
traits of brave soldiers, who have been led to fight their way
through desperate difficulties, is their enthusiasm and confidence in facing others even more formidable. It sometimes
seems nothing short of an infectious madness, in which the
mind is abnormally alert to everything but danger, and physical strength and endurance become amazingly multiplied. To
arouse that kind of enthusiasm, and keep it alive despite
discouragements, has ever been a prime object of all skillful
commanders.

Here were Clark's men — some seventy Americans and
sixty Creoles — soaking wet, cold, famished, without a pound
of food, with scant ammunition, fatigued by eighteen days
and nights of almost incredible toil and exposure, facing a
well-fortified enemy, supposed to be greatly superior in numbers, and well supplied with cannon, ammunition, and food;
yet of these men, in this situation, Bowman's Journal says:
'Never was men so animated with the thoughts of revenging
the wrongs done their back settlements!', and Clark, that
'Every man now feasted his eyes and forgot that he had
suffered anything!'

'The plain between us and the town [wrote Clark] was not a perfect level. The sunken ground was covered with water, full of
ducks. We observed several men on horse-back out shooting them,
within half a mile of us, and sent out as many of our active young
French men to decoy and take one of them prisoner, in such manner
as not to alarm the others, which they did. The information we
got from this person was similar to [that given by] those we took on
the river, except that the British that evening, had completed the
wall of the fort &c; that there were a good many Indians in town.

'Our situation was now truly critical; no possibility of retreating
in case of defeat; in full view of the town, that at this time had upwards of six hundred men in it, — troops, inhabitants, and Indians.
The crew of the galley, though not fifty men, would have been now
a reenforcement of immense magnitude to our little army, if I may
so call it. But we would not think of [difficulties.] The idea of
being made prisoner was foreign to almost every man, as they ex-

pected nothing but torture from the savages if they fell into their hands. Our fate was now to be determined, probably in a few hours. We knew that nothing but the most daring conduct could insure success.

'I knew that a number of the inhabitants wished us well, many luke-warm to the interest of either [side]; and also learned that the Grand Chief, Tobacco's Son, had openly declared, in council with the British, that he was Brother and Friend to the Big Knife. These were favorable circumstances, and as there was little probability of our remaining until dark undiscovered, (as great numbers of fowlers go out, ...that we now see and hear through the plains around us), I determined to begin the career immediately, and wrote the following placart to the inhabitants, and sent it off by the prisoner just taken, who was not permitted to see our numbers:

'"To the Inhabitants &c.

'"Gentlemen: Being within two miles of your village with my army, being determined to take your fort this night and not being willing to surprise you, I take this step to request of such of you as are true citizens and willing to enjoy the liberty I bring you, to remain still in your houses, and that those, (if any there be) that are friends to the King of England will instantly repair to the fort and join his troops and fight like men and that if such should hereafter be discovered that did not repair to the garrison, they may depend on severe punishment. On the contrary those that are true friends of Liberty may expect to be well treated as such. I once more request that they may keep out of the streets, for every person found under arms on my arrival will be treated as an enemy.

'"G. R. CLARK."

'I had various ideas on the supposed result of this letter. I knew it could do us no damage; that it would encourage our friends, cause the luke-warm to be decided, and astonish our enemies; that they would of course suppose our information (as to their numbers &c) good, and our forces so numerous that we were sure of success;... that the army was from Kentucky [the Falls of Ohio] and not from the Illinois, as it would be thought impossible to march from thence, and that my name was only made use of [to deceive them], (this they firmly believed until the next morning, when I was shown to them by a person in the fort that knew me well), or that we were a flying party that only made use of this stratagem to give ourselves [opportunity] to retreat. This latter idea I knew would be soon done away. Several gentlemen sent their compliments to their friends, under borrowed names, well known at Vincennes, ...[of] persons supposed to have been at Kentucky. The soldiers all had instructions that their common conversation, when speaking of our numbers, should be such that a stranger overhearing must suppose that there were a thousand of us.

'We anxiously viewed this messenger until he entered the town, and in a few minutes could discover by our glasses some stir in every street we could penetrate into, and great numbers running or riding out into the commons, we supposed to view us, which was the case. But what surprised us [was] that nothing had yet happened that had the appearance of the garrison being alarmed, — no drum, or gun. We began to suppose that the information we got from our prisoner was false, and that the enemy already knew of us and was prepared.

'Every man had been impatient. The moment was now arrived. A little before sunset we moved and displayed ourselves in full view of the town, crowds gazing at us. We were plunging ourselves into certain destruction or success; there was no midway thought of. We had little to say to our men, except inculcating an idea of the necessity of obedience &c. We knew they did not want encouraging, and that anything might be attempted with them that was possible for such a number, — perfectly cool, under proper subordination, pleased with the prospect before them, and much attached to their officers. They all declared that they were convinced that an implicit obedience to orders was the only thing that would insure success, and hoped no mercy should be shown the person that should violate them, but such immediately put to death. Such language as this from soldiers to persons in our situation must have been exceedingly agreeable.

'We moved on slowly in full view of the town, but as it was a point of some consequence to make ourselves appear as formidable [as possible], we, in leaving the covert that we were in, marched and counter-marched in such manner that we appeared numerous. [When] raising volunteers in the Illinois, every person that set about the business must have a set of colors given him, [which] they brought with them to the amount of ten or twelve pair. These were displayed to the best advantage, and as the low plain we marched through was not a perfect level, but had frequent risings in it (of seven or eight feet higher than the common level, which was covered with water), and they generally run in an oblique direction to the town, we took advantage of one of them [and] marched through the water under it, which completely prevented our men being numbered. But our colors showed considerably above the height, as they were fixed on long poles procured for the purpose, and at a distance made no despicable appearance. As our young Frenchmen had, while we lay on Warrior's Island, decoyed and taken several fowlers with their horses, officers were mounted on these and rode about more completely to deceive the enemy. In this manner we moved and directed our march in such a manner as to suffer it to be dark before we had advanced more than half way to the town. We then altered our direction and crossed ponds where they could not have suspected us, and about eight o'clock gained the heights back of the town; and as there was yet no hostile appearance, we were impatient to have the cause unriddled.

'Lieutenant Baily was ordered with fourteen men to march and fire on the fort. The main body moved in a different direction and took possession of the strongest part of the town. The firing now commenced on the fort, but they did not believe it was an enemy, until one of their men was shot down through a port as he was lighting his match. ... The drums now sounded and the business fairly commenced on both sides. [Says Bowman's Journal: 'Fine sport for the sons of Liberty!']

'We now found that the garrison had known nothing of us; that having finished the fort that evening, they had amused themselves at different games and had retired just before my letter arrived, as it was near roll-call. The placart being made public, many of the inhabitants were afraid to show themselves out of doors, for fear of offense, and not one dared give information [to the garrison.] Our friends flew to the commons and other convenient places to view the pleasing sight, which was observed from the garrison and the reason asked, but a satisfactory excuse given; and, as part of the town lay between our line of march and the garrison, we could not be seen by the sentinels on the walls.

'Captain Shannon [afterwards Clark's quartermaster] and another being some time before taken prisoners by one [of their scouting parties] and that evening brought in, the party had discovered at the Sugar Camp some sign of us. They supposed [us] to be a party of observation that intended to land on the height some distance below the town. Captain Lamothe [with twenty men] was sent to intercept [us.] It was at him the people said they were looking, ... when they were asked the reason of their unusual stir. Several suspected persons had been taken to the garrison, among them Mr. Moses Henry. Mrs. Henry went, under the pretense of carrying him provisions, and whispered him the news and what she had seen. Mr. Henry conveyed it to the rest of his fellow prisoners, which gave them much pleasure, particularly Captain Helm, who amused himself very much during the siege and I believe did much damage. [It would be interesting to know how the doughty captain "amused himself" and what the damage was.]

'Ammunition was scarce with us, as most of our stores had been put on the galley; ... but fortunately (at the time of its being reported that the whole of the goods in the town were to be taken for the King's use) ... Col. Legras, Major Bosseron [1] and others had buried the greatest part of their powder and ball. This was immediately produced, and we found ourselves well supplied by those gentlemen.

'The Tobacco's Son, being in town with a number of warriors, immediately mustered them and let us know that he wished to join us, [saying] that by morning he would have a hundred men. He received for answer that we thanked him for his friendly disposition, [but] as we were sufficiently strong ourselves we wished him to desist, and that we would converse on the subject in the morning, ... and as we knew that there was a number of Indians in and near the town that were our enemies, some confusion might happen if

[1] Their titles were won later.

our men [and his] should mix in the dark; but hoped we might be favored with his counsel and company during the night, which was agreeable to him.

'The garrison was now completely surrounded and the firing continued without intermission (except about 15 minutes a little before day) until about nine o'clock the following morning, by the whole of our troops, (joined by a few of the young men of the town that got permission), except fifty men kept as a reserve in case of casualties happening, which [were] many and diverting in the course of the night.

'I made myself fully acquainted with the situation, fort, town, and the parts relative to each. The cannon of the garrison was on the upper floors of strong block-houses, at each angle of the fort, eleven feet above the surface, and the ports so badly cut that [although] many of our troops lay under the fire of them, within 20 or 30 yards of the walls, they did no damage, except to the buildings of the town, some of which they shattered. . . . Their musketry in the dark employed against woodsmen covered by houses, palings, . . . ditches, the banks of the river &c was but of little avail and did no damage to us, except wounding a man or two. . . . Breastworks were soon made by tearing down old houses, gardens, &c, so that those within had very little advantage of those without the fort, and [the garrison] not knowing [our] number. . . thought themselves in a worse situation than they really were. . . . As we could not afford to lose men, great care was taken to preserve them sufficiently covered, and to keep up a hot fire, in order to intimidate the enemy, as well as to destroy them. The embrasures of their cannon were frequently shut, for our riflemen, finding the true direction of them, would pour such volleys when they opened that the men could not stand to the guns. Seven or eight of them in a short time got cut down. . . . I believe, if they had stood to their artillery, that the greatest part of them would have been destroyed in the course of the night. . . . Sometimes an irregular and as hot a fire as possible was kept up from different directions for a few minutes, and then only a continual scattering fire at the ports as usual, and a great laughter immediately commenced in different parts of the town, by the reserved parties, as if. . . [only part of our men] fired on the fort a few minutes for amusement, — as if those continually firing at the fort were. . . regularly relieved.

'Conduct similar to this kept the garrison eternally alarmed. They did not know what moment they might be stormed, or sapped, . . . they could plainly discover that we had flung up some intrenchments across the streets and appeared to frequently [be working] very busily under the bank of the river, which was within thirty feet of the fort walls. The situation of the magazine we well knew. Captain Bowman began some works to blow it up, in case our artillery should arrive; but, as we knew that we were daily liable to be overpowered by numerous bands of Indians on the river, (in case they again heartily joined the enemy, the certainty of which we were yet unacquainted with), we resolved to lose no time, but to get the fort in our possession as soon as possible, and, ...if the vessel did not arrive before, to undermine the fort the ensuing night, and fixed on the spot and plan of executing this work, which we intended to commence the next day.

'The Indians of the different tribes that were inimical had left the town and neighborhood. Captain Lamothe continued to hover about it, in order if possible to make his way good into the fort. [Our] parties continued in vain [trying] to surprise him. A few of his party was taken, one of which was Maisonville, a famous Indian partisan. Two lads that captured him led him to a post in a street and fought from behind him as a breastwork, supposing that the enemy would not fire at them for fear of killing him. ... They were ordered by an officer...to untie and take him off to the guard, which they did, but were so inhumane as to take part of his scalp on the way, but happened to do him no other damage. [Maisonville, it will be remembered, had been reported to Clark's men as leading a party of Indians to recapture and perhaps scalp Captain Williams' brother. The fate of the latter being unknown to the Americans, the wonder is that Maisonville's life was spared.]

'As almost [all] the persons that [were] most active in the [Indian] department of Detroit were either in the fort, or with Captain Lamothe, I got got extremely uneasy for fear that he would not fall in our power, knowing that he would go off, if he could not effect his purpose in the course of the night. ...A re-enforcement of twenty men, although considerable to them, would not be of great moment to us, in the present situation of our affairs; and, knowing that we had weakened them by killing or wounding many of their gunners, after some deliberation on the subject we concluded to risk the reinforcement in preference to his going again among the Indians. As the garrison had at least a months provisions, ...in the course of that time he might do us much damage. A little before day [therefore] the troops were withdrawn from the fort, except a few parties of observation, and the firing totally ceased. Orders were given that in case [he] approached, not to alarm or fire on him, without a certainty of killing or taking the whole [party.] In less than a quarter of an hour he passed within ten feet of an officer and small party that lay concealed. Ladders were flung over to them and they mounted them. As they mounted our party shouted. Many of them fell from the top of the walls, some within, and others back; but, as they were not fired on, they all got over, much to the joy of their friends. ...The firing immediately commenced on both sides with double vigor, and I believe that more noise could not have been made by the same number of men, but a continual blaze around the garrison until a little before day.'

The western country had rarely known a cannonade, and never before so noisy a battle; but Clark's aim, he said, was to keep the 'garrison eternally alarmed,' and 'get the fort in our possession as soon as possible.' His soldiers — rough men, most of them — confident of taking the 'Hair-Buyer General,' and 'animated with the thoughts of revenging the wrongs done their back settlements,' no doubt enjoyed making the night hideous. The terror of the French women and children amidst this pandemonium may be imagined.

'A little before daylight...our troops were drawn off to posts prepared for them, about 60 to 100 yards from the garrison, from which a loop-hole could scarcely be darkened [but] a rifle ball would pass through it. To have stood to their cannon would have been destroying their men without a probability of doing much service. Our situation was nearly similar. It would have been imprudent in either party to have wasted men, without some decisive stroke required it. Thus the attack continued until about nine o'clock in the morning of the 24th.

'Learning that the two prisoners they had brought in the day before, had a considerable number of letters with them, I supposed it was an express [from Gov. Henry] that we expected about this time, which I knew to be of the greatest moment to us, as we had not received one since our arrival in the country. Not being fully acquainted with the character of our enemy, we were doubtful that those papers might be destroyed; to prevent which I sent a flag demanding the garrison to [surrender] and desiring Governor Hamilton not to destroy them, with some threats in case he did, should he fall into my hands. [The message sent with the flag read as follows:

"'*Sir:* In order to save yourself from the impending storm that now threatens you I order you to immediately surrender yourself up with all your Garrison, Stores, &c, &c., for if I am obliged to storm, you may depend upon such treatment justly due to a Murderer. Beware of destroying Stores of any kind, or any papers or letters that is in your possession, or hurting one house in the town, for by heavens if you do there shall be no mercy shewn you.

'"G. R. CLARK."'

'His answer was: [Gov' Hamilton begs to acquaint Col. Clark that he and his Garrison are not disposed to be awed into any action unworthy of British subjects.

'H. HAMILTON.'][1]

'The firing commenced warmly for a considerable time, and we were obliged to be careful in preventing our men from exposing themselves, as they were much animated, having been refreshed during the flag, and frequently mentioned their wish to storm the

[1] From *Bowman's Journal,* Congressional Library; *Illinois Historical Collections.* VIII, 160.

place and put an end to the business at once. This would [have been] at this time a piece of rashness. Our troops got warm. The firing was heavy through every crack that could be discovered in any part of the fort. With cross-shot several of the garrison got wounded; . . . no possibility of standing near the embrasures. After some time, towards the evening,[1] a flag appeared with the following proposals:

['Lt. Gov[r]. Hamilton proposes to Col. Clark a truce for three days, during which time he proposes there shall be no defensive works carried on in the garrison, on condition that Col. Clark shall observe on his part a like cessation of any offensive work; that he wishes to confer with Col. Clark as soon as can be and further proposes that whatever may pass between them two and any other person mutually agreed upon to be present, shall remain a secret till Matters be finally concluded as he wishes that whatever the result of their conference may be to the honor and credit of each party. If Col. Clark makes a difficulty of coming into the fort, L[t] Gov[r] Hamilton will speak to him before the Gate. 24th Feb'y 1779.'] [2]

'I was greatly at a loss to conceive what reason Gov. Hamilton could have for wishing a truce for three days on such terms as he proposed. Numbers said it was a scheme to get me into their possession. I had a different opinion and had no idea of his possessing such sentiments, as an act of that nature would infallibly ruin him, but was convinced that he had some prospect of succors, or otherwise extricating himself, although we had the greatest reason to expect a reenforcement, in less than three days, that would at once put an end to the siege. I did not think it prudent to agree to the proposal and sent the following answer:'

['Col. Clark's compliments to Mr. Hamilton and begs leave to inform him that Col. Clark will not agree to any other terms than that of Mr. Hamilton's surrendering himself and Garrison Prisoners at discretion. If Mr. Hamilton is desirous of a conference with Col. Clark, he will meet him at the Church with Capt. Helms. 24th Feb'y 1779.' [3]]

Clark must have waited anxiously to know what answer would be made to this demand. Surrender had already been refused during the night; and broad daylight having now revealed the smallness of the besieging force, the alarm which had affected many in the fort during the night must in great measure have passed away. Hamilton had ample provisions to stand a six months siege; he had at Detroit about five times as many men as Clark, and several thousand Indian allies might soon be brought to his relief. Clark said he was

---

[1] Clark means towards noon — 'evening' — according to old Virginia usage, commencing then and including afternoon.

[2] *Bowman's Journal, supra; Illinois Historical Collections*, VIII, 161.

[3] *Bowman's Journal*, Congressional Library; *Illinois Historical Collections*, VIII, 161.

extremely uneasy lest these savages be gathered to trap him; and to avoid that he had allowed Lamothe and his twenty men to re-enter the fort. His overdue galley, with its forty men and cannon, had not been heard from, and might never arrive. As assault upon the fort, even if successful, would involve a terrible loss of men — if unsuccessful, a still greater one; and in either case the besiegers might soon become the besieged. Time therefore was pressing. His main hope was to intimidate the garrison, and his dictation of unconditional surrender was evidently designed for that purpose. While all outside the fort — Americans and French alike — awaited Hamilton's reply, their anxiety to learn the result, the general silence, and the fixing of all eyes on the fort gate may be imagined. At length it opened, and out came Hamilton himself, in the striking red uniform of a British colonel of regulars, with him his Indian leader, Major Hay, and prisoner, Captain Helm. The three passed on to the Catholic church, and there met Colonel Clark, with Captain Bowman. The supreme moment had arrived. The young American commander knew that upon this conference hung the fate of his men and of his whole campaign.

At this critical moment a dramatic episode occurred which Clark promptly seized upon and used with telling effect to intimidate the garrison and disgust the Indians with their British allies. He said:

'Sometime before, a party of warriors, sent by Mr. Hamilton against Kentucky, had taken two prisoners, [and] was discovered [approaching Vincennes.] A party [under Captain Williams] was immediately detached to meet them, which happened in the commons. They conceived our troops to be a party sent by Mr. Hamilton to conduct them in, — an honor commonly paid them. I was highly pleased to see each party whooping, halloing, and striking each others breast as they approached in the open fields. Each seemed to try to out-do the other in the greatest signs of joy. The poor devils never discovered their mistake until it was too late for many of them to escape. Six of them were made prisoners, two of them scalped, and the rest so wounded, as we afterwards learned, but one lived.

'I had now a fair opportunity of making an impression on the Indians, that I could have wished for, — that of convincing them that Governor Hamilton could not give them that protection that he had made them to believe he could. In some measures to incense the Indians against him for not exerting himself to save their friends,

ordered the prisoners to be tomahawked in the face of the garrison.
[Captain Williams asked and was allowed to dispatch them.] It
had the effect that I expected. Instead of making their friends
inveterate against us, they upbraided the English...[for] not trying to save their friends, and gave them to understand that they
believed them to be liars and no warriors. [To Clark's men, this
summary execution was almost a matter of course, for these savages
were just returned from a raid to butcher their friends and relatives, including, they thought, Captain Williams' brother.]'

'Governor Hamilton produced signed articles of capitulations,
that contained various articles, one of which was that the garrison should be surrendered on their being permitted to go to
Pensacola on parole, &c. After deliberating on every article I
rejected the whole. He then wished that I would make some proposition. I told him that I had no others to make than what I had
already [made], — that of his surrendering as prisoners at discretion; that his troops had behaved with spirit; that they could
not suppose that they would be worse treated in consequence of it,
notwithstanding their viewing us as savages; that if he chose
to comply with [our] demand, though hard, perhaps the sooner the
better; that it was in vain to make any proposition to me; that he
must be sensible that the garrison would fall, and that both of us
must [view] all blood spilt, for the future, as murder; that my troops
were already impatient and called aloud for permission to tear
down and storm the fort; if such a step was taken, many of course
would be put down, and the result of an enraged body of woodsmen breaking in must be obvious to him. It would be out of the
power of an American officer to save a single man. [This was unquestionably true. With the innumerable massacres of their
relatives and friends, the long pent-up fury of the assailants had
been gathering for this storm. Once in hand to hand conflict with
such hated enemies, nothing could have restrained them from blood-
thirsty revenge.]

'Various altercation took place for a considerable time. Captain Helm attempted to modify our fixed determination. I told him
he was a British prisoner, and it was doubtful whether or not he
could with propriety speak on the subject. [He had been well
treated by Hamilton.] Governor Hamilton then said that Captain
Helm was from that moment liberated and might use his pleasure.
I informed the Captain that I would not receive him on such terms;
that he must return to the garrison and wait his fate; and told the
Governor that hostilities should not commence until the minute
after the drums gave the alarm.

'We took our leave and parted but a few steps before the
Governor stopped and politely asked me if I would be so kind as to
give him my reasons for refusing the garrison on any other terms
than those I had offered. I told him I had no objections to giving
him my real reasons, which were simply these: that I knew the
greatest part of the principal Indian partisans of Detroit were with

him; that I wanted an excuse to put them to death, or otherwise treat them as I thought proper; that the cries of the widows and fatherless on the frontiers, that they had occasioned, now required their blood from my hands, and that I did not choose to be so timorous as to disobey the absolute commands of their authority, which I looked upon as next to divine; that I would rather lose fifty men than not to empower myself to execute this piece of business with propriety; that if he chose to risk the massacre of his garrison for their sake, it was his own pleasure, and that I perhaps might take it into my head to send for some of those widows to see it executed. Major Hay paying great attention, I had observed a kind of distrust in his countenance, which in great measure influenced my conversation during this time. On my concluding, "Pray, Sir," says he, "who is it that you call Indian partisans?" "Sir," I replied, "I take Major Hay to be one of the principal." I never saw a man in the moment of execution so struck as he appeared to be, — pale and trembling, scarcely able to stand. Governor Hamilton blushed, and I observed was much affected at his behaviour in the presence. Captain Bowman's countenance sufficiently explained his disdain for the one and sorrow for the other. I viewed the whole with such sentiments as I suppose natural to some men in such cases. Some moments elapsed without a word passing on either side. From that moment [my] resolutions changed respecting Governor Hamilton's situation. [Hamilton's courage and mortification had won Clark's quick sympathy.] I told him that we would reconsider the matter and that I would let him know the result; if we thought of making any further proposals [other than] of his surrendering at discretion, he should know it by the flag; if not, to be on his guard at a certain [signal] by drum; in the meantime no offensive measures should be taken; agreed to and we parted.

'What had passed being made known to our officers, it was agreed that we should moderate our resolutions. The following articles were sent to the garrison and an answer immediately returned.

["'1st. That Lt Govr Hamilton engages to deliver up to Col. Clark Fort Sackville as it is at present with all stores, Ammunition &ca.

'"2d. The Garrison will deliver themselves up Prisoners of War & to march out with their arms, accoutrements, Knapsacks &ca.

'"3d. The Garrison to be delivered up to-morrow morning at 10 o'clock.

'"4th. Three days to be allowed to the Garrison to settle their accounts with the traders of this place and inhabitants.

'"5th. The officers of the Garrison to be allowed their necessary baggage &ca.

'"G. R. CLARK."

'"POST VINCENT 24 Feby 1779.

'Within the limited time Capt. Helm returned with the Articles signed thus:

'"Agreed to for the following reasons — The remoteness from succors, the State and Quantity of provisions &c, the Unanimity of Officers and men on its expediency, the Honble terms allowed, & lastly the confidence in a generous enemy.

'"H. HAMILTON

'"Lt Govr & Superintendent." [1]]

'The business being now nearly at an end, our troops were posted in several strong houses around the garrison and patrolled during the night to prevent any deception that might be attempted, and the remainder, off duty, lay on their arms; and for the first time for many days got some rest. [Certainly they needed it.] . . .

'One reason why we wished not to receive the garrison until the following morning, was its being late in the evening be[fore] the capitulation was signed, and the number of prisoners that we should have when compared to our small force. We doubted the want of daylight to arrange matters to advantage, and, as we knew we could now prevent any misfortune happening, . . . supposed it prudent to let the British troops remain in the fort until the following morning. We should not have had so much suspicion as to make use of so much precaution, but I must confess that we could not help doubting the honor of men that could condescend to encourage the barbarity of the Indians; although almost every man had conceived a very favorable opinion of Govr Hamilton, and I believe that what affected myself made some impression on the whole. [When he penned these lines, Clark little suspected the ill return his generous sentiments toward his prisoner had received in a narrative Hamilton wrote to vindicate himself to his superiors.[2]]

'The morning of the 25th approaching, arrangements were made for receiving the garrison and, about 10 o'clock, it was delivered in form.' Hamilton wrote: 'Our little Garrison surrendered Prisoners of War the 25th of Feby. and marched out with Colours flying, lighted match, & fixed bayonets, honors which, tho stipulated, Colo.^l Clark has in the handsomest manner declared due to the spirit of the few Men who defended the Fort.' [3]

One can picture the scene as Hamilton led his well-drilled scarlet clad regulars of the King's Own Regiment between the lines of Clark's bedraggled men, while all Vincennes looked on and old Captain Helm, amidst loud huzzahs, hoisted the American flag he had formerly refused to pull down.

From that day to this, the great country north of the Ohio

[1] *Bowman's Journal,* Congressional Library; *Illinois Historical Collections,* VIII, 168.

[2] *Michigan Pioneer Collections,* IX, 489.

[3] *Royal Institution,* London, *American MSS.,* vol. 12, no. 45. Hamilton adds: 'I must tender this testimony to the Officers and men under Colo.^l Clark's command, that they have treated our Officers & Soldiers as men of honor should.' (*Id.*)

has been ours! Not a white man professing British allegiance was left in it south of the Great Lakes basin. Throughout the rest of the Revolution the civilized inhabitants recognized no other than American government, for despite every effort of the British to reconquer it they were never able to regain a foothold in it.

Clark had already made treaty allies of all the Indians in the Mississippi Valley north of the Ohio except the Miamis, Delawares, and Shawnees; and soon after Hamilton's surrender the Miamis and Delawares sued for peace, while even the Shawnees were awed into inaction.[1]

[1] Colonel Clark wrote Governor Henry, April 29, 1779: 'Those nations who have treated with me have behaved since very well, to wit, the Piankeshaws, Kickapoos, Ouiatenons on the Wabash River, the Kaskaskias, Peorias, Michegamies, Foxes, Sacs, Illinois, and Pottawatomies, nations of the Mississippi and Illinois rivers. Part of the Chippewas have also treated and are peaceable. I continually keep agents among them to watch their motions and keep them peaceably inclined. ...There can be no peace expected from many nations while the English are at Detroit. I strongly suspect they will turn their arms against the Illinois, as they will be encouraged. I shall always be on my guard, watching every opportunity to take advantage of the enemy, and if I am ever able to muster six or seven hundred men, I shall give them a shorter distance to come and fight me than this place. Those Indians who are active against us are the Six Nations, part of the Shawnees, the Miamis, [who soon afterward, like the Delawares, sued for peace], and about half the Chippewas, Ottawas, Iowas, and Pottawatomies, nations bordering on the lakes.' (*Illinois Historical Collections*, VIII, 172.)

CHAPTER XIII

DETROIT CLARK'S MAIN OBJECTIVE

'WE yet found ourselves uneasy, [said Clark.] The number of prisoners we had taken, added to those of the garrison, when compared to our own numbers, [was so large] that we were at a loss how to dispose of them so as not to interfere with our future operations.

'Detroit opened full to our view, — not more than 80 men in the fort, great part of them invalids; and we found that a considerable number of the principal inhabitants were disaffected to the British cause. . . . The Indians on our route, we knew, would be more than ever cool towards the English. . . . [With] possession of Detroit, and a post of communication at Cuyahoga, supplies might always be easily sent. . . from Pittsburg, and Lake Erie we might easily have in our possession; which would completely put an end to all our troubles in this western quarter, and perhaps open a door to further advantageous operations. Those were the ideas that influenced us at present. . . .

'A complete company of volunteers from Detroit, . . . mostly young men, was drawn up and, when expecting to be sent into a strange country and probably never return to their connexions, . . . told that we were happy to learn that many of them were torn from their fathers and mothers and forced on this expedition; that others, ignorant of the true cause in contest, had engaged from . . . being fond of enterprise, but that they now had had a good opportunity to make themselves fully acquainted with the nature of the war, which they might explain to their friends; and that as we knew that sending them to the States, where they would be confined in jail, probably for the course of the war, would make a great number of our friends at Detroit unhappy, we thought proper, for their sakes, to suffer them to return home, &c. A great deal was said to them on the subject. On the whole they were discharged on taking an oath not to bear arms against America, until exchanged, and received an order for their arms, boats, and provisions to return with. The boats were to be sold and [proceeds] divided among them when they got home.

'In a few days they set out, and as we had spies that went among them as traders, we learned that they made great havoc to the British interest on their return, publicly saying that they had taken an oath not to fight against America, but they had not sworn not to fight [for America] &c; and things were carried to such a height [at Detroit] that the commanding officer thought it prudent not to take notice of anything that was said or done. (Mrs. McComb, that kept a boarding house, I understood had the assurance to show him the stores she had provided for the Americans.)[1] This was the completion of my design in suffering this company to return. Many others, that we could trust, we suffered to enlist in the corps, so that our charge of prisoners was much reduced.

'Finding that ten British boats, loaded with goods and provisions, were daily expected down the Wabash, for fear of [their] getting intelligence and returning, on the 26th, Captain Helm, Majors Bosseron and LeGras, with forty volunteers, were sent in three armed boats in pursuit of them.'

'We could now augment our forces in this quarter to about four hundred men, as near half of the inhabitants of Vincennes would join us. Kentucky we knew could immediately furnish perhaps 200 men, as there was a certainty of their receiving a great addition of settlers in the spring. With the aid of our own stores [on the galley], which we had learned was safe, added to those of the British, there was not a single article wanting for such an attempt; and supplies might be got at Detroit for some time. We privately resolved to embrace the object that seemed to court my acceptance without delay, giving the enemy no time to recover the present blows they had received; but wished it to become the object of the soldiery and inhabitants before we should say anything about it. But immediately it became the common topic among them, and in a few days [they] had arranged things so that they were, in their imagination, almost ready to march. They were discountenanced in such conversation, and such measures taken as tended to show that our ideas were foreign from such an attempt; but at the same time was taken every step to pave our way.'

At last, three days after Hamilton's surrender, the armed

---

[1] See Mr. McComb's statement to Mrs. General Jessup about providing such stores. (*Draper MSS.* 10 J 23 1-b.)

Soon afterwards Captain Helm wrote Clark: 'It gives me Great Satisfaction to think of your Intention against Detroit. You must be the man to take that place. I have had intelligence since I wrote you. there is not above one hundred men in the garrison. . . . Pray neglect no time on your Expedition, . . . I know your activity to be Great. I think you may depend on the greatest part of this village to go with you. You may be assured your name Strikes Terror to both English and Indians. Send no man but yourself, if you think proper of the Expedition. Weau [Ouiatenon] & Ome [Miami] is ready to receive you with Joy. Your health and mine [was drunk] by the whole village, before the Commandt Officer, and by many of the officers of the Garrison.' (*Draper MSS.*

49 J 42; *Illinois Historical Collections,* VIII, 316.)

Captain Bird, the able British military engineer who built the Detroit fort, declared it indefensible. (*Michigan Pioneer Collections,* x, 626.) So, twenty-nine days after Hamilton's surrender, did his successor, Lernault, who begged a large immediate reënforcement 'to defend the town, or old fort, and not abandon it in case of an attack.' (*Id.,* x, 421.) He said that 'the Canadians are exceedingly assuming; not one will lend a hand to strengthen the fort'; that he had 'little hopes of any assistance from either the Canadians or Indians'; and that 'all the Canadians are rebels, to a man.' (*Id.,* IX, 328). So great was the disaffection at Detroit that General Haldemand sent him authority to establish martial law and to execute offenders, or send them prisoners to Niagara, 'to assure the fidelity of the rest.' (*Id.,* IX, 408; x, 328, 347.)

galley arrived at Vincennes, 'the crew much mortified, although they deserved great credit for their diligence.' On their way up the Wabash they had taken up a messenger with Governor Henry's long expected dispatches, which said that Clark's battalion would be completed, and a reënforcement (of five hundred men under Montgomery)[1] sent in the spring. This news, said Clark, gave him and his officers both pleasure and pain, — pleasure in the prospect of so large a reënforcement, but pain because they feared to wait for it to march against Detroit.

'A council was called on the subject. I laid before the officers my plans for the immediate reduction of Detroit and explained the almost certainty of success. ...If we waited the arrival of the troops mentioned in the packet, the enemy in the meantime might get strengthened and probably we might not be so capable of carrying the [place] with the expected reenforcements as we should be with our present force in case we were to make the attempt at this time; and in case we should be disappointed in the promised reenforcement, we might not be able to effect it at all.

'There were various arguments made use of on this delicate point. Every person appeared anxious to embrace the present opportunity, but prudence appeared... [to require us] to wait for the reenforcement. ...In short, the enterprise was deferred until the [20th day] of June, to rendezvous at [Vincennes.] In the meantime every preparation was to be made, procuring provisions &c; and, to blind our design, [it was arranged] that the whole of our troops except a small garrison, should march immediately off to the Illinois.'

'Never,' he wrote Colonel Mason, 'was a person more mortified than I was at this time to see [slip] so fair an opportunity to push a victory, — Detroit lost for want of a few men!'[2] Writing Governor Henry, he said he could have taken it with five hundred,[3] and the British archives now make this plain; while the capture would have cut the great water route between the British and their Indian allies and, as he said, been 'the salvation of all our inner frontiers.'

Amongst Governor Henry's dispatches was a resolution of the Virginia assembly commending Clark and his men for their 'extraordinary resolution and perseverance in so hazardous an enterprise' as the capture of Kaskaskia, and thanking them for 'the important service thereby rendered their coun-

---

[1] Montgomery to Clark, July 7, 1779, *Draper MSS.* 49 J 58.

[2] *Illinois Historical Collections*, VIII, 146.
[3] *Id.*, 172.

try.'[1]   The Governor also enclosed an act of the Assembly [2] (December, 1778) creating the new 'County of Illinois,' to include 'all citizens of this Commonwealth who are already settled, or shall hereafter settle, on the western side of the Ohio'; and he informed Colonel Clark that Captain John Todd was appointed civil governor, with title of Colonel and County Lieutenant.   Thus was established the first American government northwest of the Ohio; and the only one recognized there until, five years later, Virginia ceded the region to the United States.

'March 5th Captain Helm, Majors Bosseron, and LeGras returned from their tour up the [Wabash] river with great success. They came up with the enemy in the night. [Discovering] their fires at a distance, they waited until all was quiet, surrounded and took the whole prisoners without firing a gun. Those gentlemen were so off their guard, and had so little apprehension of an enemy in that part of the world, that they could hardly persuade themselves that what they saw was real. This was a valuable [acquisition], seven boats loaded with provisions and goods to a considerable amount. The provisions were taken for the public and the goods divided among the whole [troops], except about £800 worth to clothe the troops we expected to receive in a short time. This was very agreeable to the soldiers, as I told them the state would pay them in money their proportions and that they had plenty of goods.'

An amusing appropriation of the credit for this capture appears in the letter of Moses Henry, the blacksmith prisoner, who wrote Colonel John Gibson: 'I had the pleasure, after being relieved, to be sent on an expedition up the Wabash, to meet a certain number of Boats, with stores & merchandise, which I took, together with the chief Judge of Detroit who was sent with Governor Hamilton to Williamsburg.' [3]

On March 7th, Clark sent Captains Williams and Rogers with twenty-five men to conduct to Virginia about an equal number of his prisoners, including Governor Hamilton. There the 'Hair-buyer General' found much less kindly treatment than he had received from his young captor, for he was put in irons for his barbarities.[4]

---

[1] *Draper MSS.* 48 J 44–5; *Illinois Historical Collections,* VIII, 74–5.

[2] Hening's *Virginia Statutes; Illinois Historical Collections,* II, 9.

[3] *Michigan Pioneer Collections,* XIX, 422.

[4] To avoid threatened retaliation on American prisoners in British hands, Washington advised milder treatment of Hamilton, but for a time Governor Jefferson and his executive council refused, saying they had evidence in Hamilton's own writing of his instigating Indian cruelties, and they were determined to

The capture of Hamilton, the chief representative of British power in the west, had electrical effect upon the Indians. Shortly afterwards chiefs of the Ouiatenans, Miamis, and Pottawatomies (the three formidable nations between him and Detroit) came to Vincennes, 'making great protestations of their attachment to the Americans, begging...to be taken under the cover of our wings, and that the roads through the lands might be made straight and the stumbling blocks removed, &c.' This of course exactly suited Clark's plan to march unhindered through their country against Detroit, and a friendly treaty was soon made with them. Five days later he and nearly all his troops left for Kaskaskia, to gather men and supplies for the Vincennes rendezvous in June and the march on Detroit.

On the return of the victorious little army to Kaskaskia — fifes and drums playing, banners flying, and not a man missing — one can imagine the transports of the emotional Creoles gathered to greet their heroes. It would be interesting to know if Terese de Leyba was there. After a time of general rejoicing, Colonel Clark addressed the people, praising the conduct of his volunteers and introducing the new civil governor, Colonel John Todd. On all sides prospects seemed bright: The British had been driven far away; the Creoles were proud to be 'Sons of Liberty' and citizens of Virginia; they viewed her troops as brethren and Clark as their liberator; and they confidently looked to see him free their kinsmen at Detroit. They gladly volunteered to serve with him and gave liberal supplies for the coming rendezvous at Vincennes. The road for the march thence against Detroit was open. With his own troops, French volunteers, five hundred men expected from Virginia under Montgomery, and 'three hundred good men from Kentucky' promised by Colonel John Bowman,[1] Clark could fairly count on a force of twelve hundred men. He said: 'We were now going on in high spirits,' yet he had his misgivings. He wrote Governor Henry:

make an example of him. Finally, however, Hamilton was released from irons, paroled, and allowed to return to England. There, unfortunately for his own reputation, he wrote a long narrative vindicating his military conduct which, along with his own earlier letter still existing, proves him both untruthful and mean-minded. (*Michigan Pioneer Collections*, IX, 489.) Although his brave conduct at Vincennes had won the quick sympathy of Clark and his officers, Hamilton lacked the moral courage to bear his defeat with dignity.

[1] *Illinois Historical Collections*, VIII, 150, 299.

'There is one circumstance very distressing — that of our money being discredited...by the great number of traders who came here in my absence, each outbidding the other, giving prices unknown in this country by five hundred per cent, by which the people conceived it to be of no value, and both French and Spaniards refused to take a farthing of it. Provision is three times the price it was two months past, and to be got by no other means than my own bonds, goods, or force. Several merchants are now advancing considerable sums of their own property, rather than the service should suffer; by which I am sensible they must lose greatly, unless some method is taken to raise the credit of our coin, or a fund be sent to New Orleans for the payment of the expenses of this place, which would at once reduce the prices of every species of provisions; money being of little service to them, unless it would pass at the ports they trade at. I mentioned to you my drawing some bills on Mr. Pollock in New Orleans, as I had no money with me. He would accept the bills, but had not money to pay them off, though the sums were trifling, so that we have little credit to expect from that quarter.[1] Public expenses in this country have hitherto been very low, and may continue so if a correspondence is fixed at New Orleans for payment of expenses in this country, or gold or silver sent.'[2]

No such correspondence was fixed, however, nor was any gold or silver sent. Virginia, like the other states, was fast heading for insolvency.

It was at this time that Clark, in order to supply his troops for the proposed march, took a step which was as imprudent as it was patriotic. He directed his Conductor General, Shannon, to 'purchase all...stores necessary for the use of the army, and give the respective persons furnishing the same notes entitling them to draw on the commanding officer for cash.'[3] This was done; the Conductor General drew a great number of bills on the state which Clark accepted and

---

[1] So early as June, 1779, one of Clark's bills on Pollock for 2771 piastres was protested and demand made for payment. (*Illinois Historical Collections*, v, 98. See also William Wirt Henry's *Life of Patrick Henry*, III, 233.)

[2] *Illinois Historical Collections*, VIII, 173.

[3] Virginia State Library '*Illinois Accounts*' MSS., *Shannon's Order Book*, March 7, 1779. For example of bills accepted and paid by Clark, see *Illinois Historical Collections*, VIII, 328, giving two for 7698 livres and 3836 dollars respectively, 'for peltries furnished the state of Virginia for...purchasing provisions for said state as per account.'

The later history of these bills and Clark's efforts to get the state to relieve him of the burden of them, appears pretty fully in his various petitions to the Assembly, in his correspondence with his brother Jonathan, and in the Assembly Journals. Many copies, abstracts, and references to them as well as a vast number of other papers relating to Clark and western history are in the author's duplicated, bound, and indexed manuscripts which he expects to donate to two public libraries for the use of future writers.

personally indorsed, thus becoming bound to pay a great number of Virginia's obligations — obligations which she never denied, nor ever paid.

By late May came a shocking disappointment. Montgomery arrived at Kaskaskia with his anxiously expected reenforcement; but, instead of 'five hundred' properly equipped men, there were only one hundred and fifty, and those half clothed and half starved. Their long delay and sad plight was caused by their having been diverted to join an expedition against the Cherokees in western North Carolina.

'Things immediately put on a different appearance [said Clark]. We now lamented that we did not march off from Vincennes to Detroit; but, as we had a prospect of considerable reenforcement from Kentucky, we yet flattered ourselves that something might be done. ...At least we might maneuver in such manner as to keep the enemy in hot water and in suspense, and prevent their doing our frontiers much damage. Went on with procuring supplies, and did not yet loose sight of our object; and, in order to feel the pulse of the Enemy, I detached off Maj^r Linctot...and a company of volunteers up the Illinois River, under the pretense of visiting our friends, to cross the country and fall at the [Ouiatenan town] and return to [Vincennes], making his observations [on] his Route. This we expected would perfectly cover our designs, and, if we saw it prudent, we might on his return proceed.'

Early in June Montgomery and his men and the supplies were sent to Vincennes in boats, and the rest of the troops marched over-land; while Clark himself, 'with a party of horse, reached [that place] in four days, where the whole safely arrived in a short time after.'[1] There all his hopes were dashed. He tersely wrote: 'Instead of 300 men from Kentucky, their appeared about 30 Volunteers commanded by Captn McGary. The loss of the expedition was too obvious to hesitate about it. Col. Bowman had turned his attention against the Shawnee's Town and got repulsed and his men discouraged.'[2]

John Bowman had spoiled everything. Bent on winning laurels for himself, instead of marching his promised men to join Clark at Vincennes, he carried them against the Shawnees. Those Indians, although unfriendly, had been awed by the capture of Hamilton, and were by no means inclined to war. Bowman gained no coveted glory, but he antagonized the

[1] *Illinois Historical Collections*, VIII, 300.   [2] *Id.; Draper MSS.* 49 J 52.

savages generally and utterly destroyed hope for an unob-
structed march through their country against Detroit.[1]
Clark's fixed policy had always been to avoid conflict with
the Indians and demand only a free road to the British;
but now, as he said, he could only 'maneuver to keep the
enemy in hot water and suspense.' How he did this amusingly
appears in the letters of the British officers. They show the
Indians fearful and the British themselves in a state bordering
on panic. To confuse them, many conflicting rumors of Clark's
strength and purposes were circulated by his French friends
through the enemy's country; and to add to the alarm, several
small detachments of troops were sent out towards the distant
British posts. The effect was amazing.

May 2, Major de Peyster, commanding at Mackinac, sent
reports of Clark's men building boats near Milwaukee
(nearly four hundred miles from where they really were), and
that they would soon arrive at Green Bay and cross Lake
Michigan to take the British fort at Mackinac![2] Another
body of Americans was reported at Chicago, and De Peyster
at once began strengthening his Mackinac fort and tearing
down buildings in the town to prepare for a siege.[3] Two
months later he reported Clark as having abandoned his
march against Mackinac and gone down the Mississippi to
Natchez,[4] and soon afterwards that nine hundred men, with
artillery, and three hundred horse, were marching from Kaskaskia to Vincennes, and that Montgomery, with six hundred
more, was on his way to join them.[5] To intercept another
imaginary force of four hundred horsemen under Linctot (who
had just thirty), De Peyster sent out three hundred whites and
Indians under Lieutenant Bennett; but such was now the
Indian fear of the Big Knives that Bennett was deserted. He
reported: 'We have not twenty Indians in our camp who are
not preparing for leaving us.'[6] Further east, Captain Bird,
endeavored to raise a force of Indians south of Lake Erie, but

---

[1] Roosevelt strangely fails to comprehend this larger significance of Bowman's
unfortunate expedition. He says: 'The
defeat caused intense mortification to the
whites, but in reality the expedition was
of great service to the Kentuckians,
though the Kentuckians never knew it.'
(*Winning of the West*, II, 248.) He
imagines it prevented an impending
raid by Bird with 200 Indians — a raid

which was most unlikely, and, in any
event, would have been comparatively
insignificant.
[2] *Michigan Pioneer Collections*, IX, 379–
80; XIX, 415.
[3] *Id.*, IX, 387.
[4] *Id.*, IX, 384.
[5] *Id.*, IX, 390; 393; XIX, 442.
[6] *Id.*, IX, 393; XIX, 455–6.

found it impossible. He wrote: 'The savages are very uneasy; fain would council,'[1] and said that notwithstanding 'the fair promises made by the chiefs, not a man will turn out to war, except a little band of...twenty or thirty led absolutely by Girty. ...Our enemies will meet with little or no opposition in their progress to Detroit.'[2] Even as far east as Pittsburg, the Indians were cowed. Washington's former land agent there, Colonel Crawford, wrote him: 'Col. Clark's affairs have changed the disposition of the Indians much. They have done very little mischief this summer.'[3] In another direction, Gautier, the British Indian agent, took two hundred and eight Indians against the Virginians in the Illinois, expecting to be joined by many others on the way; but he was coldly received by the tribes he had expected to reinforce him. They even compelled him to give up one hundred and twenty American prisoners and himself to beat a hasty retreat. 'I believe,' he said, 'if they had been stronger they would have seized me and delivered me to the Bostonians.'[4] Reading these British reports, one feels the pathos of Clark's regret: 'Detroit lost for want of a few men!'

Having again been forced by John Bowman's folly to abandon his cherished design, he distributed most of his troops between Vincennes, Kaskaskia, and Cahokia, and himself, with the remainder, went to the Falls of Ohio. There he had ordered a fort to be built on the southern bank, in what is now Louisville, which became his headquarters during the rest of the war.[5]

While Clark was still at the Vincennes rendezvous, the Virginia Assembly

'Resolved that the General Assembly have a high sense of Col⁰. Clark's important services in the reduction of Fort St Vincents. That the Governor be requested to transmit to him by the hands of Lieu^t Rogers an elegant Sword in the name of the Genl. Assembly & in Testimony of ye merit of his Services.'[6]

[1] *Michigan Pioneer Collections* x, 334.
[2] *Id.*, xix, 413.
[3] *Draper MSS.* 15 S 227.
[4] *Michigan Pioneer Collections*, xix, 397. The British and Indians sometimes called the Americans 'Bostonians,' no doubt because the first protracted siege of the war was at Boston.
[5] To attract settlers and recruit troops, the state conveyed to Clark 168,000 acres of land from which he could grant them bounties. These he accounted for later and reconveyed to the state the ungranted acres. (Jefferson to Clark, Jan. 29, 1780. *Illinois Historical Collections*, v, 144; Butler's *Kentucky*, 113.)
[6] *Virginia State Library, Journal House of Delegates*, p. 14, June 12, 1779. December 14th following the sword was sent Colonel Clark with a highly compli-

Captain Joseph Bowman had been raised to the rank of major, but shortly after the rendezvous he died in consequence of an explosion of ammunition. His loss — the first sustained by the little army — was keenly felt by all the men, and perhaps by no other more than by Colonel Clark, who placed great dependence in him.

About the time of Clark's return to Louisville, Jefferson, who had succeeded Patrick Henry as Governor of Virginia, ordered him to build a fort near the mouth of the Ohio. The importance of that point for military and trade purposes was obvious; but Jefferson's main object in ordering it fortified was neither commercial nor military, but political, and to forestall any claim on the part of Spain to the country north or east of it. Clark wrote him: 'I am not clear but the Spaniards would fondly suffer their settlements in the Illinois to fall with ours for the sake of having opportunity of retaking both.'[1] The lands at the mouth of the Ohio being subject to overflow, he built the fort a short distance below, on the eastern bank of the Mississippi, and called it Fort Jefferson.[2] In more propitious times it would have been an exceedingly valuable post, for it commanded both rivers, but the times were far from propitious.

Here it seems well to pause a moment to consider what Clark had already accomplished. Our leaders were not ignorant of the danger threatening eastern America from the British and Indians in the west, and, because Detroit was the enemy's western post of first importance, Congress had considered plan after plan for its reduction. Throughout the war, it maintained at Pittsburg by far the largest and best equipped military force west of the Alleghenies. Its successive commanders — General Hand, General McIntosh, Colonel Brodhead, and General Irvine — were all experienced officers of

mentary letter by Lieutenant-Governor Page. (*Draper MSS. 52 J 68.*)

[1] *Virginia Calendar State Papers*, **I**, 326.

[2] The founding of Fort Jefferson has repeatedly been represented as a blunder, because it was said it brought on a war with the Chickasaws. Some have attributed the alleged mistake to Jefferson, others to Clark. In truth, as the contemporary records clearly show: (1) the building of the fort was ordered by Jefferson for political reasons far outweighing any objections based on apprehended conflict with the Chickasaws, for he wished by actual possession to maintain a right to the country against Spain (*id.*), and, furthermore, (2) the Chickasaws were already at war with us before the fort was built. Clark wrote: 'Its notorious they had done a great deal of mischief for two years before and the building of the post actually stopt a formidable invasion...by them.' (Clark to Harrison, Oct. 18, 1783. *Virginia State Library.*)

mature years who had won more or less distinction in the seaboard armies; but not one of them secured so much as a foothold across the Ohio. None accomplished much more than a defense of the Pennsylvania frontier. In 1778 when, unknown in the east, Clark had taken Kaskaskia, Congress abandoned its plans to capture Detroit, but ordered General McIntosh to 'proceed without delay to destroy such towns of the hostile Indians [towards Detroit] as will most effectually chastise and terrify the savages on the frontiers.' [1] He marched against them with over a thousand men, including Brodhead's Eighth Pennsylvania.[2] Shortly afterward, Brodhead said his regiment contained eight hundred effectives, and 'must be considered one of the best in the line.' [3] Yet McIntosh accomplished nothing; his campaign was a costly failure.

The truth is that all these commanders contemplated only frontal attacks on the enemy, which involved many and great difficulties of transportation and supply, as well as severe fighting. The result was nearly always the same — a maximum of effort and outlay, but a minimum of achievement. There would be a desultory conflict and a few Indians killed, but the rest would hover about the invading army — threatening ambuscades and cutting off stragglers and supply trains. Then would come a shortage of food, making further progress impossible, and finally the inevitable retreat, mortifying to the troops and encouraging to the savages.

It was the singular merit of Clark's plan of campaign that he avoided any such frontal attack, and also the difficulties of supplying an army in a cross-country march over wilderness hills and streams. Instead, starting from the same point, he took advantage of the Ohio current for transportation, passed by the hostile Indians, gained their rear where he would most surprise them, and there, ignoring them, made his attack upon far weaker white foes and won possession of a cultivated country where his troops could find support. Although only twenty-four years of age when he planned his campaign, he saw clearly — what these more experienced continental commanders evidently did not see — that the British posts could be more easily conquered with a small force than the numerous and scattered Indians with a large one. He saw also,

---

[1] *Journals of Congress.* (Claypoole, Philadelphia), IV, 426–7.

[2] Hassler's *Old Westmoreland*, 80.

[3] *Pennsylvania Archives*, VII, 465, etc.

and early explained to Governor Henry, that once those posts
were taken, the savages might find his friendship better than
his enmity. The result was that whilst the others were planning their large, costly, and fruitless expeditions, Clark, with
less than two hundred men, actually reduced all the British
posts south of the lakes without the loss of a man. 'Although
brave troops take pride in their heavy battle losses, bloodless
victories are best, and bloody ones often discredit their
commander.'

Professor Albert Bushnell Hart pronounces Clark's campaign to reduce the British posts 'far the most adventurous
and daring campaign of the Revolution.' It was much more
than that; it was perhaps the most brilliantly conceived and
executed. No other more clearly or repeatedly shows how
imaginative forethought, keen and quick reading of the motives controlling men, — civilized or savage, — painstaking
forehandedness, and quick adjustment of changing means to
rapidly changing situations can take the place of superior
forces and overcome obstacles apparently insurmountable.

Of all the direct results of the Revolutionary War in the
west, the two most important were (1) the conquest of the
country north of the Ohio, and (2) the settlement next year of
a large population — 20,000, it is said — south of it in Kentucky; and each was necessary to supplement the other.
The conquest, by promising safety to settlers, opened the way
for many new Kentucky settlements, which in turn, by furnishing fighting men and supplies, made the conquest permanent; and both results hung upon Clark's victory over
Hamilton. The little battle of Vincennes, though insignificant
in numbers engaged, unheralded at the time, and until of late
almost ignored in printed history, was the pivotal event upon
which hung our possession of the Revolutionary West, with
all that it has meant in the nation's history; yet, amazing
though it seems, the man who won it is to-day almost unknown
to his countrymen! In a once popular volume — *The Generals
of the Revolution* — a long list of them is given, accompanied
by laudatory sketches, but his name is not in the list. Winsor
says that no year of the Revolution was 'so barren of results'
as 1779 — the year Vincennes and Hamilton were captured
and the British driven forever from the Mississippi Valley![1]

[1] *Narrative and Critical History*, VII, 55.

The Revolutionary War in the west might almost be called Clark's War. Throughout in chief command for the State which carried it on, its boldest conceptions, its only great offensives, and its paramount achievement were distinctly his. His campaign to reduce the British posts, whether originality of conception be considered, or disproportion of means to ends, or success in execution, or results secured, was assuredly one of the most brilliant in American annals. In civil affairs also he disclosed both resourcefulness and judgment surprising in one so young. Perhaps no other part of his career called for a higher order of ability than his handling of the French at Kaskaskia and of the Indian horde at Cahokia.

In this connection, the aid he received from the 'inner-frontiersmen' should be recognized. Their victory over the Shawnees at Point Pleasant in 1774 made possible the settlement of Kentucky the next year. Again, by quelling the Cherokees in 1776, the effective expeditions of the Virginia and Carolina frontiersmen probably prevented the abandonment of Kentucky. Furthermore, the inner-frontiersmen of the upper Ohio and Holston regions furnished the larger part of Clark's fighting men.[1]

The scant recognition their services have received in history, although regrettable, has been almost inevitable; for their contributions to the outstanding achievements of the war were oftenest indirect and scattered, and it is only the movements of the battle front which engage much attention in history. When, however, the borderers were in the front, as they were in three of the most decisive battles of the Revolution — Saratoga, King's Mountain, and Cowpens — their really brilliant work, though seldom appreciated, has not been ignored. In truth, every frontiersman who fought the Indians along the inner frontiers, and every farmer, stockraiser, or miller there who furnished supplies for the armies, east or west, helped both to make Clark's conquest possible and to win the eastern war; just as his soldiers and the advanced settlers of Kentucky, by holding the western Indians

---

[1] During the Revolution the western 'inner-frontier' of Virginia was, roughly speaking, its great Valley, embraced within the extensive counties of Frederick, Shenandoah, Augusta, Botetourt, and Fincastle, and their offshoots, Washington, Montgomery, and Rockbridge. Their records all abound with names of men connected with the settlement and defense of Kentucky and with Clark's conquest north of it.

in check, protected the inner frontiers and contributed indirectly, but essentially, to the success of the seaboard armies.

Under the leadership of two remarkable Virginians, James Robertson and John Sevier, the frontiersmen on the Holston rendered brilliant service in defending their part of the frontier against the southern Indians. Two more interesting or strongly contrasted personalities would be hard to find. Robertson, calm and resolute, belonged to a superior type of men for whom the grandeur, solitude, and even the dangers of the wilderness had singular fascination. Washington was one of them, Clark another. All fit Joutel's description of La Salle: 'He was a man of regular behavior, of large soul, well enough learned and understanding in the mathematics, designing, bold, undaunted, dexterous, not to be discouraged at anything, ready at extricating himself out of any difficulties, no way apprehensive of the greatest fatigue, wonderful in adversity.' [1]

Sevier was of different mould. With his Huguenot strain, he was 'the Game-cock of the Tennessee' — a most dashing and brilliant Indian-fighter, and one of the heroes of King's Mountain. Handsome and big-hearted, he was idolized by his followers and affectionately known as 'Nollichucky Jack.'

[1] J. P. Dunn's *Indiana* (American Commonwealth Series), 7.

CHAPTER XIV

GREAT KENTUCKY IMMIGRATION: GATHERING CLOUDS

OF all the conflicts over our western country, none was more important in the nation's history than the one now to be considered. This was the resolute and often seemingly hopeless struggle of Clark and his men to hold the country they had won, and defend Kentucky during the last four years of the Revolution. That period of our western history has been little noticed, little understood, and never at all adequately treated. A few striking events of popular interest, such as expeditions against the Indians, inroads by them, and picturesque individual exploits, have been narrated with evident relish and much invention; but some important underlying conditions and events have oftenest been unnoticed, and when noticed, greatly distorted. The same is true of Clark's career during the same period and afterwards. No connected or trustworthy account of it has ever been written. The truth about him still lies almost completely buried in the unpublished writings of his time, which evidently have been seldom more than superficially investigated by those who have essayed to write of him; yet his later public services were even more strenuous and hardly less important than the earlier ones, and required far more self-sacrifice.[1]

Until about the time he left Vincennes for the Falls of Ohio, the lot of his men had been one of great strain and hardship,

---

[1] We have had a number of excellent investigators of the source materials of western history who did not write, and many more excellent writers who did not investigate. Draper was a wonderful investigator, accurate and impartial, but he wrote poorly and little. His collection of Clark papers at Madison, Wisconsin, is unique in extent and priceless in value.

The *George Rogers Clark Papers* (VIII, *Illinois Historical Collections*), by James Alton James, is an admirable collection containing most of the previously unpublished writings by and to Clark, and some others concerning him, up to October 1, 1781. A second volume of the series is promised, and it is to be hoped will be as meritorious. The present author's collection of Clark papers, besides including nearly all those published by Professor James, contains originals and transcripts of important papers not used by him, and also a great number relating to the period from October 1, 1781, to Clark's death in 1818. Most of them were gathered when the author hardly expected to be able to do more than annotate the more significant ones and leave them to some historic library for the use of later writers.

but also of compensating success and inspiring prospects. They lived during the *renaissance* of political liberty. The liberal doctrines of Rousseau, Locke, Montesquieu, and other political theorists were almost as familiarly discussed by intelligent men in the parlors of colonial America as in those of London and Paris; and we may be sure Clark had heard much of them from Mason, Jefferson, and other friends amongst the ardent champions of political liberty. The growing passion for free government and 'the rights of man,' (especially in America, where provincial and frontier conditions intensified it), was not unlike the zeal for religious liberty during the century before; and when the high-handed measures of George the Third and his parliament threatened America with tyrannous taxation, this passion, as John Adams said, burst forth in the colonies 'in a flame of fire.' Naturally, it most stirred the souls of young men; and nearly all of Clark's men were young. When Vincennes was taken, he was only twenty-six, Joseph Bowman the same; Bayly, Shelby, Williams, Brashear, Worthington, Quirk, Montgomery, Rogers, all were young men; and all were proud to be Sons of Liberty and to prove their republican principles by devoted service against 'the Tyrant King.' Some amongst them evidently appreciated the greatness of the cause they were battling for, and knew they were actors in a drama in which heroism and success would deserve to be gloriously recorded. Reading the letters of Clark's officers, we are repeatedly impressed with their spirit of patriotic devotion. To that, and not to their selfish interests, he invariably appealed in his calls on them for service; and loyally nearly all responded; for, with most of them, the war was evidently one with a high ideal — rough, no doubt, and bloody, but for Liberty!

But after the capture of Vincennes a different story of Clark and his men remains to be told, and it will explain many important events in his later career which few seem to have understood. They had won possession of a vast country, but to hold it without reënforcements or supplies seemed hopeless; and day by day the troops found themselves steadily weakening, not only in numbers but in *morale*. The fire of enthusiasm, which upheld them during the period of their brilliant exploits, had died out, and only grim determination led the officers and some of the men to stay in the service.

Many of them, too, were physically wrecked, for they had served under conditions calculated to undermine health. No wonder that Clark wrote: 'A number of our men now got sick. Their intrepidity and good success had, until this, kept up their spirits; but, things falling off to...little more than common garrison duty, they more sensibly felt the pains and other complaints that they had contracted during the severity of the late uncommon march, to which many of those valuable men fell a sacrifice, and few others ever perfectly recovered.' [1]

To add to their distress, the winter of 1779–80 proved to be one of unexampled severity. It was long called the 'Hard Winter.' A quaint contemporary narrative says it 'begun about the first of November and continued until nearly March. The turkeys were all dead; the buffaloes had got poor; people's cattle mostly dead; no corn, or very little in the country. The people was in great distress; many in the wilderness frost-bit; some dead. Some eat of the dead cattle and horses. When winter broak, the men would go and kill buffaloes and bring them home to eat; but they were so poore a number of people would be taken sick and did actually die for want of solid food.' [2]

Pioneer life, even without human enemies, is everywhere rude and hard; but for the settlers and soldiers in the west during the Revolution there was savage war, and in its wake came famine and pestilence. The Indians forced all to crowd into the forts, with such horses, cattle, hogs, and poultry as they could bring in; but there they were subjected to dangers no less real and only less dreadful than those threatened by their savage foes. Without change of raiment, perhaps for weeks or months at a time; usually with only one spring to supply water for man, beast and fowl, as well as for bathing, butchering, cooking, and washing; with no sewerage to carry off disease-breeding filth; with no way properly to separate the sexes; often with no physician, surgeon, or needed medicines, though many were the wounded and sick; with game-meat and corn for their almost unvarying food, day after day for weeks and months together, and these often exceedingly scarce; the wonder is not that sickness became common, but that it was not more fatal. Fortunately, the first three

---

[1] *Illinois Historical Collections*, viii, 294.   *MSS.* 57 J 13; *Colonial Men and Times*,
[2] *Danl. Trabue's Narrative*, *Draper*   by Lillie Harper.

posts in Kentucky — Harrodsburg, Boonesboro, and Logan's — and most of the later settlements there were located in the high and healthful Bluegrass region; but, for strategic reasons, the soldiers of the 'Illinois Regiment' were always quartered in malarial river posts. That was equally true of Kaskaskia, Cahokia, and Fort Jefferson by the Mississippi, of Vincennes on the Wabash, and of the Falls of the Ohio. Malaria, with its chills and fevers, attacked nearly all and permanently wrecked the health of many. That tenacious disease is now little dreaded, for quinine is an effective cure; but quinine was then unknown and the only supposed remedy was liquor, which is now known to be no remedy at all, but often more destructive than the disease.

During 1779 the finances of the Confederation became chaotic, and its paper money nearly worthless. An American dollar, which a year before had passed at twenty-five cents, by January, 1779, had dropped to half that value, and by the end of the year to two and a half cents; the next year it was worth only one tenth of a cent. A Mexican silver dollar would buy a thousand dollars of the United States! Yet 'issues followed faster and faster, till depreciation brought the bills so low that to print them cost more than they were worth.' To uphold them, laws were passed making them legal tender in payment of debts, and punishing creditors who refused to accept them; so that a member of Congress afterward said; 'For two or three years we constantly saw creditors running from their debtors, and the debtors pursuing them without mercy!' 'He was reckoned an honest man who, from principle, delayed to pay his debts.' Suspicion supplanted confidence, and business was paralyzed. Coins almost disappeared. Staple products of each locality became the measures of value in trade. In Virginia, taxes and debts were paid and purchases made with tobacco. In the west, peltries were the common substitute for money; one bought corn, salt, or powder with bear skins, deer hides, or the like; and when even these substitutes were wanting, primitive barter was resorted to.

With neither money nor credit, government and people alike suffered at the hands of the unscrupulous. The inevitable result followed, general demoralization, public and private; for 'a debased currency, with quantities of unreliable paper, affects the moral life of every family throughout the land; it makes possible cunning and dishonesty,— on a large scale amongst those who have, and on a small scale amongst the poorer classes; it sows, broadcast, discontent and lawlessness.' John Randolph once said: 'The four hundred men who went out to David were in debt, the conspirators with Catiline were in debt, and I defy you to point me to a desperately indebted people anywhere who ever bore a regular, sober government.'

We love to think of our Revolutionary fathers as patriots, devoting themselves and their all to the great cause of freedom; and we may rightly be proud of those who were such heroes; but all were not patriots, for human nature was much the same then as now. Broad-visioned men knew the greatness of the cause of independence and to it dedicated themselves and their all; but they were the few; — the dull, the ignorant, the inconstant, the selfish, and the unprincipled were the many. For every man who contributed beyond his means, probably ten shirked giving at all, and many sought only personal profit at public expense. No one can read aright the history of that period without realizing the truths here stated, nor without exalted admiration for the ability of some, and the devotion of all the real heroes of the Revolution; but to appreciate their patriotism one must also realize the burden they bore by reason of the shortcomings of their far more numerous fellow citizens. The letters of the time abound in gloomy complaints of the loss of virtue among the people, and reading them one gets the impression that the writers were morbidly pessimistic; but in truth there was cause for their despondency. The dissensions and jealousies, sectional and personal, growing out of these conditions, now seem almost incredible. Hardly a single eminent man of that time, from Washington down, escaped outrageous traduction. In the general demoralization both the Continental Congress and state legislatures rapidly retrograded, not only in ability, but in character. Although they still contained some able patriots, small, self-seeking politicians more and more took the places of the great men who had been at the helm when the storm of revolution came.

Aside from the general demoralization, the western people had financial troubles peculiarly their own. One early source of suspicion and bitter complaint arose from an act of Congress concerning two issues of paper money amounting to seven million dollars. They were found to have been counterfeited, and were recalled for cancellation, the holders being required to present them for redemption at certain offices east of the Alleghenies before June 1st following, after which they were to become worthless. Clark's men had been paid with this money, and the Illinois French had freely received it in exchange for their goods. As both soldiers and inhabitants were then entirely cut off from communication with the east and knew nothing of this act of Congress, they failed to present their money for redemption within the time limited, and found it waste paper on their hands. The French inhabitants, seeing the things they had sold for worthless money being used by the soldiers, suspected them of imposition, and angrily charged them with it. In fact, the soldiers were doubly losers. They not only lost their pay by receiving depreciated money, but could purchase necessaries only by giving their personal bonds, or by personally endorsing bills on the state, which they were afterwards compelled to pay. In this situation, in order to feed and clothe their troops, Clark's officers commanding in the Illinois were compelled to order impressments, while some of the cold and hungry soldiers helped themselves to fuel, hogs, and cattle of the French without waiting for impressment orders, and then trouble came. Soon the soldiery and inhabitants were almost at war, and after a few weeks the soldiers became the weaker party.

Hardly less disastrous to the western people than the evils mentioned was the long and bitter controversy in the Continental Congress over Virginia's claim to the country west of the Alleghenies.[1] For years before the Revolution the region had been the field of a lucrative fur trade, carried on mainly by Pennsylvanians. Strong Philadelphia merchant

[1] Virginia's charter, granted in 1609 by King James I, covered all the country west of the Alleghenies and north of the North Carolina line. Originally it extended to the Pacific, but was restricted to the line of the Mississippi by the treaty with France in 1763. The Carolinas and Georgia also had charter claims extending to the Mississippi, which were little disputed, while Massa-chusetts and Connecticut feebly asserted claims to long narrow strips of western territory within the charter bounds claimed by Virginia. The western land controversy in the Continental Congress, however, was almost wholly over the Virginia claim. The whole controversy is treated at length in the author's work on the *Revolutionary West in Diplomacy and Politics*, now in preparation.

firms kept trains of fur-traders and supply-carriers going and coming through the French and Indian towns; and they feared Virginia would cut them off from this trade. She was already the wealthiest and most populous of the states, and if she were allowed to control so vast a territory, the smaller northern states feared she would soon grow rich and powerful enough to domineer over them; and that, they thought, would be worse than British rule. They strongly insisted that she must give up all claims to lands west of the Alleghenies, and fought hard to secure Articles of Confederation which would empower Congress to decide all state boundary disputes and thus make the whole western region the common property of all. For six of the eight years of the Revolution they refused to confederate unless Congress were given that power, but this Virginia stoutly opposed. To justify their refusal many technical arguments were advanced against the validity of her charter title — some of them quite far-fetched. The strongest was the very real danger of her dominating power. Even granting Virginia's legal claims, Mr. Wilson of Pennsylvania said: 'Pennsylvania has no right to interfere with those claims, but she has a right to say that she will not confederate unless those claims are to be cut off.' [1] Yet without confederation there was imminent danger that the Revolution would collapse and the revolutionists be punished. One member said: 'If we don't confederate, we shall all hang!' [2]

In all this bitter conflict, the shrewd and sleepless promoters of the Indiana and Vandalia companies were at work influencing Congress to force Virginia's surrender of her western charter territory; for they were playing for enormous fortunes, and confidently looked to Congress to confirm their pretended Indian titles. But for their ceaseless scheming, the controversy would probably have been settled early during the Revolution. At length, however, the need for confederating became so pressing that, despite their opposition, Congress in July, 1778, adopted Articles of Confederation and recommended them to the states for ratification. A majority of the states did ratify them, and thereupon Congress implored the remaining ones to do so, saying: 'The confederacy can alone establish the liberty of America.'

[1] *Diplomatic Correspondence of the Revolution.* (Wharton.)   [2] *Id.*

The adopted Articles were all Virginia could wish, for they gave Congress no power whatever to decide state boundary disputes and thus restrict her charter territory. On the contrary, such disputes were required to be decided by a court of impartial judges, who were to be fairly chosen and sworn to decide according to law and evidence. Furthermore, one of the articles expressly provided that 'No state shall be deprived of its territory for the benefit of the United States.' Virginia's victory seemed complete; her opponents had virtually given up their effort to make her surrender her western claims. They evidently did this, however, only because at this time there was little hope that the trans-Allegheny country could be wrested from the British, and it seemed hardly worth contending for.

In July, 1778, Congress abandoned finally its plans to capture Detroit, but the members did not then know that on the fourth day of that same month Clark had taken Kaskaskia. Even had they known it, probably few of them would have thought that his small force could hold it, or dreamt of his conquest extending further. Slowly the backward states ratified the Confederation Articles, until, on February 22, 1779 (the very day when, unknown to Congress, Clark's men were struggling through the deep waters of the Great Wabash to take Hamilton), the twelfth state, Delaware, ratified. This left one state only, Maryland, refusing. New York's ratification, however, was made on condition that the Articles should not go into effect until all the thirteen states should ratify them, and two more years were to pass before Maryland would do so.

This was the situation when, in the spring of 1779, news reached Congress of Hamilton's surrender. At once the western land controversy revived surprisingly; for, more than ever, the west seemed to be a prize worth contending for. Clark's victories promised safety to settlers there, and a great immigration and rapid rise of land values were expected. The desire of eastern people to get homes and fortunes in the west became a contagion. One of them wrote: 'People are running mad for Kentucky hereabouts.' Thousands went there. Others, led by Robertson, founded an advanced settlement at what is now Nashville, Tennessee.

To her charter title to the country north of the Ohio, Virginia had now added another title by conquest, but as her claim grew stronger, so also did opposition to it from the northern states. Most of them, joining Maryland and the land companies, again sought to have Congress appropriate the whole western territory for all the states. Congress plainly had no sort of title to any lands there, but resourceful land company promoters and their confederates trumped up a pretense of title for New York, and contrived to make that state *seem* to convey it to Congress. It was based on nothing better than the old fiction of Six Nation Iroquois' conquest and ownership of the whole trans-Allegheny region, and also upon the false assumption that the pretended title of those Indians devolved upon New York because they lived in that state. The ingenious methods used to carry out the scheme to arm Congress with this preposterous claim will appear fully elsewhere,[1] and can be given only passing notice here.

A vaguely worded bill which was 'railroaded' through the New York legislature, was so framed as apparently to authorize her delegates in Congress to fix her western limits and to cede to Congress an undefined region west of those limits. In reality the delegates were not authorized to cede a foot of land that New York ever owned. On the contrary, the legislature gave them explicit directions delimiting the state's bounds and expressly forbidding them to cede any lands within those bounds. Those instructions the delegates did not see fit to disclose to Congress. Instead they exhibited only a certified copy of the legislative act, and then delivered a deed so drawn as to appear to convey an unlimited western territory. Thereupon the confederates brazenly asserted that the whole trans-Allegheny region belonged to Congress. In truth, both the claim set up for New York, and the pretended cession, were merely a political trick to give Congress an excuse for appropriating the western charter lands of Virginia and the states south of her.[2]

---

[1] Author's *Revolutionary West in Diplomacy and Politics*, in preparation.

[2] The scheme of imposition was probably understood by only two or three confederates amongst the members of the New York legislature, and by only a few in Congress. The alleged western title of New York was not only a preposterous fiction, but the cession deed gave no intelligible description, or any bounds of the region pretended to be ceded by it. It was not legally a conveyance at all, but merely a 'quitclaim,' which neither asserts nor implies a title which peradventure the grantor might have or afterwards acquire. Legally the deed signified only that New York would not afterwards lay claim to the nebulous territory mentioned as ceded. See *Report of Regents of University on*

Here let it be understood that the land-scheme promoters by no means confined their influence to Congress. Their emissaries busied themselves mightily in stirring up opposition to Virginia's government amongst the people west of the mountains. In this they were much helped by the great immigration which in 1780 followed upon Clark's victories of the year before. Most of the people went to Kentucky. Writing from near Louisville, May 5, 1780, Colonel Floyd said: 'Near 300 large boats have arrived at the Falls this spring with families. . . . We have six stations on Beargrass with not less than 600 men. [That may have meant over 3000 people.] You would be surprised to see 10 or 15 waggons at a time going to and from the Falls every day with families and corn.'[1] By the summer of 1780 Kentucky's population was said to have swollen to twenty thousand. What it really was no one knew, for it was in a state of flux, and no record was kept; but, whatever the exact figures may have been, the increase was surprising when they were compared with the one hundred and two hard-pressed men and boys who made the whole fighting population in early 1778.

With this rush of immigrants the character of Kentucky's population greatly changed, and not for the better. The pioneer element was submerged by the newcomers, who were usually both unwilling and worthless for military service. Many, indeed, came west to avoid such service, or to escape taxation. A large part of them were Pennsylvanians, who carried with them their deep-seated prejudice against Virginia, and were quite ready to oppose her land grants and government. Virginians also came in great numbers, however, and most of them cordially disliked the Pennsylvanians and upheld their own state's claim to the country. The Pennsylvanians — largely Germans — came down the Ohio in flat-boats, the Virginians usually by the mountain passes. All alike were intent on getting lands; but they found the most valuable ones already taken up by Virginians earlier in the field, and a great number of large tracts idle and held by non-residents only for future rise in value. The land-hungry newcomers regarded these absent proprietors in no friendly light, and showed an ugly agrarian spirit. Many of them ' squatted ' on

Boundaries of New York, I, 149-54; General Philip Schuyler's letter, *id.*, 137. [1] Floyd to Colonel Wm. Preston, *Draper MSS.* 177 CC 124.

the lands of the non-residents and defied ejection. Nor did they stop there. Soon they were also disputing Virginia's jurisdiction, and in this stand they were encouraged by the land company promoters, who secretly instigated them to petition Congress to claim the country and make it a new state.[1] Thus arose the 'New-State Movement,' which soon gained many adherents in Kentucky, including even some prominent Virginia settlers.[2] Clark and his officers did all they could to stay the disaffection, but never could completely suppress it. Some of the insurgent conspirators tried to win over leading military men bearing Virginia's commissions; but greatly to their credit, although they had borne the brunt of war and suffered most from the state's neglect, to a man they remained loyal to her. Proposals were even made to seduce Clark to head the insurgents, but he scorned and rejected them. Writing to his father (August 23, 1780) he said: 'The partisans in these countries are again soliciting me to lead them as their Governor-General, as all those from foreign states are for a new government; but my duty obliging me to suppress all such proceedings, I shall consequently lose the interest of that party.'[3] He was soon to feel the effects of their resentment.

Amongst an impoverished people, coming from intensely jealous sections and divided in allegiance, there was envy of the few who had means, irritation under governmental restraint, evasion of taxation, resistance of military orders, hatred of the soldiers who enforced them, and a growing desire to break loose from a remote and weak state government. Clark, as Virginia's commanding officer, and his troops, being sworn to the state's service, necessarily stood in the way of the conspirators, and soon became the special objects of their hostility — hostility which was intensified by the fact that the

---

[1] For one of them see *Papers Continental Congress*, no. 48, p. 79, Library of Congress.

[2] One of the most active of the new-state conspirators was Colonel Arthur Campbell, now county lieutenant for Washington County, which then embraced what are now extreme southwestern Virginia and southern West Virginia. The unlovable Scot, not content with trying to separate his own mountain county from Virginia, busied himself stirring up disaffection also in Kentucky. At his instance a separatist meeting was called by Colonel John Donelson at Harrodsburg 'to set aside the rights to land in this country under the land laws of Virginia' (*Draper MSS.* 9 DD 34), but it was broken up by the soldiers under command of Major McGarry. By this interference McGarry made many vindictive enemies who were to make trouble for him afterward.

[3] Original letter in *Rogers Clark Ballard Thruston's MSS.*: *Illinois Historical Collections*, VIII, 453; English's *Conquest of the Northwest*, 40 (facsimile).

soldiers had to be fed and clothed, and the discontented inhabitants compelled to share the burden. One may imagine
the opposition of such people to letting their corn or cattle
be taken for the troops, their devices to hide what they had,
and the conflicts that arose when seizures were attempted.
In almost every settlement personal encounters and bitter
enmities resulted — enmities many of which lasted long after
the war and hard times were over, and even passed as family
feuds to succeeding generations.

Another cause of dissension was the division of Kentucky
this year (1780) into three counties — in the southeast
Lincoln, north of it Fayette, and west of both Jefferson. The
seat of government for the whole 'District of Kentucky' was
Harrodsburg in Lincoln County, which had a larger population than both the other counties, and, being farthest from
the northern Indians, was comparatively free from their
attacks. This division was necessary both for convenience and
efficiency of government, but it led to unfortunate jealousies
between the counties. Soon each was bitterly complaining
that it was called on for more than its fair share of military
service and supplies. The county lieutenant and chief militia
officer of Lincoln was Colonel Benjamin Logan, of Fayette,
Colonel John Todd, and of Jefferson, Colonel John Floyd.[1]
Colonel Clark was a state officer commanding state troops and
had no authority over the county militia.

[1] Floyd was appointed by Jefferson on the recommendation of Clark, who described him as the man 'known to be the most capable in the country, — a soldier, gentleman and a scholar whom the inhabitants from his actions, have the greatest confidence in.' (*Illinois Historical Collections*, VIII, 500.)

CHAPTER XV

FOUR BRITISH OFFENSIVES TO RECOVER THE WEST

EARLY in 1780 the British planned four formidable expeditions to reconquer the entire western country. One, consisting of about a thousand men, mainly traders and Indians, was organized by Major Sinclair, commandant at Mackinac.[1] It was to descend the Mississippi and sweep the Americans and Spaniards from both sides as far down as Natchez; for in 1779 Spain also had declared war on Great Britain. Sinclair was so confident of success that he made various dispositions of the country in advance of its reconquest, and promised the traders the exclusive fur trade of the Missouri Valley. He wrote General Haldemand: 'Serg^t Phillips...will garrison the fort at the entrance of the Mississippi; Captain Hesse will remain at [St. Louis]; Wabasha (a great Sioux chief) will attack... the Rebels at Kaskaskia. ...The two lower villages of the Illinois are to be laid under contribution for the support of their different garrisons, and the two upper villages are to send cattle to LeBaye [Green Bay] to be forwarded to this place to feed the Indians on their return.'[2] Wabasha and his Sioux were to descend the Mississippi 'with all dispatch, as low down as the Natchez, and as many intermediate attacks as possible shall be made.'[3] In support, Sinclair said, another expedition under 'Captain Langlede, with a chosen band of Indians and Canadians, will join a party assembled at Chicago, to make his attack by the Illinois River, and another party sent to watch the Plains between the Wabash and the Mississippi.'[4] A third British and Indian expedition under Captain Bird — an able and active leader — was to go from Detroit through the Shawnee country, gather savages on the way, capture Clark's fort at the Falls of Ohio, and then fall upon the settlements of central Kentucky.[5] From the south, a fourth and even more powerful

[1] Sinclair succeeded De Peyster, who had succeeded Hamilton at Detroit.

[2] *Michigan Pioneer Collections*, IX, 549.

[3] Sinclair wrote that on May 2d, 'Seven hundred and fifty men, including traders, servants, and Indians, proceeded, [with another party sent out from Mackinac] down the Mississippi for an attack on the Spanish and Illinois country.' (*Id.*, 548.)

[4] *Id.*

[5] On June 1, 1780, De Peyster at Detroit wrote Haldemand: 'There are now about 2000 warriors fitted out from this place to reconnoitre the Ohio and Wabash.' (*Id.*, 398.)

British force under General Campbell was to come by sea to Pensacola, and after subduing Spanish Louisiana, was to proceed up the Mississippi and unite with Sinclair's expedition from the north.

The situation of the Americans was certainly alarming; but Clark met it with tremendous energy. When the storm broke he was at the Falls of Ohio. The first British stroke was down the Mississippi, against Cahokia — the next across the river at St. Louis, about three miles farther up. Montgomery, then commanding in the Illinois, learned of the impending attack and sent hurried messages to Clark for help. He afterward said: 'We were threatened with an invasion. Genl. Clark, being informed of it, hurried his departure, with a small body of troops from the Falls to the mouth of the Ohio, when he received other expresses from the Spanish commandant and myself. Luckily he joined me at Cahokia, time enough to save the country from impending ruin.'[1] Before the enemy appeared, Clark crossed the river to St. Louis to concert measures of defense with De Leyba. It is said 'the Spanish commandant offered him command of both sides, but Clark declined[2] . . . until he could ascertain where the assault would be made. He continued only about two hours in St. Louis when he returned to Cahokia.'[3] During this short visit he doubtless saw his sweetheart, Terese, but time and duties were pressing, — the occasion was one of extreme danger, — and the lovers could hardly have had opportunity for more than tender greeting and farewell. 'The enemy appeared in great force within twenty-four hours after his arrival' at Cahokia,[4] and made a sharp attack, but were beaten off.[5] They then took to their boats and rowed up the river toward St. Louis. Signal guns were soon firing at that place, but high winds prevented their being heard at Cahokia.[6]

[1] *Virginia Calendar State Papers*, III, 443.

[2] General William Clark's memorandum to similar effect, *Draper MSS.* 48 J 9.

[3] Brackenridge's *View of Louisiana*, 122; *Wisconsin Historical Collections*, XVIII, 406.

[4] *Virginia Calendar State Papers*, III, 443.

[5] *Michigan Pioneer Collections*, XIX, 559. The British reported the American loss as 'an officer killed at Cahokias and five prisoners.'

After fully discussing the Cahokia and St. Louis attacks, Professor James Alton James says: 'In conclusion . . . the attack on St. Louis was but one phase of a comprehensive plan on the part of the British authorities for the conquest of the west. It was the only one projected during the entire war which promised to succeed, and its failure was chiefly due to the influence of George Rogers Clark.' (*Proceedings of Mississippi Valley Historical Association*, II, 210.)

[6] Even had the signals been heard and

The attack on St. Louis was more serious. De Leyba made a stout resistance and the enemies were beaten back from the town; but in the adjacent country they killed, wounded and captured many people on their farms. Amongst the wounded was said to have been De Leyba, who died shortly after the attack. His successor, Navarro, reported the Spanish loss as 22 killed, 7 wounded, and 70 prisoners.[1] Most of these prisoners were no doubt tomahawked or carried by the Indians into slavery, for the British reports show only eighteen prisoners accounted for, but 'forty three scalps brought in.'[2]

The British attack from the south was foiled by Galvez, the capable young Spanish governor of Louisiana. He not only stopped General Campbell's invasion, but attacked the British posts on the lower Mississippi and Gulf shore, and after a time reduced the whole region to Spanish control. Meanwhile Captain Bird at Detroit was gathering his great force of Indians to strike Kentucky.

After the enemy's retirement from Cahokia and St. Louis, Colonel Montgomery wrote:

'A number of prisoners and deserters left the enemy, confirming a report that a body of near a thousand English and Indians were on their march to the Kentucky country with a train of artillery; and the General [Clark], knowing the situation of that country, appeared to be alarmed and resolved to attempt to get there previous to their arrival. At the same time he thought it necessary that the enemy, . . . retreating up the Illinois River, should be pursued, so as to attack their towns about the time they might have been disbanded, distress them, convince them that we would retaliate, and perhaps prevent their joining the British emissaries again. Previous to my knowledge of the above resolution, I had informed Genl. Clark of my desire. . . to return to my family. It was then he informed me of his resolution, and that the public interest would not permit of my request being granted; . . . that I must take command of the expedition to Rock River, while he attempted to interrupt the army marching to Kentucky. . . . He left Cahokia the fourth of June with a small escort for the mouth of the Ohio [Fort Jefferson] on his route to Kentucky. I immediately proceeded to the business I was ordered, and marched

boats been available for crossing the river, it would have been folly for the Americans to leave the fort and town of Cahokia to follow an enemy many times stronger than themselves, as one writer has suggested they should have done.

[1] *Wisconsin Historical Collections,* xviii, 406.

[2] *Michigan Pioneer Collections,* xix, 559, but Sinclair, writing Bolton July 4, 1780, said: 'They have brought off forty three scalps, & thirty four prisoners, blacks and whites, & killed about 70 persons; but they were beat off in their attacks on both sides of the river, at Pencour [St. Louis] and at Cahokia.'(*Id.,* 529.)

three hundred and fifty men, mainly French and Spanish, to the lake — open on the Illinois River, and from thence to the Rock River, — destroying the towns and crops proposed, the enemy not daring to fight me, as they had so lately been disbanded that they could not raise a sufficient force.'[1]

This prompt counter-attack was well conceived. It enabled Clark to utilize the French and Spanish desire to avenge the massacres at St. Louis, whilst its boldness covered his own weakness and impressed the Indians.

Meanwhile, in order to beat Bird to the Falls and protect Kentucky, 'Col. Clark, ...before he had well breathed after the fatigue of his expedition up the Mississippi [to defend Cahokia], hurried off to the relief of the beleagured posts.'[2] Arriving at Fort Jefferson he ordered such men as could be spared to go in boats to the Falls, and himself made a quick overland journey afoot, over three hundred miles, to that place. Knowing the intervening country was infested by Indian bands, and that men could not be spared for a war party to march openly through them, he took only two companions, the three disguised as Indians, and set out, making many detours and having several narrow escapes.[3]

Bird, learning that Clark was at Fort Jefferson, resolved to attack the Falls before his young opponent could get there. He wrote his superior at Detroit (June 3rd):

'Col. Clark will not be able to join the Rebels assembling at the Falls before the 15th. of this month. He has certainly 200 soldiers with him. I could wish...to proceed immediately to the Falls. ...It is possible, before Col. Clark's arrival, they may raise 800 men, probably they may raise 600, certain they can raise 400. It is possible we may beat 800, probable we can beat 600, certain we can beat 400. Col. Clark's arrival will add considerably to their numbers, and to their confidence; therefore the Rebels should be attacked before his arrival. Now it is possible he may return by the 14th, probable by the 22nd, certain by the first of July. Tho' possible for us to get to the Falls by the 10th of this month, certain by the 14th.

'The Indians have their full spirits, the ammunition, and everything plenty, and in the state we could wish it. After taking the Falls, the country on our return will be submissive and in a manner subdued; but if we attack the nearer forts [in Fayette County] first, as

---

[1] *Virginia Calendar State Papers*, III, 443.

[2] English's *Conquest of the Northwest*, 688.

[3] 'Fort Jefferson 10th June (1780) Col. Clark and 2 men set off to go by land to the Falls of Ohio.' (*Journal of B. Smith*, Virginia Boundary line commissioner, *Draper MSS.* 46 J 18.)

we advance, we shall have a continual desertion of Indians, our ammunition expended, and...our difficulties will increase as we advance, and Col. Clark will be at the Falls, with his people collected to fight us. ...

'I have another reason for attacking the Falls: Should we succeed, we can ambuscade Mr. Clark as he returns. ... If this plan is not followed, it will be owing to the Indians, who may adopt others.'[1]

Bird passed through the Shawnee country and arrived at the Ohio River over a hundred miles above the Falls, with a few whites and over seven hundred Indians; but, receiving an erroneous report that Clark was already at the Falls, the Indians, who had a wholesome fear of him, refused to go there. 'After two days of counciling,' said Bird, 'whether they would proceed immediately to the Falls, or attack the forts on Licking Creek, the Indians determined for Licking Creek, and tomorrow by day-break we move up the stream.'[2] He was much disgusted and said: 'Their attack on the little forts, — their numbers being so great, — is mean of them;'[3] but no persuasion could make them go where they thought Clark was in command. Thereupon Bird marched them to the Licking forts, where the settlers were mainly Pennsylvania Germans.

Ruddle's Station was the first to receive the blow. It was surrounded, and the settlers, after defending themselves from daybreak to noon, surrendered 'on condition,' Bird himself said, 'that their lives should be spared and themselves taken to Detroit.' He gave the promise in good faith, and the Indians confirmed it; but, despite his efforts to protect his prisoners, he said the savages 'rushed in, tore the poor children from their mother's breasts, killed a wounded man and every one of the cattle, leaving the whole to stink.' Then three other stations in turn suffered a like fate. 'The same promises were made,' said Bird, 'and broke in like manner.' Such was Indian warfare and such Indian faith. 'The Rebels,' he said, 'ran from the next fort and the Indians burned it. They then heard the news of Col. Clark's coming against them & proposed returning.'[4]

With between three and four hundred prisoners, 'some sick and some wounded,' Bird started on his return to Detroit. The cattle having all been killed, he said, and 'the Prisoners in

---

[1] *Michigan Pioneer Collections*, XIX, 527, etc.
[2] *Id.*, 533.
[3] *Id.*, 534.
[4] *Id.*, 539.

danger of starving,' [the] 'Indians almost all left us within a day's march of the enemy. It was with difficulty I procured a guide through the woods. I marched the poor women and children 20 miles in one day over high mountains, frightening them with frequent alarms to push them forward. [Think of that twenty-mile journey through a rough and tangled forest and over high mountains, for women and children — without food and kept in mortal terror by frequent threats! One can imagine their exhaustion when their first supperless night's rest came, if indeed any rest came to the mothers.] In short, Sir, by water and land we came, with all our cannon, &c. 90 miles in 4 days, — one day out of which we lay by entirely — rowing 50 miles the last day up stream.' [1]

Yet this was but the beginning of the journey of 'the poor women and children,' for thus far they had traveled only ninety of the four hundred miles to Detroit. Over one month later De Peyster, now commanding there, significantly wrote: 'Captain Bird arrived here this morning with about one hundred and fifty prisoners, mostly Germans who speak English, the remainder coming in, — for in spite of all his endeavors to prevent it, the Indians broke into their fort and seized many. The whole will amount to about three hundred and fifty.' How many of the remaining two hundred ever came in, — how many dropped by the way, — we do not know. How many of those who surrendered at the four stations were carried off by the savages, how many were tomahawked, to what hellish brutalities the women were subjected, can only be surmised from what is proven of Indian cruelty. [2]

There was of course plain need for a retaliatory stroke against the Indians, to convince them that swift punishment would follow such onslaughts; yet, when Clark arrived at Harrodsburg he found the motley crowd greatly excited about land entries in the newly opened land office, but — the enemy having left — little concerned about the war! [3] Some refused

[1] *Michigan Pioneer Collections,* xix, 539.

[2] History and romance have made familiar stories of the Cherry Valley raid in New York and the Wyoming massacre in Pennsylvania. Bird's raid was much more destructive than either, the loss of life greater, and its horrors far more appalling; yet because it occurred far from the northeastern printing presses, few have ever read of it. In the Cherry Valley raid the number of killed is given as 48, captives from 30 to 40, and they nearly all soon released. (*History of Mohawk Valley,* by Nelson Green, S. J. Clarke Publishing Co., Chicago, pp. 900.)

[3] The excitement over lands may be imagined when it is understood that on the first day the office was opened, over sixteen hundred thousand acres of

to defend the country because they said they had no lands; others said 'let those who claim the lands come fight for them'; others that the state paid Clark's soldiers to defend the country — let them do it! Seeing that strong measures were necessary, he asked the register of the land office to close it. This the register declined to do; whereupon Clark usurped authority, ordered the office closed, and called for recruits. This closing of the office greatly incensed those who had come west only to get lands, or speculate in them. Many prepared to saddle their horses and leave for the east; but orders were issued to 'stop any person from going...by putting their horses in the service, . . . and taking their arms and ammunition.' [1]

These summary methods proved effective. Soon Clark gathered about a thousand men, and crossing the Ohio, marched some two hundred miles against the chief town of the Shawnees on the Scioto. The Indians retreating, he destroyed their town and crops and then pursued them to Piqua — a town on the upper Miami — where they were well sheltered and made stout resistance, but were out-flanked, driven slowly back, and after five hours, hot battle, completely routed. Here, too, their wigwams and crops were destroyed. The whites lost fourteen killed and thirteen wounded — the Indians some three times as many. [2]

During the fight a sad event happened which illustrated the tragedy of Indian war. In the party which in 1776 had carried the powder from Pittsburg to Kentucky was Clark's young first cousin and boyhood playmate, Joseph Rogers, who was supposed to have been killed when the party was waylaid by Indians. He had not been killed, however, but was captured, taken to the Shawnee town, and was there when Clark attacked it. During the battle young Rogers, dressed as an Indian, threw away his gun and ran towards the whites, crying

choice tracts were entered. (Floyd to Preston, May 5, 1780, *Draper MSS.* 17 CC 124.; I. Hite, Jr., to I. Hite, *Author's MSS.*; xxi, *Kentucky Historical Society Register*, January, 1923; Fleming's Journal, *Draper MSS.* 2 ZZ 74-75, holograph.)

[1] *Virginia State Library, Illinois Regiment Papers.*

[2] Clark to Governor Jefferson August 22, 1780, *Illinois Historical Collections*, viii, 450; *Draper MSS.* 8 J 136. Like nearly all successful attacks on the Indians, this raid was greatly magnified and extolled by early writers, and has been by many later ones. It is even represented as one of Clark's brilliant achievements, and descendants of men taking part in it still refer to it with pride. Certainly it was a necessary and valuable service, but as a military performance insignificant compared with his others.

out: 'Don't shoot! I'm a white man! I'm a white man!', but he fell, mortally wounded by his friends. He sent for Clark and after an affectionate meeting died in his arms.[2]

[2] Writing of the battle to his father, Clark said: 'This will be handed you by Mr. James Sutton who has accompanied me on a late successful Expedition against the Shawnees in which he done himself much honour. The particulars of the Expedition he will give you; also the fate of poor Joseph Rogers, who lost his Life in the Moment it might have been [in] his power to Render... his Country great service — his fate was fixed — no p[ossibility] of saving him.' (August 23, 1780, *Illinois Historical Collections,* VIII, 453.) The incident is described in a written account of the Rogers family by Joseph Rogers' namesake, Joseph Rogers Underwood, who was a distinguished judge of the Kentucky Court of Appeals and U. S. Senator. Copy from original is in author's MSS. One of Joseph Rogers Underwood's grandsons is the present United States Senator from Alabama, Oscar Underwood.

CHAPTER XVI

CLARK'S LAST EFFORT AGAINST DETROIT

NOTWITHSTANDING the failure of the four British campaigns and the punishment of the Shawnees, the Indians in general were far from being pacific. They saw they could get nothing from the Americans, almost as poor as themselves, and looked to Detroit for supplies and leaders. As long as that hatching-place of Indian war remained in British hands, the Americans might expect destructive inroads. Knowing this, Clark determined to try again to get an adequate force to take it, and with that view journeyed to the Virginia capital. There he laid his plan before his friend Jefferson, now governor. Jefferson was convinced of its feasibility and gave his ever-willing coöperation; for he fully understood the importance to all the states of winning that British key to the western country.[1] He had Clark made a brigadier general, promised him two thousand men, and zealously worked to supply him with every necessity. He also asked General Washington for an order on Colonel Brodhead, the continental commandant at Pittsburg, for cannon and the loan to Clark of Colonel John Gibson's regiment at that place. Washington readily agreed, saying:

'I have ever been of opinion that the reduction of the post of Detroit would be the only certain means of giving peace and security to the whole western frontier, and I have constantly kept my eye upon that subject; but, such has been the reduced state of our Continental force, and the low ebb of our funds, especially of late, that I have never had it in my power to make the attempt. I shall think it a most happy circumstance should your state, with the aid of the continental stores which you require, be able to accomplish it. I am so well convinced of the general public utility with which the expedition, if successful, will be attended, that I do not hesitate a moment in giving directions to the commandant at Fort Pitt to deliver to Colonel Clark the articles which you request.'[2]

---

[1] Moreover, although he knew his state was about to give up the whole country north of the Ohio, and had even advised her giving up Kentucky to save the Confederation, he was willing for her to bear the burden of the attempt. Perhaps no act of his life better illustrates his breadth of view and patriotism.

Jefferson to Madison, Feb. 20, 1784. Ford's *Writings of Jefferson*, IV, 244; Dunn's *Indiana*, 182.

[2] Sparks' *Writings of Washington* (Boston, 1837), VII, 341–45. Jefferson to Washington, Ford's *Writings of Jefferson*, III, 57–59.

Jefferson also wrote Clark, saying:

'Can that post be reduced, we shall be quiet in future on our frontier, and thereby immense treasures of blood and money be saved; we shall be at leisure to turn our whole force to the rescue of our Eastern Country from subjugation; we shall divert through our own country a branch of commerce which the European States have thought worthy of the most important struggles and sacrifices; and, in the event of a peace on terms which have been contemplated by some powers, we shall form to the American Union a barrier against the dangerous extension of the British Provinces of Canada, and add to the empire of Liberty, an extensive and fertile country.'[1]

While Clark was absent from the west, troubles fast accumulated there for both inhabitants and soldiers. In the French towns conditions became almost chaotic. At Kaskaskia the garrison under its successive commanders, Montgomery, Rogers, and Williams, struggled hard to maintain the post, but finally had to abandon it, (February 1781) and go to Fort Jefferson.[2] From Vincennes the commandant, Captain Bayly, wrote:

'Sir, I must inform you once more that I cannot keep Garrison any longer without some speedy relief from you. My Men have been 15 days upon half allowance; there is plenty of provisions here, but no credit. I cannot press being the weakest party. Some of the Gentlemen would help us but their Credit is as bad as ours. Therefore if you have no provisions send whisky which will answer as good an end.'[3]

---

[1] *Draper MSS.* 51 J 13. Until of recent years this significance to the east of the war in the west was grasped by few eastern or even western historians. In truth, Washington's problems in the eastern war cannot be comprehended without realizing the vitally important support he received from the frontiers and from the diversion in his favor made by carrying on the western war north of the Ohio. Writing to Jefferson about this time, Clark said: 'However foreign it may be to most people in power, it is beyond all doubt that our possessions in the Illinois and Kentucky have been the salvation of all our interior frontiers since the commencement of the war, and have enabled them to give that assistance against the British armies they have done. I know a number of gentlemen dispute this assertion, but if the war should continue two years and no army should march from some part of the States into the enemies' country, they will be con-

vinced of their error.' (*Draper MSS.* 14 S 64; *Virginia State Library*.)

Washington is reported to have said, in 1778: 'I will retreat, if beaten, to the mountains of Virginia; I will, if beaten there, retreat across the Alleghenies; but never will I lay down my arms til independence comes.' The spirit of this declaration was Washington's, but if he made such a statement it must have been to encourage his supporters or to deceive the enemy; for no man knew better that a retreat over the Alleghenies would have proved a very disastrous one for defeated and pursued soldiers, unfamiliar with the pathless forest or Indian warfare, and deprived of sustenance from the farms and factories of the east. They would have found the Indians in the forest far more formidable than the British armies near the Atlantic.

[2] *Illinois Historical Collections*, VIII, 581; *id.*, VIII, cxxiv.

[3] *Id.*, 581. Whiskey, like peltries,

South of the Ohio the people were hardly better off than their French friends north of the river. At Fort Jefferson a powerful force of Chickasaws, led by the half-breed Colbert, surrounded the sick and starving garrison and demanded a surrender. That being refused, a vicious attack followed, lasting three days. At its height, and when the defenders seemed doomed, Colbert was wounded, and a well directed shot from an iron six-pounder loaded with bullets played havoc amongst the savages, who thereupon withdrew.[1] During the excitement of the attack a young girl displayed cool judgment and courage worthy of remembrance. A cow and her calf were outside, and the saving of them meant the saving of children's lives. 'While the men were parleying what to do, and hesitating to expose themselves, Nancy Ann Hunter ran into the open space and taking up the calf brought it within the enclosure, the cow following, while shots of the savages whistled by and cut her clothing, herself unharmed.'[2]

Although the Chickasaws were beaten off, the people were scourged by still deadlier enemies — want and disease — 'numbers daily dying.'[3] Seeing nothing but starvation and death where they were, many of the inhabitants and some of the soldiers left, going down the Mississippi, never to be heard from more. The few remaining sank their cannon in the river and, crowded into a few rough boats, were taken by Colonel Montgomery to the Falls, where he took command. He wrote the governor:

'After a dangerous and disagreeable voyage up the Mississippi, I arrived at Fort Jefferson on the 1st. of May last, when I found the Troops in a very low and Starving Condition, nor was there any goods or any Property wherewith to purchase. From the Illinois nothing could be expected, the credit of the State being long since lost there & no supplies coming from this place, occasioned an Evacuation of that Post, which for want of Provisions, took place on the 8th June last.

was commonly used as a substitute for money.

[1] *Draper MSS.* 31 J 73; 51 J 41.

[2] *Filson Club Publications*, No. 27.

[3] Before the abandonment Captain George, commanding, wrote: 'We are reduced to a very small number, . . . and numbers daily dying.' (*Virginia Calendar State Papers*, I, 382). Even dauntless and fun-loving Captain Helm wrote most gloomily of the situation, but in a lighter vein added that he was 'sitting by Captain George's fire with a piece of light-wood and two ribs of old buffalo, which is all the meat we have seen these many days. Excuse haste, as the lightwood's just out and mouth watering for part of the two ribs. Capt. George gives his compliments, but has neither light nor paper.' (*Id.*, 383.) Paper was one of the scarcest of needed articles in the west.

'Since my arrival here, I find things in the same Condition — not a mouthful for the troops to eat, nor money to purchase it with; and ...the credit of the government is worn bare. The counties of Lincoln and Fayette particularly, tho able to supply us, refuse granting any relief without the cash to purchase on the spot. ...I am constrained to billet the troops through the country in small parties, for want of necessaries, except a small guard to keep the garrison; so that unless supplies soon arrive I fear the consequences will be fatal.'[1]

A council of the regimental officers resolved to send this letter to the governor, but to do so called for an 'express,' and they had no money to pay for one; for expresses to the distant capital at Richmond were very expensive. Even before hard times reached their height, one express cost Colonel Clark nearly $200, specie; and the charges multiplied many times as the war progressed. Finally Major Quirk volunteered to undertake the dangerous task.[2]

In eastern Virginia one obstacle after another arose to prevent the expedition against Detroit. A main one was the untimely invasion of Virginia by the British army under Bene-

---

[1] *Virginia Calendar State Papers*, II, 313. Montgomery said the Illinois Regiment 'since its being raised, — its now going on three years, — have drawn no pay in these parts, nor only scarce clothing for the troops, which is the reason of many of the Best of our men deserting every day.' Quartermaster Shannon said they were also 'destitute of all kinds of military stores and none to be purchased. ...To procure necessaries for the troops...my own bonds were given, and if the money should not come, I expect no mercy from the creditors.' (*Shannon's Letter Book*, Virginia State Library, C 273.) Next month he wrote Clark: 'You know when you left us if the enemy had approached our situation would have been desperate; and you may rely on it that we get weaker every day, — not one stroke towards fortifying the post since your departure. ...It appears as if the inhabitants here and on Beargrass, if assistance do not come early in the spring, would entirely move off. ... There is not sufficient soldiers here at present to furnish assistance in cutting and securing beef, without speaking of the necessary guards for waggons for hauling corn, tar, &c.' (*Id.*) Nearly all the horses had been run off by the Indians, and the few remaining had to be

kept in the stations, where they consumed the scant supply of corn so sadly needed by the people. Colonel Floyd wrote the governor from the Falls: 'We are all obliged to live in our forts in this country, and notwithstanding all the caution we use, forty seven...have been killed or taken prisoners by the savages, besides a number wounded, since January. ...Whole families are destroyed without regard to age or sex; infants are torn from their mothers' arms and their brains dashed out against trees. ... Not a week passes, and some weeks scarcely a day, without some of our distressed inhabitants feeling the fatal effects of the infernal rage and fury of those execrable hell-hounds. ...A large proportion of the inhabitants are helpless indigent widows and orphans, who have lost their husbands and fathers by savage hands and [are] left among strangers, without the most common necessaries of life. ...The confidence of the people in General Clark's vigilance, his enterprising spirit, and other military virtues, together with their inability to move, have barely been sufficient to keep this country from being left entirely desolate.' (*Virginia Calendar State Papers*, II, 48.)

[2] *Virginia Calendar State Papers*, II, 313.

dict Arnold, and the approach of another under Cornwallis. The two thousand men promised Clark were imperatively needed at home, and even he was called on to take part in the defense. It is interesting to learn that with a body of raw militia he gave Arnold's army the only check it received.[1]

Another cause of his recruiting troubles was the evident design of the northern majority in Congress to ignore Virginia's claim to the western country and appropriate it for all the states. If that was to be done and Virginia deprived of any special benefit from the expedition to take Detroit, her people could see no reason why their state alone should assume the burden. By the end of 1780 she was in dire distress; her treasury was empty; her best troops had been sent to fight in other states; many had gone under Lincoln to the relief of Charleston and had been surrendered by him; Gates had been defeated at Camden and De Kalb killed; Arnold's army was ravaging her plantations, plundering and burning public and private property, and about to enter her capital; Cornwallis with a strong British army was approaching. In imminent danger of subjugation, and pleading with the states north of her to come to her relief, Virginia was in no condition to carry on a political struggle with them, but needed to conciliate them. At last, when Arnold's army was within a few miles of Richmond — when public property there was being hurriedly rushed to places of safety, the state officials about to flee, and all was confusion — her Assembly (January 2, 1781) offered to surrender to Congress the whole region north of the Ohio.

With that offer one might suppose her opponents would have been satisfied and thereafter been content to leave her West Virginia and Kentucky; but not so, for it was there that the land company promoters were looking for fortunes. By this time they had gained surprising influence in Congress, which would not accept Virginia's offer of the princely domain north of the Ohio unless she would also give up West Virginia and Kentucky.

[1] At Hood's Ferry, January 6th, the British 'landed their whole army in the night, Arnold attending in person. Colonel Clark of Kaskaskies had been sent with 240 by Baron Steuben, and, having properly disposed of them in ambuscade, gave them a deliberate fire which killed 17 on the spot and wounded 17. They returned it, in confusion, by which we had 3 or 4 wounded, and our party, being so small, without bayonets, were compelled to retire on the enemy charging with bayonets. They (the British) fell down to Dobb's.' (*Governor's Letter Book for 1781*, 30, Virginia State Library; also H. Burk's *Virginia*, 457.)

In this situation few men could be induced to join Clark's expedition. Some of the recruiting officers refused to enlist men, and the governor was constrained to overlook their disobedience. He then wrote Clark to recruit his two thousand men in the ever-troubled Pittsburg region, and the effort to do so was earnestly made, but in vain. The Virginians and Pennsylvanians there were rent with discord, and the Pennsylvania partisans opposed the expedition because it was organized by Virginia.[1] Pittsburg, too, was the western headquarters of leading promoters of the land companies, and they doubtless lost no opportunity to obstruct the recruiting.[2]

[1] The following letter of Colonel Neville to Clark throws an interesting light on the conditions in southwest Pennsylvania at this time:

WOODVILLE 14th *April* 1782
DEAR GENERAL

I arrived at Woodville the day you left Whelan I was very sorry I had not the pleasure of seeing you before [you] set out upon your Expedition and am also sorry you had to deal with such a set of rascals as was...in this part of the country. I mean the leading men of Washington [and] Westmoreland Counties [Pennsylvania] Who I am informed did everything in their power to prevent your Campaign. I have had at least forty Quarrels on the subject. Some times they made you a Flour Merchant, at other times a Land Jober and Trader for the State of Virginia &c &c ...and tho I am unfortunate enough to fall in to Pennsylvania I shall live and Die in the Interest of Virginia. They have brought a number of suits in Washington Court agst Colo Cox for his assistance to you and it was once expected he would be ruined, but two or three suits are determined in his favor, which will perhaps be a precedent for the rest.

Those very people who refused to go with you turned out in large bodies this winter and killed ninety odd of the poor Moravian Indians, the Greatest part Women and Children, and another party fell on the Indians at Fort Pitt and put five to Death and wounded the Sixth who is since dead and now threatens Col Gibson his Squaw and Children. I am now [on] the very Frontier and expect a very troublesome Summer.

Mrs. Nevil recd your kind letter from Whelan and is greatly obliged to you for

the Friendly advice you Gave her, and found the Times Turned out just as you mentioned. —

your Brother and my perticular Friend John is Married to Miss Hite. I hope he may be as happy as any man in the World: he justly merits it.

Should you ever Come into this Quarter again I hope without ceremony you will make my Cottage your home, for be assured My Dear General no man regards the Name of Clarke more than myself.

Mrs. Nevill and the Girls present their Compliments to you and Accept the same from

Your Humb Ser t
JOHN NEVILL

The Honble Brig r Genl George Clarke Favored by Capt. Oldham.

(*Draper MSS. 52 J 18.*)

Colonel William Croghan's letter (*id.,* 11 S 61) gives a graphic account of the sequel of the massacre of the Moravians and the torture and death of Colonel William Crawford by the relatives of those Indians.

[2] When Cornwallis was overrunning Virginia and Lafayette was struggling hard to save it, Pendleton wrote Madison: 'Our people are made very angry by a report that Pennsylvania, instead of forwarding their troops with that celerity which their duty and the situation demanded, were throwing out insulting speeches — that Virginia was too grand; better be humbled by the enemy, and such like. What consequences this may produce, I know not, but they will be chargeable to the companies of Land Jobbers who, for their own interest, are poisoning the minds of the people by their fallacious publications. I am sorry

Furthermore, Colonel Brodhead, the commander there was ambitious to reduce Detroit himself, was intensely jealous of Clark, and did much to discourage enlistments.[1] Despite Washington's orders, he even refused to allow Gibson's regiment to join the expedition.

The crowning obstacle to Clark's recruiting was the passage of a resolution by the Virginia Assembly (June, 1781) authorizing the executive 'to put a stop to the Expedition lately ordered against Detroit, and to take all necessary steps for disposing of, or applying to other uses, the stores and provisions laid in for that purpose.'[2] The resolution was offered by Patrick Henry, and was said to have grown out of an unfortunate enmity which had arisen between him and Governor Jefferson, who considered it a reflection on his administration.[3]

This resolution, wrote Clark, 'seemed to alarm this country; the Greenbrier militia returned; the drafts in this country dispersed; great numbers returned to Virginia that were for the enterprise.'[4] From Wheeling he wrote Jefferson:

'Whoever undertakes to Raise an Army in this Quarter will find himself disappointed, except the laws was in greater force and not depending on the will of the populace. This Country calls aloud for an Expedition, wishing me to put it in Execution, but so strangely infatuated that all the methods I have been able to pursue will not draw them into the field. We have made draughts to no purpose. Governor Reed [of Pennsylvania] wrote to them, but to no effect. From the time I found I was to be disappointed in the troops ordered by Government, I began to suspect the want of men, which is now the case, when everything else is prepared. ...I have relinquished

that line [of Pennsylvania troops] was not forwarded, as for want of them the Marquis Lafayette was obliged to abandon Richmond, which he left Saturday and retired on this side Chickahominy.' (*Washington-Madison Papers*, May 21, 1781, Thos. Birch & Sons, Catalogue 694.) Amongst the 'fallacious publications' Pendleton refers to was an ingenious, but decidedly disingenuous, pamphlet written by Thomas Paine to attack Virginia's western charter title, and entitled '*Public Good: Being an Examination of the Claim of Virginia to the vacant Western Territory, and the Right of the United States to the same; to which is added proposals for Laying off a New State to be Applied as a Fund for Carrying on the War, or redeeming the National Debt*,' printed December 30, 1780. It

was charged, and was probably true, that for writing it he was promised 12,000 acres of the Indiana Company's lands, although Conway's *Life of Paine* disputes this. See Morgan's letter and Alvord's note, *Illinois Historical Collections*, v, 210.

[1] See *Frontier Defense on the Upper Ohio*, Thwaite and Kellogg, Draper Series, vol. 3, *Frontier Advance*, vol. 4, and Retreat, vol. 5, by Kellogg.

[2] Virginia State Library, *Journal House of Representatives*, June 21, 1781.

[3] But Virginia's offer to surrender the northwest to Congress seems a sufficient explanation of Henry's wish to stop an expedition from which the state would get no special benefit.

[4] *Draper MSS.* 14 S 71.

my expectation relative to the plans heretofore laid [against Detroit.] If I find a prospect of completing my forces in any other country, I shall do it and make my strokes according to circumstances.

'I do not yet condemn myself for undertaking the expedition against Detroit. I think yet, had I near the number of men first proposed, I should have carried it. I may yet make some stroke among the Indians before the close of the campaign, but at present really to be doubted. I have been at so much pains to enable us to prosecute the first plan, that the disappointment is doubly mortifying to me; and I feel for the dreadful consequences that will ensue throughout the frontier if nothing is done.'[1]

When Washington learned of Clark's difficulties, he wrote him saying: 'I feel not only for the public disappointment, but for your own, as I doubt not you had the affair much at heart and that you would have executed it with your usual ability and address had you been able to have found the means.'[2]

To stop desertion, and still hoping to be reënforced from Kentucky, General Clark descended the Ohio with such men as he had, leaving word for another delayed body, under Colonel Lochry, to follow. Lochry did follow, with about a hundred men in boats, but was attacked by a large force of Indians, and all but one man killed or captured. The disaster is briefly described in the journal of one of the surviving prisoners, Lieutenant Anderson:

'Aug. 24th. Colonel Lochry ordered the boats to land on the Indian [or north] shore, about ten miles below the mouth of the Great Mayamee river, to cook provisions and cut grass for the horses, when we were fired on by a party of Indians from the bank. We took to our boats, expecting to cross the river, and were fired on by another party in a number of canoes, and soon we became a prey to them. They killed the colonel and a number more, after they were prisoners. The number of our killed was about forty.'[3]

Lochry was an ardent supporter of Clark's expedition, and was bringing a much needed reënforcement; yet, so bitter was the feeling of the Pennsylvania partisans towards Clark that many attributed the disaster to his neglect of Lochry, and some even charged that he planned the massacre! This pre-

[1] Colonel Floyd wrote from the Falls: 'I begin now to be greatly discouraged on account of our defenceless situation, especially since I heard the expedition was set aside. I fear this step will be fatal to the inhabitants here without your immediate interposition.' (Floyd to Jefferson August 10, 1781. *Draper MSS.* 51 J 80; *Virginia Calendar State Papers,* III, 294.)

[2] Library of Congress, *Letters of Washington,* B vol. XIII, Pt. III, 483–84.

[3] English's *Conquest of the Northwest,* 725.

posterous charge well illustrates the unreasoning violence of
prejudice and traduction in that hornet's nest of dissention
during the Revolution. It was the first widely circulated falsehood about Clark, but by no means the last. The real cause of
Lochry's disaster is now made plain by letters passing between
him and Clark, which were taken by the Indians, but are fortunately preserved in the British Museum.[1]

On the way down the river Clark's drafted men continued
to desert, so that when he reached the Falls the few remaining
were found wholly inadequate for any offensive operation.
Thus ended his last attempt to carry out his cherished project
to capture Detroit, 'in the execution of which,' he soon afterwards wrote Jefferson, 'my very soul was wrapt, as leading to
others of equal importance.'[2]

How different Clark's journey down the Ohio this year from
the one three years before, when he was on his way to take
Kaskaskia! Then, despite his small force and unknown dangers ahead, glorious prospects opened before him; he was, as
he said, 'elevated with the thoughts of the great service we
should do our country.' Now, his plan to take Detroit having
failed, all hope for further achievement seemed gone; and well
might he say: 'I feel for the dreadful consequences that will
ensue throughout the frontier if nothing is done.' Nothing was
done, and throughout the west years of suffering and disaster were to follow.

[1] They show Clark making every effort
to assist Lochry to join him, waiting for
him long after the appointed rendezvous, sending back to him boats, men,
and provisions. They show Lochry and
his men going 397 miles down the river
in high spirits, when he made an imprudent landing and suffered his defeat and
death. See *Lochry's Letters to Clark*,
British Museum, Add. MSS. 21845, ff.
122–23, and *Major Wall's Receipt Book*,
Virginia State Library.

[2] *Draper MSS.* 14 S 64.

CHAPTER XVII

APATHY AND FORT-BUILDING CONTROVERSY

WHEN General Clark reached the Falls he called a meeting of the principal militia officers of Kentucky, to learn what support they would give for a necessary expedition to quell the Indians. The three counties were represented by their county lieutenants — Colonel Logan for Lincoln, Colonel John Todd for Fayette, and Colonel Floyd for Jefferson. Colonel Trigg also appeared from Lincoln, and Colonels Pope and Cox from Jefferson. At this meeting there arose an issue over the building of new forts on the Ohio which, although seemingly local and temporary, mightily affected the history of the west and Clark's later career.

Because the northwestern Indians who invaded Fayette and Lincoln had usually come through the Shawnee country, the people of those counties erroneously believed the Shawnees were their most dangerous foes and demanded special protection against them. (See map, page 25.) They complained that Fort Nelson at the Falls was too far down the Ohio to protect them, and insisted that if only one fort could be maintained it should be higher up the river and more in the line of Shawnee invasion of their counties. In reality, the Shawnees were not their most dangerous enemies, but the tribes living north and northwest of the Falls, outnumbering the Shawnees perhaps twenty to one.[1] The Shawnees mainly directed their attacks against the whites on the upper Ohio.

General Clark's responsibilities of course included the protection of all the three Kentucky counties, and also holding on to the Wabash and Illinois country; and for both purposes the Falls was the point of greatest strategic value. It not only lay between all three counties and their most formidable

[1] Every considerable invasion of Kentucky, after Hamilton's capture, was by these northwestern Indians — Miamis, Ouiatenans, etc. Bird's raid was made with them. Though he passed through the Shawnee country, few Shawnees joined him. The same was true of Caldwell and McKee's invasion two years later, although the Kentucky people and early writers believed it was by the Shawnees and led by 'Girty the Renegade,' who was more cordially hated by the pioneers than any other enemy, and was made ubiquitous and a bugaboo for their children.

enemies, but was the one place on the Ohio where a garrison
was necessary to keep the river open for transportation, since
boats were compelled to stop there for over land carriage of
cargoes, and without military protection would have been an
easy prey for the savages. A garrison there was absolutely
necessary if he was to have authority north of the Ohio; or if
he was to carry on military operations there; or if he was to
retain the very useful aid of the French and friendly Piankeshaws there.

His address to the militia colonels has been preserved, and
was an earnest appeal for patriotic coöperation.[1] In view of
his disappointment over the failure of the Detroit expedition
and his anxiety to protect the western people, the address was
truly pathetic; for, read between the lines, it shows he had
small hope of receiving the support he asked. He said:

'For a series of years I have made strong study to support and
protect the back settlements of our states, — not from any particular
attachment I had to them, but knowing the very great advantage
they were of to the Whole Continent, as a Barrier against the Indians more valuable than is generally conceived by the Continent at
large. I have taken every measure in my power to support them,
sparing no trouble, fatigue, or dangers to accomplish whatever offered to Advantage, — Sensible that nothing would put a Stop to
the war so vigorously prosecuted by the Indians but the Reduction
of the British Indian posts and possession of Lake Erie.' [Then,
after stating his recruiting difficulties and the inadequacy of his
present small force for any aggressive campaign, he said the Indians
have] 'many reasons to dread the proposed Enterprise; but, if
nothing of importance is done, they will take it for granted that we
are not able to prosecute the War. Encouraged, they will come on
with double Vigour. I dread the issue.'

Referring to the opposition of the land company promoters
and new-state malcontents to the government and settlement
of Kentucky, he said:

The Public Clamour against the settlement of your Country being
such, I have never ventured to say much in your defense, as it might
have deprived me of the opportunity of doing as much for you as I
wished; but I know, and always knew, that this Department was of
more real Service to the United States than half of all their Fronteer
posts, and [has] proved of great Importance by engaging the attention of the Enemy, that otherwise would have spread Slaughter and
Devastation throughout the more Interior Fronteers, and deprived

---

[1] *Draper MSS.* 51 J 84; *Illinois Historical Collections*, VIII, 596.

them of giving any assistance to our Eastern Armies; and, more than
probable, the Alleghany would have been our Boundary at this time.[1]
But to give you a full detail of my Ideas on this Subject is unnecessary.

I would not wish that you should think that I mean to flatter you
by what I have said...of your settlements. I could never have condescended to undertake any enterprise that only promised advantage
to a particular part of the community. The general good was what I
aimed at, as only consistant with my own sentiments. It was immaterial to me from what part of the fronteers I raised my army,
could I have got one, as there was but the one Common Enemy to
act against.[2]

Finding myself disappointed on the Monongehela, I have come to
you, and should be glad to know what you would wish to be done.
The forces ordered by government to be furnished by your country,
added to those I have, are not sufficient to execute anything of moment. A greater number must be called to the field. I wait, as a
spectator, to see what a country is determined to do for itself when
reduced to a state of desperation. I am ready to lead you on any
action that has the most distant prospect of advantage, however
daring it may appear to be. Your situation is truly desperate. The
evacuation of Fort Jefferson has already happened; that of [Vin-
cennes] will shortly take place, — it being out of our power to keep
them any longer. Of course the Indians in those countries must, to a
man, embrace the British interest, and you will have several thousand warriors more to contend with than formerly. ...

From some late circumstances, I am apprehensive this will be the
last piece of service that I shall have it in my power to do for you in
the military line, and could wish it to be as complete as possible.
[For reasons which will presently appear, he had resolved to resign
his command.] My situation being desperate, similar conduct would
be agreeable. A full conveyance of your ideas I shall expect. I am,
Gentlemen, with esteem,

Your obed^t Servt   G. R. CLARK

Sept. 5, 1781

The minutes of the meeting show that all the officers joined
in an appeal to the state for an expedition against Detroit in
the spring; but that Clark's proposal for a volunteer one
against the Indians was rejected. All the Jefferson County
officers and Trigg of Lincoln favored it, but Logan and Todd
opposed it, saying they thought 'it would be best to decline an

---

[1] This language — merely repeating
what he had early and often said before
— pretty plainly disposes of the assertion of Hinsdale and other writers that
Clark 'probably had no conception of
the remote bearings' of the western
warfare he was waging. Even so early

as 1776, indeed, he had disclosed a clear
conception of them in his memorial to
the Virginia Assembly when asking for
a county government for Kentucky.

[2] Virginians had no doubt objected to
his bringing Pennsylvania troops into
Kentucky.

expedition this season altogether, and to erect a strong garrison at the mouth of Kentucky, thereby to enable parties of 50, 100, or 200 to visit the enemy in the winter season (and have their retreat secured to them) and, by distressing them, force them to offer peace.'[1]

Two days after the meeting, Logan and Todd in a joint letter told General Clark 'To call upon them for necessary militia to assist' in building the new fort at the mouth of the Kentucky, and said they 'are willing to furnish corn and buffalo beef as far as in their power.'[2] He accordingly at once began preparations for building the fort and called on them for their quotas of men and supplies; but, after returning to their counties, and no doubt finding their people opposed to lending any aid, they answered that they had changed their minds! They wrote him they had 'expected that the new fortifications would be built and garrisoned, if not wholly, at least principally by the regulars. The assistance you require we are quite ready to give, but we have no intrenching tools and our militia are still very thin, and what there will be, much busied in securing their crops.'[3] General Clark probably thought these were poor excuses to evade service. 'Besides,' said they, 'we have some disagreeable news relative to the unfriendly disposition of the Cherokees and expectation of hostilities, either against the southern settlements of this county, or the Cumberland.' Yet there was no Cherokee raid,

[1] *Draper MSS.* **51 J** 85; *Illinois Historical Collections*, VIII, 596.

[2] *Draper MSS.* 51 J 87.

[3] See also Todd to Governor, Oct. 21, 1781, *Virginia Calendar State Papers*, II, 562, saying: 'On parting with General Clark we expected to furnish assistance in building the Garrison at the Mouth of Kentucky from the Militia but expected it to be built principally by Regulars and wholly garrisoned by them; since which a Requisition has come to Col. Logan and myself to furnish Tools & build the Garrison and afterwards defend it by men drawn from the Body of our Militia until he shd have leisure to relieve them which we are satisfied wd not happen in any short time.

'On consulting with Col. Logan we concluded to defer building the Garrison because we had no intrenching Tools, no professed Engineers, no money & we conceived it to belong to men who draw constant pay to garrison it. The Result of our Consultation we sent to the General with a promise to lay the matter before your Excellency or the Gnl Assembly. If the State had no Troops on pay we should have no cause to remonstrate; but — when they had Troops, & those Troops kept in the more interior & secure posts whe[re] so much has already been expended — to augment the Expence by putting the Militia on duty at a place distant from 60 to 120 Miles from home we conceive to be impolitic.'

This statement seems hardly fair when Todd must have known that General Clark's state troops were neither paid nor half fed; and that the 'interior posts' in Jefferson, which he refers to, so far from being 'secure,' were the most exposed of all and suffering far more frequent and destructive attacks than his own county, or Lincoln.

and moreover those Indians were so poorly provided with guns and ammunition, and so well held in check by the Holston settlers, that no formidable raid was to be seriously apprehended. They had never made one into Kentucky before, and never made one afterwards.

Logan and Todd concluded their letter by informing General Clark that, 'upon the whole, as Jefferson County must be excused from their part of the fatigue of building and defending the new garrison, and as it is solely intended for our defense, on calculating the cost we conclude we are willing to forego the many advantages which would attend it, for this season, and think it better to defend ourselves near home. We therefore, upon full consultation and mature deliberation, recommend to you that the design be dropped until we can learn the will of the Assembly now sitting.'

What Todd and Logan really wished was to get the Assembly to order new forts built by General Clark for the special protection of their counties, but without their assistance. The building of the fort at the mouth of the Kentucky was dropped; no fort there was ever built; of far greater moment, no protective campaign was undertaken. The savages, finding little to gain or fear from the discordant Kentuckians, became more alarmingly aggressive. At the very time General Clark was appealing to the county officers for coöperation against them, the northwestern Indians were on the warpath; and the brunt of their attack was borne by Jefferson County. Within a week after Logan and Todd wrote their letter, Colonel Floyd, while patrolling with a scouting party near the Falls, wrote this hurried note to General Clark:

Friday 14th ½ past 10 o'clock [*September* 14, 1781.]

Dear General: —

I have this minute returned from a little excursion against the enemy, and my party, 27 in number, are all dispersed and cut to pieces, except 9 who came off the field, with Capt. Asturgus mortally wounded, and one other slightly wounded. ...I don't know yet who are killed. W. Ravenscroft was taken prisoner by [near] me. A party was defeated yesterday near the same place and many women and children wounded. I want satisfaction. Do send me 100 men, — which number, with what I can raise, will do. The militia have no good powder; do send some.

Yours &c &c   JOHN FLOYD [1]

I cant write; guess at the rest.

[1] *Draper MSS.* 51 J 89; *Illinois Historical Collections*, VIII, 604.

Thirteen men were killed in this encounter. Two weeks later Floyd wrote: 'I believe upwards of thirty persons have been killed and captured in this county since I wrote you the other day.' This loss, with the killed he had previously mentioned, was over a fifth of all the militiamen of Jefferson County.

Disappointed in his efforts to get help from Fayette and Lincoln, for either expedition or fort building, General Clark was also deeply hurt at this time by a resolution of the Virginia Assembly 'to call to account certain officers and others in the western country' for 'waste and misapplication of public property.' As he had been in chief command and presumably responsible for any such abuses, and as no particular persons were named in the resolution, he naturally thought it was aimed at him; and his feelings may be conceived. He had devoted almost his whole young manhood to the state's service, and as he said, 'been at uncommon pains' to save her expense; and the resolution cut him to the quick.[1] He sent Major Crittenden [2] to Richmond with a resignation of his command and a letter to the governor, saying:

'All hopes of enterprise in this department are totally laid aside this campaign. However great the disappointment may be to me, I could wish it to center there, and the effects not so generally felt; as I am sure they will be if some speedy and spirited step is not taken.

[1] Colonel Davies, the war secretary of the new governor, Benjamin Harrison, had written Clark previously: 'Some of the inferior officers, in their detached commands through that extensive country, have, I fear, taken advantage of their remote situation from your immediate presence and suffered the most ruinous waste and abuses to take place.' (*Draper MSS.* 52 J 14.) In reply Clark wrote: 'In a department where business hath been as Various and Extensive as this hath, there can be no Doubt of many Errors being committed, many hath been detected. But by Report I believe there is more noise made about it than is necessary, principally originating from the little men that is sometimes sent to government from this quarter. [Who these 'little men' were will appear presently.] Jealous of their importance, [they] Embrace that declamatory principal, so very agreeable to such bodies, supposing by striking at the principal characters of their Country, that Strangers will View them as men of consequence. The Credit that is given to such characters near the helm of affairs, I can assure you Sir, hurts the Interest of the State generally. The expenses in this department hath been considerable, but had it not been for them, and the consequential service, we should have been obliged before this to have spent five times as much in the defense of our frontiers, and, Except some Expenses that have proved unnecessary, as a citizen I am satisfied with the proprietary of the Whole.

'Accounts have been long prepared for settlement, but I doubt the arrival of Auditors. I have examin'd nearly the whole, and Expect to finish the Remainder on my Return to Fort Nelson.' (*Virginia Calendar State Papers*, III, 347.)

[2] Father of John J. Crittenden, U.S. Senator and author of the famous 'Crittenden Compromise' of the slavery issue.

...An expedition against the Shawnees would avail little, ...and appears trifling when compared with the other [against Detroit], in the execution of which my very soul was wrapt, as leading to others of equal importance. ...

'Two thirds of those [Indians] formerly in our interest have already taken the hatchet this spring. ... Kentucky, without succors, with the addition of two or three thousand warriors let loose upon them, with all the assistance that can be given them by the British, must inevitably fall a sacrifice, except strongly fortified. If the mischief were to centre here, the consequences might not be so alarming; but other parts of our country will feel the effects.' Clark then again urged an expedition against the Indians and said: 'To enable you the better to lay your plans, I have sent Major Crittenden to wait on you. ...I have lost the object that was one of the principal inducements to my fatigues and transactions for several years past. My claim appears to have run out. I find myself enclosed with a few troops in a trifling fort, and shortly expect to hear the insults of those who have, for several years, been in continual dread of me.'[1]

The enemies whose insults he expected were the separate-state conspirators, instigated by the 'Philadelphia gentry,' as he called the Vandalia and Indiana promoters.

In a second letter to Governor Harrison he said:

'I find nothing more in our power at present than to endeavor to keep possession of St. Vincennes the ensuing winter. From *political* views that, with this post, will require all our troops to garrison.[2] I shall arrange everything in this department to the best advantage and wait with impatience for an answer from your Excellency [about the resignation] which I expect within fifty days. If my services are any longer necessary to my country I shall yet take pleasure in doing that you should order or recommend. If not, I should be glad [to know] how soon I was at liberty. But Sir I must again most earnestly recommend it to you to put an army into some part of the enemies country as early as possible, — not from any private views or hopes of my own, — I feel for the distresses I know to be hovering over our frontiers. Cap[t] Rob[t] Todd is appointed paymaster to our Regiment. They have received no pay for several years. I hope your Excellency will be favorable & furnish him with money for that. purpose.'[3]

While Crittenden was on his way to the governor with

---

[1] October 1, 1781. *Illinois Historical Collections*, VIII, 605; *Draper MSS.* 14 S 64.

[2] Here again Clark refers to the importance of *possession* of the northwest country in the expected peace negotiations which would determine whether that region would be American or British. His letters repeatedly show him fully alive to it. In the previous letter he had referred to the danger of the British 'regaining the Illinois,' and said 'many other reasons might be offered for the expedition besides allusion to the terms of peace.'

[3] *Draper MSS.* 14 S 71.

Clark's resignation and letters, so also was a letter from Todd to the governor.[1] Todd tried to justify his and Logan's refusal to aid in building the fort they had demanded, attacked General Clark's military policy in maintaining his one fort at the Falls, and recommended three others higher up the Ohio at the mouth of the Kentucky, Licking and Limestone. Logan went as a delegate from Kentucky to the Assembly, and at Richmond no doubt supported Todd's recommendations. He also had written to Governor Harrison, saying:

'As to the present distresst situation of this County I shall say but little about it, as it appears the conducting of the war in this Western County is invested in General Clarck, who I expect hath give you every necessary intelligence. If some method is not fell upon Early the ensueing Spring to repel the enemy, I hope your Excellency & the Honorable Councill will grant me the liberty & send me instructions to raise two companies of light Horse for defense of this county.' [2]

Logan did not wish these new troops put under Clark's command for the general defense, but under his own command, solely for the defense of Lincoln. From this time opposition to Clark by militia officers of that county and Fayette became most bitter.

Governor Harrison referred to the Assembly the appeal of the Illinois Regiment officers for an expedition and the letters of Clark and Todd. A committee reported that it had conferred with Major Crittenden and was warned 'that the country of Kentucky is in the greatest danger of being annoyed, if not totally subjugated, by the British and Indians from Detroit, and the tribes between that post and the Ohio, if an expedition is not carried on against them'; but, the committee said, it 'appeared from concurrent opinions of other persons acquainted with the country, [no doubt Todd was one and Logan another] [3] that it might be defended by... garrisons at the following posts; — the Falls of Ohio; the mouth of the Kentucky river, the mouth of Licking Creek, and the mouth of Limestone Creek; that the defense of these posts would require six or seven hundred men and two gun boats at each... which might be manned from the respective

[1] *Virginia State Library, Illinois Papers* (loose).
[2] *Virginia Calendar State Papers*, II, 665.

[3] Two other bitter enemies of Clark were members of the Assembly from Kentucky — John May and Captain Isaac Hite, Jr.

garrisons.'[1] Thereupon the Assembly *'resolved*, that the proposed expedition against Detroit ought not for the present to be attempted, [but] that some plan of defense ought to be adopted for the security of the inhabitants of this state residing in Kentucky, and that the Executive do, from time to time, take such measures for that purpose as circumstances may admit.'[2] This was mere evasion of its own responsibility by the Assembly, and an attempt to shift it upon the governor, but Governor Harrison declined it. He was ever singularly sensitive to blame and most cautious to avoid being held responsible for any misadventure. He knew the desperate plight of the Kentucky people and how little he had done to save them, and probably feared he would be held accountable for any disaster they might suffer. Thereupon the Assembly itself ordered General Clark to erect the three forts, but it neither gave nor proposed giving any help in money, men, or supplies. How the forts were to be manned by six or seven hundred men, when he did not have a fifth of that number; or with whose money or credit they were to be built; or how the six gunboats were to be built, equipped or manned, the Assembly did not indicate.

In accordance with the resolution, Harrison ordered Clark to 'act entirely on the defensive for the present'; but in order 'to secure the country,' directed him to 'strengthen and garrison the following posts, viz: the Falls of Ohio, the mouth of Kentucky river, the mouth of Licking Creek, the mouth of Limestone Creek to effect which [he was] authorized to call on the three counties of Jefferson, Lincoln and Fayette immediately for as many men as will make up, with his Regulars, a body of *three hundred and four*, rank and file, properly officered.'[3]

Apparently the Governor assumed that all General Clark had to do, to get these three hundred and four men, was to call on the three counties for them. He did not explain how, if the *three* new forts ordered 'would require six or seven hundred men,' Clark was to garrison them and the Falls fort also with only three hundred and four. Harrison then said: 'The unfortunate situation of the country in money matters and the deranged State of our Finances put it, for the present, out of

---

[1] Virginia State Library, *Journal House of Delegates*, Dec. 11, 1781.
[2] *Id.*
[3] *Draper MSS.* 51 J 100.

our power to furnish the General with a shilling of money, either for carrying on his Operations, or for discharging his old debts,' meaning the state's debts Clark had become personally bound to pay. Such were the impossible demands upon the young general, and such the support given him by the state. Soon afterward Harrison wrote him about his tendered resignation, saying:

'Major Crittenden delivered a verbal message to the Board from you respecting the resolution of the last Assembly. It was a matter of great surprise to us, as we could not conceive how Gen. Clark could take that resolution as aimed at him, whose character has ever stood unimpeached. You must be sensible that great abuses have been committed and that it was necessary to bring offenders to public justice. At such only the resolution points. I have my hopes that on cooler reflection you will think with me & have no more unhappy moments on that subject. A resignation at this time would be extremely injurious to the state inasmuch as it would throw the whole back country into confusion & perhaps occasion its loss; the thought of which will, I am sure, induce you, if you have [not] done it already, to lay aside your resentment. ...I have now, Sir, only to assure you that I have the highest confidence in you.'[1]

Harrison also said: 'The plan of the gunboats I very much approve. They will certainly render essential service.' He refers to Clark's plan for the state to build and arm four large and swift 'row-galleys' to patrol the Ohio above the Falls and shield Fayette and Lincoln from Indian attack, and make the upper river safe for travel.

On receiving the Governor's conciliatory letter, General Clark replied:

'I am satisfied concerning the verbal message alluded to in yours, finding that [the Assembly resolution] was not aimed at me. I wish those who see the resolution may not think so, as it's known that most public transactions in the Western Depart'mt pass'd through my hands. Such an idea must be painful to me, well knowing the Exertions I have used to save the public monies. Abuses have taken place, and I ardently wish for the arrival of the Auditors to adjust the accounts. Examples are not wanting, which would have taken place before this time had I not put the Construction I did on the resolution. What hurt me was the idea I had of its being so pointed. Not but what I think it the duty of government to call all persons to account for their conduct. I hope it will always do me credit, and I shall be careful that no person that comes under my notice go without their deserts, if in my power.

[1] *Draper MSS.* 51 J 101.

'The repeated disappointments I have met from government occasion me to enter on the business you propose with some regret, but shall lay aside every reflection and commence anew. But in what manner to conduct myself, I am really at a loss to determine, [being] without either money or credit; and the saleable public property I have on hand such that I cannot spare without a probability of getting it replaced, which I do not yet discover.

'We are reduced to the necessity of a defensive war and wish to be able to repel those [Indians] I expect we shall have to contend with. If we are fortunate this Spring, a small reenforcement and a few supplies may Enable us, perhaps, to turn the scale on them after harvest. The post of Licking will be immediately Established and others as soon as circumstances will permit. [He did not foresee that his calls on Fayette and Lincoln for help, though now authorized, would be disobeyed.] Pray give me all the Immediate assistance in your power. Hostilities have already commenced, and I wish the predictions in my last to you may not come to pass. This year you may Rely on it that every Exertion will be made, and I hope such as will answer the purpose; but our circumstances at present are such that it's impossible to give a just idea of what will be done.'[1]

Clark's only available fund was a fast dwindling supply of flour, bought at Pittsburgh for the Detroit expedition. By selling part of this, he was able for a time to give his men a scanty support and do something toward strengthening the Falls fort; but seeing that the flour supply must be replenished, or the fort abandoned, he bought of a trader seventy thousand pounds additional, giving his own bond for the price (something over $6000, *specie*), and to secure payment mortgaged — and lost — three thousand five hundred acres of his best remaining lands.[2]

He next requested that the 'specific' taxes from the three Kentucky counties be applied to meet his needs.[3] The Assembly was willing, but by a blunder ordered only those from Fayette to be so used. He promptly called attention to the mistake, but such was the inattention of the Richmond officials to western affairs that a whole year passed before the error was corrected. Meantime he was powerless to build the forts, for he had no authority to call for specific taxes from Lincoln or Jefferson, and the people of Fayette would resist being alone required to deliver them.

[1] *Virginia Calendar State Papers*, III, 68.
[2] *Draper MSS.* 52 J 53; *id.*, 61.

[3] *Virginia State Library* (part omitted from Clark's letter to Governor in *Virginia Calendar State Papers*, III, 347).

CHAPTER XVIII

IN THE EAST, PEACE: IN THE WEST, WAR

IN view of the straits of Virginia's western people and troops, it may seem strange that the British did not recover the country north of the Ohio; but Great Britain also was financially unable to carry on offensive operations. Like winded game-cocks, the enemies faced each other without strength to renew the struggle; and so they remained until at last the British abandoned the disputed field forever.

It is important here to understand that Clark and his men rendered a most important service in the general war for independence by aiding to force Great Britain to financial exhaustion. Her whole western war was mainly waged by her Indian allies, and the burden upon the British treasury was very heavy. General Haldemand was constantly complaining of the enormous outlays of Hamilton and his successors to supply the Indians with arms, powder, lead, food, blankets, and liquor. When the Americans suddenly appeared in their midst, these outlays were of necessity greatly increased. The urgent demands for more troops, more supplies, and, on the other hand, the reluctant but unavoidable acquiescence of the commander-in-chief, told one of the most significant stories of the Revolution. The diplomatic correspondence leading to the treaty of peace shows plainly that Great Britain lost the war by sheer lack of money; and that was in large measure due to her expensive Indian warfare in the west. The carriage of every pound of supplies from Quebec or Montreal to the distant British posts and scattered Indian towns multiplied many times its original cost; for transportation up the rivers and lakes and over land was laborious and dangerous, and had to be paid for accordingly. The British official reports show a great number of lake transports — pirogues, batteaux, and larger vessels — carrying not only supplies for the British garrisons, but astonishing amounts for the savages. Throughout the war Indian bands — sometimes numbering only a score or less, at others many hundreds — were fitted out and sent in rapid succession against Clark's men on the Mississippi,

Wabash, and Ohio and against the Kentucky settlements and inner frontiers.[1]

After Cornwallis' surrender, in October, 1781, the British gave up hope of subjugating America, and ceased active military operations; but the case was far different with their savage allies, who became more belligerent than before. They learned that Virginia had forbidden offensive expeditions against them; attributed this to fear; and, feeling that their homes were safe, felt free to attack those of the whites across the Ohio. They learned, too, of the coming peace, and knew that if they were to save their homes and hunting grounds from the land-grasping Americans, they must strike them before losing their British allies. Nor were they nearly so impoverished by warfare as the western Americans. Their needs were few; the British at Detroit still supplied them with guns and ammunition; the wilderness furnished them game, clothing, vegetable foods, and fuel; the streams yielded them

---

[1] The outlays of the British were great even before Clark's disconcerting movements compelled more hurried and wasteful efforts to meet his expected attacks. Thus, the British Military Inspector wrote: 'The meeting of the Indians in December 1777 cost the British government £14,000, besides presents sent by Sir Guy Carleton, to the amount, as I am informed, of £20,000 more, New York Currency, — rum and ration not included.' (*Michigan Pioneer Collections*, IX, 371.) The official British reports show that at Detroit alone eighteen great councils with the Indians were held, and many others were held elsewhere. In July 1778, Hamilton's Indian Agent there, Major Hay, wrote that 'five thousand souls [Indians] will be dependent for their support on this place.' (*Id.*, 441.)

Besides supplies sent up the lakes — many of them imported from England — great quantities were bought from traders at the western posts. At one time Haldemand wrote De Peyster: 'The very enormous expense attending the purchase of Indian presents at the several Posts in the Upper Country, owing to the avidity of the traders who supply them, has determined me to attempt a diminution of it by supplying them from England.' (*Id.*, x, 393.) But the remedy was of no avail. The unavoidable cost of carriage and the great number of savages to be supplied necessarily made the burden immense. Plan as they would, in that day of slow and costly transportation the British found it ruinously expensive to conduct a war against an alert enemy in a wilderness some five thousand miles from England and a thousand or more from their Canadian base at Quebec. In addition to costly supplies for his troops and Indians, Governor Hamilton, in the one year 1778, received in money drafts £79,195, New York currency. (*Id.*, xx, 94.) During the war he and successors at Detroit received in such drafts £433,898, while the commandants at Mackinac received £637,976, making a total for those two posts of £806,901, which was then a very great sum, although only a fraction of the actual cost of the Western war. (*Id.*)

On the American side, Clark, with only £1200 of Virginia paper money and a few boats and supplies, set out on his expedition against Kaskaskia, captured the Illinois towns, and won over Vincennes without receiving another penny or pound of supplies from the Virginia government. His men were fed, clothed, and armed for their future achievements partly by the French enemies he had converted into friends, partly by Oliver Pollock, and in much larger part by the advances and bonds of Clark himself, and his officers.

fish; and, now that the Big Knives were forbidden to invade their country, they were free to hunt, fish, and grow their needed crops undisturbed. So, while Virginia's people east of the mountains suffered greatly from poverty and disordered government, her western people, after Cornwallis surrendered, not only suffered far more from those ills, but were also subjected to dreadful savage war. This difference cannot be ignored in judging how far her western citizens had just cause to complain that they were left to bear the brunt of the war.

Virginia still claimed they were her citizens and claimed their country. The war was her war — not theirs only; and the duty to serve in it and furnish means to carry it on was no more the burden of her western than of her eastern citizens. Yet when Virginia's western people implored help from the east they were told there was no money in the state treasury. All through history, however, states without money in their treasuries have managed to carry on wars by impressing the properties of their citizens; and this the western people thought should have been done in the eastern counties. True, many there were in want and rags, but others had considerable means and some even wealth that could have been levied on to equip and support the five or six hundred needed troops. The occasion plainly called for earnest appeals by Governor Harrison and the Assembly for voluntary contributions and service, and for extreme measures of taxation; but no such appeals were made and no such measures taken.

The fault, however, was that of the state's government rather than of its eastern people, whose psychology must be allowed for as well as their distress. They were simply too harassed by their own serious troubles to realize the far more dreadful straits of their distant kinsmen, or their own duty to make greater sacrifice to relieve them. It would be most unjust to assume that they were aware of both, but remained callously unconcerned. On the contrary, had their sympathy been strongly appealed to, and their duty to serve and contribute of their means been clearly presented to them, the state government could no doubt have secured the needed supplies and men, and also gained public support for necessary additional taxation. Indeed, the state treasury undoubtedly received from taxes many times more than would have sufficed to relieve the western situation, but expended its funds for other and far less imperative purposes.[1]

Without a dollar of state money to pay for expresses to Richmond, General Clark had repeatedly managed to send them to warn the governor of a powerful impending attack at the Falls fort, and plead for aid; but always there was the same response — no help! Governor Harrison wrote him that Kentucky would have 'nothing to depend upon for the present, but the virtue of the people. That has been tryed with Success on many Occasions & I hope may be again, when they are informed that the Assembly are closely engaged on the subject of Finance and they mean to do justice to the public creditors.'[2] In other words, Virginia's western people and Clark's handful of troops were to bear the whole brunt of the state's war without present aid from the state government, and with only a general promise of help in the future — a promise which time and again had been made them only to be broken.[3]

The state's treatment of her western state creditors at this time was a constant source of irritation. Few of them were promptly paid; few indeed were ever paid. At first they were usually put off because funds were lacking, but they fared much worse after the Virginia assembly offer to cede Congress the country north of the Ohio on condition that Congress should reimburse Virginia its expenses and liabilities incurred in conquering and holding it. As Congress was known, however, to be little inclined to paying its debts, it was feared that it would evade reimbursing Virginia fairly unless she could

[1] The state's failure to aid her hard-pressed western people and to pay her western creditors is not flattering to Virginia's state pride, and it has generally been shunned by Virginia historians. It probably explains the fact that, with few exceptions, they have generally ignored Clark's patriotic services and sacrifices for his state, and failed to give him the place he undeniably earned in the unrivalled galaxy of her great men of the Revolutionary era.

[2] *Draper MSS.* 51 J 101; Virginia State Library, *Governor's Letter Book.*

[3] To another of General Clark's appeals for immediate assistance, the governor replied: 'Our circumstances as to money matters are as wretched as they were when I wrote you by Major Crittenden, and will continue so until fall, when, I hope, our prospects will brighten greatly. I am glad to hear the people are pleased that government intend to be punctual in their money engagements. If they give credit to it, why are you in want of necessaries? A moment's reflection would show them that it was much more to their advantage to wait a few months for payment, and then receive hard money, than to receive trash immediately.' (March 24, 1782, *Draper MSS.* 52 J 11.) Apparently Governor Harrison would not see that they no longer had any confidence in promises from the state of hard money, or anything else.

support every item of her claim with an unimpeachable voucher. To guard against this a commission, headed by Colonel William Fleming, was ordered to go west to secure proof and report all such outlays and liabilities, and meanwhile, payment of western military claims was virtually suspended. Nevertheless, a great number of sorely distressed creditors implored immediate payment, and many went to Richmond to demand it. The governor and assemblymen were so beset by them that they came to look upon the whole brood of western claims as nuisances to be shunned. Referring to them in a message to the assembly, Governor Harrison said:

'[They] must rest till we get a report from the Commissioners sent into the Western Country. This may be expected early in the Spring, when I shall be surrounded by Clamourous Creditors who have long been kept out of their Money, and who will lose all patience if they are not paid as soon as they produce certificates of the balances that are justly due.

'I cannot inform the Assembly with any accuracy what sum the demands may amount to, tho' I have some reason to think they will not fall short of four or five Hundred Thousand Specie Dollars. The rage of Conquests, ill planned Expeditions, & too great Confidence in Men seem to have brought this enormous debt on the State.'[1]

Even when western military claims were adjusted and approved by Colonel Fleming's commission, the state government generally delayed and ultimately refused to pay them.

It was over a year before the commissioners reached Kentucky where, amidst all the dangers and distractions of savage war, their investigations were subject to almost interminable interruptions and delays. Indeed, they were never completed, although many successive commissions were appointed for the purpose.[2]

The commissioners were instructed to demand original vouchers from all disbursing officers, with clear proof of every

---

[1] Virginia State Library, *Governor's Letter Book*, 196. This reference to 'ill planned expeditions' was manifestly a hit at Jefferson and Clark.

[2] With the best of intentions each of these succeeding commissions tangled the western military accounts. Unfamiliar with the voluminous and incomplete papers of its predecessors, each usually attempted to rearrange the vouchers and restate the accounts, until all became inextricably confused. Historians who have referred to them have been generally misled into gross errors. Thus Oliver Pollock's advancements to Clark have been many times multiplied by writers who supposed Pollock's advancements to Virginia and Congress were made to Clark, and assumed that Pollock paid bills drawn by Clark which in fact were never paid.

item of outlay; but to produce these was often impossible. Military supplies during four years of war were necessarily purchased in many places, and by many different men — often by barter; often hastily in time of great danger; sometimes by men who could hardly write, or find paper and ink wherewith to write. The commissioners found it impossible to collect complete vouchers from soldiers scattered through a vast territory and fully occupied with the imperative demands of war. Some had died, many could not be found; some of the disbursing officers, for want of more competent ones, were wholly ignorant of correct accounting, though none more skillful or brave in war. Some were suspected of dishonesty, because their accounts were unintelligible or incomplete and they could not produce proper vouchers — others because sheer necessity had forced them to draw bills on the state for what seemed exorbitant prices. Peculation, it should be said, however, was comparatively rare, and was usually confined to men of the non-combatant trader class, some of whom had been employed to secure military supplies.

Most of the officers — nothing daunted by the failure of the state to pay for their services, or even to repay their money outlays in her behalf — and many of their French friends, personally endorsed the state bills, or gave their personal bonds to procure supplies for the troops. Few of them were ever relieved of these obligations, or reimbursed either by the state, or the United States, which later undertook to pay them. Shannon, Helm, Father Gibault, Cerré, Montgomery, Vigo, Bosseron, LeGras, Linctot, McCarty, Floyd, and many others were thus sorely embarrassed or ruined. When the holders of claims on the state presented them at Richmond (sometimes after journeying five hundred or a thousand miles, and after long months of weary waiting), they were oftenest referred to the roving commission of western accounts in some unknown part of the great west.

The Virginia Assembly was not only loath to use any of the state's revenues to pay debts contracted in the western war, but conveniently assumed that Virginia's obligation to pay them had been shifted upon Congress by her unaccepted offer to cede the region north of the Ohio on condition of reimbursement. Far worse, it was assumed that her offer to cede that country relieved the state of her duty to protect, or even govern, her citizens there. In December 1781 the Assembly deliberately allowed the act for the government of the County of Illinois to expire and refused to renew it, notwithstanding the French inhabitants there, when they became citizens of Virginia, had received her solemn promise of protection and just government. Of all people, they knew least of self-government and were least qualified to establish one; yet they were left without laws, or any legislature to make them; without peace officers to preserve order, without judges to punish crime; and cruel misrule by the conscienceless strong followed. The French applied to Clark as their ever trusted friend, and he did all he could to help them; but he could do no more than represent their distress and needs to the state government and urge their relief, and his appeals were unheeded.[1]

In Kentucky also, in 1782, government was almost hopelessly disordered, for the land company emissaries had for two years been active in stirring up disaffection. General Clark wrote Governor Harrison (May 2, 1782):

'By the exertion of many of the principal officers of the country, that deserve credit, we are like to reduce the people to subordination, — in short they begin to suspect those that first confused them as their greatest enemies. I believe in a short time it will be dangerous for a man to speak of a new Government in this Quarter, except among a small party of blackguards. The body of the people now seem to be alarmed for fear Virginia will give up their interest — [that is, cede Kentucky to Congress.] ...If the country can be saved from the impending blow, a remembrance of our past anxiety and trouble will give pleasure.'[2]

Clark was soon to learn that this apparent suppression of the new-state conspirators was only temporary, for opposition to Virginia and to his own authority was but approaching its height.[3] Only four days after he wrote this letter, the controversy in Congress over the western country reached its culmi-

---

[1] Alvord says: 'neither at this time [1778] nor later, when there was most just cause to criticize the military force, did the French utter a word of complaint against him, for he had won not only their esteem but their affection, so that they never held him responsible for the evils that crowded upon them.' (*Illinois Historical Collections*, II, XLIX.) The treatment of the French of the Illinois and Wabash by the United States after it acquired the Northwest Territory in 1784 (both before and under the Ordinance of 1787) makes one of the darkest chapters in American history.

[2] *Virginia Calendar State Papers*, III, 150.

[3] *Id.* III, 555.

nation, and a dramatic one. A packed committee made a report on the several western state claims, and also the claims of the Indiana and Vandalia Companies to West Virginia and eastern Kentucky. Had the report been written by the promoters themselves, it could not have met their desires more fully. It rejected Virginia's claim and recommended that her cession of the region north of the Ohio be rejected; it upheld the fictitious title of the Six Nation Indians to the whole disputed western region; it upheld the claim set up for New York, and recommended that Congress accept the pretended cession from that state; and finally it upheld the Six Nations grant to the Indiana Company of a great part of West Virginia.

The report did not openly recommend that Congress should recognize the validity of the Vandalia Company's claim to all the rest of West Virginia and all of Kentucky east of the Kentucky River; but it did so covertly. The committee said it would be

'incompatible with the interests, government, and policy of these United States to permit such immoderate and extravagant grants of land to be vested in individual citizens,' [but it was careful to add:] 'In order to do the strictest justice to such of the said Vandalia Company as are and shall remain citizens of these United States, the committee recommends payment to them of their full shares and proportions of all their purchase money, expenses and charges accrued on said lands, by distinct and separate grants out of the Vandalia lands, to the full amount thereof.' [1]

The enormous 'expenses and charges' these grasping American promoters of the Vandalia Company would have claimed on account of their long course of political corruption in London and America can be imagined; and no one could have disproved the correctness of their figures. In all probability they would not only have got their own 'full shares,' but also the shares of their deserted British associates, and by 'grants out of the Vandalia lands' have become lordly proprietors of nearly all the good lands of West Virginia and a third of all Kentucky.

When the western people were told that without their consent they were to be torn from Virginia and made territorial subjects of Congress; that their Virginia land grants were to be treated as void; that West Virginia and all Kentucky east

[1] (*Journal Continental Congress; Old Journal of Congress*, VII, 263.)

of the Kentucky River were to be given to the land companies, and all the rest of the western country treated as the common property of all the states, their indignation may be imagined. They had got their land grants from Virginia under the firm belief that they were within her charter bounds; under this belief they had dared the wilderness, cleared the land, and made their homes; unassisted, and even impeded by the northern states and Congress, they had held the country against the British and Indians; they had known no other government than Virginia's; and to have their homes wrested from them and themselves subjected to the rule of a discredited Congress and for the benefit of the northern states and 'land jobbers' could hardly fail to provoke resistance.

A flood of protests poured upon the Virginia Assembly. One only will be quoted here, because the most significant. This was a memorial from Kentucky, signed by most of the leading military men there including General Clark, Major Crittenden, Captains Helm, Chapline, Williams, Brashear, Baily, and George, by Daniel Boone, Squire Boone, Bland Ballard, and some seventy-odd others. They said that they

'have been greatly alarmed at finding that Congress has not only refused the cession offered them [of the region northwest of the Ohio]...but a committee of that august body, appointed for the purpose, is prejudicing the public against the claim of Virginia and to prepare your memorialists for paying twenty pounds sterling for their own lands!

'Your memorialists do conceive, from the spirit of the Constitution of America, that if the country they possess does not of right belong to Virginia, the property of course must be vested in themselves, and that Congress has no right to any part thereof; and when your Memorialists, through your Honorable House, make a request to Congress for a new state and to be received into the Union, they are then, and not before, subjects of another state. ...

'What your memorialists at present wish is Virginia's protection to them, as part of the state entitled to its privileges, or an information what they may expect. Justice is what they claim, and what the equity of their pretensions will allow them. They view themselves as Virginians, and they hope, as such, what is alluded to will not be given up without their consent. They also know that it is through them, and those they claim as citizens of their detached country, that the greatest part of the western waters [country] is not now in possession of their most inveterate enemies, and could easily prove the importance they have been to the United States.' [1]

[1] This paragraph bears the unmistakable earmarks of Clark's authorship.   (*Virginia State Library*, 'Kentucky Petitions,' B 438, l.f.)

Had the congressional committee's report been adopted and Kentucky abandoned by Virginia, Congress and the land companies would have found the imposition of a new government on the Kentuckians and taking their lands from them an exceedingly expensive and doubtful undertaking. Amongst themselves they were bitterly discordant, but in resistance of this great wrong they would probably have united to a man, except a few new-state confederates of the land companies. Although General Clark had once reluctantly withdrawn his resignation of command, he now renewed it, saying: 'The following is a request I make of your Excellency, which is to be relieved from this department. My reason for this...must be obvious to you and so reasonable that I hope it will meet with your approval.'[1] His reason, as he afterward explained, was that he wanted to be free to oppose the appropriation of Kentucky by Congress.

The report of the packed Congressional committee was not adopted, however, for while it was under consideration a startling *dénouement* came. Mr. Lee of Virginia, seconded by his colleague Mr. Bland, moved Congress 'that previous to any determination relative to the cessions of the western lands, the name of each member present be called by the secretary; that, on such call, each member do declare, upon his honor, whether he is, or is not, personally interested, directly or indirectly, in the claims of any company, or companies which have petitioned against the territorial rights of any one of the states, and that such declaration be entered on the Journal.'[2]

This motion caused panic amongst the delegates favoring the land company scheme; it killed the committee report! 'The members were not willing to stand the searching inquisition of this motion. It was parried and the report of the committee postponed from time to time until May 6th, when it was postponed indefinitely.'[3] Motion after motion was made by the Virginia delegates to force Congress to act on it, but in vain. They could never bring the land-scheme advocates to meet the honor test, and the efforts of the promoters to use Congress for their nefarious purposes ended. Thereafter they

[1] *Virginia Calendar State Papers*, III, 216.
[2] *Life of Patrick Henry* (W. W. Henry), II, 92 *et seq.*; *Journal Continental Congress* XVII, 808 *et seq.*
[3] *Life of Patrick Henry* (Henry), II, 92-93; *Journal Continental Congress*.

mainly directed their activities to stirring up opposition to Virginia in West Virginia and Kentucky.[1]

[1] Hinsdale, in his *Old Northwest* (224) makes no mention of this pregnant motion to uncover the methods of the land company promoters, but closes his discussion of the committee report by saying: 'To follow it through the Journal is a wearisome undertaking, especially as the land issue soon became complicated with other subjects, as the national finances.' For the very reason, however, that the land issue did become complicated with the national finances — and it was complicated with other no less fundamental public concerns — it is necessary to pursue the subject if we are to understand our history. Winsor, in his *Western Movement* (200) makes no mention whatever of Lee's searching and effective motion, but simply says: 'The report as a whole was never acted upon, since it was seen that the cession movement could get on better without such friction' as would ensue from attempting to enforce its approval.

CHAPTER XIX

INSUBORDINATION AND THE BLUE LICKS DISASTER

REVERTING to military affairs in Kentucky in 1782, General Clark wrote Governor Harrison:

'We have received very alarming accounts from the enemy at Detroit. They last fall collected chiefs from the different hostile tribes of the Indians and instructed them not to disturb the frontiers, and particularly Kentucky, until towards spring, — until then to form small parties and take prisoners to hear what was going on, by which conduct the whole country would be off their guard: that the whole would embody in the spring, reduce this post, and lay the whole country waste, and make one stroke do for all. They are actually making every preparation at Detroit, and the conduct of the Indians has been agreeable to their directions. This information, through various channels from the Illinois, cannot be doubted.'[1]

A month later Colonel Floyd wrote imploring aid from the Governor and Assembly, and said the enemy's design to attack the Falls (Fort Nelson) was

'so well authenticated that it cannot be doubted. ... Our whole strength at this time [in Jefferson County] is three hundred and seventy men, who, according to the best calculations I can make, have about eight hundred and fifty helpless women and children to take care of, and [are] very generally deprived of every possible means of removing back to the settlement. ...

'One fourth of the militia is called for by Gen[l] Clark, for the purpose of fortifying the fort against a siege; but from the immediate danger in which everyone conceives his own family, the authority of militia officers, at such a distance from government, grows every day weaker and weaker; and the new-invented ideas of a separate state, — calculated on purpose for disaffection and an evasion of duty, — are so many causes to retard the necessary business and seem to threaten us on all sides with anarchy, confusion, and I may add, Destruction.

'But even to suppose that the works can be completed before the arrival of the enemy, it is then impossible that Gen Clark, with the inconsiderable number of troops he now has, can defend it; and a dependence on Militia, scattered over three extensive counties, under the circumstances before mentioned, is depending upon a very great uncertainty.'[2]

[1] *Virginia Calendar State Papers*, III, 87.

[2] *Id.*, III, 121.

Again, May 2nd, Clark sent an express to the Governor
telling him: 'The apprehensions of the designs of the Detroit
Gentry on this country is reduced to a certainty. They have
their eyes on this post. ...If they carry their point, its consequence is obvious.'[1]

These appeals brought no help, and since fort building was
impossible and offensive expeditions prohibited, Clark's only
weapon was diplomacy. Considering the pitiful weakness of
his little force, the success of his maneuvers was surprising.
With the aid of leading Frenchmen and the friendly Piankeshaws, he kept up a constant flow of misleading reports
amongst the enemy Indians, and made them and the British
believe he had a powerful army about to march against Detroit. Thus, the British commander there wrote: 'Two thousand French troops are destined for Detroit, as early as possible, to take the route of the Falls of Ohio. It would be highly necessary, if you can spare two or three companies of Rangers,
that they were sent early, in order to keep up the drooping
spirit of the Indians. At all events Mr. Clarke will enter the
Shawnese Country with a larger body than ever.'[2]

General Clark also builded great hopes upon his proposed
little pioneer navy — armed rowboats, larger and swifter than
anything afloat on the river and able to run down and destroy
an enemy craft. They offered several advantages over forts
for the protection of the people of Fayette, since they could
be built under the protection of the Falls garrison, could be
placed anywhere a fort could be built, would fully serve the
same purpose, yet could be moved rapidly to any point on the
river where the Indians were expected to cross for attack or retreat. He wrote the Governor: 'Our greatest dependence is in
armed boats, but cannot fit out a sufficiency of them in time
without the supplies you promis[d], and those mentioned in my
last, arriving in time. If it was possible for the troops, with
those articles, to arrive some time in April, I should be under
no kind of apprehension of their doing much damage to the
country; but without [them] the consequences are to be
dreaded. Pray Sir be as liberal as possible in your reënforcements.'[3] No troops, however, were sent out; and almost none

[1] *Virginia Calendar State Papers*, III,
150.
[2] March 20, 1782, *Michigan Pioneer
Collections*, XX, 4.

[3] March 7, 1782, *Virginia Calendar
State Papers*, III, 87; *Draper MSS.* 11 J
17.

of the promised supplies, and they too late to do more than prevent desertion of his few remaining men.

Governor Harrison undertook to have the boats built on the upper Ohio, but 'Col. Davies, the war secretary, informs the Executive that Major Hardins is willing to supply the boats on the Ohio for Genl Clark, if the money can be furnished to pay for them;' [1] to which the governor replied: 'I am sorry to inform you we have but 4 shillings in the treasury and no means of getting any more.' [2] Failing to get the four armed boats built by the state, Clark, with Floyd's assistance, managed to build one at the Falls. Armed as well as might be (for lack of promised rigging they tried to make ropes of pawpaw fibre[3]) it was partially manned by such few men as Clark could enlist for it, or dared spare from his garrison. He wrote Harrison: 'We have...a galley on the stocks, that will be finished in about twenty days, that I think will do business. She is seventy three feet keel, calculated for navigation of the Ohio, to have forty six oars [and] one hundred and two men. One six, two fours, and a two pounder is her proposed metal. We have great dependence on the cannon you promised us arriving in time.' [4] 'Open, small boats will by no means answer the purpose of crusing on the river, as they are liable to be ambuscaded when they come near the shore, or in the narrow parts of the river; but on the galley, gunnels...play on hinges and raise her sides so high that she can lay within pistol shot of the shore without the least danger.' [5]

This war-boat — the Leviathan of our first western American navy — was sent under Captain George to the mouth of the Licking, opposite the present site of Cincinnati. There it proved thoroughly effective in preventing the savages from crossing the river anywhere near it, for they feared being trapped on the Kentucky side; but, like nearly all Clark's well-laid plans during this demoralized time, his naval one was blocked by discord. He could get no aid from the state or Kentucky militia to build or man additional boats. The armed galley was sent to the Licking for the special protection

[1] *Virginia Calendar State Papers*, III, 113; cf. Virginia State Library, '*Executive Papers Apr 1782*,' Hardin to Davies, April 25, 1782.
[2] *Virginia Calendar State Papers*, III, 133.
[3] Floyd to Clark, May 12, 1782, *Draper MSS.* 52 J 21.
[4] *Virginia Calendar State Papers*, III, 150.
[5] *Id.*, 207, 210, 214.

of Fayette and Lincoln, yet when militia from those counties were called for to make up a sufficient crew, only a small company of disgruntled men from Fayette came, commanded by a Captain Patterson. Their conduct appears from the following letter from Captain George to Colonel John Todd:

BIG BONE CREEK, *July 19th*, 1782

Sir:

I wrote you on the 12th inst. that Capt. Patterson had joined me with thirty eight Men (officers included) It is now with the greatest pain I inform you that since this party has had any Connection with us there has been nothing but murmuring and grumbling on their part. . . . First they insisted on being allowed double Ration of Flour. This was granted them; . . . then they must be allowed to march on shore and not work at the boat; . . . that was granted them, and indeed every Indulgence they could desire. . . . At last this morning they have determined to go off at all Events (although their Tour is not out this seven days.) I shall inform Gen[l] Clark of the particulars and obtain his directions; in the meantime I beg you will take the most effectual Methods of bringing those People to Justice for their mutinous and disobedient conduct.

I am sir Your most ob[t] Serv[t]

ROBERT GEORGE[1]

Col. John Todd, Co-Lieut of Fayette.

To this letter Captain George appended the following interesting entries from his journal:

'July 14th. Capt. Patterson came into the Cabin and said that unless his men were furnished with two pounds of flour, each man, per day and was allowed what beef they could kill, he would be dam'd if any man of his sho[d] stay on board. He also insisted to draw *back* rations at the same Rate, from the time his men came to the mouth of Kentucky. . . .

'July 15th. This morning Capt. Patterson & Mr. McGuire and his Lieu[t] came into the Cabin and said the Militia to a man refused to come on board; alleging that Militia could not be made Salors of, with other like excuses; and these officers declared that in their Opinion that the men would sooner fight than come on board.

'July 19th. Captain Patterson came on board this morning and said his men had gone off before day, but at 8 o'clock we discovered not less than 10 of them in the skirts of the woods on the River bank, altho Capt. Patterson said there were not left but himself, his two officers, and one spy.

'ROBERT GEORGE'[2]

By midsummer 1782 the situation of the Kentucky settlers plainly offered only two alternatives — coöperation or dis-

[1] *Draper MSS.* 52 J 25. [2] *Id.*

aster. An unprecedented force of British and northwestern Indians was collecting in the Shawnee country, under Captains Caldwell and McKee, to attack the Falls fort. McKee wrote that they had gathered 'the greatest body of Indians... that have been assembled in this quarter since the commencement of the war, and perhaps never may be in higher spirits to attack the enemy.' [1] Several small advance bands were already raiding in the Kentucky country, and Captain Estill with twenty-five men, in Fayette, had been defeated and himself slain. In this alarming situation, General Clark, notwithstanding Governor Harrison's prohibition of offensive operations, called a council of the county lieutenants to consider a counterstroke, but his proposal fell on deaf ears. Fortunately the British had been led to believe he was marching a strong army against Detroit, and therefore delayed their attack — as one of their officers said, to 'wait to see the event of Mr. Clark's expedition, should it appear to be intended against that post.' [2]

At last the enemy's blow came, and although the real objective was the Falls, the blow fell upon Fayette. It found the disorganized militia of that county, and of Lincoln also, hopelessly unready. Despite every warning of the coming invasion, not even scouting parties had been kept out to watch and report the coming of the enemy. The result was a complete surprise and a costly disaster.

Caldwell and McKee had sent Indian scouts from the Shawnee country towards the Falls to learn Clark's movements, and they reported that his army was 'assembled to come this way, and in a few days would be on their march to the Shawnee Towns.' [3] (See map, page 25.) Thereupon other scouts were sent to discover more surely in what direction this imaginary army was moving. They reported that they 'had discovered the Enemy on their march below Big Bone Lick,' on the Ohio a few miles below the mouth of the Licking. Undoubtedly they were Captain George's galley men and Patterson's unruly recruits. Other scouts reported 'that three days ago, upon crossing the Ohio near the mouth of the Big Miamies River [opposite the Licking] they again discovered a body of the enemy, whom they suppose to be an advanced party.' [4]

---

[1] *Michigan Pioneer Collections*, xx, 49.
[2] *Id.*, xx, 29.
[3] *Id.*, xx, 32; cf. *id.*, 4, 13, 27.
[4] *Id.*, xx, 32, 33.

Thereupon urgent calls for more Indians were sent out, and meanwhile McKee wrote that other scouts reported

'they had viewed the Enemy from the top of the Hill near the mouth of the Miamis, three days ago, and that they had two large boats in their front, from which two cannon were fired every evening upon coming to their camping ground, and that they also saw a number of Indians with them. [Really Captain George's half naked and sunburnt men.] They say they are the most formidable Army that has yet come into their Country, and from their appearance must intend more than attacking their Villages. The lowness of the Miami will retard their progress so much that we are in hopes we shall have time to collect ourselves. July 23d, Captain Caldwell is Just come up with the Lake Indians, but is apprehensive that the reinforcement with Capt. Brandt will not arrive in time. However, whatever force we are able to collect, we shall endeavor to keep between them and Detroit, which must undoubtedly be their object from all accounts.' [1]

This report of armed boats and Clark's great army at the mouth of the Licking greatly disconcerted the Indians and made them keep well away from that place. No fort there could have more effectually answered the purpose. Said McKee: 'When the return of the scouts from the Ohio informed us that the accounts we had received were false, this disappointment, notwithstanding all our endeavors to keep them together, occasioned them to disperse in disgust with each other.' [2] The Shawnees refused to march against Clark. 'Upwards of three hundred Hurons and Lake Indians,' however, advanced with Caldwell and McKee to a point on the Ohio some seventy miles above the Licking and opposite Limestone Creek.[3] Here, McKee said, 'we remained, — still in uncertainty with respect to the Enemy's motions, — and it was thought best from hence to send scouts to the Falls, and that the main body should advance into the enemy's country and endeavor to lead out a party from some of their forts, by which we might be able to gain some certain intelligence. Accordingly we crossed the Ohio and arrived [August 16th] at one of the Enemy's Settlements call'd Bryant's [or Bryan's] Station.' [4]

This station, it should be understood, was near the extreme southern border of Fayette County and most remote from the

[1] *Michigan Pioneer Collections*, **xx**, 33.
[2] *Id.*
[3] *Id.*, p. 49.

[4] *Id.*; *Register Kentucky State Historical Society*, vol. 24, no. 70. p. 47, January, 1926, as to name.

Indian country, being over a hundred miles march from the
Ohio where the enemy crossed. They had been allowed to
traverse, undiscovered, almost the entire breadth of the county.
Had Colonel John Todd kept out proper scouting parties, the
coming of the enemy would have been known well in advance
of their arrival, for they followed a well-known route and their
numbers made discovery sure. Perhaps he did try, but was
powerless to secure scouts; for military commands were not
only commonly, but openly disobeyed. Certain it is that the
presence of the Indians was not discovered until they had surrounded and attacked Bryant's Station, and even then their
number was grossly underestimated.

Meantime, on the night of August 15th, Colonel Levi Todd
— a colonel of the Fayette militia under his brother — having
learned that a party of men had been defeated by some
Indians on the upper Blue Lick, ordered twenty men to go
there. They started the next morning, but, about an hour
later, a hurried messenger reported the Indians at Bryant's.
He thereupon set off after his men, overtook them by twelve
o'clock the next day, and carried them to the relief of that
place — some mounted, some afoot. As they approached, the
Indians fired on them, killed two, and routed the unmounted
men, but most of the horsemen succeeded in getting into the
fort.[1]

The county lieutenant of Lincoln, Colonel Ben Logan, was
supposed to be at Harrodsburg; but his next in command,
Colonel Trigg, happened to be in Fayette, and to him Colonel
Levi Todd sent a note asking him to assemble Lincoln militiamen and come 'quick as possible to Lexington.'[2] Trigg sent
the note to Logan, with an endorsement stating that he had
taken it upon himself to order half of the Lincoln militia companies to march at once to Lexington, where he would await
them.[3]

Meanwhile, the Indians set fire to outhouses at Bryant's and
continued their attack until the next day, the 17th., when they
retired, evidently hoping the Kentuckians would pursue and
offer them an opportunity to take prisoners and gain desired
intelligence of Clark's movements.[4] In pursuance of this plan,

[1] L. Todd's Letters, *Virginia Calendar
State Papers*, III, 300, 333.
[2] *Draper MSS. 52 J 35–7.*
[3] *Id.*

[4] *Michigan Pioneer Collections*, XX, 49;
Virginia Calendar State Papers, III,
300, 333.

they moved in a leisurely manner northeastwardly some
twenty-five miles or more to the 'Blue Lick,' where they
crossed the Licking River to some rising ground in a sharp bend
of the stream, and prepared for battle. Here they were about
thirty miles northeast of Lexington.[1]

Trigg, having gathered about a hundred and thirty men
from Lincoln, marched them to Bryant's, where he was joined
by some hastily summoned Fayette militia, under Colonel
John Todd, who took command of the whole force, amounting
to one hundred and eighty-two men, 'all on horseback.'[2]

Meanwhile, Colonel Logan had received Trigg's letter on
the night of the 17th., and hastily assembled one hundred and
fifty-four more men of Lincoln. At noon on the 19th., they
arrived at Lexington, 'finding the people there quite unconcerned and at their common divertions!' He 'spent some time
shewing them their Error, to little purpose, himself being
weakened by the conversation of the Lexington and Bryant
Inhabitants ridiculing the pursuit, saying there was a sufficiency of men gone with Col. Todd, which caused many of
the volunteers to delay.'[3]

This plainly shows the utter demoralization of the militia,
and want of any real military discipline or authority. Even
the fourth day after the Indians had appeared at Bryant's,
the militiamen — officers and privates alike — seem to have
been completely at sea as to the enemy's strength and design,
and the inhabitants indifferent.

Before Logan reached Lexington, however, Colonel John
Todd, with fifty two men from Fayette and Trigg's one hundred and thirty from Lincoln, on the 18th. 'pursued the enemy
as far as Reddles that Eavening. 19th, continuing the pursuit, discryd them off the heights of Licking, on the opposite
side, some distance back of the Blue Licks, [and about twenty-
five miles northeast of Lexington.] Crossing ye River, an action immediately commenced, and in five minutes a Total
Rout on our side. Fifty of the Lincoln and 16 of the Fayette
Troops fell,' including Colonels John Todd & Trigg, two majors, and four captains.[4]

---

[1] Robert Johnson's *Map of Kentucky*
(holograph); *R. C. Ballard Thruston's
MSS.* Louisville, Ky.
[2] *Id.*; *Draper MSS.* 52 J 35-7.
[3] *Id.*

[4] *Draper MSS.* 53 J 35; Levi Todd to
Robert Todd, Aug. 26, 1782, *Virginia
Calendar State Papers*, III, 333, and to
Governor, Sept. 11, 1783, *id.*, 300; and
Boone's Account, *id.*, 275.

Major Madison, of Trigg's command, described the pursuit
and battle more fully:

'18th Aug[st] Col. Todd and Trigg arriv[d] at Briant's Station, about
ten o'clock, when they were informed by Capt[n] Craig that the Enemy
had Retreated about Ten in the morning; that their numbers was
inconsiderable; that he was sure they might be overtaken and...
defeated by the party present, to wit 182 men. The pursuit immediately took place, following the Indian trail to Riddles, near
Miles, where it was discovered that the Enemy was far superior to
the number supposed, and, by information of Capt. Hay to Col.
Boon, a large party of the Enimy was also discovered at the upper
Blue Licks, 8 miles from the Lower. The principal officers appeared
to be confused in their council, — each afraid to speak Candidly for
fear of being suspected of Timidity, but the whole moved forward,
apparently without order. Orders then issued for the whole, when
an attack should Commence, to ride in among the Enemy before a
gun was fired. Continuing the Route untill near day, then halted
untill sun-up on the 19th, when four miles from the Lick. Then,
marching in three parallel lines to the heights opposite the Blue
Licks, where, on discovering party of the Enimy, the whole appeared to be in the utmost confusion, each viewing the other with
that consternation foreboding destruction. No Genl order given
after this period. The spies venturing across the River Reconoitering
the Lick, found the Enimy that was discovered, had gone on. Maj
Mogary [McGarry] crossed with his division, after which Colo Trigg
with his, and Col. Boon following.
'Raising the heights on the opposite shore, the spies still advancing
returned in full speed, [and] informed the party that the Enimy was
but a small distance. The cry for action was the[n] given. The whole
Moved on in the order they then were, without ever forming, — the
front getting Repulsed before the Rear got near the Enemy. A gen[l]
Rout took place. Having an unguarded ford to Retreat through, the
Victory became compleat, on the side of the Enemy.'[1]

The river at the Blue Licks runs first south, then turns in a
half circle to the west and then runs north. It thus forms a
U-shaped loop containing about two hundred acres of land,
which was well wooded. Across the northern, or open end of
the loop, Caldwell and McKee formed their main battle lines,
about half a mile long, but in a long hollow which extended
southeastwardly from the front of their left wing they threw
out a hidden flanking detachment, which seems to have en-
filaded Trigg's men, throwing them back on Todd's and caus-
ing the stampede of the whole.[2] It was a pell-mell attack and
a complete rout.

[1] *Draper MSS. 52 J 35-7.*
[2] Colonel Levi Todd, soon after the de- feat, wrote his brother: 'The ground was equally favorable to both sides.' As he

This was the greatest disaster that had befallen the Kentucky people during the entire war, and they were appalled. Plainly they were themselves to blame, for, with such formidable enemies to contend with, obedience to military orders and concert of action were imperative; yet there had been neither. One result of the defeat could have been foreseen by any one knowing the conditions then prevailing. Each surviving officer, and the defenders of those who were killed, sought to put the blame on some other. All sorts of charges and counter-charges were made by the adherents of the respective Lincoln and Fayette officers. Many attributed the defeat to Colonel John Todd's incapacity. Others charged that Colonel Logan had negligently, or even intentionally, failed to go promptly to Todd's relief. The counter-charge was made that notice to Logan of the presence of the enemy had been purposely delayed, to prevent his displacing Todd as commander and gaining the credit for an expected victory. Others asserted that the defeat had been caused by the reckless conduct of Major McGarry, of Lincoln. It was said that when the troops reached the Licking and learned the enemy were on the other side, some of the officers hesitated to attack, but that McGarry called on all who were not cowards to follow him, and, putting spurs to his horse, dashed into the stream, and caused all to rush into the enemy's trap. McGarry vigorously denied this, but he had made many enemies among the new-state partisans whose seditious meeting he had forcibly dispersed, and it was said they were his detractors.[1]

While only part of the Indians gathered to oppose Clark

was in the centre he probably knew nothing of the hollow, or of the flank attack from it. See map of battlefield, *Draper MSS.* 52 J 35-7. Various and conflicting accounts of the battle appear in printed works, e.g., Collins' *History of Kentucky*, II, 657-64.

[1] Soon after the battle, in order to vindicate himself, McGarry on August 28th wrote to Colonel Logan: 'Sir: I understand I am much sensured for incouraging the men to fight the Indians when we came up with them. I should have informed you of a grand Scheam that was planned, when I saw you, only I thought perhaps it would cause a Riot, and you may Judge the matter yourself, only it is hard to Judge dead men.

you saw Trigg did not write to you untill he was sure you could not come up with us, and Todd took Capt. . . . Craigs word for the number of Indians, so we marched in order to gain great Applause with men, as it was well known [MS. torn] you would [have] had the command, as all the men was of our county, and their Scheam met with sad misfortune, which I am sorry for. so I suppose you have heard of my bad conduct, perhaps by some person that was concerned in the scheam, and if you think I am faulty I should be fond to have a hearing of the matter, Sir if anything should happen we have not 1 lb of lead.' (*Draper MSS.* 52 J 35-7.)

were thus easily defeating the unruly Fayette and Lincoln militia, the troops at the Falls were hard at work strengthening their fort. Floyd, who was out with a scouting party towards the east, learning of the Blue Licks defeat, wrote Clark: 'I have this moment received notice that Girty, with 600 savages, attacked Boon's garrison'; and that during the siege it was reinforced by 150 men from Lincoln, on which the enemy retreated to Licking, pursued and overtook them, a bloody engagement ensuing. 'We lost 70 men including Col⁵ Trigg, Bowman and Boone & other officers.' [1] Floyd added that he expected a severe attack 'this night, or early in the morning,' and asked for powder and lead, as his men had almost none.

This distorted report was doubtless the first news General Clark received of the Blue Licks disaster, and with it came notice of the enemy's near approach to the Falls. Several other alarming reports followed, and then Floyd wrote him that the savages 'had attacked Kinchelow's Station [near the Falls] and taken [thirty-seven] prisoners,' but that the enemy's 'whole number does not exceed 150 and perhaps not so many.' [2] He added: 'If you think we can defeat them, let no time be lost in letting me know it, that I may collect all the men who are able to march. I am now convinced that they are on their retreat, so that it will not be any great risque in drawing the Men from the Stations. I am also convinced that the Enemy have [deliberately given] time to give us an Opportunity to attack them & it is truly mortifying to think they should miss it; yet I am sensible of the Evill consequences that might attend our engaging them to a disadvantage.' These Indians were evidently those McKee and Caldwell had sent to the Falls to learn about Clark's movements.

[1] *Draper MSS. 52 J 34.*   [2] *Id., 52 J 40.*

CHAPTER XX

RECRIMINATION AND TRADUCTION

ALTHOUGH many and bitter were the complaints of one another amongst the Fayette and Lincoln survivors of the Blue Licks battle, they soon united in finding a scapegoat to saddle with responsibility for their defeat. This was General Clark, although the affair was solely their own, and he had nothing to do with it. He had no authority over them or their militiamen, except to call upon them to aid in fort building, and he was not within a hundred miles of the battle; but some one suggested that he had caused the disaster by not building the new forts! This charge — conveniently acquitting themselves — was circulated by some of the surviving officers of Fayette and Lincoln, and a hue-and-cry raised in those counties against Clark as the responsible cause of the disaster. It was taken up by many other people there, already unfriendly to him. It is often but a step from enmity to slander, and from one slander to another, and a surprising number of preposterous falsehoods were circulated about him, first in Lincoln and Fayette, and soon afterward at the state capital — all within a few weeks after the Blue Licks defeat. In writings which may still be read, he was charged with tyranny, ambition, vanity, cowardice, peculation, drunkenness, idleness, and even collusion with horse thieves! None of these writings — some of them anonymous — were intended ever to come to his knowledge, and few probably did. So far as known, only two of them did, and he promptly disproved the charges in them and discredited their authors.[1]

As General Clark knew nothing of the Blue Licks affair, except from hearsay, he could of course make no proper report of it to the governor. That was the duty of the senior commanding officer, Colonel Logan, who twelve days after the

[1] The only one worth mentioning here is in *Virginia Calendar State Papers*, III, 358, about intermingling certain flour belonging to one Elliott with flour belonging to the state. As to this, see deposition of Commissary Major Walls before Colonel Fleming explaining the intermingling as due to an accident during a storm, and that the state got Elliott's fine flour for an equal number of kegs of less weight of coarse flour and Elliott was the loser. Clark had nothing to do with it. (Author's transcript, R 684.)

battle wrote the governor an account of the engagement in which he endeavored to fix the blame on Clark. After telling of his own actions and the defeat (as shown in the footnote below) [1] he said:

'I am inclined to believe that when your Excellency and Council become acquainted with the military operations in this country, that you will not think them so properly conducted as to answer the general Interest of Kentucky. From the accounts we have received by prisoners who escaped this spring, we were confident of an invasion from the Detroit Indians. Common safety then made some scheme of defense necessary, for which purpose I was called upon by Gen[l] Clark to attend a council; and, after consulting matters, it was determined to build a fort at the mouth of Licking, and shortly I received his orders for 100 men to attend this business, with a certain number from Fayette. Before the day of rendezvous I was instructed to send the men to the Falls of Ohio, in order to build a strong Garrison and a row Galley, thus weakening one end to strengthen another and the upper part of the country was left exposed, and the enemy, intercepting our designs, brought their intended expedition against the frontiers of Fayette. [Logan could not say, however, that he had heeded any such orders, and his statement gives the very misleading impression that the enemy only invaded 'the *frontiers* of Fayette'; whereas in truth they had been allowed to penetrate, unobserved, almost to the southern boundary of the county.] The immense expenses incurred by the State in this western country, we

---

[1] 'Sir: I beg leave to present your Excellency & Council with one of the most melancholly events that has happened in all this Western Country. On the 14th inst: Capt. Holden from Fayette, pursued a party of Indians who had made prisoners of a couple of boys in his neighborhood; he overtook them and was repulsed with a loss of four men. On the 16th a considerable army appeared before Bryant's Station, under the command of the noted Simon Girty, and many other white men; they attacked the Station closely, and defeated different parties endeavoring to throw in assistance, but without much loss on our side. An Express was immediately despatched to Col: John Todd, who at that time was in this County in the neighborhood of Col: Trigg — On the 17th, at night, I received a letter from Col: Trigg, wherein he informed me of what had passed. Orders were immediately given for every man to turn out, and on Sunday the 18th I crossed the Kentucky with a considerable detachment, & the day after arrived at Bryant's, where I understood the Indians had raised the siege & were followed by Col: John Todd, with 135 of the Lincoln militia under Col: Trigg and 45 of the Fayette under Col: Bowman — Dreading the consequences that might ensue from this precipitate affair, I immediately pushed within a few miles from Bryants. We were met by about 25 men, who informed — of a total defeat at the *Big Blue Licks* on *Licking*. I covered their retreat, and marched back to Bryants, where I collected 470 men, and the 24th went to the battle ground and buried 43 — our loss in this action is 50 missing from Lincoln, and 15 from Fayette, among whom are Colls: Todd and Trigg (Trigg was quartered) Major Harlin, Capts: McBride, Gordon, Kinkaid & Overton, & Lieuts: Givings, Kennedy, McMartry, Rogers & McGuire, and Mr. Joseph Lindsay our Commissary. 'From the situation of the ground, on which our men were drawn upon (the plan whereof I have taken the liberty to enclose) I hardly know how it was possible for any to escape.' (*Virginia Calendar State Papers*, III, 280-81.)

know is enough to prevent the government from giving us any further aid; but when your Excellency and Council are informed that the people have never been benefitted by these expenditures, we still hope your compassion will be extended to a detached, distressed part of your country, as it is not in the power of the People to answer the misapplication of anything by a proper officer.'[1]

This insinuation was evidently aimed at General Clark and indicates an ugly enmity toward him; for Logan undoubtedly knew the Assembly had passed an act to investigate 'misapplications of public monies and supplies' in Clark's western military department.

Logan's letter does not tell the Governor of Clark's repeated calls for the militia of Fayette and Lincoln to help build the new forts; or of their refusal to help; or of Clark's building of the row galley at the Falls for the special protection of Fayette and Lincoln; or of the fact that it was actually stationed at the mouth of the Licking; or that it fully answered the purpose of a fort there. He gives the impression that the galley was built only to protect the settlement at the Falls and also that because no fort had been built at the mouth of the Licking the Indians passed into Fayette by *that* route. He wrote this letter twelve days after the battle, when he should have known — but evidently did not — that the galley had been stationed at the Licking and that the Indians had not crossed the Ohio there, but some seventy miles above, at Limestone.

Following fast upon Logan's letter, the 'Officers, Civil as well as Military, of Fayette County,' also wrote the Governor saying 'If something is not speedily done we doubt Kentucky will wholly be depopulated. The Executive, we believe, thinks often of us & wish to protect us; but, Sir, we believe any military operations that for 18 months have been carried on [meaning by General Clark] in consequence of orders from the Executive have rather been detrimental than Beneficial. Our militia are called on to do duty in a manner that has a tendency to protect Jefferson County, or rather Louisville, a town without inhabitants, a fort situated in such a manner that the enemy coming with a design to lay waste our country would scarcely come within One Hundred Miles of it, & our frontier open and unguarded.'[2] These Fayette officers then pray the

---

[1] *Virginia Calendar State Papers*, III, 280.
[2] *Id.*, 301.

'building of a garrison at the mouth of Limestone and another at the mouth of Licking.' No doubt they had by this time discovered that the Indians had not come against them by the Licking route, and therefore they do not, like Logan, attribute their defeat to the lack of a fort at the mouth of that river. They doubtless had also learned that Clark's row galley was there and had kept the Indians well away from that point.

Unluckily for Clark's reputation at the capital, three of his most malignant enemies were at this time members of the Virginia Assembly — Colonel Arthur Campbell, John May, and Captain Isaac Hite.[1] May represented Jefferson County, while Hite was a member with Logan from Lincoln. When Colonel Campbell learned of the Blue Licks disaster, he may or may not have reflected that it had been in large measure due to the sedition and strife in Kentucky which he had himself been so active in promoting. He was not slow, however, in using the opportunity to censure the men who had opposed his insurrectionist conspiracies, and especially Clark, against whom he ever nursed his old enmity. Two weeks after the battle he wrote Governor Harrison's war secretary:

'Never was the lives of so many valuable men lost more shamefully than in the late action of the 19th of August and that not a little thro' the vain and seditious expression of a Major McGarry. How much more harm than good can one fool do. Todd and Trigg had capacity but wanted experience. Boone, Harlin and Lindsay had experience but were defective in capacity. Logan is a dull, narrow body from whom nothing clever need be expected. What a figure he exhibited, at the head of near 500 men, to reach the field of action six days afterwards and hardly wait to bury the dead, and when it was plain that part of the Indians were still in the country. General Clarke is in that country, but he has lost the confidence of the people and it is said become a sot; perhaps something worse.'[2]

This falsehood about Clark's drinking — for such it certainly was — first appeared in this letter of Campbell, but it was soon widely spread at Richmond. What Logan, May, or Hite may have told their fellow-members in the Assembly, or the governor, or others, about the young general we do not know. What reports others may have circulated we do not know, nor could he. The Blue Licks disaster and responsibility

[1] This Captain Isaac Hite of Kentucky is not to be confounded with his cousin, Major Isaac Hite, of the Virginia continental army, or his uncle, Isaac Hite, Sr., merchant of Frederick County, Virginia.

[2] *Virginia Calendar State Papers,* III, 337.

for it were no doubt much discussed amongst legislators and other officials; and if the Kentucky delegates charged the disaster to Clark's neglect, or drinking, the charge was pretty sure to be accepted, circulated and given credit by gossips, without the least inquiry to learn whether it was true or false.

Before these letters reached the governor, Colonel William Christian, who was the first person in eastern Virginia to learn of the Blue Licks defeat, informed him of it. He sympathized deeply with the Kentucky people, described their desperate situation, and proposed to Governor Harrison to raise five hundred mounted volunteers from the country west of the Blue Ridge and go to their relief by attacking their Indian enemies.[1] He said Colonel William Preston and Colonel William Campbell — of King's Mountain fame — offered their assistance. All he asked of the governor was that the volunteers' horses and accouterments, if lost, should be 'paid for at some future day.'

In reply to this appeal Governor Harrison said the plan would be a good one, if there were money for it; that the Assembly had not taken off the restriction of offensive operations, nor left it in the power of the executive to employ more than a small part of the revenue in defense of the state, even in the greatest emergency; that he thought it best to wait until spring, or till the sense of the Assembly could be known; that it was probable the Indians had gone off, and that they would not return again that winter, 'but lest I should be mistaken, have sent orders, if assistance should be wanted for the defense of the country' to call on the county lieutenants of three mountain counties![2]

Governor Harrison, on first learning of the Blue Licks defeat, evidently feared he would himself be blamed for it, because he had neglected repeated warnings of the dangers threatening the Kentucky people and had made no great effort to relieve them.[3] When, however, he received the letters

[1] *Virginia Calendar State Papers*, III, 331.

[2] Virginia State Library, *Governor's Letter Book*, October 9, 1782. 'Sence writing the above I have received official information of the disaster in Kentucky.'

[3] There can be no doubt that he knew the danger. On May 22, 1782, he wrote Captain William Harrison censuring him for selling powder intended for Clark, and said: 'What may be the consequences, I Know not, as it seems certain that the quarter where he commands will be powerfully attacked this spring. If he should be overborne for want of ammunition, will the excuse you make of want of money, justify you in this country, or to the world?' (*Draper MSS.* 10 S 31.)

from Logan and others in Kentucky attributing the disaster not to his neglect, but to General Clark's in not building the new forts, he readily accepted their version and joined them in casting the blame on Clark. He wrote Colonel Levi Todd (October 14th): 'In December last Forts were ordered built at the mouth of the Ky river &c. Why this has not been done Gen. Clark will account. I am apt to think if he had obeyed his orders, this Disaster would not have happened; as the approach of the enemy would have been known in time for the people to have collected in sufficient numbers to have driven them back. These orders are repeated, and I trust will be executed; if they are not, I shall look on it as the Duty of the higher officers in Kentucky to inform me of it.' [1] Though the 'orders are repeated' for building the forts, Harrison still ordered no men, money or supplies sent to build them.

To Logan he wrote the same day: 'Gen. Clark's conduct in not erecting strong forts at the mouth of Ky. &c, as he was ordered to do in December last, surprises me much. The Executive saw the importance of these posts for the protection of the Country, and gave orders accordingly, and I had not the least suspicion that they were not obeyed till the receipt of your letter.' [2] In view of all the letters he had received from General Clark this statement seems very extraordinary.

To the letter of the Fayette officers Governor Harrison made similar reply, adding: 'Kentucky is as much the object of my care as Richmond, and I shall show it on all occasions.' [3] He next wrote Colonel Fleming — chief commissioner of Western Military Accounts, who was about starting to Kentucky — saying:

'I gave the General orders in December last to build forts at the mouth of the Kentucky, Licking, and Limestone and to garrison each of them with sixty eight men. If he had obeyed the orders, it is probable the late misfortune would not have happened, as the country would certainly have been alarmed, if not protected, and have had it in their power to have met the Enemy with more equal force. The orders are again repeated; and I desire you will use your endeavors with him to fix his attention on the occasion, and will not again overlook a breach of duty. If you find it necessary, you'll please insinuate this to him.

'I have had too much reason to complain of General Clark on

[1] Virginia State Library, *Governor's Letter Book*, 7. [2] *Id.*, 20. [3] *Id.*, 10.

other accounts, besides what Colo Bowman says of the French
horses, which story I can hardly believe to be true. If you find it is,
I beg you will use your endeavors to moderate the resentment of the
French. ...A report, much to his prejudice, prevails here of his
being so addicted to liquor as to be incapable of attending of his
Duty, by which the public interest suffers much. I must beg the
favor of you Gentlemen to inquire into this in a private way, and let
me know your sentiments.'[1]

From these statements of the governor, Colonel Fleming
doubtless went to Kentucky ready to believe all sorts of
charges against General Clark, and expected to find him addicted to drink, neglecting the public business, and, as Logan
had insinuated, even guilty of 'misapplication' of the public
funds. In fact, Fleming's Journal shows that he was at first
suspicious of Clark; but after meeting him and learning the
true state of affairs in his department, all such suspicion
entirely disappeared. He and his colleagues not only found
nothing to censure in the general's military or personal conduct, but endorsed his military plans, approved his accounts,
and in many ways showed their esteem for him. They found
it had been impossible for him to build the forts ordered, for
lack of means.[2]

Undoubtedly Governor Harrison was right when he wrote
Fleming that 'a report prevails at the capital of his [General
Clark] being so addicted to liquor as to be incapable of attending to his Duty'; but it is no less certain that the report was
utterly false and due to traduction by Clark's enemies. The
governor himself will presently be found stating he was fully
satisfied of this. In truth, so far from being addicted to liquor,
General Clark, both before and during this period of vilifi-
cation and for years afterwards, was an exceptionally temperate man. Amongst the hundreds of extant letters mentioning
him and written by his contemporaries — enemies as well as
friends — not one intimates that he had ever been intoxicated, although in his day virtually everybody drank liquor
and doubtless he did in moderation. Otherwise, so rare an
exception to the common custom would likely have attracted
attention and been remarked in some of these letters. On the
other hand, had he been given to excessive drinking, that fact

---

[1] Virginia State Library, *Draper MSS.*
48 J 71.　　　　　[2] *Draper MSS.* 2 Z.Z. 69 *et seq.*; *id.*, 52
J 74.

would even more surely have been mentioned, especially by his enemies.

Within three months after the Blue Licks defeat, General Clark was warned by a friendly member of Governor Harrison's council [1] that the falsehood about his drinking was being circulated at Richmond; but he was not told who its authors were, and soon afterward Governor Harrison wrote him that he was fully satisfied the charge against him was unfounded and due to traduction by his enemies. After that General Clark no doubt thought the slander was effectually scotched and required no attention; but he did not realize that it would prove perennial.

He probably had no friends at the capital to defend him; for he had left eastern Virginia when a youth and, except short visits to further his military plans, had never returned there. Unfortunately his friends Mason and Jefferson were at this time bowed down by domestic sorrows and withdrawn from public life and society. Shortly before the Blue Licks disaster he had written Jefferson confiding his wounded feelings over the treatment he had received from the state — evidently referring to the assembly resolution about 'misapplication of public monies and supplies,' which he erroneously thought was intended to reflect on him. For months the letter was unanswered, for Jefferson's wife was hopelessly ill, and she died on September 6th, 1782. His biographer says he was 'tender and assiduous in his care of her as it was possible for a man to be. ...For three weeks after she died he did not leave his room; afterwards he had recourse to long wanderings in the solitary wood-paths of the mountains.' [2]

One of Jefferson's first three letters after his wife's death — probably the first [3] — was a reply to Clark (November 26, 1782) saying:

I perceive by your letter you are not unapprised that your services to your country have not made due impression on every mind.

[1] James Monroe.

[2] *Life of Jefferson*, 71, in *American Statesmen Series*, J. T. Morse — none too friendly a biographer.

[3] Jefferson wrote no letters from May, 1782, to the date of his letter to Clark. On the same day he wrote Livingston briefly acknowledging an appointment as envoy to France, and to Chevalier de Chattelux. To the latter he said: 'I received your letters of   and June 30th, the latter on October 17th. ...It found me a little emerging from the stupor of mind which had rendered me as dead to the world as she whose loss occasioned it.' (November 26, 1782, *Writings of Jefferson*, Congressional Edition, I, 321 *et seq.*)

That you have enemies you must not doubt, when you reflect that you have made yourself eminent. If you mean to escape malice, you should have confined yourself within the sleepy line of regular duty. When you transgressed this, and enterprized deeds which will hand down your name with honor to future times, you made yourself a mark for malice to shoot at. Of these there is enough, both in and out of office. I was not a little surprised, however, to find one person hostile to you, as far as he has courage to show hostility to any man. Who he is you will probably have heard, or may know him by this description of being all tongue, without either head or heart. In the variety of his crooked schemes, however, his interest may probably veer about so as to put it into your power to be useful to him; in which case he will certainly be your friend again, — if you want him. That you may long continue a fit object of his enmity and for that of every person of his complexion in the state, which I know you can only by continuing to do good to your country and honour to yourself, is the earnest prayer of one who subscribes himself, with greatest truth and sincerity.

Your friend & Serv[t]

TH: JEFFERSON[1]

Few things in Jefferson's life better disclose his goodness of heart than the constancy of his esteem and affection for his much harassed friend. Years afterward he said: 'No man alive rated him higher than I did.'

[1] Ford's *Works of Jefferson*, III, 304, where the letter is erroneously mentioned as addressed to James Steptoe.

CHAPTER XXI

CLARK RESIGNS COMMAND: THE REVOLUTION ENDS

LITTLE suspecting that he was himself being blamed for the Blue Licks disaster by Logan and others, General Clark on October 18th wrote Harrison:

'The works at the Falls was forwarded by every means in our power, until they were supposed sufficiently strong to withstand an attack from the Enemy, but not yet compleat. Those preparations, ...and the measures taken to let the Enemy know that we were fully acquainted with their design, (which in fact we were), I believe has saved the western country. By their losing all hopes of reducing the Falls, they divided their force, sent some to Wheeling,[1] and the main body to make a diversion on Fayette County; and had it not been for that imprudent affair at the Blue Licks, the country would have sustained little damage.

'I learn that Col. Logan has sent you a full account of the whole transaction. The conduct of those unfortunate Gents was extremely reprehensible. The enemy continues to sculk in small parties in different parts of the country, but do little damage at present. The movements of the enemy last spring and summer put it entirely out of our power to establish the posts at the mouth of the Kentucky, Licking, &c; they may be begun this fall.'[2]

General Clark might have added that the opposition to his calls for men had put the fort building out of his power; but he was ever reluctant to blame others and most guarded when he did. His remarks about the 'reprehensible' conduct of those responsible for the defeat are perhaps the severest comment he appears ever to have made on the conduct of other officers.

Taught by the Blue Licks defeat, the people of Fayette and Lincoln at last awoke to the fatal consequences of discord, and instead of refusing to join General Clark in an expedition against the Indians, now urged him to lead them on one; and this he did. Although offensive expeditions had been prohibited, he knew this one was necessary and he did not hesitate to encourage it. He had not yet received Governor Harrison's letter blaming him for the Blue Licks affair and, sup-

[1] The Shawnees did go against the Wheeling settlements, but were not sent there by their British leaders, as Clark supposed.

[2] *Virginia Calendar State Papers*, III, 345

posing he still had his confidence, evidently assumed that the
necessity for the expedition would insure its approval. He
therefore wrote Harrison (October 22nd): 'It is planned, and
the rendezvous appointed for the mouth of the Licking, the
first day of November. I expect a thousand men. If it is attended with success, I make no doubt it will save the effusion
of much blood the ensuing year.'[1]

When Harrison got this letter he sent Clark this characteristic reply: 'I suppose the desire of the people, for revenging
themselves on the savages for the loss of so many valuable
friends, was the cause of your undertaking an expedition;
otherwise it was certainly wrong to do it without consulting
me. I have some reason to apprehend that it will rather pro-
long than shorten the war.'[2]

With over a thousand men Clark crossed the Ohio, marched
rapidly against the principal Shawnee towns and destroyed
them. Writing soon afterward to the governor, he said:

'Col. Floyd, with three hundred men, was ordered to advance to
bring on the action, or attack the town. Major Walls, with a party
of horse being previously detached, by a different route, as a party
of observation. Although Col. Floyd's motion was so quick as to get
to the town but a few moments later than those who discovered his
approach, the inhabitants had sufficient notice to effect their escape
to the woods by the alarm cry that was given on the first discovery,
to be heard at a great distance and repeated by all who heard it. Of
course our parties only fell in with the rear of the enemy. The quantity of provisions burnt far surpast any idea we had of their stores of
that kind. The loss of the enemy was ten scalps, seven prisoners, and
two whites retaken, — ours one killed, one wounded. ...The British
trading post at the head of the Miami and carrying place to the
waters of the Lakes shared the same fate, by a party of one hundred
and fifty horse commanded by Col. B. Logan. Property to a great
amount was destroyed.'[3]

[1] *Virginia Calendar State Papers*, III,
216.

[2] Virginia State Library, *Governor's
Letter Book*, 255.

[3] *Virginia Calendar State Papers*, III,
381. The importance of this expedition
has been greatly exaggerated by early
and even late writers. Roosevelt thinks
it prevented any 'threatened serious
invasion of Kentucky afterwards.' (*Winning of the West*, III, 85.) In fact, such
invasion was decidedly serious afterward. The defeat of the Shawnees did
discourage the growing hostility of other
tribes, but the main cause of their becoming less aggressive for a while was
that the Revolutionary War was virtually ended for the British, and they
ceased openly to encourage the Indians
to attack the Americans. McElroy's
Kentucky in the Nation's History (113)
also says: 'The great war period of Kentucky history had closed with Clark's last
Shawnee expedition, ...and in no instance again assumed the dignity of real
warfare.' On the contrary, the savage
warfare soon became more alarming.

In all Clark's expeditions against the Indians, Lincoln County, which contained over half of Kentucky's population, furnished most of the men; and for that reason Logan, who was their senior militia officer, was always accorded secondary command.

When Governor Harrison learned that the expedition had been successful, his attitude about it completely changed, and he wrote General Clark:

'I...very sincerely congratulate you on the success of your expedition against the Indians. The officers under your command deserve the highest praise. ... It will teach the Indians to dread us and convince them we will not tamely submit to their depredations. It has ever been my opinion the attacking of them in their own country is the only way to keep them quiet and save expense, but I have unfortunately differed in sentiments from those to whom I am amenable. ...I have now, Sir, to return you particular thanks for your spirited and judicious conduct through the whole course of your expedition, and to assure you that we shall ever entertain the highest sense of the important services you have rendered your country.'[1]

On returning from the Shawnee towns General Clark visited Lincoln County, where he learned that complaints had been sent to the governor about him in connection with the Blue Licks affair. As he had never received anything but high praise from the governor, however, he evidently felt he had his confidence and thought the complaints needed no attention. Without mentioning them, he wrote Harrison:

'I had great prospect of getting the post at the mouth Licking built and garrisoned by [the] army, on our return; but found it would be exceedingly disagreeable to them to be detained. If in my power, your orders shall be executed, but how these posts are to be supplied I cannot as yet conceive. Nothing can be got on the credit of the state, the expenditures of government for a considerable time being on private funds. I have, by disposing of some Lands that I was possessed of, laid in a tolerable store at the Falls; but if divided between three or four posts will be but trifling.' [Clark then suggests 'an excursion against the Wabash nations in the spring, which would ...perhaps silence the whole in this quarter,' and adds:] 'If you should think of putting any such thing in execution, I shall yet receive pleasure in making every preparatory stroke in my power, before I leave the country, which I hope will be the last of March.'[2]

---

[1] Virginia State Library, *Governor's Letter Book*, 18. He sent also a similar letter of congratulations to Logan. (*Id.*)

[2] *Virginia Calendar State Papers*, III, 386.

Hardly had this letter left him when General Clark received the following amazing one from Governor Harrison, written over a month earlier:

Sir: — No official accounts from you of the situation of the part of the country committed to your care have reached me for several months, for which I am at a loss to assign a reason. Government can never be administered properly unless the officers of it are regular in their description of the wants and distresses of their departments.

If the disappointments you have met with in your proposed plans have occasioned this inattention and neglect, the reason is by no means a good one; because circumstances may alter, and one time enable Government to do what they could not at another.

I have received letters from Col Levi Todd and other respectable characters in Kentucky, giving an account of a powerful invasion by the Indians, and an unfortunate battle fought with them by Col John Todd on the 19th of August, in which that worthy gentleman and many others of the most valuable inhabitants have fallen. These are circumstances so much within your line of duty, that I cannot help expressing my very great surprise at your silence.

In my letter of the 20th. of December last, you were directed to erect forts at the mouth of the Kentucky river, the mouth of Licking Creek and at the mouth of Limestone Creek and to garrison each of these posts with sixty eight men, to cover and protect the country. Whether you have complied with these orders or not, you have not thought fit to advise me; but I have every reason to suppose from other information that they have altogether been neglected, to which much of the present misfortune is to be attributed, as such establishments would have been a great curb to the Indians; the country might from these posts have been alarmed at the approach of an enemy, and, with the assistance of the garrisons, better enabled to repel their attacks. These reasons governed the executive when they gave the orders, and induced them to fix on you to execute them, and it gives me great pain to find that you have disappointed us in our expectations. The same reason that dictated the former order still governs us, and I insist that they be carried into immediate execution.

If the Indians have not left the country, or you have good reason to expect their return this fall or winter, you'll apply to the commanding officer of Washington, Montgomery and Botetourt counties, who have orders to send you any number of men you may call for, not exceeding two hundred.[1]

As the marching militia will not only be attended with very great inconvenience to the individuals, but with great expense to the

---

[1] If the 'unlimited powers to call upon the militia of Jefferson, Fayette, and Lincoln,' which General Clark had already received from Governor Harrison, had not enabled him to get men for fort building, he was not likely to get them from the distant and no less disaffected counties of Montgomery, Botetourt, and Washington. Campbell's seditious influence was great there.

State, I trust you will not call for them but in case of urgent necessity. Economy now may put it in our power in the spring to take more decisive measures; however, I would by no means have any consideration of this sort interfere with the safety of the people and only mention it to you as a secondary consideration.

The commissioners of western accounts, that are sent into the part of the country where you are, are men of prudence and judgment and it may not be amiss to consult with them on this occasion. Before these Gentlemen all the accounts of your military expenditures in every department are to be laid, in order to their being adjusted and reported on, and, when this is done, I shall expect your attendance here for a final settlement of them. You will excuse me for again repeating my request to be informed by every opportunity of the material circumstances that may happen in Kentucky, and what progress you make in the discharge of the several matters entrusted to you. I am &c.,

BENJAMIN HARRISON [1]

General Clark was far from being a man of the bloodless type to bear intended wrong without resentment and the unjust censure in this letter must have angered him mightily. Firm self-control and the desire to be fair were, however, amongst his most marked characteristics, and he never wrote in passion. He had always respected Governor Harrison and now sent him the following magnanimous reply:

LINCOLN, *Novr. 30th*, 1782

Sir:

I had this day the pleasure of receiving your letter, dated 17th of October, which for a few moments I was at a loss to comprehend. But on recollecting some circumstances, find that on the supposition of your taking many reports and party memorials, [which] I learn have been handed to your Excellency, for granted, can see that your duty required such a letter to me. I unfortunately have not copys of my former letters to Government with me, and [am unable] to send in pursuit of the person I expect to be the bearer of this, who has already set out, ...so that it is not in my power to be as minute as I could wish.

I have always made it a point to inform Government of every circumstance I thought necessary for them to know, except the importance of it was [of] too trifling a consequence to be at the expense of an express, and no opportunity offering. In short, it is almost impossible at this distance to acquaint you of the various circumstances attending so critical and extensive a department as this. For many months past it was impossible to have got a letter to you without a strong guard, except by chance.

I have in a former letter, I think, given you satisfactory reasons

[1] *Draper MSS. 52 J 50; Virginia State Library, Governor's Letter Book.*

why the posts alluded to were not built. Preparations were made early in the spring for the expedition of your orders, but a full prudence directed that we should not enter on too large a scale. The fortifications at the Falls was first to be repaired, proceed to Kentucky, from thence to Licking, compleating our works in Rotation; but, in the execution of this business I had not only to counteract the designs of the enemy, but a powerful party endeavoring to subvert the Government, of which, I have reason to believe, great part of those who give your Excellency so much intelligence belong. Those, and many other recent circumstances, caused me to meet with difficulties in drawing out the Millitia, hardly to be surmounted with the assistance of many worthy Gentlemen in office.

I found it was impossible to build those forts without the greatest probability of sacrificing a party, as not less than six or seven hundred men could have kept possession of the mouth of the Licking after six days, being within eighty six miles of the body of the enemy; and the clamours of even those people whom I suspect to have made their complaint to you was that such post could not be supported and [was] of no consequence, — though I believe it not to be the real sentiment of the whole, but rather to disappoint the design to save themselves from duty.

Receiving repeated intelligence from the enemy, we endeavored to fix on the most likely plan to save the country. Colo. Todd's Militia was excused from all other duty but that of keeping out proper Scouts and Spies on the Ohio and Elsewhere to discover the approach of the enemy, to give [time] to imbody a sufficient force to repel them, as it could not be previously done, not certainly knowing in what quarter they would make their stroke. Instead of those necessary duties being done, on which their salvation apparently depended, the enemy was suffered to penetrate deliberately into the bowels of their country, and make the attack before they were discovered. This, I believe, is what is wished to be blinded, and the neglect to be one of the principal springs to that mad pursuit and carnage of the Blue Lick, as the reverse of fortune could have obliviated their former neglect.

I must confess that I have been deficient in my duty in not giving you an account of every circumstance attending this unhappy affair, but hope to be excused, as it was owing to my delicacy in affecting the memory of the gentlemen who fell, not conceiving it to be of singular advantage to government, and knowing it would fix an eternal stigma on others' characters.

But as the scales have turned, to the amazement of many, I shall immediately collect every circumstance relating to the whole affair for your perusal.[1]

[1] This he never did; at least we find no letter indicating it. Perhaps he was too much occupied to prepare it. More likely the improved conduct of some of those men in his recent expedition against the Shawnees, and his characteristic aversion to censuring others, prevented his writing such a report. Some of the blamable ones, too, had been his friends and had been killed. Washington himself was not more careful than Clark to avoid misjudging others.

You will pardon me, Sir, for informing your Excellency that you will hereafter find that you are greatly imposed on by party. I am persuaded if you are acquainted with the true character of many of those Gentlemen that you speak of, that you will have no further allusion to them.

You have complained that Gentlemen do not give information of shameful neglect, committed I suppose by me. Their is no Gentleman of his own knowledge knows of any, except those little Gentlemen I have before hinted of. Nothing but the zeal I have for the public interest, and the idea I have of your goodness, would induce me to venture to tell your Excellency that, as long as you countenance those kind of people, you encourage enemies in the state and keep your government in confusion; but I know your situation and how difficult it must be for you to discriminate.

Instance what was the design of the memorial I learn you received from Fayette County: to cover their misconduct and a prelude to a major's commission for a trifler, and a colonel's for a person something more deserving, to the prejudice of a valuable man, Mr. Swearinger, who had been absent some time and was daily expected, which would have prevented their design. To my certain knowledge, they now dread the Execution of what a few of them were deluded to pray for again — Col. Donelson, who was last spring chairman of the Committee that endeavored to subvert the government and cost us so much trouble to overset, since bearing a commission.

As for expenses, disappointments, the want of public credit, neglect, mal-conduct in persons employed, &c, &c, — I have perhaps experienced greater anxiety for the welfare of the State than most of the men in it, as the changes of government have been so frequent that it would, of course, put it out of their powers to so fully feel all those misfortunes attending its interest, as one continually engaged in its service. To enumerate all the various circumstances attending mine, what man in the state would not have cast [off] allegiance to it, [and] overset its Government in this Quarter? [1]

Unfortunately the rest of this letter has been lost. It breaks off just at the point where we could most wish it had been continued. In his situation and with his influence, a less faithful man would most likely 'have cast off allegiance to the state and overset its Government'; and probably there was never a day, from the time when the new-state conspirators proposed to make him their 'Governor-General,' that he could not easily have done it. He was the recognized leader of the Virginians, who were the militant part of the Kentucky population and ready to fight for their freedom and their lands.[2] To the

[1] *Draper MSS.* 52 J 50, holograph.

[2] Virginia would almost certainly have let the Kentuckians go, for she had neither the means nor the motive to oppose Congress and reduce them to obedience by force. What effect Kentucky's independence would have had upon our hold of the Northwest Territory can only be

last, however, he remained true to his mother state. If there was never a day when he could not have overset her government in Kentucky, there was never a day when he would contemplate doing it.

On receiving this letter, Governor Harrison briefly replied:

Sir: Your several favors of the 30th November this Moment come to hand as the Dispatches were ready to close. I can only acknowledge the receipt of them, and forward an order on the Counties for any Specifics that may be in them. I am fully satisfied you have been traduced, but as you had it in your Power to prevent any bad effect from such representations by keeping me fully informed of the Steps you had taken and your inability to carry your orders into Execution, you must attribute any thing that may be disagreeable to you to your own Inadvertence but of this I shall write more fully in my next. I am Sir &c.[1]

In another letter again directing Clark to make bricks without straw by building forts without men, money or supplies, Harrison said: 'I agree with you that the command you have is not a proper one for a gentleman of your rank, and therefore accept your proposal of resigning. Before you leave it, I wish you to regulate the regular Corps and reduce the number of officers to the number of privates.' [2] In reply Clark wrote:

'In my last letter I flattered you with the prospect of our attempting one of the Forts on the Ohio immediately. I was too sanguine in my hopes. Without funds from you for the purchase of provisions, enough could not be provided to march a sufficient body of men to the spot. Corn is the only article of provision that could be got in tolerable plenty, — a bushel of which could not be got on the credit of the state.

'I can't certainly conceive what reason your Excellency could have for supposing that I should have been backward in having your orders respecting those forts executed, if in my power. One of them, in particular, would add greatly to my interest;[3] and, supposing me fond of command, I then of course should prefer the greatest number possible.

'I thank you, Sir, for your permit of retiring. The smallness of

surmised. Freed from Virginia's weak government, the new state might have offered lands to settlers on easy terms and thus gained sufficient population and vigor to repress the Indians. If not, the Wabash and Illinois French would probably have returned to their British allegiance and the Northwest Territory been reunited to Canada. Many letters

show their willingness to desert the Americans.

[1] Virginia State Library, *Governor's Letter Book* (1783), p. 60.
[2] *Id.* (1782), 255.
[3] It would have been near his Salt Lick land on the Kentucky River, and by protecting settlers, would greatly have enhanced its value.

command could not have been my reason, for it is certainly extensive, but quite a different cause.

'Every exertion in my power [has] been made, for many years, for the defense of this department. Knowing the safety of all our frontiers depends on it, of course [I] took pleasure in encountering the greatest fatigues, leaving nothing in my power undone, either by dividing the councils of the Indians, taking necessary excursions into their country to distress our enemy and cause the Friendly to keep so, and attempting to destroy the interest of that numerous clan of partisans, of pretended Proprietors, residing in Philadelphia, that was endeavoring to divide the counsels of the people here, and at the same time destroying their interest at the seat of Government, more effectually to complete their disaffection to the state. As soon as I found they were likely to carry their point, I at once saw the destruction of the country, if the war should continue, and of course wished not to be a witness to the great success of their attempts against me, as the greatest stroke they could possible make [was to] put it out of my power to save the country. I wished to be clear. These were my reasons.'[1]

Harrison next wrote Clark as follows:

'I am sorry you have taken my permission to retire in the light you have done. The smallness of the command was my only reason. I am fully impressed with the services you have rendered your country on many occasions, and have often lamented that the Situation of the State should be such as to put it out of my Power to enable you to gain fresh laurels. That you have some enemies is certain, and that they have misrepresented you is certain; but their representations have never had sufficient weight to injure you materially with the Executive.[2] They knew you had orders to build Forts for the Protection of the Country; as it was not done they had some cause to complain; and you not informing me immediately why the instructions were not carried into Execution gave a force to the clamors that would have not have been attended to if you had been explicit in time, as you have since. I shall be glad to see you as soon as your Affairs will permit you to come to Richmond.'[3]

Unaware of Governor Harrison's letters to others reflecting upon him, General Clark evidently accepted these friendly assurances at face value, overlooked the governor's effort to shift blame from himself, and apparently always regarded him as a friend.

[1] *Virginia Calendar State Papers*, III, 453.

[2] In view of his letters to others reflecting on Clark's conduct, this assertion seems surprising. Clark's grievance was *not* the permission to resign his command (he had repeatedly asked and earnestly desired that), but the unjust censure of his conduct in not building new forts, and casting on him the blame for the Blue Licks defeat, for which he was not in the remotest degree responsible.

[3] *Draper MSS.* 52 J 84; Virginia State Library, *Governor's Letter Book*, 95.

During this harrowing last year of the war, General Clark suffered a loss like that of General Lee when Stonewall Jackson died. In April he learned that 'Colonel Floyd, one of his brothers and another person, going to the salt works were fired on by Indians, Col Floyd mortally wounded, his brother's horse shot under him, and the third person shot dead'; and 'Col Floyd, with his brother's assistance, got to the salt-works.'[1] Two days later Floyd died. Clark had lost a most capable second and loyal friend, the Kentucky people a mainstay in time of danger, the nation one of the very finest of its forgotten Revolutionary heroes.

[1] Colonel Fleming's Journal, *Draper MSS.*, 2 Z.Z. 69.

CHAPTER XXII

VIRGINIA AND HER WESTERN CREDITORS

AFTER making arrangements to turn over to Major Walls the command of the remnant of his Illinois Regiment at the Falls, General Clark journeyed over the Mountains to Richmond to present his accounts to the Governor. They had already been investigated and approved by the Commissioners of Western Military Accounts headed by Colonel Fleming, who reported on only two items of his claim: namely, for his officer's pay and for reimbursement for his flour purchase for his troops at the Falls.[1] The state's far greater obligations to him on account of his innumerable personal endorsements of her military supply bills were not included in the report, but were left for future adjustment. The commissioners reported as follows:

'It appears to the Commissioners that their is due to Genl George R Clarke for flour &c furnished the garrison of Fort Nelson, one thousand two hundred and four Pounds 6/5½ for his pay as Colonel from the 2d January 1778, untill the 22d January 1781 £1101...for his pay as Brigadier Genl from the 22d January 1781, untill the 26th June 1783, £1092: 10: 0 in all three thousand three hundred and ninety seven Pounds 16/5½ as pr account and vouchers received.'[2]

Soon afterward the Governor's Council ordered the Auditor to grant General Clark military certificates for his officer's pay to January 8th, 1782, and 'warrants on the military fund for what became due him after that date and a warrant for any moneys due him exclusive of his pay.'[3]

It thus officially appears that for all his years of service, from the time he started on his expedition against Kaskaskia to the end of the Revolution, he had never received one penny of his officer's pay! Nor had he asked for any![4] Far greater

---

[1] *Draper MSS.* 46 J 24–5; Virginia State Library, *Executive Council Order*, July 1, 1783.

[2] *Report of Fleming's Commission*, Virginia State Library. After long delay he received land for this officer's pay, but it was worth nothing like the amount of the pay and he lost nearly all of it in

paying the debts he had contracted for the state.

[3] Virginia State Library, *Executive Council Minutes*, July 1, 1783.

[4] Washington rightly deserves the nation's gratitude for serving through the Revolutionary War without pay; Clark not only served six years without pay,

than his officer's pay, however, were his outlays in taking up a great number of Virginia's military supply bills. These were not ordered paid, but left unsettled. Far worse for him, he was not relieved of his liability as surety upon many other bills which he had been unable to pay. Instead, he was left throughout life harassed and humiliated by suits on these state bills. He was powerless to restore his shattered fortune by engaging in some profitable business, for had he made money it would only have been seized by the holders of these state bills, who were rarely the men who had furnished the supplies, but speculators who had bought up the bills for almost nothing.[1] Had there been a bankruptcy law he might have sought its relief from them; as it was he was left liable at any time to be thrown into prison for not paying these debts of the state.

Nor was his own financial ruin all he had to bear, for he had to witness the distressing poverty of friends whom he had induced to assume, like himself, the burden of the state's debts. Many of them had received bills personally endorsed by General Clark, and in their distress appealed to him. Thus, a Pittsburg merchant who had furnished supplies for his Detroit expedition wrote him:

Dr. Sr:
'No in my Great Distress I send you thes lines. Everything that I have is going to be sold for Some Debt that I contracted for part of the goods that you Got from me. ...If you Do Not Relieve me now I am a ruined man, but I hope you have Gratetude and Onner to

---

but sacrificed his all. In 1780 he did ask the Assembly for a tract of land on the north side of the Ohio to compensate him for what was then owing him by the state; but the grant was not made. An Assembly committee reported favorably on his petition, extolled his 'great service, not only in reducing the British posts, ...but saving the inhabitants of the western frontiers of this and the neighboring states,' and recommended that the grant he asked be made, but required him to pay for it £20 per hundred acres, or about £7000. (Virginia State Library, *Journal House of Delegates,* June 30, 1781.) The committee evidently intended to be generous, but the land was poor and then worth no such price, and the payment required for

it was far more than Clark could make. The Assembly, however, rejected the committee's report and refused to make the grant. Thus, notwithstanding the excessive payment required, and although the grant was asked only to relieve him from the state's own debts, and would have amounted to less than one acre in forty thousand of the northwestern lands he won for her, he was left unrelieved and throughout life bound for her debts.

[1] Many of these bills, endorsed by Clark, Pollock, and other patriots, were thus bought and held by one Simon Nathan, who was more sophisticated in political and legal methods than they, and managed to get his claims for large amounts arbitrated and paid.

make me hole. Dr Sr I hope you will Rite Emmedently to get Relief as I am in Distress Your Complien will for ever Obledge

Your Umble Servt

JOHN GIBSON[1]

A French physician and surgeon, Dr. Conard, was employed to treat the Illinois Regiment troops, and received bills on the state for his pay and medicines. These he sent to the capital for payment. Months and years passed, but he could get nothing. He went in person to Richmond to press for payment, but was referred to the western commissioners. In an amusing but pathetic memorial, quoted in the footnote, he indignantly told the story of his hard treatment.[2]

Far greater were the hardships of Oliver Pollock. He was a rich man when the Revolution began, but with uncalculating patriotism had accepted a great number of supply bills drawn on him by Congress and Virginia. To pay the bills he was compelled to mortgage and sell his property, and even give up his home; but a large debt still remained. To get Congress and Virginia to reimburse him, he set sail with wife and children for Philadelphia; but, stopping at Havana, was sued for some $57,000.00 of these debts and thrown into a debtor's prison. His wife and children faced starvation. A kind friend sent

---

[1] *Draper MSS. 52 J 56.*

[2] 'Give me leave to represent to you that five years have elapsed since I have solicited payment of my account. ... Your Excellency and Council, advised me to go to Kentucky and General Clark. I have not the means of carrying me there. What can I do on impossibility like this?

'It is everywhere allowed a sick man to complain. I am in the condition of a sick man. Such relief [is] what pains me; and I supplicate your Excellency to have my accounts examined and to consider if it is expedient, or becoming the Governor of a state, to put off payment of my just debt in the manner it is done, — never to be ended.

'Is it then that I did not take care of the soldiers, sick, and wounded? Did I not furnish them with the medicines, a very large house to lodge, and nurse the sick men? Has not the rent of said house cost me fifty dollars, hard money, a month? And who ought to pay this rent, I, a poor surgeon, or the State of Virginia? Are my services in this nothing?

Did a single sick or wounded soldier die under my care? whereas, before I entered on the service, they died as if they had been poisoned. ...

'I have nothing to do with the commissioners of Kentucky. I have no knowledge of the state. It was in the Illinois that I contracted with the officers of the Army of Virginia.

'The Commissioners allowed that they did not know the price of medicines, and they are not fitting men to judge of my account without hurting their conscience. Governor Harrison looked at me as if I was a rogue, a rascal, or a villain; and I do not know that he had any reason to do so. In a word he treated me durtily.

'These are the hardships of a man who has saved the lives of your soldiers. ... If I had carried my medicines to New Orleans, instead of selling them to General Clark's army, I could have sold them 200 per cent dearer than I sold them and could have got paid for them.' (Virginia State Library, *Illinois Regiment Papers*, loose.)

them to France, where they suffered all the miseries of poverty in a strange land, while the anxious husband and father lay in the Havana prison, ignorant of their fate. Finally Mrs. Pollock was given passage for herself and children to America. She went to Governor Harrison and piteously begged for some part of the money due from the state to her husband. She was given a pittance and her husband's claim ordered to be audited; but this was not done, for there were no paid auditing clerks, and she was left dependent on charity.

At length some of Pollock's New Orleans friends became his sureties, and got him released. He went to Congress and pleaded for what it owed him, and Robert Morris pleaded for him, but in vain. Congress did not deny that it owed Pollock a large sum. On the contrary, it commended his 'zeal and industry as commercial agent of the United States at New Orleans'; declared that 'he had advanced large sums out of his private fortune and...contracted large debts...for the service of the United States' and even 'that the public faith, justice, and humanity require that the sundry accounts should be liquidated and the balance paid'; but neither was done. It paid not a cent! The excuse it gave was that 'in some cases' his accounts embraced outlays for both Virginia and the United States, and it therefore 'Resolved, that it be recommended to the State of Virginia to cause the accounts of Mr. Pollock with that State to be adjusted,...in order that Mr. Pollock's accounts with the United States may be adjusted.' [1] Why Congress did not pay those items in the account which were *not* embraced with Virginia's and why it could not determine, as well as Virginia, what part of his outlays were for its own benefit, were not explained.

Despairing of justice from Congress, Pollock appealed to Virginia for a settlement and payment of his claim. After long delay, the claim was referred to the Auditor for adjustment; but nothing was done. At length the Assembly ordered an arbitrarily fixed sum paid him in yearly installments out of a specified fund; but when he applied for payment, the fund was found exhausted. Then the propriety of some items in his account was questioned and all payments suspended.

---

[1] *Journal Continental Congress*, Oct. 22, 1782, and MS. File; Virginia State Library, *Illinois Regiment Papers* (loose), A 163. See also *Pollock's Memorial, id.,* A 163, with Illinois Regiment Papers.

In his distress, Pollock appealed to Clark, saying: 'Let me call aloud on your Candor and Justice and desire that on this occasion you will not suffer them. Step forth, rescue your country from the Eternal Disgrace that must attend their iniquitous reward of my Exertions, as you have by Exertions on the Mississippi saved and preserved that valuable Country for the state you serve.'[1] In reply Clark wrote:

'*Sir*. ...I am heartily sorry that you should meet with such disappointment in the settlement of your accounts. I am sensible that you have no drafts on the state from me but what ought to be paid, as vouchers for every article, even to the smallest amount those bills were drawn for, is now in my possession and will show the propriety of them. [MSS. torn] ... and at the time of their being given I knew of no such thing as depreciation of currency. What reason Government has for not paying those just debts I cant account for, except its inability; but more than probable you are a better Judge than I am, being at the seat of government. I have already taken Every step in my power to get the Creditors of the State paid. ... (What method can you point out to me?) If I was worth the money I would cheerfully pay myself and trust the State; but can assure you with truth that I am entirely reduced myself by advancing everything I could raise, and except what the State owes me, am not worth a Spanish dollar.

'I wish it was in my power to step forth and save my country from the disgrace that is likely to fall on her. If I could find the means, nothing would give me such pleasure; and [it would] fully recompense all the uneasiness I have suffered on account of those persons, many of whom I know have advanced all they had on the faith of the government. ...If you can point out anything further that is in my power, I shall most Cheerfully embrace it.'[2]

Years were to pass before Pollock could even get his accounts audited. Two years after the Revolution he wrote Governor Henry (then again governor) that he was again 'in prison on account of debt incurred by advances made to the State of Virginia,' and said: 'I hope your Excellency will in turn pay the same honor to my signature as I have done *yours*, at the *critical moment* for a much larger sum, for which, and other advances for your state, I and my family are reduced to implore as a charity what is due to common justice.'[3]

Almost alone, however, amongst all the men who contributed in service or money to the winning of the west, Pollock

[1] *Draper MSS.* 52 J 26.
[2] Virginia State Library, *Illinois Regiment Papers* (loose), A 160.
[3] *Virginia Calendar State Papers*, IV, 14.

did at last receive some measure of justice from both Virginia and Congress; whereupon, being a man of remarkable commercial ability, he was able to restore his fortune and died in comfortable circumstances.

Clark's concern for the friends who had involved themselves was afterwards feelingly expressed in the following letter to Governor Harrison submitting his own account against the state.

RICHMOND *June* 16, 1783

Sir:

I am apprehensive that few persons since the Commencement of the war with America have had the same cause to address their superiors on a subject similar to that of this letter. It is with pain equal to the misfortunes that cause it that I daily view persons in this city, and reflect on others absent, that have Reduced themselves to a state of Indigence by supporting the Credit of the State to the westward, with a zeal that I at that time thought actuated the breast of Every friend to this Country. What must be the feelings of those men that advanced their property with the pleasing Reflection of supporting the General Cause, making no doubt of Speedy Reward at the End of the war, should they find that they were not to receive their payments for a series of years to come?

Since my return to this place I have discovered Various opinions respecting the propriety of those Expeditions. As it is a truth that will appear obvious to every man that will make himself acquainted with the situation of the frontiers and its Enemies, I can with the greatest boldness affirm that it hath been the Consequential Services attending those Expeditions that have saved the frontiers of this State from ruin, and prevented us from going to three times the Expense. What would have been our Situation had not the Executive prosecuted the measures he did to the westward, and through the means of her Officers silenced many of those tribes of Indians, by treaties and otherways, and kept them Either attacht to us or in Suspense until it was too late for them to Execute any plan destructive to our Interests? Had not those measures been taken, it is easy to Conceive what would have been the Consequence of four or five thousand Indian warriors, with all the assistance Brittain could give them, let loose on our frontiers for the course of seven years. Might we not with propriety suppose that part of the Blue Ridge would have been contended for, and all the assistance you have received from the Valuable frontier Country. . been lost to you?

For my own part, altho I have suffer'd Every disadvantage that a person could experience, for seven years [of] anxiety and fatigue — subject to the Clamours of Every Vilainous principal, perticularly the Enemies of this state — I could bear it with greater fortitude was I to be the only sufferer, and the Creditors of the State alluded to paid.

The whole of the western account will now be laid before you. After considering the Expense of Recruiting and supporting several hundred troops for a number of years in a Country where Every article necessary for them was Extravigantly dear, and the great number of treaties that have been held with Various tribes of Indians, every kind of military stores to purchase, expeditions against the Enemy, &c, I flatter myself you will find them, when reduced to their value, exceedingly moderate; as I know that Every attention was paid in order to have them so, where they came under my notice. But the great distance from one post to another often put it out of my power certainly to know for a considerable time what conduct was used, and many large accounts [have been] presented which the department under my command had nothing to do with; the whole of which I expect the Commissioners of western accounts will fully point out to you, as those gentlemen have been at uncommon pains to make themselves fully acquainted with every circumstance. Knowledge of the conduct of the greatest part of those creditors Enduces me perhaps to be more sollicitous for their being favoured, as I conceived the motives which [induced] them to advance their property was of the purest nature; and it must be granted they have been of Infinite advantage to the State, as they at the Earliest period showed their zeal for the cause. Otherways, the Country we had possession of must have been abandoned; Our Interest with the Indian nations totally lost; ... Kentucky (the greatest preservative of the frontiers of this state) would have been depopulated; and those numerous savages would have poured in on Every quarter of the frontier, which must have been supported by the very troops which have Rendered such signal service in the Eastern defence. Those Ideas I always had in View and thought myself happy in preventing the Evil. Many of my smaller charges against the state have no Vouchers. After you consider the Various circumstances attending the Command I was Interested with, you could not suppose it strange that only memorandums should be taken of some of them and many totally neglected; which I doubt will prove Ruinous to my private Interest, as the great Variety of other publick business solely Engaged my attention and Required all the adress I was master of to superintend the publick interest to advantage — not only the Civil Government of the people of the Illinois to attend to, Recruiting &c, disposing of troops that was difficult to support &c, but numerous tribes of Indians that had Ingaged in war against us that Required great and constant attention, as well as considerable sums of money, to support necessary Emissaryes among them, ... and latterly numerous partisans to Contend with that was Confusing the Inhabitants and nearly proved Ruinous to the department. I hope to be excused in praying for an Immediate Redress of those creditors, which I expect there is no doubt of, as this State hath Repeatedly given proof of her greatfull disposition, and which will farther Inable her with greater propriety to claim that honour she deserves for protecting through the course of the war at least one third of the western frontier of the United States.

As for the advances I have made of my own by bonds, &c, in cases where the necessary Requisitions could not be otherways obtained, from the low state of our finances, I pray for an Indemnity by your Interposition.[1]

At Richmond General Clark was received by Governor Harrison with every mark of esteem. The minutes of the Executive Council on July 1st, 1783, recite that 'The Board, considering the war to be so far concluded as to render the services of a brigadier general in the Western Country unnecessary, advise that General Clark be discontinued, and that the Governor be requested to return to that Gentleman the sincere thanks of the Board for the eminent services rendered by him to his country.'[2] Next day Governor Harrison wrote him:

In Council, July 2, 1783

Sir:

The conclusion of the war and the distressed situation of the state with respect to its finances calls on us to adopt the most prudent economy. It is for this reason alone I have come to a determination to give over all thoughts for the present of carrying on an offensive war against the Indians, which you will easily perceive will render the services of a general officer in that quarter unnecessary, and will therefore consider yourself out of command. But before I take leave of you, I feel myself called upon, in the most forcible manner, to return you my thanks and those of my Council, for the very great and singular services you have rendered your country in wresting so great and valuable a territory out of the hands of the British enemy, repelling the attacks of their savage allies, and carrying on a successful war in the heart of their country. This tribute of praise and thanks I am happy to communicate to you as the united voice of the Executive. I am, with respect, Sir, Yours &c,

BENJAMIN HARRISON[3]

In view of the unjust censure he had received from the governor, this handsome tribute must have been peculiarly gratifying to the young general. Replying, he wrote:

RICHMOND, *July 2, 1783*

Sir:

I had the pleasure of receiving your letter, of this day's date, and can assure you that no reward for past services could be so satis-

[1] *Draper MSS.* 52 J 86.

[2] Virginia State Library, *Executive Journal*, July 1, 1783; *Draper MSS.* 13 S 151.

[3] *Draper MSS.* 52 J 25; Virginia State Library, *Governor's Letter Book*, 182.

factory to me as the gratitude of my country. I am happy in the idea of having met with the approbation of your Excellency and Council. Should anything hereafter transpire wherein I could be of service to you in the promotion of the interests of your government, its execution will again enable me to enjoy some of those pleasures that I have often experienced of having rendered service to my country.

I have the honour to be your Excellency's Most obedient and humble Servant:

GEORGE ROGERS CLARK [1]

Thus ended, at thirty years of age, General Clark's career as Virginia's commanding officer in the west during the Revolution. Notwithstanding poverty and debts, he was at this time by no means dispirited, for there was much to cheer him. Although no heed was paid to his request to be relieved from the state debts, he believed that he would in time be freed from them. The charges which had been made against him of inebriety and neglect of duty he had doubtless dismissed from his mind, for even Governor Harrison himself had declared them false and due to traduction by enemies. Furthermore, he had great cause for justifiable pride, for he had every reason to believe that Jefferson was right when he wrote him: 'You have enterprized deeds which will hand down your name with honor to future times'; and no one can read Clark's correspondence without seeing that his ambition was to win and deserve fame of that kind.[2]

Shortly after he was freed from military command, a meeting of the continental and state line officers of Virginia was held at Richmond to consider methods of securing the benefit of large western land grants to them under a recent act of the Virginia Assembly. Although much the youngest officer present, they chose him as their chairman and afterwards elected him to the responsible position of superintendent-surveyor to select, survey and allot the lands granted them.[3] He entered at

[1] *Virginia State Library; Draper MSS.* 11 J 26. Governor Harrison requested him to prepare a written statement giving his views of the proper course to be pursued by the state in its future dealings with the Indians, and this he did in a long letter setting forth his ideas with force and clearness. What they were may be surmised from his previous writings.

[2] After Clark captured Hamilton, his brother Jonathan was next in command under Colonel Henry Lee in the brilliant capture of Paulus Hook and for his services received a gold medal from Congress and a letter of praise from Washington. Learning of this, George Rogers wrote him: 'It gives me the greatest pleasure to hear of your being universally esteemed in the continental army, which is justly due to virtue...My greatest happiness will hereafter be to find it shine forth in our family with double lustre.' (*Draper MSS.* 2 L 1.)

[3] The law required him to be examined and his proficiency as a surveyor

once upon his new duties, which lasted some years, and appears to have given entire satisfaction to his fellow officers.

Another and very different employment for the young general was suggested by his friend Jefferson. They had been corresponding about natural history objects in the western country, and in one of his letters Jefferson said:

'I find they have subscribed a very large sum of money in England for exploring the country from the Missispi to California. they pretend it is only to promote knolege. I am afraid they have thoughts of coming into that quarter. some of us have been talking here in a feeble way of making the attempt to search that country, but I doubt whether we have enough of that kind of spirit to raise the money. how would you like to lead such a party? tho I am afraid our prospect is not worth asking the question.'[1]

It is interesting to find Jefferson so early interested in the future of the unexplored region between the Mississippi and the Pacific, and concerned lest the British get possession of it. In reply Clark wrote him:

'Your proposition respecting a tour to the west and Northwest of the Continent would be extremely agreeable to me, could I afford it; but I have [of] late discovered that I knew nothing of the lucrative policy of the World, supposing my duty required every attention and sacrifice to the Publick Interest, but must now look forward for future support.

'Should Congress resolve to have the Western Country Explored I should take pleasure in lending all the aid in my power as an individual. It is what I think we ought to do; but pardon me when I inform you that I think our Ideas of the Business in genly wrong. Large parties will never answer the purpose. They will alarm the Indian Nations they pass through. Three or four young Men well qualified for the Task might perhaps compleat your wishes at a very tryfling Expence. A tolerable Subsistance on their return might procure them. They must learn the Language of the distant Nations they pass through, the geography of their Cuntry, antient Speach or Tradition, passing as men tracing the Steps of our four Fathers, wishing to know from whence we come. this would require four or five years, an Expence worthy the attention of Congress.'[2]

certified by the professor of mathematics of William and Mary College. The professor was the Reverend James Madison, cousin of the future president, and afterwards Episcopal Bishop of Virginia. His certificate to Clark is still preserved. (*Draper MSS.* 53 J 3.)

[1] *Draper MSS.* 52 J 93; *American Historical Review*, III, 673. Six years later Jefferson while minister to Paris got Ledyard's promise to 'go to America and penetrate from Kentucke to the western side of the continent.' (Ford's *Works of Jefferson*, v, 455.)

[2] Holograph, *Author's MSS.*

The plan Jefferson afterward adopted for the Lewis and Clark Expedition to the Pacific followed the general lines here suggested.

Most of the time while in Virginia in 1783 General Clark spent at the home of his parents. The next year they removed to Kentucky, with their younger children, Lucy, Elizabeth, William and Frances, and a number of slaves, and settled on a tract of rich land near Louisville, called 'Mulberry Hill.' Although the Indians were then generally quiet, depredations by some of them were still frequent and when nearing their destination the Clarks narrowly escaped massacre. At the new Kentucky home General Clark lived for some fifteen years after the Revolution.[1]

[1] In 1783 four of the five Clark brothers who had been serving in the war — Jonathan, George Rogers, John, and Edmund — were gathered for the first time at the old Clark home in Caroline. Richard, then twenty-three, was in the west, where he had been serving four years under George Rogers. William was a boy of thirteen. September 19th. Jonathan's first child was baptized and his diary says George Rogers and Edmund stood sponsors. John took no part in the ceremony, for he was then dying of consumption contracted while a prisoner on a British prison ship in New York harbor. When only nineteen he became a first lieutenant. His regiment distinguished itself in the battles of Brandywine and Germantown, but in the latter encounter, after breaking through the enemy's right wing and taking many British, the regiment was surrounded and captured. Young Clark was held prisoner until the end of the war, nearly six years. After his return his father sent him to the West Indies in search of health, but he got no better and next year returned home to die. October 29th. Jonathan's diary says: 'My brother John died,' and 'November 2nd. At my father's; my brother John buried.' Next day appears this entry: '3rd. Clear; at Mr. Mason's; set off for Kentucky.' He was going there to prepare a home for his parents on the land near Louisville which George Rogers had purchased for his father some years before. A year after this Richard Clark lost his life in the west.

CHAPTER XXIII

PEACE DIPLOMACY AND THE TREATY OF PARIS

LEAVING Clark for the moment, attention should be directed to the diplomacy during the Revolution with reference to the region between the Alleghenies and the Mississippi. Aside from American independence, the possession of that western region was regarded as of paramount importance by Spain, France, and Great Britain alike, and it was the object of much anxiety to all of them in their diplomatic dealings with the United States.

Florida Blanca, the minister who directed Spain's diplomacy, aimed to make the Gulf of Mexico a closed Spanish sea, and for that purpose coveted Florida and the country north of it, at least to the Ohio. Spain's ministers always feared the Americans west of the Alleghenies would grow numerous and strong enough to wrest Louisana from Spain, and perhaps even Mexico and the West Indies. D'Aranda warned the Spanish King of this danger in these prophetic words: 'This federal republic is born a pigmy; a day will come when it will be a giant, even a Colossus, formidable to these countries. Liberty of conscience, the facility of establishing a new population on immense lands, as well as the advantages of a new government, will draw thither farmers and artisans from all nations. In a few years we shall watch with grief the tyrannical existence of this same Colossus.'

Throughout the Revolution, Florida Blanca's dealings with America were directed to gaining our surrender to Spain of the region north of British Florida, and our admission of her exclusive right to use the lower Mississippi; for he knew that by closing that river she could prevent the growth of American population west of the Alleghenies. He was resolved that Spain should not recognize American independence, or send a minister to Congress, until these points were gained; and in his efforts to win them he was secretly but powerfully aided by Vergennes, the able minister of foreign affairs for France.

Vergennes' main objects were to humiliate Great Britain and aggrandize France — his methods shrewd, treacherous, and heartless. Some writers have thought him a true friend of America, but his own writings now show that he was not. His real aims in helping us to win independence were to cripple Great Britain, to exhaust the American states, to keep them disunited, to confine them east of the Alleghenies, and to make them forever dependent on France.[1]

To make clear the story of the final peace negotiations, it is necessary to go back for a moment to 1778, when Vergennes sent his confidential secretary, Gerard, with the treaty of alliance between France and the American states, for approval by Congress. With the treaty, Gerard also carried his chief's written instructions to violate it.[2] He was to persuade or force Congress to surrender to Spain a large part of our western country. This policy was dictated by no friendship for Spain, but Vergennes needed her help in the war and hoped to get it by offering France's aid to obtain what she wanted; and, above all else, Spain wanted two things; namely, first to recover Gibraltar from Great Britain, and secondly, to secure a firm foothold east of the Mississippi. Early in 1779 France and Spain made a secret treaty of alliance whereby France agreed to continue the war until Gibraltar should be restored to Spain; and it was also understood that Vergennes would aid Spain to secure a large part of our western country.

Gibraltar was besieged, but in vain; Vergennes found it was impossible to take it except by ruinous outlay, and the obligation to continue the war until it was recovered for Spain hung upon him like a millstone, which grew heavier and heavier as the war progressed and France became financially exhausted. When, therefore, the British gave signs of weakening and willingness to grant America independence, he, too, longed for peace. Yet he dared not propose one before recovering Gibraltar, lest Spain be offended and join Great Britain against France. He knew, however, that Florida Blanca desired our western country even more than Gibraltar, and would relieve France of her obligation to recover that fortress if Congress could be induced to surrender to Spain the region east of the Mississippi, and the exclusive control of the river. The inter-

---

[1] The French minister evidently hoped for the ultimate recovery of all France had claimed and lost in America. See Professor Frederick J. Turner's 'Policy of France toward the Mississippi Valley,' *American Historical Review*, x 246.

[2] *Revolutionary Diplomatic Correspondence of U.S.* (Wharton), ii, 523–26.

esting story of Gerard's efforts to get this surrender cannot be told here. Suffice it to say, his mission entirely failed, for Congress stood firm in refusing to yield a foot of our territory. Disappointed, sick, and irritable, he sailed for Europe; and with him went John Jay as our envoy to Spain.

Jay's mission was to get Spain to recognize America's independence, join the alliance against Great Britain, and make Congress a loan of several million pounds. But Florida Blanca had no thought of doing any of these things unless Spain should first get a surrender of our western country. He knew Congress was in dire need of money, and his policy was to hold out the prospect of a liberal loan, but to procrastinate until both Jay and Congress were reduced to desperation and forced to make the surrender. His treatment of our high-minded envoy makes American blood boil; but the story is too long to be told here.

After keeping Jay on the rack for many months with delusive hopes of a loan and treaty of alliance, and after desperate efforts on his part to save his country's financial credit by pledging his own to pay a flood of bills drawn on him by Congress with the hope that Spain would pay them, Florida Blanca could not force him to agree to surrender any of our western lands, or our right to use the Mississippi. Nor, on the other hand, could Jay get either loan or treaty without making the surrender. His mission was a complete failure, except in one very important respect: he learned to understand the methods of Spanish diplomacy, and that Vergennes and Florida Blanca were playing a brace game to despoil America — knowledge that was to stand him in good stead in the coming peace negotiations at Paris.

While Jay was still in Spain, Gerard's successor, Count Luzerne, became France's minister at Philadelphia. Soon afterwards Vergennes' double aim seemed nearly accomplished, for both Great Britain and America were almost completely worn out by the war and very anxious for peace. The British had been driven from the country west of the Alleghenies, but still held New York and Charleston, and they controlled the Chesapeake and Delaware entrances to Baltimore and Philadelphia. All efforts to get Congress to surrender the western country to Spain having failed, Vergennes determined to use a new kind of intimidation to force it to accept such a treaty of peace as he would make for both America and France with Great Britain; and that peace would certainly have given Spain much of the territory she coveted. With many professions of loyal attachment to the states, and assurances of his utmost efforts to secure for them all their territorial and other rights, he directed Luzerne to impress Congress with the importance of promptly authorizing commissioners to conclude a general peace in conjunction with France. Congress had already appointed Adams for that purpose; but Vergennes had found him not only provincially offensive, but unmanageable, and wished to be rid of him. Luzerne thereupon complained of Adams and arrogantly demanded that 'Congress should draw a line of conduct to that minister.' Humiliating as the demand was, Congress complied with it and appointed Jay, Franklin and Laurens as joint treaty commissioners with Adams.

Meantime, Luzerne was skilfully playing upon the fears of Congress to force it to instruct its commissioners to be wholly guided in the negotiations by Vergennes. He communicated alarming reports of armed intervention intended by Russia and other European powers to compel the belligerents to make peace under the rule of *uti possidetis*, by which each belligerent would be allowed to retain whatever territory it had won. Vergennes well knew this would cause consternation in Congress, for such a forced treaty would have left New York, Charleston, and other valuable eastern places in British possession. For fear of losing them, Congress dared not openly claim the western country by right of conquest, lest under the *uti possidetis* rule Great Britain should be given her still more valuable conquests along our Atlantic seaboard. Reading the journals and diplomatic instructions of Congress, one is constantly impressed with the fact that its members were alive to the danger in this situation.

Fear of armed intervention and loss of the eastern cities was not, however, the only fear Luzerne aroused in Congress. He alarmed it even more by repeated hints that, unless it would direct our peace commissioners to join in such a treaty with Great Britain and Spain as Vergennes would make for us, France would consider herself free to make a separate peace on her own account. This would have left the prostrated American states the easy prey of British arms. Even more alarming still was Luzerne's intimation to Congress that if it did not let Vergennes make the treaty of peace for us, France would furnish no further aid in carrying on the war. Reading of the mortifying dependence of Congress at this time upon the French King, and of its cringing obedience to the arrogant commands of Luzerne, makes an American blush; yet there seemed to be no alternative, for the starving must beg. Esau was not the last to sell a birthright for a mess of pottage.

Finally Congress yielded to all of Luzerne's demands. It directed the American commissioners to 'make the most candid and confidential communications upon all subjects to the ministers of our most generous ally, the King of France, to undertake nothing in the negotiations . . . without their knowledge and concurrence, and *ultimately to govern yourselves by their advice and opinion.*' They were in effect commanded to sign any treaty of peace Vergennes would make, provided that it should secure American independence and a continuance of the alliance with France. What territory should be embraced within the United States — whether New York, or Charleston, should be American or British, or the western country surrendered to Spain — Vergennes was to decide for us!

Had those instructions been obeyed, the United States would probably have been left little, if any, territory west of the Alleghenies; Spain would doubtless have been given dominant possessions there east of the Mississippi; American independence would have been little more than a name; the divided and bankrupt Atlantic States would have been alternately the prey of the heartless diplomacy of France, Great Britain, or Spain, and dependent on one or the other of those powers.

The humiliating instructions of Congress to our peace commissioners, to allow Vergennes to dictate the terms of the treaty to suit himself, were not followed, however. That they were not, was due to John Jay. When he reached Paris, Adams was in Holland; Laurens a prisoner in the Tower of London; Franklin, old, frail, and flattered by the attention of French savants, nobles, and royalty, and unduly grateful to the French government for its aid to America, was completely duped by Vergennes. The old philosopher credulously gave his entire confidence to the French minister, and thereby came dangerously near ruining his country. Fortunately, Jay's diplomatic wits had been sharpened by his experience in Spain, and with unerring penetration he now threaded the maze of Vergennes' treacherous scheming. Becoming convinced that the wily Frenchman had sent an agent to negotiate secretly with Lord Shelburne, the British prime minister, for a treaty which would divide our western country between Spain and Great Britain, Jay determined to circumvent him by sounding the British minister about a separate treaty between America and Great Britain. In taking this step he knew he would violate the instructions of Congress, offend Franklin, infuriate Vergennes, and perhaps endanger our alliance with France. He knew his own countrymen might believe him a traitor, conspiring with the British enemy; but he knew also that his country was at stake, and to save it he determined to hazard everything he held most dear. In American history there is no finer example of moral courage and patriotism.

The rest of this thrilling diplomatic story will be told fully elsewhere,[1] but will only be briefly mentioned here. Shelburne sent agents to Paris to treat secretly for a separate peace with America. Jay told Franklin and Adams what he had done; Adams without hesitation, and Franklin very reluctantly, approved his action and joined him in ignoring the instructions from Congress. From that time forth there were no 'candid and confidential communications upon all subjects to the ministers of our most generous ally the King of France.' On the contrary, a separate treaty of peace was made with Great Britain by which she ceded to us the whole Revolutionary West, with the right forever to the free navigation of the Mississippi to the sea.

Some writers have thought that in the Paris negotiations the Revolutionary West was deemed of minor importance, and was conceded by Shelburne only as a conciliatory compromise to effect a real reconciliation with the Americans. A more radical error would be hard to find.

For Great Britain the negotiations were conducted throughout under the directions of the prime minister, Lord Shelburne, who was called to power because his country was financially exhausted and unable to continue the war. Her people demanded peace, and he undertook to secure it. His confidential agents at Paris, Oswald and Strachey, were charged with the actual conduct of the negotiations, but under his constant supervision.

[1] Author's *Revolutionary West in Diplomacy and Politics* (in preparation).

Before our commissioners would consider other terms of
peace, they demanded of Great Britain an unqualified acknowledgment of American independence, and early in the negotiations this was conceded. Thereafter the subject of most
determined conflict between the British and American negotiators was over the question whether our western country, and
particularly the Illinois, should become British or American.
This assertion is not undisputed, but will be found abundantly
sustained by the record facts of the negotiations. Hinsdale
truly says that, next to independence, the disposition of our
western country 'was the most important question involved in
the negotiation, far transcending' all others; but he thinks this
was not appreciated at the time by Jay, Franklin, and Adams.
'It is impossible,' he says, 'to say much about the western
boundary discussions, because we know next to nothing about
them. Other controversies at Paris, far less important, were
reported much more fully; but here, the information that we
possess only piques our curiosity. The right to fish on the
banks of Newfoundland was thought more valuable in 1782
than the ownership of the valleys of Ohio, the prairies of Illinois, and the forests of Michigan!'[1] On the contrary, we may
be very sure none of our peace negotiators thought anything
of the kind, but that all of them realized the supreme importance of holding the great western country—alike for the preservation of our independence, for the restoration of our financial credit, and for the growth of a great American nation.
To suppose otherwise would be to presume a lack of intelligence on their part utterly inconsistent with all we know of
them. Franklin had long been deeply interested in the western country; Jay had long fought for it with Florida Blanca at
Madrid, and Adams stood with Jay.[2]

The British negotiators well knew that, unless we would
give up this western country, Great Britain could only recover
it by continuing the war and reconquering it. Because, indeed,
diplomacy is nearly always roundabout, and diplomatic talk
is largely palaver about legal and moral rights, there was almost endless fencing about royal and colonial territorial rights,
charter grants and repeals, royal proclamations, and other

[1] Burke Aaron Hinsdale, *The Old
Northwest* (Boston, 1899), 179-80.

[2] See numerous proofs of this in Fran-
cis Wharton's *Revolutionary Diplomatic
Correspondence of the United States*
(Washington, 1889), e.g., v, 657, 838;
VI, 23.

argumentative make-weights; but all this was merely superficial, for diplomacy does not aim at justice, but at successful bargaining. All knew the real question was whether Shelburne would continue the war to reconquer the western country — whether our negotiators would give it up to get peace.

Not only was Great Britain financially exhausted, but the fact was so well known that Oswald admitted to Franklin she could no longer carry on the war. 'Our enemies,' he said, 'can do what they please with us; they have the ball at their feet.'[1] Yet Shelburne contended desperately to the very last for at least a part of the western country, particularly the Illinois. Having long been active head of the British Board of Trade for the Colonies, and especially familiar with American affairs, he knew the great strategic value of that region, and that possession of the Illinois would enable Great Britain to build up quickly a western empire which would dominate the whole Mississippi Valley. A rich and level country, the Illinois was unencumbered with tangled forests, was already occupied by a civilized and tractable people, was comparatively free from troublesome Indians, and commanded the great trade arteries between Canada and New Orleans; and, under an orderly British government, Shelburne could confidently look for it to expand and become powerful. He doubtless expected that in due time it would drain population from the poor and demoralized Atlantic states; would detach the western Americans from those east of the Alleghenies, would absorb Spanish Louisiana, and would render the restricted eastern states an easy prey to British diplomacy or British arms.[2]

Although he asserted, with great appearance of finality, that his king was rightful owner of the whole trans-Allegheny region, he very carefully avoided seeming anxious to recover any of it. His policy was to force the American commissioners to offer a surrender of the Illinois, rather than comply with another demand which he would openly press to the utmost; namely, a demand for restoration to the loyalist (Tory) refugees of their confiscated estates, or else compensation to them. He well knew, however, that actual restoration of the estates was impossible; and that the only compensation we could possibly make the loyalists was in our western lands; and it was precisely those lands that he most wanted. His indirect and

---

[1] Wharton, *op. cit.*, v, 570.　　[2] Adams clearly saw this. (*Id.*, vi, 59.)

carefully veiled game to win them makes a most interesting and important chapter in our history. His instructions to Oswald and Strachey, and their conduct, make the game plain. The Americans were to be informed that they (1) must give up their claim of right to fish on the banks of Newfoundland, (2) must pay the debts owing by Americans to British subjects, and (3) must either restore the estates of the loyalists, or else compensate them. Other comparatively trifling issues, such as our northeastern boundary, were from time to time discussed as make-weights in argument, but these three were the main ones.

The dispute about British debts was soon settled, it being agreed that Congress should recommend their payment by the states. To attain his paramount object — a foothold in the Illinois — Shelburne gave very particular directions to Oswald and Strachey. They were not to disclose his great desire for that region, by openly pressing a demand for it, although they were strongly to assert the King's right to the whole West and especially the part north of the Ohio, formerly claimed and ceded by France. To cover his real design, Shelburne instructed them to put forward his demand for the loyalists, and only cautiously suggest our cession of the western lands, as compensations for them — not to furnish Great Britain a strategic foothold in the Illinois! To force such compensation, he told them to declare that British *honor* required it, and that even to gain peace, his King could never abandon his demand. In diplomacy, such a demand, based on honor, is intended to be understood as final and irrevocable — an *ultimatum*.

That this honor-demand of compensation for the loyalists was merely a blind to cover Shelburne's design upon the Illinois can be seen by reading his instructions to Oswald and Strachey. He directed Strachey to 'bring forward the French boundary of Canada' (down to the Ohio), and 'urge these claims and the right of the King to the...domain, *not indeed for their sake, but in order to gain some compensation for the refugees.*'[1] He also told Oswald how to conduct the negotiations, and said: 'As a resource to meet the demands of the refugees, the matter of the boundaries and back lands presents itself.' Had Shelburne cared to express his real aim plainly,

[1] Edmund G. Petty-Fitzmaurice, *Life of William, Earl of Shelburne* (London, 1875–76), III, 281. Author's italics.

he would have transposed this sentence and said: '*As a resource to meet the demands of boundaries and back lands*, the matter of the refugees presents itself.' He suggests to Oswald the method of argument to use with the Americans, saying: 'For the good of America, — whatever the government may be, new provinces must be erected on those back lands and down the Mississippi; and supposing them to be sold, what can be so reasonable as that part of the province, where the King's property alone is in question, should be applied to furnish subsistence to those whom [even] for the sake of peace, he can never, consistently with his honour, entirely abandon.'[1]

This honor *ultimatum* about loyalist compensation was much harped on by Shelburne, for he knew we could only make such compensation by giving up our western lands; and they were his heart's desire. He particularly instructed Oswald that 'An establishment for the loyalists must *always* be on Mr. Oswald's *mind, as it is uppermost in Lord Shelburne's*';[2] and it was evidently understood between them that this 'establishment' was to be in the Illinois. Franklin, reporting the ensuing negotiations, wrote: 'We had much contestation about the boundaries and other articles, which he proposed and we settled. ... They wanted to bring their boundary down to the Ohio, and to settle their loyalists in the Illinois country. We did not choose such neighbors.'[3] 'The British ministers struggled hard for two points,— that the favors granted the royalists should be extended, and our fishery contracted. We silenced them on the first by threatening to produce an account of the mischief done by those people.' Franklin, who was ever a shrewd and bold trader, set against the British demand for compensation for the royalists a demand for far greater compensation to the Americans for the wanton destruction of their towns and property. Against their demand of the lands of the Illinois, he coolly demanded the lands of Canada to recompense the despoiled Americans. This demand, however, was used only defensively and never seriously pressed. Continuing, his report says: 'As to the second [point, about fishery] when they told us they could not possibly agree to it as we requested it, and must refer it to the ministry in London, we produced a new article

[1] Petty-Fitzmaurice, *op. cit.*, III, 284.   [3] *Id.*, VI, 112–13.
[2] Wharton, *op. cit.*, V, 571. Author's italics.

to be referred at the same time, with a note of the facts in support of it.... It seemed, that to avoid the discussion of this they suddenly changed their minds, dropped the design of recurring to London, and *agreed to allow the fishery as demanded [by us].*' [1]

Again and again the fishery, the northeastern boundary, and other disputes were renewed — the fishery seriously, the other points for make-weights; but to the very last, the British negotiators insisted that the honor of their king demanded compensation for the loyalists, and declared that a 'refusal upon this point will be *the* great obstacle to peace.'[2] All the while, however, the Americans knew this demand was a mere subterfuge to get a British foothold in the Mississippi Valley. Both Jay and Adams were clear about this, and Franklin hardly less so. Adams said: 'We divided upon two points, the Tories and Penobscot [the northeastern boundary], — two *ostensible* points, for it was impossible to believe that my Lord Shelburne or the [British] nation cared much about such points.'[3] At another time Adams wrote: 'I am not sure that the Tories and the ministry and the nation are not secretly stimulated by French emissaries to insist upon Penobscot and a full indemnification to the Tories....Nevertheless, if my Lord Shelburne should not agree with us, these will be *only ostensible points. He cares little for either.*'[4] Jay early understood this and undoubtedly had explained to Adams that this demand was a mere blind to cover Shelburne's designs on the Illinois.[5] Yet, to the very last minute of the negotiations, it was insisted on as an honor-*ultimatum* from which the British king would never recede.[6] Finding the Americans immovable, however, Oswald and Strachey reconsidered their threat to break up the negotia-

---

[1] Wharton, *op. cit.*, VI, 112. Author's italics.

[2] *Id.*, V, 850. Author's italics.

[3] *Id.*, V, 872. Author's italics.

[4] *Id.*, V, 856–57. Author's italics.

[5] *Id.*, V, 850.

[6] *Id.*, V, 805, 848–50; VI, 48. These are but a very few and somewhat hastily selected quotations and citations from the diplomatic records supporting the text. To understand the subject fully it is necessary to study the history of the long conflict between Great Britain, France, and Spain over our western country for many years before the Revolution, and the struggle of Congress and Jay to foil the efforts of Vergennes and Florida Blanca to wrest it from us all through the Revolution. How any one who has made a careful and unbiased investigation of the subject can doubt that Jay, and after him Adams, read aright the treacherous policy of Vergennes towards America, seems incomprehensible, in view of Vergennes' own writings and conduct, and those of his confidential agents and confederates. Yet some, though by no means most of our historians, have represented Vergennes as a real friend of America. The subject will be treated at length in the present writer's *History of the Revolutionary West in Diplomacy and Politics*, in preparation.

tions, gave up this honor-demand, agreed to our terms, and signed Jay's draft of the preliminary treaty of peace making the center line of the Mississippi the western boundary of the United States. The Revolutionary West, with a later change of northern boundary, thus became irrevocably òurs. Because it was ours, independence became real and a blessing instead of a curse, the Federal Union and Constitution possible, and our nation great.

Richer far, in all that makes empire of real worth, than Cortez ever won in Mexico, or Clive in India, our first 'great West,' which Clark and his men won for us, would have been thrown away by the Continental Congress, at the behest of Vergennes, but for one man — John Jay.[1]

The vacillation and neglect of the impoverished Virginia government in supporting Clark were paralleled by the vacillation and neglect of Congress in supporting Jay. The dissention and sedition secretly sown by the land-company promoters to hamper Clark's every effort in the western war had their parallel in the secret conspiracies of our professed friends of France and Spain to hamper and defeat Jay in his desperate efforts to hold our claim upon the western country and the Mississippi. As Clark found those land-company promoters more formidable enemies than even the British and Indians, so Jay found the ministers of France and Spain far more dangerous enemies in diplomacy than our open enemies of exhausted England. As Clark, weakened by the indifference and inaction of the Virginia government and forbidden to carry on plainly necessary offensive operations to hold the country he had won, deliberately violated his instructions and ended active Indian hostilities by destroying the Shawnee towns, so Jay, when almost overwhelmed by the intrigues of Vergennes, unable to count on the support of Franklin, and instructed by Congress to withhold nothing from Vergennes, but to obey his directions in making a treaty, deliberately violated those instructions, secretly and alone took the vital step which circumvented the shrewd Frenchman, and saved our western country. To both Clark and Jay, the people of this nation owe a debt of gratitude they can never repay — a debt never yet duly realized. To their victories in war and diplomacy every

[1] See *Peace Negotiations of 1782-83*, New York Historical Society (Address by John Jay), Nov. 27, 1883, 114.

state between the Alleghenies and the Pacific must trace its history as a member of the Federal Union. Yet comparatively few Americans know John Jay: fewer still know George Rogers Clark.

In this connection it should be said that some writers, in estimating Clark's part in the winning of the region from the Alleghenies to the Mississippi, seem to overlook the effect of his victories in giving the Americans a vast numerical preponderance over the British in the west. Whereas before those victories Great Britain's white population, along the western Great Lakes and in the Illinois, outnumbered the opposing Americans about ten to one, the relative strength of the two sides was completely reversed at the end of the Revolution. By losing the Illinois towns and Vincennes, Great Britain had lost about two fifths of her western white subjects and had left, along the western Lakes, hardly more than thirty-five hundred — nearly all of them none too loyal or militant French Canadians. On the other hand, Clark's victories not only won over Great Britain's subjects in the Illinois and on the Wabash, but made possible the great western immigration which multiplied many times the American population and fighting strength in the west. By the end of the Revolution a cordon of American settlements, containing perhaps thirty or forty thousand people, extended south of the Ohio from southwestern Pennsylvania to central Tennessee and western Kentucky, and thence over the Wabash and Illinois to the Mississippi.

Between these far-separated American and British white opponents, there lived in the Mississippi Valley eastwardly of the Wabash only a very few Indian allies of the British — consisting almost entirely of the Shawnees in southern Ohio and the Delawares of central Indiana — together numbering perhaps less than six hundred men; and both tribes had been severely handled. It was not upon them that the British relied to carry on their offensives against Clark, but upon the far more numerous northwestern Indians near the Lakes; and for over a year before the treaty of peace Great Britain was too exhausted financially to fit them out for war, and therefore prohibited further offensive operations.

Apparently overlooking the financial and numerical weakness of the British themselves, and the small number of their discouraged Indian allies in the region between the Wabash and upper Ohio, some writers assume that this region was in British control at the end of the war, and hence infer that Clark's conquest north of the Ohio was limited to the area of his military occupation in the Illinois and Wabash country. This seems plainly an error. Actual military occupancy rarely limits territorial conquest. The winning of a single strategic point often involves domination of an extensive outlying district. Many a large region, though never entered by the conqueror's troops, has been won by winning a dominant line of approach with a superior force.

It seems neither practicable nor important, however, to ascertain the precise territorial extent of Clark's conquest. Its real import lies in its influence in bringing about Great Britain's concession of territory in the treaty of peace. In that connection the important question is whether the region north of the Ohio, or Kentucky, or the region south of it (Tennessee, western Georgia, Alabama, and Mississippi),[1] would have been conceded to us if his services had not been rendered. Would those regions have been ours or Great Britain's if he had not induced Virginia in 1776 to assert her claim to Kentucky and support the pioneers there; or if he had not conceived and induced her to authorize his expedition to reduce the British posts, and then reduced them; or if he, and others by his inducement, had not endorsed the state's bills to supply her troops and carry on the war; or if his victories had not opened the way for the great western immigration; or if he and his unpaid men had not struggled as they did through the last four years of war to hold the western country until Great Britain surrendered all claim to it? Had he failed to do those things can it be assumed that some one else would have arisen to do them?

[1] It seems pretty plain that Clark's victories led to Great Britain's giving up that southern region. Except for small settlements near the Mississippi River, it was almost uninhabited save by war-like Indians at the close of the Revolution, and was apparently given up, without discussion and as a matter of course, along with the greater and far more valuable region north of it.

CHAPTER XXIV

NEW–STATE MOVEMENT: WILKINSON'S INTRIGUES

When news of the peace became known in America, many thought with Tom Paine that 'the times that tried men's souls are over'; yet, as Fiske says, 'The most trying time of all was just beginning. It is not too much to say that the period of five years following the peace...was the most critical moment in all the history of the American people. ...In 1783 the love of union, as a sentiment for which men would fight, had hardly come into existence among the people of these states. ...The length of the war and its worst hardships had been chiefly due to want of organization. Congress had steadily declined in power and respectability; it was much weaker at the end of the war than in the beginning; and there was reason to fear that as soon as the common pressure was removed the need for concerted action would cease to be felt and the scarcely formed Union would break to pieces. There was the greater reason for such fear in that, while no strong sentiment had as yet grown up in favor of union, there was an intensely powerful sentiment in favor of local self-government. This feeling was scarcely less strong between states like Connecticut and Rhode Island, or Maryland and Virginia, than it was between Athens and Megara, Argos and Sparta.' [1]

Notwithstanding Lee's motion in 1782 had killed the packed congressional committee's report favoring the Indiana and Vandalia Companies, the promoters and their confederates continued to urge Congress to claim the whole trans-Allegheny country under the pretended cession from New York. So threatening became their influence that in February, 1784, Jefferson, fearing the loss of all Virginia's trans-Allegheny territory, urged her to give up Kentucky and all of West Virginia westward of a line drawn south from the mouth of the Kanawha. [2] But if Jefferson feared that Congress would appropri-

[1] *Critical Period of American History.*
[2] 'Because,' he said, 'the people beyond that will separate themselves; and they will be joined by all our settlements beyond the Alleghenies if they are the first movers.' (Jefferson to Madison, Feb. 20, 1784, Ford's *Works of Jefferson*, IV, 244.) But, as his proposal would have

GENERAL GEORGE ROGERS CLARK
1752—1818

From the Painting by Matthew Jouett in the possession of the Filson Club,
Louisville, Kentucky

ate even the eastern part of West Virginia, the northern states no less dreaded delay in getting joint ownership of the lands north of the Ohio which Virginia had offered to cede, for they sorely needed the money the lands were expected to yield. Many of their citizens were looking to them for homes or fortunes; and their unpaid soldiers were clamoring for lands there, instead of worthless government certificates. Congress therefore, despite protests from Maryland and the land companies, on March 1, 1784, accepted Virginia's offer of the territory north of the Ohio, on condition that she should be reimbursed her outlays and liabilities incurred in conquering and holding the ceded territory. On that day Jefferson delivered her deed of cession to the United States, and Virginia was left in undisturbed possession of West Virginia and Kentucky. This was the deathblow to the Indiana and Vandalia land scheme.

On the same day Jefferson presented Congress with his ordinance for the government of the Northwest Territory, which, except an article concerning slavery, was adopted and became the law of the territory until the more famous 'Ordinance of 1787' was substituted for it three years later. The evil results of the change in the slavery clause are pointed out in the note below.[1]

left to Virginia the region claimed by the Indiana Company, it was not likely to be accepted by Congress.

[1] Jefferson's Ordinance provided that, *after the year 1800*, there should be neither slavery nor involuntary servitude in the territory, otherwise than in punishment of crime, whereof the party should have been duly convicted. He postponed the operation of this anti-slavery provision until 1800 in justice both to the French inhabitants and to the slaves themselves. The property rights of the inhabitants had been solemnly promised them when they became American citizens, and their slaves made a very large part of their property. But by a much extolled provision in the 'Ordinance of 1787 for the Government of the Northwest Territory,' slavery was made *immediately* illegal.

Without even a day's notice to the owners of slaves — without any regard to their guaranteed property rights, without any provision for compensating them; and apparently without any understanding, or even thought, of the fatal consequence to the slaves themselves, the Continental Congress by this over-

lauded 'Ordinance of 1787' immediately freed every slave within its bounds. It ruined many of the slave owners, disorganized the whole labor system of the territory, greatly reduced production, increased the already distressing general poverty, deprived the slaves of the protection of their lawful owners (whose interest it had been to feed, clothe and protect them, and many of whom were undoubtedly humane masters) and turned loose the poor, ignorant slaves — men, women, and children — to beg, steal, or starve! They were made the easy prey of unscrupulous men. Families were scattered — many inveigled, or forcibly carried, across the Mississippi and thence taken down to New Orleans and sold into slavery infinitely worse than any they had before known. Time and again the inhabitants of the Territory — both French and American — appealed to Congress to grant a reasonable time for freeing the slaves, but Congress heeded them not.

Yet the anti-slavery provision of the Ordinance of 1787 did not prevent slavery, but only made it unlawful. It

When news of the preliminary treaty of peace with Great Britain reached the west, it was expected that the British would promptly give up Detroit and the other lake posts, and that there would be no more general Indian war. Clark did not share that view. He knew the savages did not consider themselves conquered, and that when they learned their lands were to be taken from them, they would be more hostile than ever. He wrote Governor Harrison: 'The agreeable news [of peace] with Britain I am in hopes will greatly alter the face of affairs in the back country. The prospects of our possession of the posts on the lakes will, I make no doubt, divide the councils of the Indians for some time and prevent their making any capital stroke on the settlements of Kentucky; but I have not the least idea of their quitting war until they are invited to a treaty by prospects of presents, or reduced to a peace by an armament in their own country.' [1] This proved prophetic. For over a year the Indians remained quiet, but when Congress then undertook to oust some of the tribes north of the Ohio, savage war broke out with renewed fury.

Following fast upon the news of peace, a great tide of emigration poured westward over the mountains. Thousands of soldiers from the disbanded armies, on returning to their homes in the east, found their lands run down, their horses and cattle gone, and their families and neighbors in sad plight. Many industries had been crippled or destroyed, and capital was lacking to reëstablish them. As there was little prospect of betterment in that part of the country, many sought new homes in the west where cheap lands and virgin soil promised abundant crops and prosperity.

Not every part of the west, however, attracted immigrants, for the Indians were north of the Ohio and south of the Tennessee, while West Virginia and western Pennsylvania were gen-

virtually gave immunity to those who seized negroes and ran them off for sale in Spanish territory. Congress took no step to make the operation of its anti-slavery ordinance humane. For some years it hardly made a pretense of giving the people of the Wabash and Illinois region any government at all. It seemed only interested in land sales in the Northwest Territory.

In the long history of the mistreatment by the United States of its own subjects (not excepting even the Illinois Creoles, or in later years the transplanted Cherokees of North Carolina) perhaps the most cruel of all was the treatment of the slaves of the Northwest Territory by and under the anti-slavery provision of the Ordinance of 1787. As Jefferson once said: 'To abandon persons whose habits have been formed in slavery, is like abandoning children. (Ford's *Works of Jefferson*, v, 447.)

[1] *Virginia Calendar State Papers*, III, 476–77.

erally mountainous. The main flow therefore was to Kentucky and Tennessee — particularly central Kentucky. The gently rolling plateau there, covered by a superb forest and in places carpeted with luxuriant blue-grass, was the Mecca of post-Revolutionary emigrants.[1]

The inrushing newcomers were of varying nationality and characteristics, and included farmers, cattle raisers, some mechanics, more politicians, negro slaves, a few preachers, many more lawyers — some of them men of high repute and others of the land-shark variety — a goodly number of officers from Washington's armies, and many more of the common soldiers. Some few of the immigrants had means, but most were poor. They gathered their families and small belongings and in motley parties trekked up the Valley of Virginia and thence passed through Cumberland Gap into the promised land. A shorter route for most of them was over the Alleghenies and down the Ohio, but it was less traveled because the Indians made it unsafe.

Owing to the great increase of Kentucky's population, the three original counties — Lincoln, Fayette, and Jefferson — were divided in 1785 into seven; but for military purposes they were still grouped under the three old names and will usually be referred to by those names.

Even before Congress accepted Virginia's cession of the lands north of the Ohio, it was preparing to take possession of them and offer parts for sale. On the very day of the cession, it elected seven commissioners to treat with the Indians for a general peace, and get from some of them a surrender of their lands. All the commissioners were eastern men except one, General Clark, who was nominated by Jefferson. They were directed to hold a treaty meeting with all the tribes, and, to the amazement of the western people, the place named was Albany, New York. This was sheer folly, for it was absurd to expect western or southern Indians to attend a meeting so far from their homes. They had been discouraged by the desertion of their British allies and wanted peace, but thought this treaty scheme was a trick to draw them far from home and leave their towns exposed to attack during their absence. Furthermore,

---

[1] See *American History and its Geographic Conditions*, 71, by Ellen C. Semple, and map showing population west of the Alleghenies after the Revolution. (*Industrial History of U.S.* (Coman), 136.)

without waiting for a treaty with them, Congress was passing resolutions looking to the sale and settlement of some of their lands near the upper Ohio; and to make matters worse, squatters came down the river and made 'tomahawk claims' of bottom lands there. Incensed by this intrusion, the Indians not only struck the squatters, but crossed the river and fell upon the Kentuckians, who sometimes retaliated by going over to the public lands and taking revenge on any Indians they could find.[1]

To avoid renewed Indian war, Congress plainly had choice of two — and only two — courses. One was to leave the red men their lands and prevent intrusion on them until the lands could be bought; the other to subdue the savages and seize the lands. Unfortunately, Congress did neither, but instead demanded a surrender of lands, first from one tribe and then another, yet sent no army to compel compliance. In fact, it had no army. One of its first acts after the peace with Great Britain was to discharge all its troops except fifty-five men at West Point on the Hudson, and twenty-six at Pittsburg!

Some eastern leaders were quite prone to put the blame for continued Indian warfare upon the western people themselves, notwithstanding it was they who were the sufferers. In the east people could not understand why the Indians were hostile unless provoked by the western whites; and that convenient explanation was precisely the one the savages were always ready to give when charged with depredations. In truth, their hostility was the inevitable consequence of the resolve of Congress to oust them from their lands. Western men saw this, eastern ones generally did not, for people living in old centers of civilization rarely investigate or understand distant frontier conditions. Even Jay said: 'Not a single Indian war had yet been occasioned by the aggressions of the present federal government, feeble as it is.' In pioneer parlance, this was 'sticking in the bark.' It would be nearer the truth to say that every Indian war during the last four years of the continental government was due to the weak and blundering efforts of Congress to appropriate the Indian lands.[2]

[1] These reprisals, however, were few and almost negligible compared with the frequent and destructive raids of the savages.

[2] Apparently seeing neither folly nor wrong in the course Congress pursued towards the Indians, Roosevelt says that 'the most ultimately righteous of all wars is a war with savages'; that is a 'silly morality which would forbid a course of

Other influences also operated to keep the Indians at war beside encroachments on their lands. We know how loath Great Britain and Spain had been to give up the western country, and both still hoped to win it. They saw the thirteen impoverished and discordant states, under a discredited Congress, heading fast toward bankruptcy and disunion; and they not only looked to see the early wreck of the Confederation, but secretly endeavored to hasten it. With the breaking up of the United States, Great Britain might well regain the country north of the Ohio — Spain all below the Tennessee. By the treaty of peace Great Britain had agreed to surrender Niagara, Detroit, and other northern posts, but for twelve years afterward persisted in holding them.[1]

With the tide of immigration to Kentucky in 1784 there came an extraordinary man who, more than any other, was to influence the course of western events for many years afterwards. This was General James Wilkinson, whom Professor Turner rightly declares our 'most consummate artist in treason,' and Winsor and Roosevelt, the most 'despicable character' America has produced. Small and handsome, of open countenance, pleasing voice, and charming manners, he was the most captivating and treacherous scoundrel in our history. Entering the Revolutionary Army before Boston when hardly more than a boy, he courted and rapidly won favor with the great in the army, in society, in Congress, and later in the west. He won the confidence of superiors whom he was ever plotting to undermine, and the loyalty of friends whom he was ever ready to ruin to effect his selfish ends. In time he became commander-in-chief of the American armies and held that exalted post for years, while all the time a sworn vassal and pensioner of the Spanish King. He had considerable military talent, but used it only for his own advancement.

At first he attached himself to Colonel Benedict Arnold, and

conquest that has turned whole continents into the seats of mighty and flourishing nations'; that 'whether the whites won the land by treaty, by armed conquest, or, as was actually the case, by a mixture of both, mattered comparatively little so long as the land was won'; that there was no 'alternative to these Indian wars'; and that it is idle folly to speak of them as being the fault of the United States Government. (*Winning of the West*, iv, 52–56.)

[1] Great Britain's excuse was that the United States had violated the treaty provision for the payment of debts owing by Americans to British subjects, but back of this was the desire to recover the western country, and make it a fulcrum to overturn our infant republic and oust Spain from the Mississippi Valley.

was his companion in the famous march against Quebec. Later, when a rivalry arose between Arnold and General Gates, Wilkinson deserted his chief and became Gates' aide and confidante — 'Gates' Jackal,' Trevelyan calls him.[1] During the British invasion by Burgoyne, in 1777, ending in his surrender to Gates at Saratoga, Wilkinson is said to have used his talent for deceit by taking credit for an important discovery of the enemy's position made in the night by another officer, Colonel Hardin. Hardin confided the discovery to Wilkinson, who unblushingly reported it as his own.[2] Upon Burgoyne's surrender, Gates sent him with the news of the great victory to Congress,[3] which he was invited to address, and which appointed him brigadier-general in preference to Colonel Daniel Morgan, one of the two real heroes of Saratoga, the other being Arnold. Gates, who was a scheming politician rather than soldier, was made president of the Board of War, with great powers, and he had his charming young aide given the important position of secretary to the board. Then followed the 'Conway Cabal' — the conspiracy in the army and in Congress to overthrow Washington and make Gates commander-in-chief. All through the history of the Cabal are found signs pointing to Wilkinson as its master spirit.

After a time, however, Wilkinson, realizing that Washington could not be overthrown, implicated Gates in the scheme in a talk with Lord Stirling, who promptly communicated the fact to Washington's aide, Alexander Hamilton. When Gates learned of this, he threatened to challenge Wilkinson, who seemed to have no escape from a duel, for a denial of Stirling's report would have brought a challenge from that gentleman. Wilkinson avoided fighting either, however, by claiming that what he had said about Gates was only said 'in a convivial hour' — in other words, while he was drunk. The excuse answered his purpose and there was no duel; but, knowing the cunning methods of the man, the presumption is strong that his treachery was carefully prearranged and his intoxication pretended rather than real. Many of his fellow officers, and forty-nine others, demanded that his commission as brigadier-

[1] *American Historical Review*, III, 154.
[2] Marshall's *Kentucky*, II, 51; Appleton's *Cyclopædia of American Biography*, VI, 511.
[3] *Journal of Congress* (Claypoole), III, 469, gives his report; Bancroft's *United States*, 191.

general be rescinded by Congress;[1] but before this could be done he resigned it.

When Arnold became clothier-general of the American forces, it was his quondam friend, Wilkinson, who secretly made charges of corruption against him to President Reed of Pennsylvania, and aided in driving the able and brave, but ill-governed Arnold into his well-known treason.[2] Soon afterward Wilkinson became clothier-general. For a while he flourished, but after a time was suspected of corruption and denounced by President Reed. Few men knew better when to bend before a storm, and again he avoided one by tendering his resignation, which Congress instantly accepted.[3] Washington seems to have suspected him of crookedness and wrote Congress a letter indicating it.[4] Wilkinson, with characteristic pretense of injured honor, greatly resented this and at once wrote Congress[5] demanding a copy of Washington's letter, 'which,' he said, 'involves my official conduct and integrity.' Writing to a member,[6] he declared his resignation was not due to 'conscious guilt and an apprehension of punishment,' but to 'the difficulty, if not impossibility, of obtaining a public opinion against the infallibility of General Washington.... An impeachment of his justice, be it ever so well founded, or so ably supported, would excite nothing more favorable than derision & contempt and would be esteemed a sort of impiety.' This unwilling tribute by the meanest to the noblest American is noteworthy.

After the war, bankrupt, but pretending to be 'the leader of a large commercial company in Philadelphia,'[7] Wilkinson removed to Kentucky, where he at once entered upon a daring career of speculation and political activity. His ambition was three-fold — wealth, political influence, and military eminence. The high positions he had held in the eastern army and his delightful personality gave him ready entrée to the new

[1] *Appleton's Cyclopædia of American Biography*, VI, 511.

[2] *Pennsylvania Archives* (1st Series), 449.

[3] *Journal Continental Congress*, XIX, 313.

[4] *Id.*, 374; *Papers Continental Congress*, no. 152; X, 67.

[5] *Id.*, no. 78; VI, 301; *Journal Continental Congress*, XIX, 374.

[6] McKean, April 8, 1781; *McKean Papers*, I, 46; *Historical Society of Pennsylvania*.

[7] Perkins' *Western Annals*, 263. He was not a member of the Philadelphia firm, which merely furnished him limited quantities of goods to sell in Kentucky and Tennessee. See Wilkinson's correspondence with the head of the concern, Dr. Hugh Shiell, *Kentucky State Historical Society MSS.*; photostat copies in *Author's MSS.*; also *R. C. Ballard Thruston's MSS.*

and hardly formed society in Kentucky, and won him many loyal but deluded friends. He was of course careful to court those who had best standing and greatest influence, and few of them but afterwards paid dearly in money, or trouble, for associating with him. For a dozen years after he arrived in Kentucky the main thread of our western political history was woven by his artful hand, and it always ran in crooked lines. He was ever scheming to undermine the man above him. Standing in his way to military eminence, he first found General Clark, with unrivaled reputation as a great captain and easily the man of first influence among the western people; and him Wilkinson at once began plotting to overthrow and succeed as Indian Commissioner for Congress and military leader in the west. Although seemingly only personal, few chapters of post-Revolutionary history treat of events of greater national moment than the one which will tell of Wilkinson's ingenious plot to effect this purpose; and it is a chapter which has never yet appeared in print.

After the Revolution nearly all the people in Kentucky became 'separatists' and wished it to be made an independent state and admitted into the Union. They must not be confused with the separate-state conspirators of the earlier years, 1780-83, who denied Virginia's jurisdiction and land grants in Kentucky. The new order of 'separatists' affirmed both, and wished separate statehood with Virginia's consent. This was not only necessary for Kentucky, but would relieve Virginia of the burden of governing the distant district; so the Virginia Assembly willingly gave its consent. Very properly, however, it required that before the separation should take effect Congress should assent to the new state's admission into the Confederation. This requirement was made to avoid Kentucky's detachment from the Union. The Kentucky people had to call eight popular conventions and wait for seven years (1785-92) before they could get Congress to agree with Virginia upon their admission to the Union. The northern states were little inclined to admit another southern state to impair their majority in Congress, and Kentucky was received into the Union only after a new northern state, Vermont, was admitted. Those seven years of delay were years of irritating suspense and great disorder in Kentucky.

Although, after the separatist movement began, the old

order of conspirators against Virginia's government was being pretty well suppressed, Wilkinson at first pretended to be their friend; but he treacherously communicated what he learned from them to the Commonwealth's Attorney, Walker Daniel, who was vigorously prosecuting their leaders. Daniel wrote Governor Harrison: 'I have to mention that General Wilkinson's conduct not a little contributed to convince the people that Pomeroy [a leading insurgent who was being prosecuted] was deluding them and telling them nothing but falsities. As a native of Maryland and living sometime in Philadelphia, the party was very communicative to him [Wilkinson] when he first moved down to this country. The decided, unequivocal manner in which he delivered to them his sentiments on this subject had very considerable effect. He took pains to set them right and gave me much information. I conceive we are greatly indebted to him.'[1] When this letter was written, Wilkinson had only been in Kentucky about ninety days, yet was giving 'much information' to be used in prosecuting them! What the information was, and how much of it he invented, are not known. Soon after this he openly joined the popular separatist party, and after a couple of years managed to thrust himself into apparent position as their leader.

The second Kentucky convention seeking separation from Virginia was held at Danville in August, 1785. Wilkinson promptly took advantage of it to play the agitator. As all the members favored separation, their proceedings were entirely harmonious, and they unanimously passed a resolution respectfully requesting the Virginia Assembly to pass an act of separation. But this did not suit Wilkinson's purpose. Such a stormy petrel always likes to fish in troubled waters, and to trouble the political waters was ever his aim. The other members only desired to ask the Assembly for statehood; but he wished the people to believe the Assembly would refuse it, and to lead them fiercely to demand it. To effect this end he managed to get the convention to adopt an ornate and fiery address, from his pen, recounting the wrongs they had suffered and advocating an expedition against the Indians north of the Ohio, in the territory of Congress, although such an expedition had been expressly prohibited by the state govern-

[1] *Virginia Calendar State Papers*, III, 588.

ment. The address appears in the footnote below and makes interesting reading.[1] It will presently be seen what was done about the expedition and the part Wilkinson played in connection with it.

[1] To the Inhabitants of the District of Kentucky.

Friends and countrymen:

Your representatives in convention having completed the important business for which they were specially elected, feel it their duty, before they adjourn, to call your attention to the calamities with which our country appears to be threatened — *blood has been spilled from the eastern to the western extremity of the district;* accounts have been given to the convention, [from post St. Vincennes, which indicate a disposition in the savages for general war; in the mean time if we look nearer home, we shall find our borders infested, and constant depredations committed on our property. Whatever may be the remote designs of the savages, these are causes sufficient to rouse our attention, that we may be prepared not only to defend but punish those who unprovoked offend us. God and nature have given us the power, and we shall stand condemned in the eyes of Heaven, and mankind, if we do not employ it, to redress our wrongs, and assert our rights.

The Indians are now reconnoitering our settlements, in order that they may hereafter direct their attacks with more certain effect, and we seem patiently to await the stroke of the tomahawk. Strange indeed it is, that although we can hardly pass a spot, which does not remind us of the murder of a father or brother or friend — we should take no single step for our own preservation. Have we forgot the surprise of Bryant's, or the shocking destruction of Kincheloe's stations? Let us ask you — ask yourselves — What is there to prevent a repetition of such barbarous scenes? Five hundred

Indians might be conducted undiscovered, to our very thresholds, and the knife may be put to the throats of our sleeping wives and children. For shame! Let us arouse from our lethargy; let us arm, associate and embody; let us call upon our officers to do their duty; and determine to hold in detestation and abhorrence, and treat as enemies to the community, every person who shall withhold his countenance and support, of such measures as may be recommended for our common defence; let it be remembered that a stand must be made somewhere — not to support our present frontier would be the height of cruelty, as well as folly; for should it give way, those who now hug themselves in security will take the front of danger, and we shall in a short time be huddled together in stations; a situation in our present circumstances, scarcely preferable to death — let us remember that supineness and inaction may entice the enemy to general hostilities — whilst preparation and offensive movements will disconcert their plans, drive them from our borders, secure ourselves, and protect our property. Therefore:

Resolved, That the convention in the name and behalf of the people, do call on the lieutenants, or commanding officers of the respective counties of this district, forthwith to carry into operation the law for regulating and disciplining the militia.

Resolved, That it be recommended to the officers, to assemble in their respective counties, and concert such plans as they may deem expedient for the defence of our country, or for carrying expeditions against the hostile nations of Indians. (Marshall's *Kentucky,* I, 213–15.)

CHAPTER XXV

CLARK MADE COMMISSIONER OF INDIAN AFFAIRS

AFTER various changes in its Indian treaty plans, Congress abandoned its order for a general meeting at Albany, and directed one to be held with the northwestern tribes at Cuyahoga, near Lake Erie. For that purpose, General Clark, General Richard Butler of Pennsylvania, and Arthur Lee of Virginia were chosen commissioners and instructed to get as extensive a surrender of Indian lands as possible. In ordering the treaty to be held so far north, Congress again required the impossible, for Cuyahoga was situated amidst hostile savages under British influence. The meeting place was therefore changed to Fort McIntosh on the upper Ohio. General Clark met his fellow commissioners in New York, and at their request preceded them to the west in order to invite the Indians, especially the Shawnees, to attend the meeting. The Shawnees, however, showed little inclination to do so, for they knew their lands were wanted by Congress and were suspicious and angry; and furthermore, Wilkinson had been tampering with them. Although wholly inexperienced in dealing with them, one of his first acts on arriving in Kentucky was an attempt to assume leadership in Indian affairs by opening, or pretending to open, peace negotiations with those angered Indians! One of his speeches to them is given below.[1] He

[1] Chiefs and Brothers of the Shawnee Nation:

We, the Big Knife, embrace this opportunity by one of our Great Chiefs lately from our Grand Council, your brothers, to inform you that the English and Americans have at length buried the hatchet and concluded a firm peace.

We wish you and our brothers the Red People to join your hands to the chain of friendship, thus brightened by us, your brothers of America, and your fathers, the English. We should have rejoiced to have had it in our power to send you particulars of the peace, but your eldest brother has not yet forwarded them to us, although we every day expect to hear from him.

We yesterday received the following Talk from him: 'I approve the method you have taken to support your Troops. Their term of service being now expired, by the happy conclusion of the war, you will please to discharge the whole corps.'

Thus brothers, we prove to you our sincerity in desiring peace and friendship, our warriors are discharged & gone home to their wives and children. We have buried the tomahawk; we have covered the blood which has been spilt; and we have gathered together the bones that they may no more be seen. Now, brothers, we wish you to do the same, to join your hands to ours, bury the hatchet and let war come no more amongst us for we desire to become one flesh & one blood with you.

When the peace, which the Americans and British have made, comes among you, you will find that the British have forgot you, their children. Nevertheless we wish to consider you as brothers and hold with you the chain of friendship.

Mr. Owens informed me that the Talks

knew he had neither authority nor money to treat with them, and doubtless never thought of doing so, but only aimed to confuse them and prevent Clark and his fellow commissioners from effecting a treaty with them.

When the time came for the meeting with the Indians (January, 1785), chiefs of the distant Wyandots, Delawares, Chippewas and Ottawas appeared, but no Shawnees! The tribes attending made no objection whatever to giving away lands that did not belong to them, and readily signed a treaty professing to grant to the United States nearly all the southeastern half of the present state of Ohio, including the country and towns of the Shawnees![1] The commissioners, disappointed to find themselves unable to secure any real cession of those lands, called another meeting and tried hard to get the Shawnees to come to it; but nearly a year passed before this could be done.

Soon almost daily complaints were received by Clark from Kentucky, charging him and his fellow commissioners with trifling about protecting the people there, because no treaty had been made with their nearest enemies, the Shawnees, but only with the distant northwestern tribes. These complaints were almost certainly instigated, if not actually written, by Wilkinson; for he will be found soon afterward sending just such complaints to the Governor of Virginia in order to discredit Clark and be appointed to succeed him as Indian Commissioner.[2]

Although Congress had not got an acre of the Shawnee lands from the Shawnees themselves, without waiting to treat with them, it conveniently assumed that it owned those lands and sent a 'geographer' to survey a large part of them, called

I sent you some time ago, on the subject of a Treaty, was not yet opened on account of your chiefs being absent. As soon as they have collected & considered of the matter, it will be necessary to send a runner to let us know their sentiments, that I may inform our Great Chief, who will send persons to meet them at this place at any time they may appoint to conclude a firm peace, which we hope may continue as long as the rivers and woods shall last.

Made at the Falls of Ohio, this 7th day of February 1784.

To the Chiefs and Warriors of the Shawnee Nation.

(*Draper MSS.* 12 S 1.)

[1] Dillon's *Indiana* 585; *Draper MSS.* 46 J 94.

[2] Wilkinson alone appears to have had a motive for sending those Clark received, and that he was quite capable of forging them will soon abundantly appear. Not suspecting that the complaints emanated from him, but supposing they came from many persons in Kentucky and represented a general hostility towards him, General Clark's pride might well have driven him (and it nearly did) to resign his position as Indian Commissioner. Had he done so, Wilkinson's way to succeed him would have been cleared of its main obstacle.

'the Seven Ranges.' It also sent a young lieutenant with a handful of soldiers to warn off intruders. He found many desirable tracts already occupied by squatters — generally rude and lawless people from various states who had drifted down the Ohio from Pittsburg. When ordered to leave, some of them threatened resistance, and an ugly conflict seemed imminent.[1]

In their journey down the river these squatters usually avoided the angry Shawnees by landing on the Kentucky side and afterward crossing over to the public lands. This led the soldiers to suppose the troublesome intruders hailed from Kentucky, and to look upon the Kentuckians generally as enemies to be punished, rather than as fellow citizens to be protected. On the other hand, it was charged that the soldiers actually supplied the savages with food, guns and ammunition to carry on their raids into Kentucky; and naturally the Kentuckians were hot with indignation. Another circumstance added to their irritation. They had resented the appointment of General Butler, a Pennsylvanian, as one of the commissioners to treat with their Indian enemies; and Mr. Lee having resigned as commissioner, another northern man — General Samuel Parsons, a Connecticut lawyer — was appointed in his stead. The choice of a New England man wholly unfamiliar with Indian affairs, and out of sympathy with the Kentuckians, disgusted them greatly; and soon afterward they were informed that Parsons and Butler were representing them as lawless people intentionally provoking Indian hostility. Parsons wrote that he was convinced they were 'all opposed to a treaty and are using every measure to prevent it.' [2]

[1] Their belligerent attitude is amusingly shown in the following notice from one of their leaders for a meeting to frame a constitution for their self-government:

March 12, 1785

Notice is hereby given to the inhabitants of the West Side of the Ohio River that there is to be an election for the choosing of members of the convention for the forming of a Constitution for the governing of the Inhabitants; the election to be at the mouth of the Miami River, and one to be held at the mouth of the Scioto River, and one the Muskingum River, and one at the dwelling house of Jonas Menzous — the members to be chosen to meet at the mouth of the Scioto on the 20th day of the same month.

I do certify that all mankind, agree-able to every constitution formed in America, have an undoubted right to pass into any vacant country and there form their constitution, and that the Confederation of the whole United States Congress is not impowered to forbid them; neither is Congress impowered from the Confederation to make any sale of the uninhabited lands to pay the public debts, but the Confederation has prescribed a particular mode for the payment of all public debts, which is by tax levied and lifted by authority of the legislatures of each state.

JOHN EMERSON

(*Draper MSS.* 1 W 39–44.)

[2] *Papers Continental Congress,* no. 56, 377, etc.; *Draper MSS.* 11 J 40.

The much desired treaty meeting with the Shawnees was planned by the commissioners to be held late in the fall of 1785 at the mouth of the Great Miami, near the site of Cincinnati; and, because of his reputation for handling Indians, General Clark was again requested to invite them. Although only the Shawnees were to be asked to surrender lands, he invited also the distant Delawares and Wyandots; for he designed using them to influence the Shawnees to accept such treaty terms as would be offered them. Furthermore, since no lands were to be demanded from the Delawares and Wyandots, they would be likely to restrain the Shawnees from doing violence to the commissioners, lest it embroil all the Indian tribes in war with the United States.

Three interesting accounts of the treaty proceedings are preserved — namely (1) the *commissioners' minutes*, kept by their secretary,[1] (2) *General Butler's Journal*,[2] and (3) the *Journal of Ensign Denny*, an intelligent young man who afterwards became a major.[3]

Denny's Journal tells of events leading up to the treaty meeting:

'August 29th. The Commissioners and a detachment of troops started down the Ohio in twelve small keels and batteaux, besides two large flats, called "Kentucky boats." The flats carry cattle, horses, &c., the others the troops and goods for the Indians. ...

'Oct. 22nd. Arrive at Great Miami. Best ground for our stations about a mile above the mouth. All hands set to work chopping, clearing &c., and preparing timber for block-houses and pickets, and on the 8th had ourselves enclosed. Hoisted the American flag and christened the place Fort Finney, in compliment to Captain Finney, the commanding officer.

'Dec. 5th. Generals Clark, Butler and Parsons leave us on a visit to the Falls of Ohio.

'20th. Commissioners [Butler and Parsons] returned a few days since from the Falls, disappointed at not finding more Indians come in. Those with us, about one hundred, are principally Wyandots and Delawares, with whom the treaty at Fort McIntosh was held. The Shawnees are the fellows the present treaty was intended for; they seem to hang back. ... Indians treated very kindly, ... dancing parties in our council house almost every afternoon. Very few went home sober, but those who did were sure to get drunk at night. They would come next day and peremptorily demand a quantity of rum, and on being refused they set homeward very much offended, de-

[1] *Draper MSS*. 3 U 186.
[2] *Id.*, 304.
[3] *Record of Upland County and Major Denny's Journal*.

claring that the next day should move them off, never to be seen as friends again.

'21st. Sent...Col. Harmar...a letter [saying]: "Since my last the Commissioners, after sending back the Shawnee chief to bring their nations, and other on the Wabash, &c, have taken a trip to the Rapids where they left General Clark. Whether he will return, or not, is a doubt with us; but General Butler and General Parsons say he will be up in a few days. Our reason for thinking he will scarcely return is that while here he received, almost daily, complaints from the people on the frontiers of Kentucky reflecting on him for trifling, as they think, with some of the savages while others are plundering them." ' [Not suspecting Wilkinson as the one source of these 'almost daily complaints' from Kentucky, and stung by what he supposed to be the ingratitude of the people there in making them, General Clark probably made it known that he would wash his hands of the whole treaty-making business, resign his commission, and let them handle their Indian problem to suit themselves. On reflection, however, he seems to have changed his mind.[1]]

Denny next briefly describes an early American Woman's-Rights meeting as follows:

'The Indian women assembled in our council-house and desired the attendance of the chief captain. We all turned out, heard an oration from one of their elderly ones, the conclusion of which was a request for something to warm their hearts!'

'23rd. General Clark returned from the Rapids, which was a very agreeable surprise.

'28th. The chiefs of the Delaware nation (particularly Captain Pipe) made proposals to our commissioners to send once more...to the Shawnee towns...to bring a final answer from them.

'29th. New deputation sent to bring the Shawnees, if possible, to treat.

'[January] 1786 8th. Lieutenant Doyle arrived and informed us that...they were met by a party of one hundred and fifty Shawnees. At last they were coming. After a time nearly four hundred and fifty were gathered, of whom a hundred and thirty were Delawares and Wyandots.]

'14th. We received information of the Shawnees intending to come to the council house, and that on their approach they would salute us with three rounds per man. In order to return their salute, twelve men were ordered to parade with three rounds of cartridges, and myself to command them. We waited their approach, which was very solemn. As they came up they gave us Indian music, beat on a keg drum by one of the chiefs, the whole singing at the same time.

[1] He did not soon overcome his resentment, for later, when a general Indian war became imminent and the militia officers of Kentucky unanimously called on him to take command, he will be found long holding aloof and refusing to do so.

Their line was formed in rank of file, the women bringing up the rear, all in very regular order.[1]

'Our commissioners, knowing them to be a very proud nation, thought it best to pay them the same honors and ordered preparations in a style rather degrading to the United States, which was that a party of soldiers should cook and serve out provisions to them in the council house. Now, with them the most decrepit old women are made choice of for that business, and nothing could have occasioned greater laughter than the appearance of soldiers carrying kettles of provisions to them. When the Indians saw them, they cried out: "There come the old women with warrior's coats on" &c and who knows but they conceived us all "old women" clad in uniform.[2]

'21st. Bohengeehalus, with about twenty Delawares arrived. They were saluted in the same manner. . . . Bohengeehalus is esteemed one of the greatest warriors now among all the Indians. After he had seated himself, he discovered General Clark and, knowing him to be a great warrior, rose and saluted him very significantly. Instead of taking hold of each others hands, they gripped nearly at the shoulder, and shook the left hand underneath the right arms.[3]

'This evening we were entertained with the Shawnees dancing, much in the same manner as it was performed by the Wyandots, but the assembly vastly larger. After they had gone through several of their common dances, they prepared for a war dance.

'The Shawnees have a variety of dances, but the most pleasant one is their social dance as it is interpreted. As many young men as please form a ring around the fire, move, dance, and sing love songs; the girls look on for some time; at length they rise, one after another as the spirits move them, and seize a partner. The couple stick to each other, dancing and performing every possible gesture, but still keep in the ring, singing and beating time to their music. Now, while busily engaged, the parties exchange some article of dress, or other things, as a token of their regard. The girls are very fond of getting a few of us engaged in this dance.

[1] In the original this paragraph goes before the preceding one.

[2] An Indian expressed his most insulting contempt by calling one an 'old woman.' The order was doubtless given by Parsons, who knew little of the Indians; almost certainly not by Clark, for it violated his whole theory about dealing with them; hardly by Butler, who was a real soldier, which Parsons was not.

[3] The Commissioners' Minutes say: 'Bohongehelas saluted General Clark and addressed him thus:

'"Not as a King, but as a warrior, I Bohongehelas address you. You are the head of a great nation, as I am of mine. To the Great Spirit I give thanks for having preserved us till this day when we have opportunity of speaking together.

Three weeks are gone since I assigned the hatchet into the hands of my kings. Since that time I have ceased to war and have now come to this council fire with my chiefs, our women and children, to promote the work of peace. At this council fire I am glad to see you present, because I hope that you will assist your great men, as I will mine, to settle every matter, which is to be transacted. Brother, General Clark, again as a warrior I tell you I am glad to see you and thank the spirits above who on this morning has brought us together." To which General Clark replied that he was glad to see him and his party & that his endeavors should not be wanting to promote and end the good work which was begun.'
(*Draper MSS.* 3 U 186.)

'But the war dance exceeds all. It was performed at the request of the officers. Eight or ten or the most active men stripped themselves quite naked, except the breechcloth, painted their bodies and faces so as to have a horrid appearance. Armed with tomahawk and scalping knife, they formed a circle, danced moderately to a mournful kind of tune for ten or fifteen minutes, gave the war-whoop and sat down together on seats placed for the purpose. They now hung their heads, — a dead silence for a short time. One gets up, dances and capers to the music, repeats his exploits, the injuries they have sustained, urging the others to be strong and rise and revenge themselves on their enemies. At length they are roused, one after another, until all get up, when they commence the most tremendous yelling, jumping, and figuring about in imitation of shooting, scalping, and tomahawking, exerting themselves exceedingly until a signal is given for silence. A short speech concludes.'

Despite all these appearances of good feeling, the commissioners and handful of soldiers well knew there was danger ahead. The Shawnees outnumbered the few whites many to one, and when the time should come to require them to sign a treaty giving up their lands, none could tell whether their answer would be given with pen or tomahawk. For several days the commissioners discussed the best method of dealing with them, and carefully worked out and agreed upon a bold program, just such as Clark had always pursued with the savages. Butler and Parsons no doubt recognized his superior experience and skill in handling savages and deferred to his judgment.

Every precaution was taken to prepare the Shawnees, especially the younger and more hot-blooded warriors, to submit to the terms about to be demanded of them, rather than resort to violence. At first none of the Shawnees were consulted, but only the Wyandots and Delawares were called together and the demands of the United States 'explained to their satisfaction.' Thereafter Bohungeehalus and other chiefs of those tribes supported every demand the commissioners made of the Shawnees, and by their presence and speeches made the proposed treaty possible. Next, the commissioners carefully discussed and prepared their speech to the Shawnees, and General Butler was directed to deliver it.

Before this was done, however, 'The Commissioners sent for the Shawnee chiefs and had a private conversation on the nature of the speech and their intention in framing it in this manner, that, by putting their young men in mind of the ills they have done and danger to which they have exposed their nations, it will have a tendency to induce them to listen to the advice of the Chiefs and give weight to that advice.'[1] This *privately* consulting the Shawnee chiefs beforehand, and explaining to them the proposed speech, was clever policy, for it flattered them and prepared them to hear and approve strong language from the commissioners in the public council about to be held. It tended to make confederates of them in preventing angry opposition from any of their hot-brained warriors.

Next, says Butler's Journal:

'28th The...Shawnees were called for public council, also the chiefs of the Wyandots and Delawares. ...Telapaxie, a Delaware chief, addressed...the Shawnees...and advised the head warriors ...to follow his example — that he had laid down the hatchet and would never more take it up. After he had concluded I began the address and went through it clearly. I also went into a recapitulation of all their breaches of all the treaties they had made with the United States; the mischief they had done our citizens; the distress they had involved their nations in by this conduct; and that they were now left to the mercy of the United States, which they may yet experience, if their conduct convinces us of their determination to live in peace for the future. We then closed and required their answer, which they promised when they had considered what we have said.

'Sunday 29th, the Shawnees informed us they will give us their answer today, on which the Wyandot and Delaware chiefs were called, the whole collected, and Kehenepelathy, a Shawnee captain, spoke in a very clear and masterly manner, recapitulating the substance of our address, acknowledged the truth of what we related, and hoped we would forget all that was past.'

[So far the program of the commissioners had worked perfectly. Not only had their speech provoked no outspoken opposition, but it had been approved by the Shawnee's own spokesman. But approval of the speech was one thing, acceptance of the treaty articles about to be offered them quite another.] 'The council being over, the Commissioners met in council and concluded on the Articles of Treaty.

'Monday 30th. The Commissioners met and examined the Articles, which being approved, the Chiefs of the Shawnees were sent for and the whole explained to them, also the boundary line. ... This not pleasing them, ...we agreed to enlarge the boundary from a branch to the main of the Miami River. ...This did not seem fully to satisfy them, but we would go no further.'[2] [Here was the first open dispute, and it was plain that the Shawnee chiefs were in no mood to accede to further demands on them.]

[1] *Butler's Journal, Draper MSS.* 3 U 304, etc.
[2] *Id.*

Next, the whole body of chiefs and warriors of the three nations being assembled, General Butler delivered to them the commissioners' speech stating the terms of peace they offered in the Articles. These terms were that the Shawnees acknowledged the United States to be absolute sovereigns of the whole country ceded to them by Great Britain; that the United States granted to the Shawnees lands west of the main branch of the Miami; that the Shawnees should surrender all their white prisoners; and until that was done, should leave three hostages with the commissioners. This requirement of hostages surprised and angered the Shawnees. Cunning and deceitful, they were ever willing enough to secure an advantage by making promises which they had no intention of performing; but to surrender three of their leading men as hostages to secure performance was a very different matter. In fiery mood their orator, Kehenepelithy, at once arose and spoke as follows:

'Brothers! By what you said to us yesterday we expected everything past would be forgotten; that our proposals for collecting the prisoners were satisfactory, and that we would have been placed on the same footing as before the war. Today you demand hostages till your prisoners are returned! You next say you will divide the lands! I now tell you it is not the custom of the Shawnees to give hostages. Our words are to be believed. When we say a thing we stand to it; we are Shawnees! As to the lands, God gave us this country! We do not understand measuring out the lands. It is all ours! You say you have goods for our women and children. You may keep your goods and give them to other nations. We will have none of them.

'Brothers, you seem to grow proud because you have thrown down the King of England; and as we feel sorrow for our past faults, you rise in your demands on us. This we think hard. You need not doubt our words. What we have promised we will perform. We told you that we have appointed three good men of our nation to go to the town and collect your flesh and blood. They shall be brought in. We have never given hostages, and we will not comply with this demand!'

Here the irate chief flung upon the table a white and a black belt — the white meaning an offer of peace, the black one of war! The commissioners were to choose which they would have. A critical situation, this! To withdraw their demand of hostages meant a worthless treaty; to insist on it seemed to invite immediate massacre. The commissioners conferred a short time on their answer. Clark and Parsons sat beside the table, and Butler stood by it; and on it lay the peace or war belts awaiting their reply!

'The Commissioners...resolved they would not recede from any of the Articles, whereupon [says Butler] I addressed them in this short manner:

'"Shawnees, you have addressed us with great warmth. We think the answer unwise and ungrateful. In return for just and generous proposals, you have not only given us improper language, but asserted the greatest falsehoods. You say you cannot give hostages for performance of your promises, as it is contrary to your usages, and that you never break your word. Have you forgot your breach of treaties in the beginning of the late war with Britain, between the United States and your chiefs in '75 & '76? Do you think us ignorant of those treaties? Do you think we have forgot the burning of our towns, the murder and captivity of our people in consequence of your perfidy? or have you forgot them? Don't you remember, when Col Bou[quet] come to Tuscararas that you there gave hostages? Do you forget that you gave hostages to Ld Dunmore? Do you forget that, when he had agreed to send people to collect the prisoners, that they were like to have been murdered in your towns? Recollect, and you must know that these are treaties [by which] you gave to both these great men hostages. . . .

'"We know these things to be truths, with much more we could relate equally Aggravating. You cannot therefore expect we will believe you. I tell you we cannot believe you, or rely on your words. Are the burning of the houses of our people & barbarously ravaging our frontiers, besides the repeated violations of treaties of the most sacred, nothing? Are your barbarous murders and cruelty shewn our prisoners, marks of your fidelity, or proofs of your pacific disposition, or...desire of engaging the blessings of peace in common with us? I say they are not. ....You joined the British King against us and of course [shared] his fortunes. We have overcome him. He has cast you off and given us your country, and Congress, in bounty and mercy, offer you a country and peace. We have told you the terms on which you shall have it. These terms we will not alter. . . .

'"We now tell you, if you have been [so] unfortunate and unwise as to determine and adhere to what you said, and refuse the terms we have offered, you may depart in peace. You shall have your provisions to take you to your towns, and no man shall touch you for 8 days...after this day; but, after that time is expired, be Assured that we shall consider ourselves freed from all the ties of protection to you and you may depend, the U.S. will take the most effectual measures to protect their Citizens and to distress your obstinate nation. It rests now with you. The destruction of your women and children, or their future happiness, depends on your present choice. Peace or war is in your power. Make your choice like men and judge for yourselves. We shall only add that, had you judged, as is your interest to do, you would have considered us as your friends and followed our counsel; but, if you choose to follow the opinions which you have expressed, you are guided either by Evil counsel or rashness and are blinded. We plainly tell you this country belongs to the U.S. Their blood hath defended it and will forever protect it. Their proposals are liberal and just; and you, instead of acting as you have done and persisting in your folly, should be thankful for the forgiveness and offers of kindness of the U.S. instead of the sentiments which this String imports and the manner in which you delivered it. We shall not receive it, or any other from you, in any such way.'[1]

While speaking, Butler had lifted the Shawnee belt, and now he dashed it back on the table. Clark, who was sitting, coolly brushed it off the table with his cane, and rising, put his foot on it![2] Bolder or more contemptuous counter-defiance could not have been. The tense situation may be imagined — the apprehension of the whites; the amazement of the savages. Says Denny: 'Council broke up very hastily. Some commotion amongst the savages.' They gathered in their camp and held a heated discussion, while probably all the white men held their guns ready. Fortunately for them, the cooler heads among the Shawnees prevailed over the hot-bloods, and they returned the same afternoon and begged another meeting, when their old king, Molunthy, made a short speech, presented a *white* string, doing away with all their chief warrior had said, and 'prayed that we would have pity on their women and children, &c.'

'Feb. 1st. Treaty concluded and signed. ...Five Shawnees left as hostages.'[3] This was the first surrender of lands to the United States by Indians west of the Alleghenies. It was also the first acknowledgment by any of them of the sovereignty of the United States. The security for observance of the treaty terms by the Shawnees soon vanished, however, for Denny's Diary says: '24th. Five Shawnee hostages deserted. Took with them Mr Sufferin's family, Mr Sufferin being absent on a hunting party.'

---

[1] *Draper MSS.* 3 U 394.
[2] *Denny's Journal, supra.*
[3] Dillon's *Indiana*, p. 595, gives the full treaty. *Denny's Journal* continues: '8th. The commissioners [Parsons and Butler] left us. ...Major Finney directed me to parade the company, march them down to the bank, so as to present arms to the commissioners as they passed to the boats and, when they had taken leave and hoisted sail, I gave them a platoon by way of acknowledgment.
'General Clark left us for the Rapids on the 10th. He did not trouble us with much parade, neither did he take away any of our men.' This Major Finney endeavored to prevent as much as possible.

CHAPTER XXVI

RENEWED INDIAN WAR

ALTHOUGH the masterly handling of the Indians at the Miami treaty gave Congress the Shawnee lands it wanted, its demand of them had antagonized the northwestern tribes generally. They foresaw the loss of their own lands unless they combined and struck to save them; and combine and strike they did. They formed a great league, called the 'Wabash Confederacy,' which was planned to take in all the tribes east of the Mississippi and drive out the white intruders. Soon squatters and troops north of the Ohio and Kentuckians alike were being waylaid and tomahawked. Even the French on the Wabash suffered, although the Indians were much more friendly to them than to the other whites. At Vincennes the French and Americans were themselves almost at war, and even common danger could seldom reconcile them. The Americans, being the weaker party and the special objects of Indian hatred, were forced to flee to the fort and were reduced to desperate straits.[1] For three days they were besieged by some four hundred and fifty savages, and twenty were killed — some with horrible brutality. 'Two expresses were immediately despatched by land and water to General Clark at the Falls of Ohio to inform him of their distress,'[2] and two hastily gathered companies were sent to their relief.

Nor were the Vincennes French much better off than the Americans, for Congress had left them for two years without laws, and chaos reigned. In their distress they appealed to Clark to use his influence to secure them a lawful government; but he was at this time very ill and powerless to help them. March 29th, his father wrote one of his sons: 'Your brother, George, [is] with me very sick, his complaint being of such a nature as keeps us in doubt'; and a month later, 'I thank God your brother, George, are like to get well, after a very dangerous spell of sickness. He wishes to be remembered to all his friends, but at present...not capable of writing himself.'[3]

---

[1] *Filson's Narrative, Draper MSS.* 10 CC; Small and Henry to Clark, *id.*, 53 J 32, 36; *Vincennes Petition to Congress, id.*, 31.

[2] *Filson's Narrative, supra.*

[3] *Draper MSS.* 2 L 22, 23.

The Kentucky settlements most exposed to Indian attack were near Louisville, where from the first life had been one of extreme danger. The town itself, although from the time of its founding the objective of all the most formidable British and Indian invasions, had escaped attack; but this year, 1786, the outlying settlements were dreadfully harried, and brave men feared this section of Kentucky would be abandoned. Yet the feeling of many of the people of the other counties, especially in Lincoln, against those of Jefferson was so bitter that they were not inclined to aid them. In this extremity fifty-five leading Jefferson men, headed by General Clark, joined in a pathetic address to their brethren of the eastern counties, appealing for help,[1] and sent it to Colonel Logan, the county lieutenant of Lincoln and senior militia officer in Kentucky. The reception it met from Logan was significant. He simply sent it to the governor with a letter setting forth the needs of Kentucky at large and requesting attention to them, but without a word about aiding the Jefferson people.[2] In view of their dreadful straits, his perfunctory letter seems extraordinary; but he probably knew the people of his county would furnish neither militia nor supplies to protect the people of Jefferson, but would say that was the state's duty.

How serious the situation was no man better knew than General Clark; and certainly none was less given to panic or rash statement; yet he wrote Governor Henry: 'I dont think

[1] To the Inhabitants of Nelson, Lincoln, and Fayette Counties,
Friends and Fellow Citizens:
Independent of that benevolence of disposition which should mark the character of every individual and excite to generous and noble action, there exists an implied contract between the settlers of this country to support and defend each other against the invasions and attacks of our relentless and common enemies. ...We apply to you for aid to revenge the injuries we have already suffered and to prevent those with which we are every day threatened. We regret the occasion which subjects us to the dire necessity of applying to our friends to leave their peaceful abodes...in defense of the lives of ourselves, our wives, and helpless infants who, without your kindly interposition, will probably fall a prey to savage barbarity.... We flatter ourselves that however pressing may be the calls of your domestic concerns, you will not withhold that assistance which we now most earnestly entreat of you. We have hitherto deferred making this application, hoping that our strength would be sufficient to repel our cruel invaders, but since find that inadequate. Being encompassed with dangers and every day plundered of our property, we have no recourse but to our friends. ...You need not, surely, be reminded how much you are interested in our security. Should we be reduced to the calamitous necessity of abandoning our settlements, your counties must become frontiers, and in that situation will certainly experience all those evils which we complain of now,... and from which we solicit your brotherly assistance to relieve us. (*Draper MSS.* 12 S 48.)
[2] *Virginia Calendar State Papers*, IV, 120.

that this country, even in its infant state, bore so gloomy an
aspect as it does at present. . . . Circumstanced as we are,
[with] no prospect of support, at least for several months, so
formidable and bloody an enemy to encounter, such irregularity in the country, no power to order the militia out of the
state for its protection, . . . I doubt great part of these beautiful settlements will be laid waste unless protected by volunteers penetrating into the heart of the enemy's country.
Nothing else will do.'[1]

Soon the Indian ravages extended to Lincoln and Fayette
also, and then came a general demand for an expedition
against the confederated Indians on the Wabash, and that
General Clark command it; for in the face of grave danger even
his enemies looked to him as their most competent leader.[2]
Although strongly favoring such an expedition, however, he
would not consent to lead this one. Lieutenant Beatty, of the
continental troops, who was visiting the Falls, wrote in his
diary: 'Kentucky appears to be in a perfect State of War. . . .
The people are now forming an expedition against [the In-
dians]. . . and also to defend the Americans at Post Vincent.
. . . It is doubtful whether the expedition will go or not, as
Genl Clark, who is a very popular character, will not give his
advice about it, though asked frequently.'[3]

No mere want of formal authority for the expedition de-
terred Clark from leading the proposed one; for, though generally careful to observe the law, he was ever more concerned
with substance than form, and in case of plain public necessity
ready to usurp authority. Three times he has been seen doing

[1] *Id.*, 122. See also Clark's letter to
Richard Henry Lee, President of Congress, to the same effect, *U.S. Department
of State, Papers Continental Congress, Indian Affairs*, no. 50, 279.

[2] Thus John May, who was one of
Clark's most malignant enemies, wrote
Governor Henry: 'I find it the unanimous
opinion of the inhabitants of this country
that Genl Clark is the properest person
to take command here; and notwithstanding the opinion which prevails below [in
eastern Virginia] of his not being capable
of attending to business, I am of the
same opinion as the rest of this country.
I have been with him frequently and find
him as capable of business as ever, and
should an expedition be carried against

the Indians, I think his name would be
worth half a regiment of men.' (*Virginia
Calendar State Papers*, iv, 157.) May
was 'frequently with' Clark only because they were in litigation, May
having set up a junior claim to Clark's
salt-lick land.

[3] Levi Todd to Governor Henry (*id.*,
iv, 124): 'I am of opinion it would have
been very agreeable to the District had
General Clark been commissioned a general officer for the present occasion.'
Levi Todd had been one of the Fayette
officers who had complained of Clark
after the Blue Licks disaster, but had become, and always afterward remained,
friendly to him.

that — each time risking censure, but winning victories and praise.[1] But now his situation was very different, for he was by no means sure the people, especially in Lincoln, would give him loyal support. He therefore held aloof, and waited to see how much they were in earnest for the expedition before he would consent to lead it.

Patrick Henry, again governor, was keenly alive to the danger threatening Kentucky, and he vigorously demanded of Congress that it restrain its Indian subjects and not shift the burden of doing so upon Virginia. His favorite sister's husband and his own dear friend, Colonel William Christian, had settled in Jefferson County and had just been slain by the savages; and his anxiety for his sister and her fatherless children no doubt added emphasis to his demand. If Congress failed to comply with it, he was resolved to authorize the Kentuckians to defend themselves by carrying an expedition into the country of Congress north of the Ohio. He did not doubt Virginia's right to send an army there, for the Sixth Article of Confederation expressly reserved to her the right to make war on any Indians invading her territory; and there was no question that Kentucky was being thus invaded. On May 16th he wrote the state's delegates to demand of Congress that 'a decided answer be given to the question: "Will Congress defend and protect our frontiers?"' and saying: 'If they will not, I ought to know it as quickly as possible; otherwise the lives of our citizens will be forfeit.'[2] If Congress would not protect them, he would authorize them to protect themselves by 'attacking the enemy in their towns' in the federal territory north of the Ohio. Congress made no objection to this, but would not itself do anything to restrain its Indian subjects. The Virginia delegates tried hard to get it to send an adequate force to do this, but in vain. They only asked Congress to send four hundred men and authorize its commander in the west, Colonel Harmar, to call for such Kentucky militiamen as he might find necessary to reinforce him, up to a thousand; but Congress balked at the expense.[3] Instead, it ordered to the

[1] Once in 1778, when he enlisted men to hold the Illinois and go against Vincennes; again in 1780 when he closed the land office at Harrodsburg, and got volunteers for his expedition against the Shawnee towns; and still again in 1782, when, despite Governor Harrison's prohibition, he raised a thousand men and destroyed their towns.

[2] Virginia State Library, *Governor's Letter Book*, 513–21.

[3] *Journal Congress* (Claypoole, Philadelphia), IV, 626, 657, 663.

upper Ohio only part of two small companies, and refused to allow Harmar to call for any militia, however imperative might be the need for them.[1]

Suspecting that Congress and Harmar were much more concerned about protecting its surveyors and public lands than in saving the lives of the Kentucky people, the Virginia delegates next moved it to order 'that the two companies should be subject to the commissioner of the Indian Department for the time being,' who was General Clark; but this also was refused.[2] Instead, Congress actually abolished the Indian Department,[3] and thus left some fifteen hundred war-mad Indians on the Wabash, and others who might join them, free to carry torch and tomahawk throughout Kentucky at will; for it was certain that Harmar's handful of men could not check them, even if ordered to do so. In fact they were used only to protect the public lands on the upper Ohio and never reached the scene of war. Indeed, Harmar was expressly directed to avoid war with the Indians 'if possible consistently with the interests and dignity of the United States,' and he replied: 'I shall give the officer commanding particular orders not to form any offensive operations without permission. The surveying and disposal of the western territory I take for granted to be the first and grand object of Congress!'[4] Undoubtedly Harmar was right; Congress considered the protection of its western citizens a minor consideration — the surveying and disposal of its lands 'the first and grand object.'

Finding that Congress would do nothing, Governor Henry's Council next *directed* 'the field officers of the different counties in Kentucky to concert measures for their own defense, taking as their guide in forming any military expeditions. . .the Sixth Article of Confederation.'[5] Knowing the bitter discord prevailing amongst them, he added: 'When your all is at stake I need not recommend union and cordiality among yourselves; you see the necessity of it.' On the same day he also sent word to Congress that the Kentuckians were '*in such situation as to*

---

[1] *Journal Congress* (Claypoole, Philadelphia), IV, 654.

[2] *Id.*, 657.

[3] *Id.*, 663. The resolution abolishing the commission gave as the reasons for doing so the saving of expense and intention to organize a new Indian Department, which, however, was not done.

[4] *St. Clair Papers*, II, 14.

[5] Virginia State Library, *Governor's Letter Book*, 500–03; *Library of Congress, Continental Congress, Letters of H. Knox, Sec'y.*, no. 150, II, 37, 39. (Author's italics.)

make an expedition against the Wabash towns necessary for their preservation,' and that *'it will probably take place.'*[1] Congress made no objection whatever to the expedition into its territory north of the Ohio — at least not until long afterward, and then under interesting influences which will presently appear.

In the spring of 1786, even the few federal troops at the mouth of the Miami were in great danger of destruction by the Indians; and instead of defending the Kentucky people, were soon begging protection from them. March 21st, their commander, Captain Finney, wrote General Clark: 'the defrent Nations on the Miami and Wabash are combining to take this post. . . . It will be impossible for me to obtain any assistance, except by accident, as their object will be to cut off our boats. Should I have it in my power, I will send the first express to You & hope you will send me the necessary Aid.'[2] Finney only asked for fifty men, and they 'to be under the direction of their own officers.' Clark of course had no authority over the Kentucky militia and could not send the men.

While the volunteer expedition against the confederated Indians on the Wabash was being organized, General Clark visited Lincoln County. As that populous county would furnish most of the troops, he evidently wished to learn whether the people there could be relied on for men and supplies if he should accept command. Apparently he received satisfactory assurances on that point, or else thought the public danger so great as to make it his duty to waive objections and lead the expedition;[3] for on June 25th he wrote to the western military inspector of Congress, Major Wyllys: 'I learn that you have been so kind as to send an express to the Falls, informing us of the danger to be apprehended from the Indians. They are daily doing us mischief in different parts of the country. We are about raising men to chastise them. I expect to leave the Falls on the First day of August with fifteen hundred men, determined not to return without destroying their country, or reducing them to terms of our own. . . . I hope it is in your power to join us, if not with your whole force, at least one company

[1] *Governor's Letter Book, supra,* pp. 500–05. (Authors Italics.)

[2] *Draper MSS.* 53 J 25.

[3] He afterwards wrote Jefferson: 'I felt myself constrained, from the pressing distress with which Kentucky was overwhelmed at the time by Indian hostilities, to come forward as a private citizen to exert all the influence I had possessed with the people to forward the late expedition.' (June 29, 1791. Library of Congress, *Jefferson Papers,* C 2nd Series, no. 16, Letter 86; *Draper MSS.* 16 S 79.)

of your troops. ....A few regulars is of great advantage amongst militia.'[1]

Seventeen days after this was written, the county lieutenants received Governor Henry's instructions authorizing a regular expedition and the drafting of men and supplies for it. One might suppose Clark would have been much pleased with this new authority, but he was much troubled by it, and with good reason. Although he had reluctantly consented to lead volunteers, who would furnish their own horses and provisions and march of their own free will, it was another thing to lead an army of unwilling drafted men and depend on supplies taken by force from a people so little disposed to comply with military exactions. Furthermore, although the Virginia law authorized the drafting of militiamen, it did not authorize carrying them out of the state against their will.

Wishing advice on these points, General Clark wrote to his lawyer friend, Colonel Abram Chapline of Lincoln County, who had served under him in the Illinois Regiment. Chapline answered: 'I received your letter...wherein you express uneasiness for the disappointment of the volunteer campaign.... The Article of Confederation does not prohibit us from carrying on a campaign against any nation of Indians that actually invades our country, or state, which is alluded to in the Governor's letter to the officers of the District...but I have had the perusal of the Militia Law, and can't find that we have any power to take the militia out of the state without their consent.' Chapline then adds this prophetic caution: 'Now if the officers use every exertion, and *keep the law close*, I believe a campaign is practicable; but if the contrary, you may depend we shall not do anything this fall.'[2] He evidently knew the ugly temper of the people in his own county and foresaw that impressment of men and supplies there would arouse great opposition, and that drafted men carried out of the state without legal authority would be likely to resist orders.

The militia officers met at Harrodsburg, August 12th, to consider plans for the expedition; but before proceeding further, they requested the legal opinion of the Supreme Court judges and the attorney-general on the following two questions:

[1] *Papers Continental Congress, Knox, Sec'y of War*, Letters, no. 150, vol. I, pp. 527–29. Governor Henry also wrote for such coöperation of the federal troops to Colonel Harmar, who ordered it. (Harmar to Knox, *St. Clair Papers*, II, 18.)

[2] *Draper MSS*. 53 J 40.

'[1] Whether the powers of the Executive, vested in them by the Act of Assembly, and also under the Sixth Article of the Confederation, are delegated to the Field Officers of the District; and [2] whether the Field Officers, under such delegation, have power to impress [supplies] for the use of the militia who may be ordered out in consequence of the said Order of Council.'[1]

The judges and attorney-general answered both these questions affirmatively, but they were not asked, nor did they say, whether the troops could be lawfully carried out of the state without their consent. On receiving this legal opinion the field officers held a council and passed eight resolutions[2] which, when read 'between the lines' and in the light of subsequent events, very plainly disclose serious discord.

The first resolution declared 'that an expedition against the Wabash and other inimical Indians is, at this time justifiable, necessary, and, *with the united efforts of the District, practicable.*'[3] This indicates doubt about securing such united efforts, and an appeal for harmony. Another resolution ordered '*that one half of the militia of the district be drafted*'; the draft being expected to yield about twenty-five hundred men. Other resolutions provided for an impressment 'of a pack-horse for every four men, and fifty days provisions'; 'that it shall be at the option of every man... to take with him his own horse, but it shall at all times be subject to such regulations as the commander-in-chief shall direct'; and 'that all privates who are mounted on horseback shall carry their own provisions,' and 'that the troops meet at Clarksville, opposite Louisville, the 10th September.' The officers also resolved 'that General George Rogers Clark be appointed as general officer and have command and direction of the army at this time ordered on offensive operations against our enemy Indians,' and 'that should General Clark refuse to take the command, then it shall devolve upon Col. Benjamin Logan, if present; if not, upon the next eldest officer.'

This resolution shows General Clark still uncommitted to lead this army, and also his recognized superior fitness for lead-

[1] Virginia State Library, *Box Executive Papers*, Dec., 1786; Dunn's *Indiana*, pp. 171-72.
[2] *Id.*, and *Draper MSS.* 53 J 42. The statement in the council minutes that they were 'convened in council by the general' is an evident mistake, for the council resolutions themselves show Clark had not consented to command.
[3] All italics in the resolution are the present author's.

ership in time of great danger. His selection as commander is the more noteworthy because it set aside Logan, the senior militia officer in Kentucky, whose Lincoln men would make more than half the army. They had generally been his partisans in the fort building and Blue Lick dispute, were called 'Loganites,' and were far from being friendly to Clark.

Although it was yet uncertain whether General Clark would take command, the militia officers went on drafting men and supplies; but opposition was great, and many who were called for service evaded it. On September 12th, two days after the date fixed for the rendezvous at Clarkesville, only about twelve hundred men appeared, whereas double that number had been expected. A second officers' council was held to consider the situation.[1] Colonel Logan, as senior county lieutenant, presided, and several resolutions were adopted. The first recited that 'the number of men is too small to execute the plan originally intended,' and it was therefore ordered 'that a field officer from each county return and procure, *by draft, all the delinquents and deserters* in his county, *and one half of the militia not before drafted.*'[2]

The enemy Indians were known to be gathered by the upper Wabash, only about a hundred and fifty miles northwest of Clarksville (see map, page 25), and General Clark (who was at Clarksville and probably had concluded to accept the command) advised marching directly against them.[3] He considered the twelve hundred men sufficient, and there were ample provisions on hand, including many live cattle to be driven with the army. The country to be traversed was generally level, or gently rolling, and the streams easy to cross; but the season was intensely hot and the roads dusty, and the drafted men were little inclined to undertake the disagreeable work of carrying their own provisions, or driving troublesome cattle.

Clark's advice for a direct march against the enemy was opposed by others who contended that instead of marching

---

[1] Whether General Clark had by this time consented to take command we do not know. Although the minutes of the Clarksville meeting recite that the officers were 'convened by the general,' one of them, Captain Craig of Lincoln, who was present, said the 'council was called by other officers than the general, and they resolved,' etc.

[2] The original minutes, signed by Logan as president, are in the Virginia State library, and photostat in *Author's MSS. Virginia Calendar State Papers*, IV, 205, gives only a partial abstract.

[3] *Draper MSS.* 9 J 238.

northwest about one hundred and fifty miles to the Indians,
the army should go almost due west nearly one hundred miles
to Vincennes (where it would still be some eighty-five miles
from the enemy) and wait there until it became known how
many more drafted men would be brought from Kentucky.
They also argued that more flour and cured meat could be
sent by boats to Vincennes than could well be carried by the
troops overland against the enemy.[1] Although this course
would take the army many miles out of its way, it was no
doubt strongly demanded by the unwilling drafted men.
Clark's advice was overruled and the following resolution
(including the crossed words) was offered:

'That the army be marched under the direction of the general ~~as
he may judge proper, but wish it may not be marched further than
O'Post~~ [Vincennes] ~~until it is known what reenforcements may be had.~~'

General Clark evidently let it be known that he would refuse command if he was to be thus hampered, and required
to wait at Vincennes for reënforcements which might never
come; for the objectionable words were canceled and the
resolution as adopted simply provided 'that the army be
marched under the direction of the general.' Thereupon he
took command. He had good reasons for demanding this
change, for it not only gave him direction of the army already
assembled at Clarksville, but left him free to send wherever
he thought best the additional men to be drafted in Kentucky. He did not wish those men to reënforce him on the
Wabash, but to send them against the Shawnees.

The next resolution is full of meaning: '*That the officers who
return* [to Kentucky 'for delinquents and deserters '], *as well
as those who may be left, consider themselves engaged in a common cause & give every aid to each other*, without as well as
within their respective counties, to carry into execution the
intent of these resolutions.' This unmistakably points to
serious dissension amongst these officers, for otherwise they
would never have thought of passing a resolution to 'consider
themselves engaged in a common cause' and to 'aid each
other.'

General Clark knew that the Shawnees, despite their recent
treaty promises, had joined the hostile confederacy; and, to

[1] *Draper MSS.* 9 J 238.

compel them to desert and discourage their allies, he ordered Logan to return to Kentucky, gather troops there and lead them against the Shawnee towns.[1]

As the Lincoln and Fayette people regarded the Shawnees as their special enemies, Logan readily gathered seven hundred and ninety men — nearly five hundred of them mounted volunteers — and fell upon the Shawnee towns. The attack was wholly unexpected and there was little or no resistance; for the warriors had gone against Clark and few, save some old men, women and children, were left in the towns. Without the loss of a man, Logan destroyed their houses and crops, killed ten Indians and took thirty-two women and children prisoners. Amongst the killed was the old chief, Molunthy, who had long been friendly to the Americans. He had surrendered, but, while shielding himself with the American flag and holding up the recent treaty, was shot down.[2] This killing of the old chief led to acrimonious disputes between some of the officers and later to court trials and lasting enmities.[3]

[1] Virginia State Library, *Box Executive Papers*, Dec., 1786; *Virginia Calendar State Papers*, iv, 204; *Author's MSS.*, photostat.

[2] *Virginia State Library, supra.* Logan was severely criticized for not court-martialing those guilty of this barbarous act, but said he did not because of the bad feeling it would have aroused.

[3] The facts about Logan's expedition have been grossly distorted in history. Thus, Withers' *Chronicles of Border Warfare*, p. 386, says that in carrying out his expedition he 'practically...revolted from Clark!' and Collins' *History of Kentucky* says Logan destroyed *eight* large towns, 'killed about 20 warriors, and captured 70 or 80 prisoners'!

For contemporary reports showing the Shawnee warriors gone against Clark and almost none but old men, women and children left in the towns, see *Michigan Pioneer Collections*, xxiv, 34–52; *Records of Upland, Denny's Journal*, Nov. 13, 1786; *Harmar's Report, Library of Congress, Continental Congress, Letter to Sec'y of War*, no. 150, ii, 163–64; *St. Clair Papers*, ii, 18–19; *Draper MSS.* 11 F 61 (Report of Indian Council, Mohawk Chief's speech). Even the sachems seem to have been absent attending a council of representatives of hostile tribes. (*Michigan Pioneer Collections*, xxiv, 34–52.)

This expedition gave Logan his first and only independent command, and he did not depreciate his performance when reporting it to the governor:

May it please your excellency:
You will find by the enclosed papers that in September 14, 1786 I received orders to collect a sufficient number of men in the District of Kentucky to march against the Shawnee towns. Agreeable to orders I collected 790 men and on the 6th of October I attacted the above mentioned Towns, killed ten of the chiefs of that nation, captured thirty-two prisoners, Burnt upwards of 200 dwelling-houses and supposed to have burnt 15000 bushels of corn, took some horses, killed a number of hogs and took near 1000 pounds of Indian furniture and the quantity of furniture we burnt cannot [MS. illegible] the militia was under my command and was not above not 27 days on duty. Nearly 500 of these men rode their own horses and carried their own provisions and from my orders were not entitled to have any interest in the service of a public horse. The Expedition was carried on in a rappid manner and I would venture to say the expenses will be found very moderate. I have the honour to be your Excellencies Obdt. humble servt

BENJAMIN LOGAN
C.L. of Lincoln
(*Virginia Calendar State Papers*, iv, 204.)

CHAPTER XXVII

WABASH EXPEDITION AND MUTINY

IN view of the discord at the Clarksville rendezvous, General Clark evidently found it necessary to conciliate the officers and men who insisted on going to Vincennes. He therefore sent a detachment to that place, in boats carrying meat and flour down the Ohio and up the Wabash, and himself made a cross-country march with the main body. Seven days were consumed before they reached Vincennes, although willing soldiers could have covered the longer distance to the enemy and been at grips with them in less than half that time. The Lincoln troops, whom Logan had left in command of one Colonel Barrett and who were generally drafted men, were unruly, and throughout the hot and dusty march were constantly grumbling. Many of the cattle were lost on the way — a pretty sure sign of sulking neglect of duty.[1] Captain Gaines, commanding the volunteer troop of horse from Fayette, said: 'During the march, at a place called French Lick, there was a meeting of the whole of Col. James Barret's command, respecting a horse which had been taken for the adjutant-general to ride. The Whole of them fired off their guns in defiance of the orders of the Genl, by which the horse had been taken. The Colonel, however, was arrested, tried, and Repremanded, which delayed us for a few hours; we then marched on.'[2] Such insubordination, so early in the march, and the arrest and reprimand of the commander of more than half the troops, boded ill for the success of the campaign.

As the army approached Vincennes, 'all the leading French inhabitants came out and greeted him.'[3] To quarter twelve hundred men upon the impoverished town was out of the question; for it would not only have been a grievous burden to the people, but made discipline in the army almost impossible. The troops were therefore stationed across the Wabash, notwithstanding which they were soon charged by the French inhabitants with plundering them.

---

[1] Statement of Captain Craig of the Lincoln militia. *Draper MSS.* 9 J 134.

[2] *Id.,* 9 J 238.

[3] *Id.,* p. 237. So also did the Americans.

Without waiting for the provisions on the boats, the army had an ample supply for at least a ten days' march against the Indians, who could easily have been reached in three days. General Clark therefore advised an immediate march with the provisions and ammunition on hand, with orders for the rest of the boat stores to be brought on by a detachment left for that purpose; 'but he was over-ruled by a plurality of voices, and he submitted, of necessity.'[1] Captain Gaines said: 'We remained at Vincennes 15 days waiting the arrival of the boats, exhausting full Rations of Beef and Flour, waiting to receive 5 days provisions of flour alone, as the Beef was so Rotten that it was all thrown overboard on the Passing up the [Wabash] River.'[2] Low water and no doubt sulking men had delayed the boats.[3] Captain Craig of Lincoln said they were 'Eight days waiting the arrival of the boats. The Wabash was so low as to make it necessary to send down a party from Vincennes to assist up the boats — to go into the water and drag the boats over the riffles. The drief beef in the boats got wet and injured.'[4]

At Vincennes General Clark had received from two chiefs of the enemy Indians deceptive assurances that they were not hostile and wished peace; but he knew that no reliance could be put upon them. He knew too that they were all fully informed of his coming, and he sent them this defiant message: 'You will inform the different tribes of Savages on the Oubash that they have long threatened me, saying that I dared not come into their Country. Now I am here. If they are men, let them come & fight, as such, and not be killing our Women and children, but fight Men! I send these bloody strings that they may accept of them.'[5]

To this challenge the Indians sent the following ironic reply, probably written by some British trader: 'Thou American, I am charmed to hear thee speak; probably thou art not a Chief, since thou speakest so ill. It gives me pleasure to hear thee speak. Thou hast surely more wisdom than we have, since thou hast informed us of thy being come; for our Parts, we...come without saying a word. We hope to hear from you once more.[6]

[1] Marshall's *Kentucky*, i, 250.
[2] Captain Gaines to Mann Butler, *Draper MSS.* 9 J 238.
[3] *Id.*
[4] *Draper MSS.* 9 J 134. Gaines said they waited fifteen days, but doubtless included the seven days consumed on the march. Either way, fifteen days' rations were consumed.
[5] *Draper MSS.* 11 J 108.
[6] *Id.*

With most of his army insubordinate and utterly lacking in fighting spirit; with no lawful authority over them and that fact known to them; with supplies still sufficient for a reasonably speedy campaign, but not for a slow one — the issue of the campaign was certainly unpromising. Clark's situation was a most trying one, yet something had to be done. To disband his force would have meant the butchery of Vincennes people and the over-running of Kentucky by rapidly multiplying savages. There was nothing left, therefore, but to march against the enemy, and accordingly the march was ordered. One of the insubordinate Lincoln officers said that even before starting 'it was a very difficult matter to keep peace with the men, and I believe, had we not have started at the time, in two days the men would have started home.'[1]

Colonel Barrett's malcontents debated whether or not they would go further; but they did. After two days, however, and when within a day's forced march of the enemy,[2] they mutinied and refused to march farther, 'alleging a scarcity of provisions as the reason for so doing.'[3] One of them afterward said that one of the ring-leaders asked him to 'know the quantity of provisions on hand'; to which he replied 'that we were scarce, and no chance to have any before we could reach the Indian towns.'[4] That, owing to the conduct of the mutineers themselves, the supply of flour and beef was low seems true; but they had several hundred horses to feed them in extremity, and had they been bent on victory, any man proposing a retreat would have been laughed at, or drummed out of camp. It is significant that only Barrett's Lincoln men professed to fear hunger, for the Jefferson and Fayette men insisted upon going on, and offered to force the mutineers to do so.[5]

Said Captain Gaines: 'We were surprised by hearing the cry of 'Who's for home? Who's for home?' from the same troops who had fired off their guns at French Lick, which was nearly half the Army, who actually marched off, headed by an Ensign — other officers choosing to await the result of what should be

---

[1] Robard's statement, *Draper MSS.* 11 J 79.

[2] The distances given are straight lines; of course the actual line of march was greater. The troops were near the mouth of the Vermillion River. (Captain Gaines' letter, *Draper MSS.* 9 J 238.) The Indians were supposed to be near the mouth of Pine Creek (Isaac Taylor's Letter, *Draper MSS.* 33 J 82), only a little over thirty miles from the army.

[3] *Id.*, 9 J 238, Gaines' letter.

[4] *Id.*, 11 J 79, Robard's statement.

[5] Moses Boone, *Draper MSS.* 9 J 237; *Maryland Journal*, v, 19.

determined on, although a Majority of them had determined the night before to return home. . . . As no solicitation could induce those troops to return to their duty, the whole returned to [Vincennes] in the greatest confusion, and then, by sixes, tens, or dozens, as inclination prompted, to Louisville.'[1] Another Fayette volunteer, Captain Moses Boone,[2] said: 'After about two days march from Vincennes, the Lincoln men revolted and started back—called Loganites. A large circle was formed of the remainder of the troops, and a general council held; some proposed to go and force back the Lincoln men — others urged the continuance of the campaign with what was left.'[3]

Another officer said: 'After marching about two days, the Regiment Col. Logan had left, mutinied and stopped and declared they would go no further, stating that the supply of provisions for the army was not sufficient for them to march to the Indian Towns & return home. The other Regiment, commanded by Col. Todd, being considered not sufficient to go on, with any prospects of Success or Safety, we turned and marched home.'[4]

Lieutenant Craig, of the Fayette volunteers, described the events as follows:

'Col. Levi Todd commanded the Fayette troops; a cavalry company of about 40 men was commanded by Maj. John Morrison. . . . Major Barret commanded the Lincoln men. . . . It was the Lincoln men that mutinied. Clark's troops camped opposite Vincennes on the west bank of the Wabash. Moved up from Vincennes and, a half day's march, crossed over to the east bank and progressed to about miles, estimated, from Vincennes, when Barret's men mutinied & went back; they complained that the provisions would soon give out and that there was only beef still left. Gen. Clark went among them, with his hat off, & begged them (in tears 'twas said) not to go; "Only promise me" said Clark feelingly, "to go with me two days

[1] *Draper MSS.* 9 J 238.
[2] Judge Moses Boone, long highly respected as a citizen and jurist of Indiana.
[3] *Draper MSS.* 9 J 237.
[4] *Draper MSS.* 9 J 153, Cave Johnson's statement. One of the Lincoln mutineers said that, 'after three days march, provisions gave out [evidently an over-statement], rummered 'what's the use of going and nothing to eat?' and next morning, when tents were struck & march ordered, the majority of the men wheeled and marched back. Some few

hundred kept with Clark.' (*Draper MSS.* 9 J 197, Briggs' statement.) One of the ring leaders, a captain under Colonel Barrett, afterwards gave this terse explanation: 'got out of provisions and returned.' (*Draper MSS.* 9 J 236, Farris' statement.) That provisions were scant there can be no doubt; but, so far from their having given out, they answered the army for a three days' disorderly march back to Vincennes, during which much must have been wasted for want of proper control.

march, & if I dont furnish you with as much provisions as you want, I will return with you." The mutineers derided him, — went off, and left him standing alone, then within two days march of [the] Indian towns. [The Indians, as Clark probably anticipated, were in fact considerably nearer than their towns.] Todd's men lay on high land to the right, & after Barret's men went off, Col. Todd put it to a vote among his men, whether they would go with Gen. Clark, & unanimously agreed they would go wherever Clark would say. But, upon a full consultation, Clark & the officers, as the strength of the army was so much reduced, [concluded] that it was best to return — and moved down to Vincennes.'[1]

Lieutenant Crockett said that when the mutineers 'were seen to file off and make up the line of march for home,' Clark, 'in pathetic strains, exhorted the remainder to stand by him to the end of the campaign; they raised a deafening shout and answered that they would perish with him.'[2] Several present said that Clark, in this hour of first defeat, was greatly moved, and in his agitation shed tears — whether in anger when addressing the mutineers, or afterwards, when touched by the loyalty of the Fayette and Jefferson men, was not stated. Self-control had always been one of his marked characteristics; but he was only recently recovered from a desperate illness, and his feelings were no doubt wrought to the breaking point when he found all hope of success blasted and Vincennes and Kentucky exposed to destruction.

The expedition upon which so much depended thus ended in disgraceful failure. Almost in the presence of the Indians, the army had tucked tail and made a disorderly retreat, inviting their contempt and attack. The people of Vincennes when they heard the news were appalled, and so also were the people in Kentucky.

What with the poverty of the French and American residents of Vincennes, the utter lack of law, the presence of hundreds of hungry, lawless, pillaging stragglers, and some fifteen hundred armed Indians only eighty-odd miles away, the situation there was frightful. For Clark to abandon the town and march off his remaining men would have been heartless; yet how he was to protect it was difficult to see. Certainly only extraordinary resourcefulness and quick action could do it; but he did it! In this surprising achievement his main asset was the ever loyal confidence he had won from the French. He had always been

[1] *Draper MSS.* **23 J 163.**   [2] *Id.,* Anthony Crockett's statement.

just and sympathetic toward them, and on this occasion their friendship stood him in good stead. With the aid of their leading citizen, Colonel LeGras, he lost no time in seeking an opportunity to open negotiations with the savages; and this he did, according to his invariable method, by confusing and overawing them! Situated as he was, it seems surprising that he should even have thought this possible.

When Indians were plotting war, some of them nearly always pretended to be still friendly; and it has been seen that two of the chiefs had sent him a message professing to wish peace.[1] At that time he ignored them and sent no reply; but now he was quick to seize the opportunity their message had given him to open negotiations, not only with them but with all the confederated Indians. Accordingly he sent to all of them the following speech offering them choice of peace or war, but peace only as a favor!

To the Chiefs and Warriors of the different Nations on the Ouabash, &c:

You all know that formerly we Spoke Together as Brothers. I then Explained to you the cause of the war Between the English & us. Your Chiefs assured me the cause was Common betwixt you and the [Big] Knives, seeing that if we were Conquered you should fall the Next Victim, the Intention of the English being to Reduce both to a State of Slavery. When the Americans had Reduced the English to that point that they were glad to accept of any Terms offered to [them] by us, they Ceded to us all the Lands, as far as the Lakes, to Compensate for the Loss they had done us during the war, &c. Without Stipulating anything Regarding you in the Treaty of Peace they made with us, [they] granted...all those Lands & Put you entirely off.

I now find that you are Excited by some English Traders to take up the Hatchet against us. Their intentions are to prevent the great Knives from Trading with you, & to engross the whole [trade] to themselves, at the Risk of your Women & Children. Provided they have your skins, they care no more about you. The frequent Murders your young men have Committed on our Women & Children have obliged us to take up the Hatchett, and we are determined not to Lay it down until the Roads are perfectly cleared. Our Women & Children may Cry, but the more they weep the more we shall seek Revenge. We are now in your Country and will not go far out of it till this be Completed.

I sent you the other day, by my friend Pacenne, a Red Belt to let you know that we are here. You sent back the Red with some strings of White Wampum and a pipe for us to Smoke. You also prayed to

---

[1] *Draper MSS.* 11 J 108.

hear from us before I saw you. This determined us to Return to our Road, tho we were already three days journey towards your Towns.

To Convince you we were not [devoid] of Humanity, I send you today some strings of white, sincerely inviting you to Come to a Grand Councill at Clarksville on the 20th Novr next, when we shall Endeavor to agree upon Terms of Peace & Friendship. If we cannot agree, we shall return to our Villages before we begin Hostilities; but if you do not come agreeable to the Invitation, I will Conclude that you are still for war and shall Act Accordingly. But you may Rest assured, if you do Continue the war, that we shall adopt measures without delay to send a great Many Families to take possession of your Lands and make a Conquest of them Forever, without showing you any mercy. We have already Spies all over it, and we know it better than ours, that the Road is good and not far from the Falls of Ohio. We dont say this to boast, but with an Intention to Convince you that we do not wish to deceive you, and to prevent your Reproaching us afterwards that we did not give you warning.

It would be well for you that this Letter were Translated to you According...to its Meaning. I wish you to know it without delay, and if you have any intention of Coming to Treat, let me know it without delay, and I shall provide everything Necessary for your Reception and provision. Be not afraid; there will be no danger for you in our Towns; witness Pecanni's people. I am informed that Several Traders are Stopped Among you. I expect the First Proof of your Intentions will be to let them go Immediately with their property. I am &c

CLARK[1]

General Clark well knew that this speech alone would accomplish nothing; but with it he also sent another written by Colonel LeGras. The Frenchman told the Indians that the General had returned from his march against them only at earnest solicitation of himself and their other French friends, who, he said, had pledged Clark their honor that the Indians would lay down their war hatchet! LeGras said:

'I have received the good words you sent me by Pannas and Piccane, at which I am pleased and, notwithstanding I see my blood Spill^d on every side, I wish to convince you all today that the French have a Tender Heart and that they have pity on your Women and Children.

'I no sooner heard your good words than I communicated them to all your Brothers the French, who Immediately joined me to send after the Army to invite it to Return, which, with a great deal of Intreaty, we obtained, Promising and flattering ourselves that you

---

[1] *Draper MSS.* 11 J 108. Clark's speech was endorsed by LeGras: 'It was delivered into the hands of Monsr J. DeVaudry, Senr Mast^r Interpreter, to explain it according to its proper meaning where need may be. LeGras.'

would Remain Quiet on your Lands and that the Fools would Strip themselves of their bad Designs. ...All the French with me Request of you Not to Cause us Shame. Do not make us Liars. I am Shocked to see you so long deaf and Blind. ...Had I not Stoppᵈ you this summer...from doing Mischief, the Birds of Prey would eat your Women and Children and your Towns would be Confounded with the Wilderness. ...

'Hold the war chiefs, ...acquainting them that in the days of their fore-fathers the Roads on Ouabash were clear and that of old the French and them were but one. Let us therefore follow the Examples of our Ancestors; ...They never Wished that their Women and Children should have cause to weep. ...

'Hearken therefore to the Speech your Brothers, the Americans, send you. Tho you Spill their Blood every day, they have pity. ...

'You I invite to sit down and take again the hand of your Brothers, the Big Knives, who spare your blood. Let us all have but one dish. The women and children have long enough Slept in fear. ...It is full time you Walked in the Clear Road you Formerly used if you have aⁿy regard for your women and Children.'[1]

Designedly, General Clark's speech made no reference to that of LeGras, or to any request from the French to grant the Indians peace. He simply offered them peace, if they would behave themselves! While he anxiously awaited an answer, something plainly had to be done to save Vincennes in case the savages should spurn his offer and attack the town. To prevent this, a show of force was necessary; and the only one he could make was by garrisoning the town. He therefore called a council of officers who approved this step and declared themselves 'unanimously of the opinion that a garrison at this place will be of Essential service to the District of Kentucky, and that supplies may be had in the District more than sufficient for their support, by Impressment, or otherwise, under the direction of a commissary.'[2] A commissary was accordingly appointed, and the council further 'Resolved, that two field officers with 250 men, exclusive of the Company of Artillery,...be recruited to Garrison post Vincent.'[3] Recruiting of men for the garrison at once began and about one hundred and forty were enlisted. It probably never occurred to General

[1] *Draper MSS.* 11 J 108. The speech bore this endorsement: 'Done at Post Vincennes 10th Octʳ 1786 & Delivered into the hands of Monsier J. DeVaudry Senʳ Master Interpreter to deliver according to the Sence...and Meaning where Need be. LeGras.'

[2] *Draper MSS.* 53 J 51. Their reason for mentioning the benefit to Kentucky, rather than to Vincennes, was evidently to justify impressments in Kentucky.
[3] *Id.*

Clark or his officers that any one could question the propriety
of doing this, for he was lawfully in command in time of war,
and was clearly vested with all the powers inherently belonging to a commander, including the power to fortify, enlist men,
and impress necessary supplies.[1]

Before any reply was received from the Indians, an interesting event occurred which was described in a record kept by
LeGras, that he afterward sent to Clark at the Falls and is still
preserved:

'A chief of the Piankeshaws came to the Post and told a Frenchman he wished to make peace with the Genl, if he was still here. He
was sent for, and he [the chief] asking for peace to himself and his
Young men, it was granted. He said he had not been with the others
for a long while; that their Intentions were unknown to him. He
was desired to acquaint any Indians he should meet that the Genl
was here to wait their answers to his speech. About the same time a
Young Warrior came in to shake hands with his Brother Warrior,
the General, who he understood had [laid] his Hatchet under his bed.
[In other words, had quit fighting.] On the General's saying no, for
he held it up still, the Indian stood amazed; and soon after he was
committed to the guard house, from whence he made his escape.'[2]

This action was in line with Clark's invariable policy in
dealing with the savages. As the Piankeshaws were the only
warring Indians who had asked peace, he wished to show the
other Indians that he was still at war, was not afraid of them,
would arrest any he found, and that if they wanted peace they
must send and beg for it! The prisoner's escape was probably
made easy that he might go and tell them.

Ten days passed after Clark and LeGras had sent their
speeches to the assembled Indians, and still no reply had come.

---

[1] Under the Confederation Articles,
Virginia had the right to order the expedition; it was undertaken with the authority and active encouragement of
her governor and executive council; the
Secretary of War, the military inspector
and the commander for Congress in the
west, and even Congress itself, were fully
informed of the organizing, purpose, and
marching of the expedition, and had
never objected to it. Indeed, the commander ordered his subordinates to co-
operate with Clark. (*Continental Congress, Letters of H. Knox, Sec'y of War*,
no. 150, II, 169–71.) Furthermore, the
expedition was morally justified by necessity for self-preservation.

If General Clark was authorized to
carry on the war in the Wabash country
at all, no less clearly he had the right to
establish and defend any post in it, and
to enlist every man and impress every
species of property in it necessary for effective conduct of the war. To deny
such powers to a commander in time of
war would be preposterous; and the law
does not deny them. See Frederick
Sturges Allen, in *Universal Cyclopædia*,
'Martial Law'; also Grotius' *Rights of
War and Peace*, XVII, 377. (Cambridge
Library Law Classics.)

[2] LeGras Report, *Draper MSS*. 53 J
108.

This was ominous, and an attack was no doubt daily expected, for they could have answered in half that time. Meanwhile, lack of food, clothing, and other necessaries for the troops during the approaching winter presented a serious problem. The inhabitants, although craving protection by the garrison troops, were far too needy to feed and clothe them; and the alternative of forcibly taking their slender means, or abandoning them to the enemy, was painful to contemplate. To procure flour Clark sent his commissary to the Illinois to beg it of the French inhabitants there. They were generously inclined, but their own needs were then such that little help could be expected from that quarter.

Clark next turned to Kentucky and requested Colonel Logan to take steps to procure provisions, which were abundant in Fayette and Lincoln; but Logan declined to do so. He wrote the Governor:

'General Clark...informs me...that he had ordered an Officer to recruit two hundred and fifty men, which orders was nearly complyd with. Those men were to keep possession of an American garrison at that place, and to Keep the Indians in terror until a treaty. The Proceedings, I think, was wise and Prudent. He also made application to me, as Eldest Officer in the District of Kentucky, to call a Board of Field Officers, in order to procure provisions for the Troops on the Northwest side of Ohio. I, Aledging myself not possest of any such Power, I declined that business, but thinks of my duty to lay the subject before your Excellency, hoping you and Council will do what you think in your Wisdom best.'[1]

Logan's refusal to take any steps to procure provisions for the garrison was followed within a few weeks by its dissolution. His course seems quite indefensible, for if the recruiting of the troops to garrison Vincennes 'was wise and prudent,' as he said, then their support was plainly proper and his duty.[2]

At this juncture some Spanish traders at Vincennes — of whom the principal was one Bazadone — received a cargo of

---

[1] *Virginia Calendar State Papers*, IV, 202.

[2] Logan knew the war was by no means over, but only suspended by a truce. He recognized its legality and had himself impressed men and supplies for it. He recognized General Clark as his superior officer, and under his orders had himself crossed the Ohio and attacked the Shawnee towns; yet he now declined to obey his superior's order to call a council of officers to procure provisions. Probably his attitude was in part due to a belief that impressments in his own county to support the garrison would be extremely unpopular and be resisted, for he knew the enmity of the Lincoln people toward Clark, and the Loganite mutineers were there to stir it up.

varied merchandise.[1] None of them had passports, which were
then required of all alien traders, and the want of which subjected them to arrest and confiscation of goods. The French
and Americans had little love for Spain, which was shutting
out of the lower Mississippi, mistreating all who ventured
there, and inciting the southern Indians to war; and these
Spaniards at Vincennes were charged with furnishing the Wabash Indians with ammunition.[2] If, therefore, supplies had to
be impressed to support the garrison, from whom, the Americans thought, could they be so properly taken as from these
Spanish traders? A court-martial was called to consider this
question and took action as follows:

A Court, held 18th October by order of Genl. Clark, to inquire
whether certain effects, the property of Sign[r] Thoulou, Sign[r] Basse
[Bazadone], & Sign[r] Trusseron, seized last evening as Spanish effects, being really the property of Spanish subjects, and if so whether
they ought to be confiscated.
The Court consisting of Capt. V. T. Dalton
                    "   E. S. Smith
                    "   Tho. Stribling
                    "   Tho. Mason[3]

The traders were examined under oath, through a sworn interpreter, and acknowledged they were Spanish subjects without passports; whereupon the Court unanimously ordered their
goods confiscated and ordered the commissary to put them in
one store and dispose of them, 'reserving 2 or 3 hhgs of Taffia
for the use of the troops, to be issued as rations.' The sentence was approved and signed by General Clark. In pursuance of the court order, Commissary Jones impressed Bazadone's goods;[4] gave him a receipt for them; reserved the taffia
as directed; distributed amongst the troops the clothing and
other articles they needed; auctioned the rest publicly, and applied the proceeds for their support. Under the circumstances,
the impressment seems to have been more than usually regular
and, being clearly necessary, was justifiable under military law.[5]

---

[1] Harmar says: 'A boat load valued at
upwards of two thousand pounds.' (*Continental Congress, Letters of H. Knox*, no.
150, II, 359–65.)

[2] *Virginia Calendar State Papers*, IV, 189.

[3] *Draper MSS*. 53 J 53; *R. C. Ballard
Thruston's MSS*., photostat copy.

[4] Whether any belonging to Thoulou

or Thrusseron were taken does not appear. Possibly they were partners, or
employes, of Bazadone, who alone is
mentioned afterwards.

[5] If Bazadone had been possessed of a
passport, Spain might have claimed
compensation for him, but could hardly
have done more.

Not until thirteen days after the officers' council had ordered men enlisted for a garrison, did the Indians answer General Clark's speech. Evidently they had waited to see whether he would leave Vincennes with his whole force and march off to Kentucky. They knew most of the men had already gone, but found that many remained, and that Clark himself stayed; and for him they had a wholesome respect. Two courses were open to them — they could besiege Vincennes, or accept his offer of peace; for they dared not go off to war in Kentucky while he and his garrison were so near their towns. They had no doubt been deserted by their Shawnee allies, because of Logan's raid; and, as they feared cannon and lacked a commissary, they were ever strongly averse to sieges. In this dilemma they hearkened to LeGras' and Clark's speeches and prayed for peace!

Those speeches, and above all the garrison at Vincennes, had enabled Clark to overawe and bring to terms the most formidable Indian gathering that ever threatened the western people after the Revolution. It was literally victory wrested from defeat; it neutralized the mutiny and even made an advantage of the retreat of the army; it saved Vincennes and shielded Kentucky; it gave Congress opportunity to arrange a permanent peace with the confederacy the ensuing spring. It was really one of the most brilliant and fruitful achievements of his whole career.

One after another, the confederated chiefs ('Goose,' chief of the Ouiatenans, 'Crooked Legs,' 'Loon, the Quicapou,' the chief of the 'Great Sioux,' 'Tusil' — the list is uncertain) sent him their replies, regretting they had taken up the hatchet, thanking him for opening their eyes to the truth, and saving their women and children — in a word, humbly begging peace. The only objection they made was to the time and place General Clark had fixed for the treaty council. Instead of November 20th, they proposed the last of April following, and instead of Clarksville, they asked that the place be Vincennes. Loon, the Quicapou, said: 'My elder Brother, thou Invitest us to a grand council at Clarksville. We dont know that place. It is to Post Vincents that our Fathers used to go to Speak, & we hope you will not refuse it to us, that place being the Bed of our Ancestors and of Monsr de Vincennes. Thou hast allowed for the purpose but one moon. Thou seeist, my Brother, that it is impossible for us, being obliged to provide for our Women and Children during the Winter; but in the Spring of the year we will Repair at your pleasure to Post Vincents.' Nothing could have suited General Clark better than this postponement, for it prolonged the truce he sorely needed.

This was his last dealing with the Indians, and it brings out, again, his masterly understanding and handling of them. Perhaps no man more thoroughly knew the Indians, or read their motives more surely, or knew better how to impress them and avoid conflict with them, or how to deceive them; and, like every capable captain, he deceived his enemies as occasion required. Excepting in the strategy of war, however, no man was freer from guile, or readier to trust men whom he supposed honorable. He had inventive resourcefulness quite as great as Wilkinson's; but, unlike Wilkinson, used it only for worthy ends. In character no two men were ever more strongly contrasted. Wilkinson's deceptive strategies were invariably for corrupt ends, and often directed against trusting friends; Clark's always against enemies and for worthy ends. It was the irony of fate that the traitor should come to ruin the patriot.

CHAPTER XXVIII

MUTINEERS' EXCUSES AND SLANDERS

FOR his remarkable success in preventing disastrous results from the mutiny, and in bringing overwhelming numbers of hostile Indians to beg for peace, General Clark certainly deserved high praise. Nor was the state government insensible of this. At the suggestion of the new governor, Edmund Randolph, the Assembly declared that '*whereas* the citizens of ...Kentucky have lately carried on two expeditions against the neighboring tribes of Indians and *it is reasonable that such services should be rewarded*, therefore be it enacted that commissioners be appointed to settle and adjust all claims for pay and rations... of the officers, soldiers and those employed in the staff department lately under the command of General George Rogers Clark and Colonel Benjamin Logan against the Shawanese and Wabash Indians and also the claims of all those who have furnished arms, ammunition, provisions... [etc.] by impressment or otherwise for the purpose of carrying on the said expeditions. ...And all those who have made impressments necessarily for the use of the said expeditions shall be and are hereby indemnified.'[1]

When Governor Randolph recommended and the Assembly passed this act, both were informed of General Clark's enlistment of troops to garrison Vincennes and made no objection to it. Logan had written the governor about it, and was himself a member of the Assembly. The whole object of the act was to relieve Clark and his impressing officers of liability for any technical illegality in their impressments, if made necessarily. If, therefore, the impressment of the Spaniard, Bazadone's, goods at Vincennes was necessary for the support of the troops, which seems indisputable, the assembly act certainly condoned any legal irregularity in the impressment.

Governor Randolph thought, however, that Congress was responsible for the Indian war, and demanded that it reim-

---

[1] Hening's *Statutes of Virginia*, XII, 231-34. Before the Assembly passed this act it called on the governor to lay before it the instructions for the late expedition by his predecessor, Governor Henry, thus showing its legality was considered and approved. (*Journal House of Delegates*, 106.) See also Judge Wallace to Governor Randolph, Library of Congress, *Madison Papers*, XIV, 94.

burse Virginia for her outlays in carrying on these expeditions. He wrote the president of Congress the following letter, every line of which is significant in view of what occurred later:

Sir: In the course of the last summer the inhabitants of Kentucky were compelled, for their own preservation, to commence expeditions against the Indians on both sides of the Ohio. These have been recognized by the State of Virginia. But, as I consider the federal interest to have been advanced by these movements, ... [I] submit to Congress the propriety of Virginia taking credit for the expeditions against the United States. On this ground I consign to your discretion the prisoners made by the troops; they are at present supported by us in behalf of the Union. Enclosed I transmit copies of the letters from the two commanders, General Clark and Colo. Logan.[1]

In both of these letters, let it be noted, Congress was distinctly informed of Clark's enlisting men and garrisoning Vincennes; and, although it declined to pay the cost of the expedition, it made no objection whatever to his carrying war into its territory north of the Ohio, or to his garrisoning that town. That objection it only discovered later, and in the manner now about to be disclosed.

While General Clark was handling the difficult situation at Vincennes so brilliantly, the Lincoln mutineers returned to their homes. They knew they would have to give some excuse for their disgraceful conduct, and of course found one; men of that kind never fail to find one. The only one they had given at the time of the mutiny was lack of food, and that they had themselves caused. Accordingly, another excuse was made up. This was that the mutiny and failure of the expedition were caused by General Clark being incapacitated for command by drinking! This kind of false charge — for such it certainly was — has been made about many eminent men during wars and heated political conflicts all through our history; for it is an easy and safe one to make, is readily accepted and repeated by the unfriendly, and is exceedingly difficult to trace and disprove. If this falsehood about Clark was invented by one of the mutineers, it was plainly an afterthought to avoid censure; but the real inventor was probably Wilkinson, who soon afterward circulated it in Lincoln County and used it very adroitly to discredit Clark with Governor Randolph and Congress and secure his own appointment to succeed Clark as Indian Com-

[1] Virginia State Library, *Governor's Letter Book*, 47, January 21, 1787.

missioner. False as the charge was, there were mutineers ready
to vouch for it; and, when repeated amongst their neighbors in
Lincoln, it found receptive believers amongst people there who
held the old sectional grudge against the General, growing out
of the fort-building controversy and Blue Licks disaster. Indeed, the charge was early written into history by one of
Clark's enemies,[1] and has been carelessly repeated by historians to this day. Only because of this is the subject now given
more than passing notice.

The only persons who were present at the mutiny, or during
the march, or at Vincennes, who are known to have said he was
drinking during the expedition, were three young mutineer
privates from Lincoln, of unknown character; and their statements were not given until when they were very old men, fifty-
eight years afterward![2] On the other hand, Captain Gaines
said: 'On this expedition I served in a Volunteer troop of
Horse, and it was our duty to attend the Genl. wherever he
went, and encamped near him every night during the whole
time until our return to Vincennes, where I left him with the
rest of the troop. It has been alleged that the Genl. was in a
state of intoxication during the whole time, which is certainly
incorrect or I should have seen it. And I can safely state that
he was cool and collected during the whole time up to our
return as above stated. It is my sincere opinion that, had we
marched across the country to the Indian towns, as the General wished, we would have given a good account then and
returned with the laurels in our caps, instead of Shagreen in
our faces.'[3]

None of the mutineer officers appear to have said Clark was
intemperate during the expedition. Some may have done so
privately, for the temptation was strong; but no one of them
ever stood openly responsible for it. Possibly some made it in
letters which may yet come to light; but, aside from the statements of the three mutineer privates, and mere general heresay reports such as Governor Harrison mentioned in 1782, a
diligent investigation has failed to disclose any contemporary
evidence whatever indicating that General Clark was ever

---

[1] Humphrey Marshall, author of the
first generally read history of Kentucky.
Concerning it see the present author's introduction to *Littell's Political Transactions, Filson Club Publications* no. XXXI.

[2] *Draper MSS.* 9 J 197; 207, 79. The
veracity of two of them appears decidedly questionable on the face of their
own statements.

[3] *Draper MSS.* 9 J 238.

once intoxicated, either during, or at any time before, the Wabash Expedition. Specific instances are never mentioned, but only vague general rumors. If called upon to justify the charge, all who repeated it, except its originators, could truthfully have said they only repeated what they had heard.

The reader has seen that upon the close of the Revolution the state line officers entrusted General Clark with their large interests in western military lands; and none of them, so far as known, ever complained of his neglect or conduct of the trust. As president of the Board of Commissioners charged with the survey and allotment of the Illinois Regiment lands, he had many responsible judicial duties to perform; and from none of the hundreds of persons interested in the distribution of the land, nor from any of the commissioners, was there complaint or intimation of neglect or incapacity on his part. His connection with the Shawnee land treaties in 1785–6 has been seen. He was much with his fellow commissioners, Parsons and Butler, and the military officers attending them; and in their letters, or the diaries which three of them left, no word is found intimating that he was intemperate, or neglectful, or incapable. On the contrary, their every reference to him is entirely respectful, and the diaries of Major Denny and the letters of Captain Finney disclose marked esteem for him.

Dating from the time of the hue and cry against him following upon the Blue Licks defeat, the old falsehood about General Clark's drinking and being 'incapable of attending to business' was no doubt still believed by many in eastern Virginia and elsewhere; and has been carelessly accepted and repeated by some historians. His life, however, has long been an open book for those who would take pains to read it. The indefatigable Draper and others have collected and bared to inspection Clark's public and most private letters alike, including a great number mentioning him written by members of his family, his friends, and his enemies. If he had been the 'sot' Arthur Campbell represented him in 1782, or been drinking so as to be 'incapable of attending to business' during the Wabash Expedition four years afterward, it is hardly believable that none of these many contemporary letters (especially those written by members of his own family, solicitous for his welfare, or by his enemies, anxious for his downfall) would not have mentioned the fact. Yet, so far as found, not one does, except several concocted by Wilkinson and presently to be mentioned. It is true that afterward, when he had ceased to have any command, he was driven to drink — though by no means to the extent sometimes represented. The extraordinary circumstances which led to this will appear when that period of his life is reached; and the reader will then be able to judge fairly and how far he was amenable to censure.

On returning to Louisville General Clark learned that false reports were circulated about the cause of the mutiny; and, doubtless remembering how he had been charged with responsibility for the Blue Licks disaster, suspected the mutineers were trying to saddle him with the blame. He therefore wrote at once to the Governor requesting an official inquiry into the conduct of the expedition, saying:

Sir: This will be handed you by Col. Logan. He will inform you of the Unfortunate affair of the Revolution in the army. Various reports no doubt hath spread Respecting this affair, but Sir, that the truth may appear, you will pardon me in recommending a court of Enquiry as soon as possible. Without something of this nature takes place it will be in vain to attempt anything for the future.

After the retreat, serious reflections convinced me that the state of our affairs would be worse than ever if something was not done. I had a number of troops recruited for one year, fortified myself at Vincennes, and in the course of four weeks brought the whole of the Wabash Indians to my own terms, blinding the cause of the retreat, and even making an advantage of it.

The Grand Treaty would have been held this fall, if we had known what articles to have agreed to; for the want of that knowledge from Congress, it's put off until the last of April next, to be held at Vincennes, and [it] is thought by the best judges that the greatest body of Indians that ever appeared together in that quarter will be Imbodied. Now what will be done in this case, it is impossible for me to determine; if it is prosecuted there must be a support of men, money, and provisions.

What the different Nations and myself have agreed to, is to rest quiet until the time it is expected that a final peace will take place. I should have sent you the whole proceedings if they had come to hand, [meaning LeGras' report of his own and Clark's speeches and strategy with the Indians], but, being sent by water the vessel hath not yet arrived; of course put it out of my power.

And as to the Shawnees business and other matters, I refer you to Col. Logan for Information. I am Sir Yr Excellency's Hm'ble Servt

G. R. CLARK [1]

P. Henry Esqr

---

[1] Virginia State Library, *Box Executive Papers*, Dec. 20-30, 1786. This letter has never been published, so far as known. It is undated, but was evidently written

It seems strange that of all men, Logan, the commander of the mutineers, should have been relied on by Clark to inform the Governor about the mutiny. Four years earlier he had trusted him to report the Blue Licks defeat, little dreaming of the ugly charges Logan was making against him to Governor Harrison; but evidently he had never learned of them, or else thought Logan had since become friendly and would fairly report the mutinous conduct of his own men on the Wabash. In fact, though remarkably keen in penetrating the motives of known enemies, General Clark was trustful, almost to credulity, in dealing with men whom he supposed honorable; and he was inclined to believe men were honorable. This apparent inconsistency between keenness and trustfulness is found in the lives of many able and high-minded men; for shrewdness is a matter of intellect, suspicion one of character; and such men are slow to suspect unworthy motives in others.

Logan, again a member of the Virginia Assembly at Richmond, doubtless gave his own version of the mutiny of his men — what version is not known; but he was not in the Wabash Expedition and his report of the mutiny could only have been heresay, derived mainly or altogether from his mutineers. Whether Randolph advised with him about Clark's request for a court of inquiry to investigate the mutiny and put the blame where it belonged — on Logan's men — is not known, but only that Governor Randolph paid no attention to the request, and that no trial of the Lincoln mutineers was ever ordered. Naturally they did not themselves ask one, nor did Colonel Logan. On the other hand, Colonel Levi Todd, who commanded the Fayette troops and stood loyally by Clark, did strongly demand such an investigation and wrote the Governor the letter quoted in the footnote below.[1] Justice to all concerned plainly demanded that his earnest request for an impar-

---

in October, before Logan's departure for Richmond, the date of which is shown in Judge Wallace's letter (*Draper MSS.* 9 J 244) and carried to Richmond by Logan.

[1] Todd wrote: 'Since the return of the armies from the northwest side of the Ohio, I presume many and perhaps varied accounts of the Success of one, and failure of the other have been transmitted to your Excellency.

'Since the return of the Army under General Clark, I have been convinced (and expect the Executive will deem it necessary) that an enquiry ought to be made into the causes of the bad Success of that Army, and hope this may be done by some Judicious and discerning Men of the District, not officers of that Army, by order of the Executive. I wish that facts might be fairly stated. Then, and not till then, Truth will fairly transpire, and reflections fall on those who, from their conduct, merit it. A Circumstantial investigation of the mutiny and punishment of the guilty should be granted; but, like General Clark's, it was ignored.

During the remainder of 1786, and for a considerable time afterwards, Governor Randolph never questioned General Clark's authority to carry on the war in the Wabash country, or to enlist men to garrison Vincennes; nor did he find any fault with his manner of conducting the war. Soon, however, there was a surprising change in the Governor's attitude, — brought about by two concurring causes. One was the effort of Spain's minister to get our surrender of the lower Mississippi, by setting the northern and southern states at loggerheads about it; the other a deep-laid plot of Wilkinson to destroy Clark.

tial detail cannot be given without pointing out such conduct in officers as (if properly proved) ought to prevent the like kind forever in future from them.

'For these reasons, and my being an Officer at the time, I omit saying anything more, but earnestly request that some mode of this nature may be adopted by the Executive to point out men who officiate without merit.

I have the honor to be your Excellency's
        Obdt H'ble Servt etc.'

(Virginia State Library, *Executive Communications to General Assembly*, Oct. 16, 1786 — Jan, 11, 1787; Virginia *Calendar State Papers*, IV, 182.)

CHAPTER XXIX

WILKINSON'S PLOT

FOR two years after the treaty of peace at Paris ending the Revolution, Spain, chagrined over its failure to gain our western country, or even an admission of her exclusive right to the lower Mississippi, maintained an attitude of aloofness toward the United States, and sent no minister to this country. Then her policy suddenly changed. In September, 1785, her King in person addressed a letter to his 'Great and well-beloved friends,' the Continental Congress, saying that: 'Desiring to give you proofs of the good will and consideration with which we regard you, and to provide that our respective subjects should enjoy from their mutual intercourse and commerce all the benefits which can be procured thereby, I have named the Commissary of my royal armies, Don Diego de Gardoqui, to go and reside near you in quality of my Encargado de Negocios.'[1]

A new chapter of Spanish-American diplomacy was opened with this appointment, but it was to concern the same old conflict over the navigation of the lower Mississippi. On arriving in New York, where Congress then met, Gardoqui opened negotiations with Mr. Jay, now secretary of foreign affairs. Ostensibly the Spaniard's object was to effect a commercial treaty between the two countries, and to secure it he proposed giving the Americans the privilege of trading with Spain's colonies. Nothing could have been more welcome to the financially crippled merchants, ship-owners, and ship-builders in the northern states, and many of them no doubt enjoyed dreams of fortune from this trade, and had visions of American clipper fleets returning heavy-laden with valuable cargoes from the Spanish Main. At once a strong demand for the treaty came to Congress from states north of Maryland and Delaware. They sorely needed the profits it promised them, for trade was then paralyzed by international and interstate restrictions and excessive duties. In the warehouses of Philadelphia, New York, and New England towns, bales and barrels of export merchandise lay covered with dust and cobwebs because excluded from

[1] Wharton's *Diplomatic Correspondence of American Revolution*, VI, 820.

foreign ports, while idle ships rotted in the harbors and unfinished ones lay untouched on the stocks. Nor were northern commercial and industrial ills the only ones calling for the stimulation of trade promised by the Spanish treaty. The spirit of turbulence and disunion was everywhere; Shays' Rebellion threatened the overthrow of all government in Massachusetts; Congress was utterly discredited and powerless; the Confederation seemed doomed; and all the while, Spain on one hand and Great Britain on the other looked on like birds of prey. When, therefore, the harassed people of these northern states learned that His Catholic Majesty of Spain had generously proposed 'mutual intercourse and commerce,' and would offer them 'all the benefits which can be produced thereby,' we may imagine how high were their hopes.

When Gardoqui came to discuss particulars of the proposed treaty, however, he let Jay understand that Spain would, of course, expect some fair return for this valuable trade privilege; and that return proved to be nothing less than our recognition of her exclusive right to the lower Mississippi.[1] At this Jay balked; for, although himself most anxious for the trade privilege, he had always asserted our clear right to the free use of the river, and had struggled hard to maintain it. Furthermore, the Articles of Confederation expressly forbade Congress 'to enter into any treaties,...unless nine states assent to the same.' The year before Gardoqui came to America Congress, by a vote of nine states, had lawfully authorized Jay to make a treaty with Spain, but only on condition that it should 'particularly stipulate the right of the United States to...the free navigation of the Mississippi to the ocean.' As that stipulation was precisely what Gardoqui wished to avoid, and as Jay had no power to waive it, further negotiation seemed useless; but both of them were anxious to come to terms, and parley after parley followed.

Meanwhile the northern demand for the treaty grew stronger; and at length Congress called on Jay to report the state of the negotiations. He said Gardoqui would make no treaty without a clause whereby we would agree to forbear the use of the Mississippi for twenty-five or thirty years, and Jay reluctantly recommended that this agreement be made. At once Congress was split into two hot factions — northern and

[1] *Secret Journals of Congress*, IV, 144 *et seq.*; also *Madison Papers*, V, 97 (Lippincott).

southern. The seven northern states demanded the treaty with this forbearance clause — the six southern ones protested that their navigation right should not be thus bartered away. Four of them had fertile lands extending to the Mississippi, and bitterly opposed their being made valueless, and their western citizens deprived of their only trade outlet to world markets, merely to enable the northern states to reap profits from Spanish trade.

Although the seven northern states had a majority of one in Congress, they could not muster the votes of nine states in support of the treaty Jay recommended; and thereupon they resorted to political *finesse* to carry their point. They voted for a resolution to rescind *so much only* of Jay's existing treaty-making authority as required him to '*particularly stipulate the right of the United States to the... free navigation of the Mississippi to the ocean.*' They then conveniently assumed and asserted that this left him free to make the treaty with a clause forbearing the use of the river for twenty-five or thirty years! Intensely indignant, the southern members charged that this was a mere quibble and trick to evade the Confederation Article requiring the assent of nine states. Even mild Madison 'wrote in heat to Jefferson and wondered if New England would sacrifice her fisheries for the tobacco trade of Virginia.'[1] Others asked if Pennsylvania would give up her right to navigate the Delaware to benefit the commerce of the South, or New England? Patrick Henry said he 'would rather part with the Confederation than relinquish the Mississippi,'[2] and Kentuckians advocated driving the Spaniards from Louisiana. On the other hand, many in New England advocated secession from the Confederation if the treaty were defeated. Mr. Gorham of Massachusetts declared 'the shutting of the Mississippi would be advantageous to the Atlantic states,' and that he wished to see it shut; and, although almost incredible now, his belief was not then uncommon in the northeast.[3]

When news of the proposed treaty reached the western people, there was a great burst of indignation which Wilkinson actively stimulated. Representatives of 'all the counties... on the western waters' joined in a remonstrance to the Virginia

[1] Winsor's *Western Movement*, 643–47.
[2] John Marshall to A. Lee, *Life of Arthur Lee*, ii, 301.
[3] Brown's *Political Beginnings in Kentucky*, 136, note, citing *Madison Papers*, ii, 609.

Assembly, vigorously denouncing the surrender of their navigation right as 'unconstitutional and dangerous...to their very existence.'

'Their prosperity [they said] must principally depend on the navigation of this river;...it will be impossible for their products to find a market through any other channel; [and] this project, therefore, presents to them the melancholy prospect of ruin to themselves and families. ...Born and educated under a common government, and attached to it by the strongest ties of interest and affection, (having equally participated in the hardships and dangers of the Revolution, and being equally entitled to its benefits,) they cannot but view with horror the idea of their being sacrificed and their interests sold by those whom they have considered their brethren, friends, and fellow citizens. Your memorialists are unacquainted with the merits of the commercial part of this project, but no consideration of advantages, however great they might be, could justify the United States for the violation of the federal compact, which this unquestionably would be. The citizens of these counties have the same right to the navigation of this river which the eastern citizens have to that of the James, or Potomac. ...With the same propriety, might Congress barter away their right to the trial by jury, or aliene a county, or a state, for advantages in trade, as occlude the Mississippi. ...Never have they before heard of a project being proposed — much less a treaty formed — which shut the door of commerce to one part of the community, and deprived it of its natural rights, for the benefit of the other.'[1]

While this controversy over navigation and the commercial treaty was going on, Wilkinson was evolving a scheme which was destined to settle it and also to shelve General Clark as military leader in the west. Early in 1786 a merchant in the Pittsburg region got from the Spanish governor the extraordinary and very lucrative privilege of trading with New Orleans. Lieutenant Beatty, then stationed at Fort Harmar on the upper Ohio, wrote in his diary (June 4): 'A few days ago one Col. Perré, ... from Monongehelea river, passed here with a Kentucky boat, 60 foot Keel & deeply laden, going to Natchez and New Orleans, he having permission from the Spanish Command'ts in those places. This must be a very profitable trade, as no person can carry it on but those having permission from the Spaniards.'[2] The news of Perré's trade privilege spread rapidly through Kentucky, and excited great longing for like

---

[1] Virginia State Library, 'Petitions Oct. '86–Jan. '87.'   [2] Magazine American History, I, 177.

advantage on the part of many others; and Wilkinson was one of them.

During the great ferment in the western country that year over the threatened closing of the Mississippi, he saw an opportunity for a profitable scheme of treason. He knew the Spanish dread of an invasion of Louisiana, and on that dread he resolved to play. He designed nothing less than to ignore the order of the Spanish governor, Miro, prohibiting American use of the river; to go boldly to New Orleans with a boatload of Kentucky products; to appear before Miro, and to alarm him with a wild fiction of an impending attack on New Orleans by General Clark with a great American army! Then he would offer to use his great influence in Kentucky to prevent the invasion; and, to show his good faith, would offer his allegiance to the Spanish King. Finally, as the King's emissary, he would exert himself to detach Kentucky from the United States, and make it a friendly buffer-state to shield Spanish Louisiana! In return for these services he would only ask an exclusive privilege to trade with New Orleans in Kentucky products until the Kentucky people should secede from the Union and become Spain's allies.

Wilkinson calculated that so long as he *alone* could enjoy the trade privilege, it would yield him enormous profits, for it would enable him to buy the unmarketable surplus products of his fellow Kentuckians at his own price, and sell them for many times more at the Spanish port. That, however, he would assure Miro, was merely incidental — his great object being to benefit his suffering friends in Kentucky, whose bountiful crops were rotting on their hands for lack of a market, and who were both able and determined to get one by seizing New Orleans. Spain's own interest, he would suggest, required that his trade privilege should be exclusive, since the Kentuckians would all envy his good fortune and, in order to share it, hasten to break away from the Union and ally themselves with Spain.

In truth, he never intended they should get the trade privilege at all, for that would have ended his profitable monopoly; nor did he aim to have them set up a separate state, for they would not do that unless all would share the trade privilege. His plan was rather to dangle before Miro and his royal master the promise of Kentucky's secession from the United States and dependence on Spain, while he dangled before the Kentuckians the promise of an open market for their products at New Orleans; but all the while he would delay performance of both promises so long as his purse fattened on the profits he could make on his purchases of the products of his fellow Kentuckians.

The scheme was certainly a most daring one, but the traitor planned it with consummate skill, laid its foundations with elaborate care, was quick to see and utilize every agency and event which might contribute to its success, and — amazing to record — carried it out precisely as planned! To Miro and the Spanish ministry at Madrid it was sure to prove welcome, if they thought it workable. With all western Americans, except the Kentuckians, excluded from the lower Mississippi, the lands of Congress north of the Ohio would be unsalable, and emigration from the east would avoid them and go to Kentucky. The insolvent Confederation, thus rendered unable to sell the lands upon which it relied for financial restoration, would almost inevitably fall to pieces, and there would remain thirteen small, jealous, quarreling, powerless sovereignties — some probably allying themselves with Britain, some with France, others with Spain; and Wilkinson knew the Spanish ministry would like nothing better.

In pursuance of his plan, in May, 1787, he sent a boatload of Kentucky commodities to New Orleans, and boldly followed himself. Before leaving, however, in order to avoid arrest and the confiscation of his boat and cargo, he instructed an agent there (who soon became his partner) to warn Governor Miro that to arrest so eminent an American would likely cause war and Spain's loss of Louisiana. The agent even suggested that it was probably Wilkinson's real purpose to provoke his own arrest in order to bring on a war, and that it would therefore be safer for the Governor to receive the distinguished American courteously. With Miro thus alarmed in advance, Wilkinson could pretty confidently expect an attentive hearing; and this he received. He explained to Miro the grievances and restlessness of the Kentucky people under the neglect of Virginia and Congress, their extreme need for the free navigation of the Mississippi, and their intention and ability to win it by driving the Spaniards from Louisiana. He even audaciously represented that a great American army was being mobilized for the purpose by General Clark at Vincennes, but suggested that his own influence in Kentucky was so great that, with Miro's coöperation, he could prevent this invasion. Pretending to be impelled by a desire for the welfare of the Kentuckians, he let the Governor know that he would be willing to make any personal sacrifice, even of his honor. Miro, greatly alarmed and completely fooled, soon fell in with the traitor's scheme. Thereupon Wilkinson took a secret oath of allegiance to the Spanish King, and undertook, as His Majesty's emissary, to detach Kentucky from the United States and make it Spain's ally.

Miro was of course too wily to trust Wilkinson's verbal promise, or to have no witness to it, so he called in the Spanish Intendant, Navarro. Together they heard what the American had to say, had him state his scheme in a signed 'Memorial,' and on September 25th sent it, with elaborate comments of their own, to Valdes, the Spanish Secretary of State at Madrid and President of the Council of the Indies.[1] They said of Wilkinson that

'after ten or twelve days, which he asked to be given in order to rest, and having announced that he had projects of great importance to propose, he related to us all that is contained in the annexed Memorial, on which he offered to work as he really did, delivering it to us on the 3rd of this month. He is a young man of about 33 years, although by his aspect he represents more, of exceedingly agreeable appearance, married, has three small children; in his manners and address he shows that he has received a very good education, which his uncommon talents have taken advantage of, as is evidenced in his memorial; trustworthy reports we have obtained are convincing circumstances that assure us he exerts the greatest influence in the said district of Kentucky, which would enable him to persuade the inhabitants of the country to follow his leadership in a critical moment.

'The Memorial explains itself so well that it would be presumptious on our part and wearisome to your Excellency were we to undertake to comment on it in its entirety, and we will therfore limit ourselves only to corroborating it and reporting on the truth of its principal points.

'All he relates regarding the situation of the Western Settlements up to the Apalachian Mountains is absolutely certain, as also that they are powerful on account of their numerous population, from which also results the certainty that Louisiana cannot resist their attacks, in the supposition of course that it will not be judged advisable to pledge H.M. to maintain an army here.'[2]

[1] Gayerre's *Spanish Domination*, 167, 186.

[2] *Pontalba Papers*, 4, 5. Copies in possession of the writer and Mr. R. C. Ballard Thruston.

The 'ten or twelve days' Wilkinson asked 'in order to rest' before relating his 'projects of great importance,' were pretty surely not devoted to rest; but were very industriously used in finding out just how much Miro and the other Spanish officials knew, or did not know, about affairs in the United States, particularly in Kentucky and the west; and what Wilkinson wanted to know he usually managed to learn. His Memorial was a very able paper — unique in its ingenuity, amusing in its audacious fabrications, and pregnant with great results to both his deserted and adopted countries. In it he represented one hundred and fifty thousand western Americans 'capable of bearing arms,' ready to deluge Louisiana, and Great Britain as ready and plotting to aid them. He then proceeded to advise the best course for Spain to pursue to secure Louisiana against invasion, by detaching Kentucky from the Confederation and wrecking the United States.

Such in brief outline was this long hidden record of Wilkinson's infamy. The Memorial has only recently been published, although for more than a hundred years it was eagerly sought, and supposed to be only in the secret archives of Spain.[1]

To throw light upon Wilkinson's motives and methods in seeking Clark's overthrow, it has been necessary to show his treasonable dealings with Miro in 1787; but this has carried us nearly a year beyond the time of his plot against Clark, to which attention is now invited. His capital object, it should be understood, was always the profitable trade privilege — his plot against Clark merely contributory to it. He knew that in order to win Miro to his scheme he would have to carry to New

[1] Gayerre, author of the excellent *History of Louisiana* (*Spanish Domination*) could find no better information of its contents than was given thirty years before by Butler in his little history of Kentucky. It probably remained in the Spanish archives until Napoleon had Pontalba report on the resources, history, and affairs of Louisiana, about the time Spain ceded the territory to France, and this doubtless accounts for it being found amongst the *Pontalba Papers* in France. Duplicate copies of it were secured by Mr. R. C. Ballard Thruston, president of the Filson Club of Louisville, who gave one to the writer. It has been recently published in full with the present author's introduction to *Littell's Political Transactions* (*Filson Club Publications*,

no. 31, John P. Morton Co., Louisville, 1926).

In the *Louisiana Historical Society Publications*, vol. IX, a writer gives some extracts from the Memorial and Wilkinson's oath of allegiance to Spain, which last he thinks 'a courageous, frank, and sincere expression of [Wilkinson's] convictions, based on circumstances beyond his control!'

Great as were the results of this famous Memorial, they were not comparable to those caused by Wilkinson's little-known plot to misrepresent General Clark and secure his own appointment as Indian commissioner; for the forgeries he concocted to support that killed Jay's treaty with Gardoqui and thus saved the tottering Union.

Orleans convincing proofs (1) that a great American army was gathering to invade Louisiana, (2) that his political and military standing were such that he could prevent the invasion and bring about Kentucky's secession from the Union and alliance with Spain. With a constructive ingenuity rivaling any to be found in published fiction, he proceeded to fabricate the proofs he needed to convince Miro. He contrived to make the Kentucky separatist conventions furnish him with seemingly indisputable record evidence of his political supremacy there; and, when genuine convention records did not fully meet his wants, he simply forged others.

But proof of his political influence was not enough for Wilkinson. He needed to impress Miro with the belief that he was also the American military leader in the west; for, although his political leadership might indicate ability to detach Kentucky from the Union, only proof of his military leadership was likely to convince Miro that he could stop the American army of invasion, or prevent Congress from suppressing Kentucky's secession by force. Unquestionably, however, the military man of first prominence in the west was General Clark, whose exploits were well known to Miro and other Spanish officials at New Orleans. To satisfy Miro that Clark's military influence was ended, and his own ascendant, became therefore Wilkinson's first object. Both for its effect on Miro and for his own advancement, he also aimed to prevent Clark's being reappointed Commissioner of Indian Affairs for Congress; for he keenly coveted that position for himself. In the Indian Department alone was an army likely to be needed, and the appointment would make him the chief active military officer of the United States.

In the mutiny on the Wabash, the ensuing events at Vincennes, and the stories of the mutineers, Wilkinson saw his opportunity to misrepresent and shelve Clark. Indeed, he probably had done more than any one else, or all others combined, to make the expedition fail. He had been trying to rouse the people to defy the Virginia government's prohibition and carry an expedition against the Wabash Indians; yet when the expedition was organized he did not join it! This seems strange, for he was only thirty years of age, vigorous, tirelessly active, and intensely ambitious for military distinction. His failure to take part in the expedition, however, is explained by the ad-

vantage he immediately afterward took of its collapse to undermine Clark. In the army, his opportunities for intrigue would
have been limited to a few soldiers; he would have been subject to orders from superiors, and called on to enforce military
orders instead of inciting resistance to them; but, out of the
army, he could go where and when he would, and see all the
persons he could use to further his aims — whether soldiers,
or civilians; he could secretly encourage resistance to drafts
and impressments, and foment opposition to the commander
who stood in his way.

At the very time the mutineers were representing Clark as
being incapacitated by drink, he was displaying brilliant
ability in his negotiations with the confederated Indians; but
Wilkinson knew the old falsehood about his drinking, dating
from the Blue Licks disaster, was still more or less current in
eastern Virginia; and nothing could suit his purpose better
than to revive it and give it new credit with Governor Randolph and Congress.

Again, the impressment of Bazadone's goods at Vincennes
and enlistment of men to garrison the place, gave Wilkinson
an opportunity, which he promptly seized, to fabricate a report to Governor Randolph representing the impressment as
plain robbery, and the enlistment of the garrison as only
Clark's first step toward raising a great army to undertake the
conquest of Louisiana!

No one, knowing how few were the men and supplies of the
little garrison,[1] would have given a moment's heed to so preposterous a report; but Wilkinson knew that few persons elsewhere knew anything of the real situation at Vincennes; and
that almost any wild story about a western army invading
Louisiana would find ready belief at Richmond and in Congress, then sitting in New York. He was the one alert man in
the west who kept in close touch with political events and men
in the east, where he had an extensive acquaintance and many
correspondents — several of them members of Congress. He
knew of the bitter conflict in that body over navigation and
the commercial treaty. He knew how seriously disordered
were economic and governmental conditions in the east, and
that the commercial and shipbuilding people in the north-

---

[1] The enlisted men never exceeded 140, and after a few weeks the garrison had disbanded for want of supplies.

Atlantic states would bitterly resent any spoliation of Spaniards, or invasion of Spanish territory, by the westerners as an
attempt to kill the treaty.

It was in December, 1786, during the excitement, east and
west, over the Jay–Gardoqui treaty, that Wilkinson sent to
Governor Randolph and Congress various anonymous and
forged papers containing his false charges against General
Clark. These papers were constructed with wonderful cunning to show (1) that Clark was an inebriate, utterly unfit to
handle the Indians at the treaty meeting he had arranged to
hold with them the next spring; (2) that the Spaniard's goods
at Vincennes, instead of being impressed by order of the court-
martial for the support of the troops, were simply 'plundered'
by Clark's officers and appropriated by them; and (3) that
Clark was organizing a great army to drive the Spaniards from
Louisiana. To give credit to these falsehoods, Wilkinson
tricked a number of his friends amongst the convention delegates at Danville into signing two cunningly contrived letters
to Governor Randolph, which *seemed* to vouch for the truth
of his charges. This he did by legerdemain — showing or
reading to his friends one set of 'testimonials' to accompany
and explain the letters, and then skillfully substituting
another set for the governor! It is morally certain that none
of the men who signed the letters, except Wilkinson himself, ever saw the substituted 'testimonials.' Neither of the
letters charged Clark with any lawless act, or design; but one
of them appeared to do so by referring to 'the testimonials
which accompany this'; and in the substituted testimonials
Wilkinson set forth all his falsehoods about General Clark.
In the other letter Wilkinson was recommended by his deluded friends for appointment as commissioner of Indian
Affairs for Congress and as a person 'well qualified for the
purpose and against whom no exception can be taken!'

The crooked course, by which Wilkinson tricked his fellow
delegates into seeming to assert, and Governor Randolph into
believing, his falsehoods about General Clark — makes a plot
quite as ingenious as any novelist ever devised; and it displays
constructive ability of the very highest order. It is a plot,
however, which is perhaps too complex to be followed with
interest except by critical readers, and, for that reason only, its
details will be omitted here; but are set forth in the appendix.[1]

[1] *Post*, p. 379.

Governor Randolph received from Wilkinson the two letters and the accompanying 'testimonials' on February 5, 1787. In view of General Clark's standing and public services, and his long unanswered request for an investigation of the mutiny, one would naturally suppose the governor would at once have notified him of the charges against him, and have given him an opportunity to disprove them; and this he could certainly have done. A note of ten lines from the governor would have sufficed. Plain justice required the notice, and no man knew this better than Randolph. He was a trained lawyer, and knew that it would violate the first and highest rule of justice to condemn, unheard, even the meanest criminal. Only five weeks before, he and his executive council had refused to consider a written and signed charge of malfeasance in office made by reputable men, against a minor state official, and had declared that a charge 'more formal in its nature must be exhibited on oath.'[1] Over two months had passed since he had received General Clark's letter requesting a court of inquiry,[2] and he had done nothing about it. Furthermore, even after he received the letters from Wilkinson, instead of immediately sending an express to Clark for an explanation, he allowed three weeks to pass without doing anything. Then, on February 28 he laid the 'letters and enclosures' before his executive council, whereupon the council minutes say:[3]

'The Board lament that those dispatches, pregnant as they are with subjects deeply interesting to our national character and quiet, and intended for the last assembly [they were *not* so intended, but were addressed to and intended for the governor himself] should, for the first time, on the 5th Day of this Instant, have been handed to the Governor, in Williamsburg, on his late journey to Norfolk on public business.

'From the respectability of the names subscribed to those letters they confide in the following facts: (1) that the prosecution of the treaty, proposed to be held with the Indians under the authority of Congress, will tend to the safety of our western settlements: (2) that the success of the treaty would be forwarded by the appointment of some commissioners, at least, who are resident in the parts of the country likely to be exposed to the incursions of the savages; (3) that General Clark has been, and perhaps is now, employed

---

[1] Virginia State Library, *Council Journal*, Jan. 4, 1787, 239 and 241.
[2] Virginia State Library, *Box Executive Papers*, 17, 8607.

[3] Virginia State Library, *Executive Journal*, 287–90.

in levying recruits
in nominating officers } for the support of the post at Vincennes:
and impressing provisions

[in fact, all the recruits had abandoned the post for lack of food] and (4) that General Clark hath made a seizure of Spanish property without any authority for such act. The Board therefore advises:

'1. That copies of the letters aforesaid and their enclosures be forthwith transmitted to our delegates in Congress, with an earnest request to communicate them, in whole, or part, according to their discretion, immediately to that body; to urge the speediest arrangements for a treaty to be holden with the Indians in April next, under the sanction of the federal government; and to propose, as commissioners, General James Wilkinson, Colo. Richard Clough Anderson, and Colo. Isaac Shelby.

'2. That it be notified to General Clark that this board disavow the existence of a power derived from them to the said Clark to raise recruits, appoint officers, or impress provisions.[1]

'3. That, as the seizure of Spanish property was never authenticated to this Board before the receipt of the said letters, so, had it been known at a period sufficiently early for prevention, it should have been prevented. [This might have saved the commercial treaty, but would have left Vincennes and the struggling troops to the mercy of fifteen hundred savage warriors!] But that this offense against the law of nations having been committed, it becomes the Executive to Declare their displeasure at the act, and to cause the national honor to be vindicated by the institution of legal proceedings against all persons appearing to be culpable; that the Attorney-General be consulted on the documents aforesaid and request to take himself, or to call upon the Attorney-General of Kentucky, as the case may require, to take such steps as may subject to punishment all persons guilty in the premises; that the said seizure of Spanish property be disclaimed by Government in a special proclamation. That a copy of this order be also sent to our Delegates in Congress in order that they may, if it shall be deemed expedient, acquaint the minister of His Catholic Majesty with these sentiments of the Executive; and that another copy be forwarded to Thomas Marshall, Esquire, and the other Gentlemen who concurred in the letters aforesaid.'[2]

---

[1] This statement seems most surprising in view of the following facts: (1) Governor Henry and his executive council permitted and encouraged the expedition to carry the war *into the country of the Indians on the Wabash;* (2) he *notified Congress* that it would probably be carried out, was necessary in self defense, and was warranted by the Sixth Article of Confederation; (3) the Virginia Assembly act, passed at Governor Randolph's suggestion, (a) approved the expedition, (b) declared 'the inhabitants of Kentucky were *compelled,* for their own preservation,' to carry it on; (c) declared it necessary; (d) approved the *compulsory impressment of supplies for it;* (e) granted *indemnity to those making necessary impressments;* (f) *ordered payment of the troops* engaged in the expedition; and (g) *declared their 'services should be rewarded;*' and finally (4) Governor Randolph, with the advice of his council, wrote the president of Congress that the expedition had been recognized by Virginia and had 'advanced the federal interest,' and demanded that Congress reimburse Virginia for its outlays in carrying it on!

[2] *Id.,* and *Secret Journal of Congress,* IV, 305.

The governor and council seemed far more anxious to appease 'His Catholic Majesty' than to learn from General Clark if he had any defense to offer to the charges Wilkinson had trumped up against him. Read between the lines, these council minutes themselves show that the governor and his council were not unaware of the injustice they were doing the General, however necessary for the public welfare they may have thought their action. Had Wilkinson himself prepared their resolutions, he could not have made them more completely meet his aims. Not only was Clark condemned, but Congress was urged to make the speediest arrangements for a treaty with the Indians, such as Wilkinson was ambitious to direct, and also to appoint him Commissioner of Indian Affairs! So far as the Virginia executive was concerned, his plot was completely successful.

On the same day, Governor Randolph issued the following proclamation,[1] to be publicly posted in every county in the state and spread broadcast by newspapers:

By His Excellency Edmund Randolph, Esq.
Governor of the Commonwealth,

A PROCLAMATION!

Whereas it has been represented to the Executive that *George Rogers Clark Esq.* after having, under color of an authority wrongfully supposed to be derived from them, recruited a number of men for the support of St. Vincents, had moreover seized the property, of certain subjects of His Catholic Majesty to a considerable amount. In order, therefore, that the honour of this commonwealth may not sustain an injury, from a belief that the act above mentioned has in any way received the public sanction, I do hereby declare, with the advice of the Council of State, that the said violence was unknown to the Executive until a few days past,[2] and is now disavowed; and that the Attorney-General has been instructed to take every step allowed by law, for bringing to punishment all persons who may be culpable in the premises. Given under my hand and the Seal of the Commonwealth, this twenty-eighth day of February in the year of our Lord One Thousand and Seven Hundred and Eighty-Seven.

EDMUND RANDOLPH

Four days after issuing this proclamation, the governor sent a printed copy of it to General Clark with the following short letter:

[1] *Draper MSS.* 53 J 63.
[2] Really twenty-three days — not 'a few.'

RICHMOND, *March 4th,* 1787

Sir: By advice of Council I enclose you an act of our Board, in which you will perceive certain Complaints exhibited against you. The Council, conceived themselves bound to issue the enclosed proclamation also.

I am Sir Your Mo. Ob. Serv.

EDMUND RANDOLPH[1]

The same day the Governor wrote Harry Innes, the Attorney-General of Kentucky, as follows:

Sir: I beg the favor of you to cause the inclosed advice concerning General Clark's violence, to be executed in the most speedy and effectual manner allowed by law. Perhaps the individual sufferer may find satisfaction in damages, notwithstanding a public prosecution.[2]

Never, perhaps, has wrong more gross been done to any man than was done by this condemnation of General Clark. Governor Randolph himself soon afterward denounced the injustice of convicting, without hearing, even a notorious murderer and fugitive from justice. Speaking of the right of every accused person to a fair trial, he said:

'There is one example of... violation in Virginia, of a most striking and shocking nature — an example so horrid, that, if I conceived my country could passively permit a repetition of it, dear as it is to me, I would seek means of expatriating myself from it. A man, who was then a citizen, was deprived of his life thus: from a mere reliance on general reports, a gentleman in the House of Delegates [Jefferson] informed the House that a certain man (Josiah Philips) had committed several crimes, and was running at large, perpetrating other crimes. He therefore moved for leave to attaint him; he obtained that leave instantly, ... without any proof better than vague reports. Without being confronted with his accusers and witnesses, without the privilege of calling for evidence in his behalf, he was sentenced to death, and was afterwards actually executed. Was this arbitrary deprivation of life, the dearest gift of God to man, consistent with the genius of a republican government?'[3]

---

[1] Virginia State Library, *Governor's Letter-Book,* 456.

[2] *Id.,* 56. The Attorney-General of Kentucky refused to execute the Governor's order on technical grounds. It was unfortunate for Clark, however, that he was not prosecuted; for the fabricated papers sent Governor Randolph might have been produced at the trial, and the delegates whom Wilkinson had tricked into signing the two letters would have discovered and exposed his villainy.

[3] Eliot's *Debates on the Federal Constitution* (Virginia), III, 66–67. Randolph was entirely wrong about the facts. Phillips was given notice of the charge and opportunity for defense, and furthermore, he was not prosecuted under that statute at all, but was tried in the usual way by jury under common law rules. (Ford's *Works of Jefferson,* II, 330.)

A common criminal may, as here said, esteem life the dearest gift of God; but the dearest possession of an honorable man is not life, but his good name; and it was of that which Randolph and his council were depriving Clark. Without notice of any charges against him, without being confronted with his accusers, without opportunity to defend himself he was condemned, publicly proclaimed, and ordered prosecuted as a malefactor — a disgrace far worse than death.

Had this action been due to malice towards General Clark, it would have been infamous; but it was attributable to no such base motive. Governor Randolph was an honorable, able and usually just man; in his Council were men of high repute; but nearly all men sometimes make grave mistakes and do great wrongs. In justice to him it should be said he was then one of the busiest and most harassed of men. The conduct of the disordered Virginia government was enough to overtax him. He was also deeply concerned at this time in bringing about a stronger union of the states, and was one of the most ardent champions of the new federal constitution. No doubt he thought that, unless promptly disavowed, General Clark's proceedings and designs, as Wilkinson represented them, would incense Spain, would kill the commercial treaty, would be bitterly resented in the north, might cause New England's secession from the Confederation, and would at least destroy all hope for a real federal union. He may even have thought the union so vitally necessary for the public welfare as to warrant the sacrifice of Clark to secure it. Then, too, he and most of his Council had either been members of Harrison's administration, or in close touch with it, at the time of the Blue Licks disaster, and like Harrison, were perhaps prejudiced against Clark by the false reports about him then so actively circulated at Richmond. Yet, though all these circumstances may palliate, they certainly cannot excuse the condemnation, unheard, of a man of General Clark's record of honorable service.

When Attorney-General Innes received Governor Randolph's letter of March 4, enclosing his proclamation and Council resolutions condemning General Clark and nominating Wilkinson for Indian Commissioner, we may be sure the traitor got them, or copies of them, to take to Miro when he left for New Orleans in May; for of all the reputable men whom Wilkinson deluded and used for his own ends, Innes was oftenest his easy dupe. To the Spaniard, these documents must have seemed convincing evidence of Wilkinson's eminent reputation and influence.

CHAPTER XXX

WILKINSON'S VICTIM

IT was not until April, 1787, that General Clark learned of his condemnation by the Governor and Council. Some six months had passed since he had written Governor Randolph requesting an investigation of the conduct of his expedition, and he had received no reply. He could only conclude that no reports to his prejudice had reached the capitol, or else that they had been thought unworthy of attention. It could never have entered his mind that, after authorizing his campaign on the Wabash, the Virginia executive could question his authority to post his troops at Vincennes, or any other place which he thought best suited for war purposes; or to enlist troops and garrison the place until peace came; or to make necessary impressments of goods to support them. But in April — sudden and overwhelming — he received the governor's letter enclosing the proclamation. This was his reward for years of sacrifice for his mother state! Naturally he held Randolph responsible for the cruel wrong. Boiling with indignation, he wrote this stinging reply:

Sir: I respect the *State* of Virginia. The information you have received hath already been stained with the blood of your country! Facts will prove themselves.

I am, Sir, yours,

G. R. CLARK[1]

His Excellency
Governor Edmund Randolph, pr Mr. Filson.

Thus closed, at thirty-five years of age, General Clark's military career as an officer of Virginia. For her he had given up everything and suffered much. During seven years, filled with difficulties, opposition and traduction, he had borne himself with remarkable self-control and dignity. Neither disappointments, nor the slander of enemies, nor the loss of his estate, nor even the heavy burden of the state's debts, had been able to crush him; for he still had the supreme consolation of duty well done, and honorable eminence well deserved;

[1] *Draper MSS.* 11 J 174. Author's italics.

but to be thus publicly disgraced was more than he could bear. However cruelly unjust his condemnation, it was official, public, inescapable. He knew he was now a marked man for his enemies to point and sneer at, and for his friends to pity. The greatest human suffering is the mental agony of an honorable man under disgrace; and, after a time of leaden days and sleepless nights, without some release, he would probably have been driven to insanity, — possibly suicide. Yet, although his was 'the greatest torture souls feel in hell — that they must live, and cannot die,' he probably never seriously considered suicide; for that was regarded as an unpardonable sin by the religious, and he was sincerely religious. Irresistibly driven to seek relief, he found it in the oblivion of drink.

His first fall was far the worst, and it was terrible. It lasted for weeks; and then, sobered and doubtless influenced by the distress of his parents and others dear to him, he began a long and brave fight against the disease that now gained hold of him. From this time forth, periodically (not constantly, as his enemies represented and some writers still assume, but after varying and oftenest very long intervals), he gave way to drink; but for over twenty years he led a life which, though sad, was generally temperate and becoming, until he was paralyzed and suffered a complete physical and mental breakdown. He had now given his enemies, however, undeniable evidence to color the false charge they had been making against him ever since the Blue Licks defeat in 1782; and they certainly made the most of it. Knowing he was undeniably drinking hard in 1787, and at times afterward, many persons readily believed the story of the mutineers about his drinking during the Wabash Expedition in 1786, and also the older falsehood of the same nature four years earlier. Unfortunately both slanders have been carelessly accepted and repeated in history.

On receiving Wilkinson's fabricated letters and 'testimonials,' Governor Randolph promptly sent Congress copies of them, of the resolutions of his Executive Council, and of his proclamation. Their effect in Congress was tremendous. The friends of the commercial treaty and the friends of a new federal government were thrown into panic, for it was feared Spain's resentment would kill both and cause war with that power. All alike were led to believe that General Clark was

about to descend the Mississippi with a great army to drive
the Spaniards from Louisiana! In the general consternation no
one seemed to doubt the truth of Wilkinson's audacious
fictions.[1]

The action of Congress following Randolph's communication was very significant. If the garrison troops at Vincennes had been unlawfully recruited and, as Congress erroneously assumed, were still there, then ousting them was
properly a matter for the war department. If the impressment of the Spaniard's goods was mere plundering, as Wilkinson represented, then it was a crime for legal prosecution.
It was neither the military or the criminal aspect of the
alleged lawless proceedings at Vincennes, however, which
seemed to interest the majority in Congress, but the dread
lest they displease His Catholic Majesty of Spain and thus
kill the commercial treaty and possibly provoke war. Accordingly, Wilkinson's papers and the council resolutions were
referred to the Secretary of Foreign Affairs, Mr. Jay. He, too,
was greatly alarmed by them, and on April 12 made a report to
Congress, saying:

'He presumes the design of Congress, in referring these papers to
him, was that he should report only on such matters stated in them
as respected foreign affairs. It appears from the act of the Council
of Virginia, on 28th February last, "that General Clark hath made a
seizure of Spanish property without any authority for that act,"
and that the executive of that commonwealth hath, with great propriety, directed such steps to be taken "as may subject to punishment all persons guilty in the premises."...From the temper visible
in some of the papers sent from the western country, as well as from
the intelligence they convey, your secretary apprehends that the
period is not distant when the United States must decide either to
wage war with Spain, or settle all differences with her by treaty, on
the best terms in their power.'

Jay then recommends the adoption by Congress of resolutions expressing its 'concern and displeasure' in learning that
'certain citizens of Virginia have, in violation of the laws of
nations, and of the peace and dignity of the...United States,
violently seized the property of certain subjects of his Catholic

[1] Writing to Mr. Madison and referring to Wilkinson's documents, Governor Randolph said: 'The documents to
be forwarded to you as stated in my public letter [to Congress] will prove the
truth of your suspicion that the occlu-
sion of the Miss. to Virginia would throw
the western settlers into an immediate
state of hostility with Spain.' (Library
of Congress, *Madison Papers*, Ac. 1081.)

Majesty at fort St. Vincennes'; and ordering that notice of this resolution be sent to His Majesty's minister, Gardoqui. Continuing, Jay said:

'Your secretary is convinced that the United States have good right to navigate the river, from its source to and through its mouth; and, unless an accomodation should take place, that the dignity of the United States and their duty to assert and maintain their rights, will render it proper for them to present a memorial and remonstrance to his Catholic Majesty, insisting on their right, complaining of it being violated, and demanding, in a temperate, inoffensive, but at the same time in a firm and decided manner, that his Majesty do cease in future to hinder their citizens from freely navigating that river through the part of its course in question. Your secretary is further of opinion, that in case of refusal, it will be proper for the United States then to declare war against Spain. There being no reputable way between peace and war, it will be expedient to prepare without delay for the one or the other, for circumstances which call for decision seem daily to accumulate.

'If Congress conceive that a treaty with Spain on terms proposed be eligible, the sooner such sentiments are communicated to your secretary the better. If an idea of obtaining better terms should be entertained, the sooner the question can be decided the better. ...

'With respect to prescribing a line of conduct to our citizens on the banks of the river, your secretary is embarrassed. If war is in expectation, then their ardour should not be discouraged, nor their indignation diminished. But, if a treaty is wished and contemplated, then those people should be so advised, and so restrained, as that their sentiments and conduct may as much as possible be made to quadrate with the terms and articles of it. ...

'He also takes the liberty of observing, that a treaty, disagreeable to one half of the nation, had better not be made, for it would be violated; and that a war, disliked by the other half, would promise but little success, especially under a government so greatly influenced and affected by popular opinion.'[1]

It thus appears that Wilkinson's fiction about Clark's imaginary army made Jay pause in his negotiations with Gardoqui and cast upon Congress the responsibility of choosing between the commercial treaty and war. That responsibility Congress never met. Instead it temporized. To lead the southern and western people to believe their navigation right would be defended against Spain, and, at the same time, to convince the northern people that every effort would be made to secure the commercial treaty, Congress was moved to direct Jay to go to Madrid and negotiate for both navigation

[1] *Secret Journal of Congress,* IV, 301.

and treaty. Nothing, however, came of the motion. The
northern delegates, alarmed by Wilkinson's inventions, feared
to force the commercial treaty, and it was dropped forever.
For this result of his scheming, save for his villainous motive,
the nation would owe him great gratitude.

Congress ordered no investigation whatever to learn what
General Clark had really done at Vincennes; but, assuming
that the garrison troops were still there, on April 24 passed
the following resolution aimed at them:

'Resolved, That the Secretary of War direct the commanding officer of the troops of the United States on the Ohio, to take immediate
and efficient measures for dispossessing a body of men who have, in a
lawless and unauthorized manner, taken possession of Post St. Vincents, in defiance of the proclamation and authority of the United
States, and that he employ the whole, or such part, of the force at his
command, as he shall judge necessary, to effect the object.'[1]

This resolution was hardly more than a gesture to satisfy His
Catholic Majesty, for long before it was passed the little
garrison at Vincennes had dissolved for want of supplies.

No formal *amende* was made by Congress to Spain, as Jay
had suggested, for doubtless Gardoqui let it be known that
he did not care for one. Nor did Congress do anything to take
advantage of the truce and treaty meeting with the Wabash
Indians which General Clark had so skillfully arranged. On the
faith of his arrangement with them the confederated Indians
had adhered to their truce agreement and refrained from hostilities; but, as the day for the meeting approached, they
could learn nothing of preparations for their reception, nor
could any one tell them when, if at all, the meeting would be
held. Naturally they believed they were being tricked, and
soon they were again on the warpath. On April 16, 1787,
Captain Finney estimated there were 8000 Indians fitted for
war and reported parties 'set out to strike the Kentucky settlements.'[2] From the unprotected French settlements, north
of the Ohio, to the mountains of eastern Kentucky and Tennessee, numerous warrior bands left their trails of destruction.

[1] *Secret Journal of Congress*, IV, 328;
Madison to Randolph April 22, 1787,
Madison Papers, Library of Congress,
Ac. 1081. Three months earlier Ran-
dolph had sent Congress Clark's and
Logan's letters about the garrisoning of
Vincennes and Congress had made no ob-
jection until the passage of this resolution.
(Library of Congress, *Papers Continental
Congress, Virginia State Papers*, II, 71.)

[2] Library of Congress, *Continental Congress, Letters Sec'y of War*, no. 150, II,
323-25.

Within twelve days after the peace treaty meeting should
have been held at Vincennes, Colonel Logan wrote Governor
Randolph: 'There is no doubt but the western Indians is at
war; the murders they are almost every day guilty of in some
parts of the District [are] too tedious and out of my power to
give a particular account of';[1] and there were many other
like reports of destructive Indian invasions.

The resolutions of the Virginia Council and Congress, condemning General Clark, had accomplished Wilkinson's first
object in his scheme to fool Miro and get the trade privilege.
Little he cared about blasting the good name and ruining the
life of a great and good man. He led the Spaniards to look to
him as their friend; he outwitted the experienced and wily
Miro; he killed Jay's commercial treaty, and thus perhaps
saved both the Mississippi and the Confederation; he balked
the adroit Gardoqui and rendered abortive Spain's whole
diplomatic policy in America; and, for all this, he received the
coveted privilege of trade with New Orleans and a yearly
pension from the Spanish King! Furthermore, during all this
time, and for years afterward, he was contriving to supplant
every military superior, and rose, step by step, to be commander-in-chief of the armies of the United States!

During the summer of 1787 Governor Randolph was having
Virginia's account made up against the United States, for her
outlays and liabilities incurred in winning and holding the
country north of the Ohio; and to do this he found it necessary
to get information from General Clark. Unwilling, however, to
ask this from one whom he had so deeply offended, he re-

---

[1] *Virginia Calendar State Papers*, IV,
286. Logan's letter continues: 'It appears to me nothing will put a stop to the
Western Indians but carrying a Body of
troops into there country. For my own
part, I have been almost silent in regard
to the Indians for some time, Rather giving way to some Gentlemen [meaning
especially Wilkinson] who would wish to
be popular; but I find, as well as they,
that it is out of their power to do a great
deal. It is now evident that some person
ought to exert themselves. I intend to
use my influence against the Western
Indians...and have hopes to succeed.'
Logan evidently was jealous of Wilkinson, and himself hoped to be appointed Commissioner of Indian Affairs

under Congress. After learning of Wilkinson's nomination, he wrote Governor
Randolph, bitterly: 'I have lately been
inform'd that a private Recommendation
had been made by Colo. George Muter,
Judge of the District court, and Harry
Innes, Attorney General of said Court,
for four gentlemen to be commissioned
by Congress to transact Indian affairs in
the District of Kentucky. If this be the
case, as I have reason to beleave it is, I
cannot help remarking the partiality of
these men; for Colo. Muter has spoake to
me since and said, if I did not go to meet
the Shawnees, no business could be done
by any other person with that nation.'
(*Virginia Calendar State Papers*, IV, 266.)

quested Colonel Logan to obtain it, saying: 'The commissioners appointed to adjust the claim...have required that the state shall produce as evidence in support of her claim the following vouchers:... General Clark's *first entries and original books*, and his accounts of goods taken from the enemy.'[1] Colonel Logan showed the governor's letter to General Clark, who wrote a reply which will presently be quoted. First, however, a few words concerning the history of his original papers will be interesting.

In November, 1779, nine months after capturing Hamilton, Clark gave his conductor-general, Shannon, this order: 'You will please to proceed forthwith to Williamsburg in order finally to settle all your Public Accts, as well as mine which I have put in your hands for that purpose. ...As soon as possible wait on the Governor.... I will expect you back with all possible dispatch.'[2] Shannon did as he was ordered. He took all Clark's original vouchers, consisting of over twenty thousand papers, setting forth innumerable items of receipt and disbursement, turned them over to the state auditor, and took his receipt to Clark for them. Soon afterwards General Arnold invaded Virginia, captured Richmond, and burned the public buildings. In the panic and confusion, Clark's papers were supposed to have been burned, and were certainly lost.

Two years later, in 1781, when it became known that Virginia was about to cede the Northwest Territory to Congress on condition that it should reimburse her outlays and liabilities incurred in conquering and holding the territory, the Virginia Assembly (fearing that Congress would evade making this reimbursement unless the state could support its claim with unimpeachable vouchers), ordered commissioners, headed by Colonel Fleming, to go to Kentucky to settle General Clark's military accounts, and directed them to demand of him his *original* book entries and vouchers for every item of his receipts and disbursements. It was of course impossible for him to produce such originals, for they had been left in the auditor's office. Even outlays of which he had kept memoranda, he could only prove by his own oath, or the oaths of others; and it was of course impossible for him to remember more

---

[1] Virginia State Library, *Governor's Letter Book*, 152.

[2] Virginia State Library, *Shannon's Order Book.*

than a fraction of the numberless items of which he had kept
no memoranda.

Before he came to ask the state for payment of the large
balance due him, he was thus compelled to make out an
entirely new account, and to procure such duplicate vouchers
as he could. This required enormous labor and time; and at
best the account could cover only part of his outlays and
liabilities. When the infinite variety of items involved are
considered, the difficulties he labored under while again preparing his account, amidst all the distractions of war, even an
approximation to completeness and accuracy could not be
expected. Yet, despite all these embarrassments, he carried
to Richmond in 1783 a remarkably correct account of a great
number of his outlays for the state during the previous five
years — many of them made directly by himself, many
through Shannon, and many through other officers. That he
was able to do this brings into strong light the falseness of the
charges, then being sent to Governor Harrison and circulated
at Richmond, that he was 'a sot' and 'incapable of attending
to business!' Despite his preoccupation with the demands
of war, he was in truth a remarkably careful and business-like
man in his attention to public money affairs, and neglectful
only of his own.

Of the correctness of his restated account there is now unexpected corroboration; for in 1913 — one hundred and
thirty-three years after he received the auditor's receipt for
his vouchers — there were found, amidst the dusty chaos of
an unused room of the auditor's building in Richmond,
seventy large packages of those original vouchers — over
twenty thousand of them, containing many times that number
of items of his outlays and endorsements for the state! They
had not been destroyed by Arnold's British soldiers. The Virginia officials simply never made any thorough search for
them. It was easier to disclaim knowledge of them than to
hunt for them, so it was assumed they were irretrievably lost,
and General Clark was left the burden of restating his account and supporting it with such proofs as he could obtain.
If he forgot and failed to take credit for any outlay, or liability
for the state, the loss was his; for the state had charged him
with every penny he had received. Certainly the scales of
justice for measuring his claims were unfairly weighted

against him.[1] Yet, in none of his many extant letters can be found one bitter word of complaint of the state's neglect of his claim, until nearly ten years after the Revolution when, after repeated petitions for relief, he became convinced that justice to him was not intended. Even then none is found save in his private letters to his brother Jonathan.[2]

Governor Randolph's own official records plainly showed the loss of those original military accounts in 1781, yet in his letter to Logan he asked that General Clark produce them. Evidently by that time the General had learned something of the way he had been misrepresented to the governor, and therefore no longer felt so bitterly towards him as when he wrote the three-sentence letter beginning: 'Sir: I respect the *State* of Virginia'; so he replied to the request in the following dignified letter:

LOUISVILLE *October 8th*, 1787

Sir:

'A few days past Colo. Logan gave me the perusal of a letter of yours to him on the subject of the Western Accts, wherein you desire him to collect all the Books and papers he could, to assist in the settlement with the United States, and if possible to get Mr. W. Clark[3] to attend you with them, to cast what light he could on the subject. I can assure you, Sir, that the whole of the papers belonging to the Dep[artmen]t (some duplicates only excepted) was delivered to the Commissioners and I believe by them lodged in the Auditor's office. I have spoke to Mr [William Marston] Clark on the subject; he declines undertaking [the] business, as it is impossible for him, or the present commissioners, to Elucidate them, as those of Kentucky

---

[1] Having restated his account, with such duplicate vouchers as he could procure, he petitioned the Assembly to be allowed to prove by his oath other items of his account for which he had left his vouchers with the auditor. (Virginia State Library, *Journal House of Delegates*, 23.) A committee reported favorably on his petition, saying: 'It appears...from a certificate of the auditor's of public accounts, bearing date the 20th day of January 1780, that said George Rogers Clark produced to them vouchers for the disbursement of 14,598 dollars on public account, which were examined by them and lodged in their office and afterwards lost in the invasion of this state by Arnold; and in the account of said Clark, the same could not be settled. It also appears to your committee that from the nature of the service in which said Clark was en-

gaged, he had it not in his power to procure vouchers for a variety of disbursements of the public money,' and the Assembly '*Resolved*, that the auditors of public accounts ought to allow the several charges in the account of the said Clark, amounting to 11,599 dollars, for which he hath no vouchers, upon his making oath that the said sum was bona fide paid and expended for public uses.' (*Id.*, 56, 66, 69.) With this action of the Assembly, General Clark had promise of a just settlement and payment of at least part of his claims; but no more than promise, for they were never settled nor paid.

[2] E.g., May 11, 1792, *Author's MSS.*, copied in English's *Conquest of the Northwest*, 789.

[3] William Marston Clark, a cousin of George Rogers.

and Illinois are blended. I know of no other method that you could adopt to get the business tolerably executed, but that of being at the Expense of sending the whole of the papers to this place, where there is the only persons living that can cast any light on them.

When I reflect on these Ac[coun]ts, and the great expense that hath already attended, and [will be] likely to attend the settlement of them, and the various Circumstances attending the Reduction and defense of those count[r]ies, and all its great consequences — it then appears more obvious to me what mischief false informers, envious, lucrative, and malitious persons have in their power to do a country, when listened to, at a great distance from the seat of government. To such length hath it been carried respecting this country, that, in order to save it in the year 1782, we were obliged to lay aside all attention to Instructions and act discretionary, [he means in carrying on the forbidden expedition against the Shawnees], which answered the salutary purpose. We dared do this as the salvation of the country was of more importance to us than the commissions we bore. And, when all the attending numerous Indian treaties, and the support of an active war for seven years, shall have been reduced to specie, it will be found, if I am not mistaken, [to] amount to a less sum than has already been spent on this [commission [1]] since the war, owing to our frugal manner of living and the want of almost every necessary.

After suffering the fatigues that I have undergone — bearing so many malignant pen's fraying, and yet have to pay large sums of money for supplies that the state could not get credit for, — [a] person might reasonably suppose that of course I must be unhappy. The reverse hath taken place. Conscious of having done everything in the power of a person under my circumstances, — not only for the defense of the country, but to save every expense possible, — I can with pleasure view countries flourishing that I have stained with the blood of its enemies, — pitying mine when I deign to think of them as citizens, otherways with the utmost contempt, as it is impossible I can have any, except those under the description alluded to. I am

Your Excellency's Humble Servt,

G. R. CLARK [2]

His Excellency Edmund Randolph
    Govr. of Virginia.

---

[1] In the original the word here *seems* to be 'communication', which could not have been intended. He probably meant (if he did not say) 'Commission,' and referred to the enormous expenses incurred by commissions through a series of years, including salaries, traveling and living expenses of commissioners, clerk hire, cost of attending witnesses, depositions, etc., which must have aggregated an enormous sum. Examining the vast mass of papers of these commissions, one can well understand how great these expenses must have been and that Clark's estimate was probably correct.

[2] *Virginia Calendar State Papers,* IV, 346.

CHAPTER XXXI

CLARK AT MULBERRY HILL

THE year 1788 opened with prospects dark indeed for the American people. By midsummer the Confederation ceased to exist; and thereafter nine months passed before a government was formed under the Federal Constitution. In the interim there was no real union of the states, and not much prospect of any. Everywhere were poverty, interstate and sectional jealousies, bankrupt state governments failing to function, and general demoralization, almost inconceivable in this day. Only chaotic conditions seemed ahead. For many months after the new constitution was submitted to the states, few believed it would be adopted — fewer still that it would remedy existing ills. It had been framed without authority and was vigorously assailed in every state. With thirteen disordered and quarreling sovereignties — each suspicious of the others, and some systematically legislating to cripple others — there seemed small hope that they could be brought into union. Thousands of men of tried patriotism lost all confidence in popular government, thought republican institutions unworkable, and, like John Adams, preferred the rule of the select few. Many more regretted the loss of the peace, order and prosperity they had enjoyed under royal rule; and not a few wished for a monarchy. Washington was urged to become a dictator. From Congress Madison wrote Randolph: 'The existing Confederacy is tottering to its foundation. Many individuals of weight, particularly in the eastern district, are suspected of leaning towards monarchy. Other individuals predict a partition of the states into two or more confederacies. It is pretty certain that if some radical amendment of the single one cannot be...introduced, that one or the other of these resolutions — the latter no doubt — will take place.'[1]

Thousands looked for asylums under the more orderly foreign governments. Numberless letters of the time show the anxiety of the writers to remove themselves and their

[1] Library of Congress, *Madison Papers*, Ac. 1081.

families from a country where they could see only dissension and suffering ahead; but whither? That question was one to make them pause. Everywhere, except in America, kings ruled; but it was not aversion to royal rule that made the main difficulty in seeking expatriation. All had lived under a king, and far more happily than they expected to live under their own disordered government. They had not become Revolutionists because of opposition to monarchy, but to arbitrary taxation. True, that opposition had developed rapidly during the war; but before the conflict even men who became the most radical of revolutionists had been reared to feel and had sincerely professed submission and devotion to the crown and deference to the nobility — not indeed to the individuals representing those institutions, but to the institutions themselves.

But where should the American who dreaded the dark future in his own country go for asylum? To France? — few had money for the voyage, or knew the language, or could earn a living there. To England or Canada? — both were overrun with bitter Tories, and neither offered a welcome for hated Americans. The most available asylum was Spanish Louisiana. It was their next neighbor, was accessible at comparatively small expense, was rich in natural resources, was settled mainly by friendly French, and many Americans already resided there. At this time, too, Spain was inviting immigration from the States and offering 'concessions and accommodations.' The result of all this was that a great number of Americans sought permission to settle in Louisiana; many went there; companies were formed to take others there in great number. Some went without waiting to learn on what terms they would be received as Spanish subjects; others demanded to know the terms before they would consent to become such.

One of those who contemplated removing to Louisiana was General Clark. With health impaired by years of strain and exposure, bankrupted by the state debts, humiliated by suits on them, and liable at any day to be arrested and imprisoned for them, he was forced to live on the bounty of his family. Like the blind Belisarius, he was a dependent for his daily bread in the empire he had saved. It was impossible for him to earn money, for it would only have gone to pay the state's debts, held generally by speculators who had bought them up for almost nothing. Naturally he sought escape from his troubles.

He wrote to Gardoqui proposing to found a colony of Americans on the west bank of the Mississippi, opposite the mouth of the Ohio; but he demanded liberties so far from pleasing to the Spanish government that nothing came of the project. His proposal was that Spain should grant him for the colony about a hundred miles square of territory and guarantee the following rights to the colonists: (1) 'that each head of family, who becomes resident within such territory, shall have a thousand acres of land, with one hundred to each person of the family'; (2) 'that it be guaranteed that they shall not be disturbed as to their religion'; (3) 'that his Majesty shall name the governor, whose term shall not be vacated but for ill conduct'; (4) 'that after three years time from the establishing of the colony, the inhabitants shall elect six councillors or assistants to the governor, which council they shall elect every three years.'[1] This provision for an elected council, which would be an effective check on the governor, was no doubt suggested by the example of the executive council of Virginia, which had long played that important part under Virginia's government. The provision preventing the governor's arbitrary removal by the King was also an important one, and was probably suggested by the long struggles of the American colonies to free their judges and other officers from royal control.

With these guaranties of religious and political freedom, the colonists might well look for virtual self-government, security and the opportunity to prosper, provided the guaranties were faithfully observed by the Spanish King; and plain self-interest would probably have made him observe them, for had he violated them he would have found it an expensive and difficult undertaking to govern by force a colony of Americans on the upper Mississippi a thousand miles above New Orleans. In his letter submitting the colonial proposition to Gardoqui (February, 1788) General Clark said: 'neither property nor character is safe in a government as unsettled as that of the United States,' and that 'if you give a favorable reception to the matter and promptly conclude concerning it, his Majesty will immediately secure a numerous and flourishing colony of

[1] Clark to Gardoqui, *American Historical Association Report*. (1896,) II, 967.

faithful subjects.' Undoubtedly this assurance was given in good faith; but no less certainly General Clark and his associates well knew Spain's reputation for duplicity, and for that reason were careful to provide against arbitrary oppression, by demanding definite guaranties of the essentials of liberty. These guaranties, however, the Spanish government would not give. Indeed, it soon changed its policy and would neither invite nor allow American immigration, which it feared would soon make Louisiana American.[1]

As this colony project of General Clark and his associates, and the terms he demanded of Spain, have been little understood, and their motives grossly misrepresented, it should be stated that from the time of the Revolution until now the free right of expatriation has been an American doctrine, for which in 1812 we waged war against Great Britain. The propriety of expatriation depends on the motive which leads to it; and, of all men of his time, certainly not one had less cause than Clark to remain a citizen of the state of his birth, or had more impelling motives for leaving it. Yet because, like so many others, he proposed seeking an asylum in Louisiana, where he could earn a living and be freed from Virginia's debts, some uninformed and reckless writers of western history have represented him as an unpatriotic soldier of fortune, a near-traitor, 'quite willing to do his fighting in behalf of Spain instead of against her!'[2]

His colonization project having fallen through, General Clark contented himself as best he could with his retirement at Mulberry Hill.[3] Of his life there we get many glimpses in his

[1] General Clark's brother, William, said the Spanish government offered him the land, but he would not accept the offer without the privileges he demanded and which it would not give. (*Draper MSS.* 48 J 9.)

[2] Roosevelt's *Winning of the West*, IV, 163.

[3] 'Mulberry Hill' was a fine tract containing about a mile square of elevated land overlooking the town of Louisville, and at that time covered by a noble forest. Though, judged by present standards, the residence was small and crude, when built it was considered an unusually spacious and complete one for Kentucky. As the residence site, with nearly fifty acres surrounding it, is now a public park of the City of Louisville, called

'George Rogers Clark Park,' and it has been proposed to restore some of its old features, a more particular description of the place as it formerly appeared may not be amiss. All the improvements have long since disappeared.

The residence was a steep-roofed log house with great stone chimneys at the side ends, contained six rooms — two of them garret rooms with dormers — and a rather wide central hall on each floor, besides large pantry and store rooms in the rear, and a small front porch and a larger back one. The kitchen was separate and about fifty feet northeast from the eastern corner of the main house. The 'quarters' of the negroes, of whom Mr. Clark owned twenty-four at the time of his death, were well built of stone and

letters and those of his near kindred and friends. He wanted
for no mere physical comforts, for not only his parents but his
brothers and sisters had ample means and were devoted to him;
but his proud spirit must have been galled by the thought of
dependence on them. Their very sympathy was hard to bear,
for it was a constant reminder of the wrongs that occasioned
it. Bitter indeed must have been his thought of them, but
he tried to forget and rarely mentioned them. His thoughts
about public affairs and his own appear almost alone in
his letters to Jonathan. In former years he had reflected
with natural pride upon the great national significance of
his military services; but now they recalled the ingratitude
and disgrace they had brought upon him, and only gave pain.
Therefore, he wrote, he avoided everything reminding him
of them. His priceless letters and public documents, shed-
ding light on western affairs and his own career, were treated
as waste paper — many of them burned, many more lost.
The 'elegant sword' voted him by the Virginia Assembly for
his victory over Hamilton, he broke and cast away.[1] Some

brick and were about fifty feet northeast
of the kitchen. Glass panes were in the
small windows of the main house, and
tradition says they attracted many cu-
rious people from considerable distances;
for window glass, being difficult to bring
safely over the mountains, was almost
unknown in the west. The residence and
kitchen were in a yard enclosed by a 'five-
plank' fence, and, until within the memory of persons still living, contained a
number of fine forest trees. From the front
gate and stile a broad avenue ran north-
westwardly some third of a mile or more
to a lane (still called Clark's Lane) and
then westwardly to the public road. In
the center of the avenue was the carriage
way, and on each side of it two rows of
locust trees, between which ran a foot-
path. Northeast of the avenue were cultivated fields, on the other side a superb
primitive forest with many great tulip
poplars, walnut, ash, and other valuable
trees. It was destroyed and the wood
used for fires, or sold, by the Federal
troops during the Civil War, when a
large army encamped there. It was at
this time that all the buildings, save
the main residence and kitchen and stone
spring house, were accidentally burned
to the ground. Fifty years later this
part of Mulberry Hill was taken for an
army camp by the United States during
the World War. The officers who selected
the site probably did not know that it
had been the home of George Rogers
Clark, William Clark, and their parents,
for they named the camp 'Camp Zach-
ary Taylor.' The old stone spring house,
then the sole relic of the buildings of its
early occupants, was torn down and the
fine never-failing spring filled up; the latter no doubt for hygienic reasons; but
why the stone building should have been
destroyed we do not know.

That Mulberry Hill is now a public
park and will always be preserved as once
the home of George Rogers Clark has
been due to an appreciation of his character and services and the generous public spirit of three brothers (his great-
nephews), Charles Thruston Ballard,
Rogers Clark Ballard Thruston (born
Ballard) and Samuel Thruston Ballard.
They purchased the site from the United
States government and presented it as a
free gift to the city's Board of Park Commissioners for the use of the public.

Photographs of the main residence
(after it had become greatly dilapidated)
and of the spring house, are in the Filson
Club collection and are reproduced in
English's *Conquest of the Northwest.*

[1] Mercer to Croghan, *Draper MSS.* 55
J 79; English's *Conquest of the Northwest.*

part of it may still be embedded in the earth at the bottom of the Ohio. The complimentary resolution, sent him on the same occasion, had become a bitter irony and was probably burned, for it was not found amongst his papers after his death. In 1781 the Virginia Assembly had rejected his petition to be relieved from the state debts by a compensating grant of land north of the Ohio, but it voted him a second sword![1] This also had become a hollow compliment and was possibly thrown away, for no trace of it has been found.

At Mulberry Hill General Clark spent much time in the woods, and found there diversion in his favorite nature study, for the region abounded in flora, fauna and geologic remains of great interest for the naturalist. He wrote Jonathan: 'For several years I have lived quite retired, ...reading, hunting, fowling, corresponding with a few chosen friends in different parts of the continent, and attending to private business, without concerning myself with that of the public.[2]

Who the 'few chosen friends' were, we do not know; for he did not keep copies of his own letters and very few of those he received during that period were preserved. One unfinished one, which he wrote to the *American Museum* concerning ancient Indian mounds, was however fortunately found among his papers. It gives an interesting glimpse of one of the needed indoor diversions which occupied his mind while he was living on his father's farm, and shows that, even during the strenuous years of wilderness war, he had found interest in contemplating a subject so remote from his exacting military business as the origin of those prehistoric remains.

Peletiah Webster, in a long article in the *Museum*, had absurdly attributed the many mounds in the Ohio Valley to De Soto and his men. Replying to him, General Clark says that in Webster's

'long account of the march of De Soto through these Cuntreys he is brought to Lexington, taken to the mouth of the Muskinghum, across to the Mississury &c &c, fortifying the Cuntrey he passed through; and all those amence works are ascribed to him. I think the world ought to be undeceived on this point. So great a Stranger to the western Cuntrey as Mr. Webster appears to be, ought to have in-

---

[1] Virginia State Library, *House of Delegates Journal*, Dec. 21, 1781.

[2] *Draper MSS.* 2 L 29. His sister Lucy, referring to this period, said General Clark 'used to spend much time in reading, had a fine favorite horse he used to ride.' (*Draper MSS.* 10 J 8.)

formed himself better before he ventured to have palmed his conjectures on the World.

'I dont suppose there is a person living that knows the Geography and Natural History of the back Cuntrey better, if so well, as I do myself. It hath been my study for many years. I have made the calculation and venture to inform you that, if their was paved Roads from each of those fortifications to the other throughout the western Cuntrey, that De Soto could not have Visited the whole of those works with his army in four years, allowing him the common Season for marching. Those works are numerous in every part of the western cuntrey, but more so in the Pittsburg Cuntrey than else where. There you will find them on tops of High Mountains   they are larger as you desend towards the Mississippi   there is not a place on the ohio that we have attempted to fortify, from Pitt down, but we find antient works. Soto might have been on the Ohio but no vestiges remain to prove it   as for his being the author of those Fortifications it is quite out of the question: they are more numerous than he had men, and many of them would have required fifty Thousand men to have ocupied   Some of them have been fortified Towns, others Incampments entrenched, but the greatest part have been common Garrisoned Forts, Many of them with Towers of earth of considerable height to defend the walls with arrows and other missive weapons. That they had commerce is evident because the mouth of every River hath been fortified; whare the Land was Subject to floods it hath been raised out of the way of water. that they ware a numerous people is also evident, not only from their numerous Works, but also their habitations raised in low Lands . . .

'the works on the Mississippi near the Caw River is one of the largest we know of   the Kaskaskias Chief Babtiste, gave me a history of it   he said that was the palace of his forefathers when they covered the whole [country] and had large towns; that all those works we saw there was the Fortifications round the Town which must have been very considerable . . .

'I had Some whare seen some antient account of the Town of Kohokia formerly containing 10,000 M[en]. Their is not one of that nation at present known by that name. Being frequently at that place, recollecting this Story, I one day set out with a party Gentⁿ. to see whether we could discover signs of such population. We easily and evidently traced the Town for upwards of five miles in the beautiful plain below the present Town of Kohokia. Their could be no deception hear because the remains of antient works was thick. . . .this Town appear[s] to have occupied that part. . .the nearest the River but not on it, as their is a strip of lower Land. Fronting nearly the sentor of this Town on the Heights is [a] pinicle. . .frequently Visited by Strangers as a mear curiosity. My visit was perhaps from a different motive. . . .

'I think the World is to blame to express such great anxiety to know [who] it was that built those numerous and formidable works and what hath become of those people. They will find them in the

Kaskaskias, Peorias, Kohokias (now extinct) Piankishaws, Chicasaws, Cherokees and Such old Nations   Th[ey] say they grew out of the ground where they now live and that they were formerly as numerous as the Trees in woods, but affronting the great Spirit he made war among the Nations and they destroyed each other   this is their Tradition and I see no reason why it should not be received as good History — at least as good as a great part of ours. At what time this great revolution Should have happened, which certainly hath taken place in this Quarter, I never could get any satisfactory Acc[t]. only that it had been the case, as it is beyond their Calculation of time; but I am convinced that it is Anterio[r] to five Hundred years and I dont think it difficult to make a tolerably Satisfactory conjecture of the time at least within a few Ages.'[1]

It is interesting to find that Clark's theory was then new, and for nearly a hundred years afterward was generally rejected by archæologists; but it is now almost universally accepted.[2]

It was about the time of his *Museum* letter that General Clark was visited by an accomplished young Virginian, John Pope, who was making a tour of the western country and who published a very entertaining journal of his travels. He wrote:

'Dec. 1, 1790. I shall proceed on to Louisville and rouse up General George Rogers Clark who, the Kentuckians say, hath ac-

[1] *Draper MSS.* 11 J 184; Schoolcraft's *Indian Tribes,* IV, 133.

[2]. Dr. Daniel G. Brinton, late Professor of American Archæology at the University of Pennsylvania, says: 'Many hundreds of the mounds have been carefully opened and their contents studied. They indicate a degree of civilization higher, indeed, than that of the native Indians, who occupied the locality when it was first visited by the whites, but not in advance of what was found in many portions of the area of the U.S., and generically strictly within the limits familiar to the red race. ... They were wholly within the 'polished stone age.' ... It is evident that they had extensive commercial intercourse in various directions. ...

'The period when the mound-builders flourished has been differently estimated; but there is a growing tendency to reject the assumption of a very great antiquity: There is no good reason for assigning any of the remains in the Ohio Valley an age antecedent to the Christian era; and the final destruction of their towns may well have been but a few generations before the discovery of the continent by Co-

lumbus. Faint traditions of this event were still retained by tribes who occupied the region at the advent of the whites.' (*Universal Cyclopædia,* VIII, 281.)

Dr. W. H. Holmes, Ethnological Curator of the National Museum, says: 'During the second half of the [19th] Century ...a gradual change took place in the views of students regarding the mound builders, and at the close of the century there was practical unanimity in the view that the builders of the great earthworks were the ancestors of the Indian tribes found in possession of the general region.' (*Bulletin 60, Bureau of Ethnology Smithsonian Institute,* Part I, 15–16.) 'Little that is specific can be ascertained regarding the character of the buildings which must have crowned mounds so great as those of Cahokia.' (*Id.,* 106.) The famous Cahokia mound is now being excavated by Professor Warren K. Moorehead of Phillips Academy, Andover, under the auspices of the University of Illinois. For particulars of this excavation, see *Daily Science Service Bulletin* (Washington), quoted in the *Literary Digest,* May 19, 1923.

tually been in a profound slumber for upwards of four years without the least symptom of wakefulness whatever. [This, and Pope's following journal entry, show how exaggerated and persistent were the misrepresentations of Clark still being circulated.] Dec 15 Arrived at his house under an apprehension that he had forgotten me. He immediately recognized me and without ceremony entered into familiar though desultory conversation, in which I was highly pleased with the Atticism of his wit, the genuine offspring of native genius. On serious and important occasions he displays a profundity of judgment aided by reflection and matured by experience. I cannot dismiss this gentleman without observing that some years since he shone forth in all the glory of military prowess. He appeared from his plans and successes to have possessed an intuitive knowledge of the maneuvers and designs of the Enemy.[1]

The year before Pope's visit, General Clark began writing the unfinished 'Memoir Letter,' which has been so often quoted in the preceding pages. The circumstances under which he was led to write it, and the use intended to be made of it, have been much misunderstood. Because, long after his death, a contemporary said it was written at the request of *Presidents* Jefferson and Madison; a hasty writer erroneously asserted that it was written after Madison became president, 'and therefore some thirty or forty years after the events of which it speaks.'[2] The correspondence leading to the writing of the Memoir should put an end to the error.[3] In fact, the Memoir was begun by General Clark in 1789, at the request of Mr. Madison and United States Senator John Brown of Kentucky. It was left unfinished in 1791 and was found amongst his papers after his death, nearly thirty years later. It discloses remarkable accuracy of memory and statement.

When, in 1787, he was proclaimed a malefactor by the Virginia governor and council, his friend Jefferson was in France, where he lived for five years amidst the excitements of the French Revolution. After his return to America, late in 1789, he was no doubt told that Clark had brought his troubles upon himself by drinking, and by lawless conduct at Vincennes. Inquiry must have convinced Jefferson that this was true, for the letters and 'testimonials' Wilkinson had sent Governor Randolph were set forth in the proceedings of Congress and

[1] Pope's *Tour of the Western and Southern Territorys, 1790–91.* (Richmond, 1792.)

[2] Roosevelt's *Winning of the West*, II, 176, note.

[3] *Draper MSS. 53 J 80 et seq.*

seemed unanswerable; and none could deny that, after his public condemnation, Clark had taken to hard drink. Jefferson must have learned this with profound regret, for he admired and loved him; but he could do nothing for him. Delicacy forbade even an expression of his sympathy. On the other hand, Clark, in his lonely hours, must many times have suffered poignant regret over the loss of his faithful friend's esteem.

Upon his return to this country, Jefferson was called to Washington's cabinet and became engrossed with the great affairs of the new Federal government. Late in 1790 the cabinet was much agitated over the disastrous defeat of General Harmar's large army by the northwestern Indians.[1] Nearly two thirds of the fourteen hundred badly organized and badly led troops were volunteer militia from Kentucky, who after the defeat found themselves left without food or ammunition in the enemy's country, to make their way home as best they could. Amongst the Kentucky people, indignation over the government's neglect of their volunteers alternated with alarm for the safety of their own homes; but soon they demanded another expedition to end savage hostilities, and large numbers volunteered to serve the next year under General St. Clair. Impelled by the public danger, General Clark left his retirement sufficiently to use his influence in support of this movement.

Jefferson thought of having Clark given command and in March 1791 wrote to Judge Innes of Kentucky:

'Our endeavors the last year to punish your enemies have had an unfortunate issue. The Federal Council has yet to learn by experience, — what experience has long ago taught us in Virginia, — that rank and file fighting will not do against Indians. I hope this years experiment will be made in a more auspicious form. Will it not be possible for you to bring Gen¹. Clark forward? I know the greatness of his mind, and am more mortified at the cause which obscured it. Had not this unhappily taken place there was nothing he might not have hoped; could it be surmounted his lost ground might yet be recovered. No man alive rated him higher than I did, and would again were he to become again what I knew him. We are made to hope he is engaged in writing the account of his Expeditions North West of Ohio; they will be valuable morsels of History, and will justify to the world those who have told them how great he was.'[2]

---

[1] For a full account see Perkins' *Western Annals*, 337 *et seq.*

[2] *Draper MSS.* 53 J 90.

In reply Judge Innes said:

'Since the reception of your Letter I have seen Genl. Clark and find he is writing the History of his Expeditions & will complete the work in the course of this summer. I entertain the same Ideas of his greatness that you do and consider him as a singular loss to the Western Country. I took the liberty of showing him your Letter, from a hope that it might cause him to reflect upon his present folly. He was perfectly sober, was greatly agitated by the Contents, observed it was friendly, & shed Tears — A sympathetic touch seized my soul and I could not forbear accompanying him.'[1]

A most touching scene, this — the humiliated hero, unable to control his agitation when he read the kind words of one whom he had long loved and whose good opinion he had always specially valued. Amongst all his friends, the two men whose approval he probably had most treasured were Mason and Jefferson — particularly Jefferson, who was nearer his own age, shared more of his interests, and had kept in closer touch with him after he went west. Perhaps the greatest hurt he suffered from Randolph's proclamation was from the belief that he had lost Jefferson's esteem; and, as if to confirm that belief, four years had passed without a word from him.

A month went by and then Clark wrote Jefferson the following letter:

JEFFERSON CITY *June 29th* 1791

Dear Sir:

Judge Innes has admited me to a perusal of part of a Letter of yours to that Gentleman, which strongly evidenced your friendly recollection of me. I have in consequence signified to the Judge by Letr the high sense I had entertained of yr partiality in my favor, and beged him to have imparted to you the heartfelt respect and gratitude which I have ever felt and still entertain for Mr. Jefferson, as well for his personal qualifications as for his uniform favourable propensities towards me.

At the time of having perused that part of your Letter above alluded to, I deemed it obligatory on my feelings to have expressed by Letter to the Judge the gratitude I entertained for the friendly remembrance of an old servant to your government, with which you was pleased to honor me. Since then, Sr, I have considered that the terms of the Letter were such and so friendly as to have demanded at my hands that this acknowledgement, however inadequate, Should be personally addressed to yourself, but untainted with the sordid desire of cultivating your patronage from selfish views. I am above that design but when duly called on I shall never be above the service of my Country at the risque of Life and reputation.

[1] *Innes Papers*, Library of Congress, May 30, 1791; *Jefferson Papers, id.*

Blood and Treasure might have been and yet may be saved. The little Factions of these Western countries, so incident to all Infant Settlements, have induced me to spurn at competition & rivalry. My pride soared above them, and although long since retired into the vale of private life, in which the eye of observation is genly more acute, disinterested, and clear sighted, yet I felt myself constrained, from the presence of distress with which Kentucky was overwhelmed at the time by Indian Hostilitys, to come forward as a private citizen and to exert all the Influence I had possessed with the people to forward the late expedition. On no public occasion shall my exertion be wanting. My country and yourself may at all times, command me.[1]

[1] *Jefferson Papers*, Library of Congress, C. 2d Series, no. 16, Letter 86.

CHAPTER XXXII

THE LOUISIANA EXPEDITION

AFTER some five years of retired life at Mulberry Hill, impending war with Spain caused General Clark to take active part in a public affair of great moment. When the people of France overthrew their monarchy and formed a republic, the national sympathy of America went out to them as friends and fellow freemen struggling against tyranny. Grateful for their aid during our own Revolution, and proud to see the influence of our pioneer example in free government extending to Europe, an overwhelming majority of the people of this country were for aiding the French, then fighting against nearly all the great monarchies of Europe. Many indeed thought we were bound to do so by treaty. When Spain joined their enemies, strong popular sentiment, nearly everywhere in the American states save in New England, favored war with that power. The French of Louisiana were eager to throw off Spain's galling yoke, and our western people were fired with desire to help them — never doubting that a sister republic there would gladly open the Mississippi.

At this juncture there arrived in this country the French revolutionist, Genêt, who had been sent by the Republic of France as minister to the United States. He was received with wild enthusiasm at Charleston, and thence made a triumphal progress to Philadelphia, where he was welcomed with bonfires and fêtes. Intoxicated by these popular demonstrations, he conducted himself much as if this country and his own were already allies in war with Spain. He issued letters of marque for vessels to leave American ports to attack France's enemies, and planned an uprising of French revolutionists in Louisiana. Republicans everywhere in America, especially in the west, wished success for the revolution there; for they looked upon it as a stroke for liberty — a blow aimed at despotism in the Mississippi Valley. They saw the French and many American settlers in Louisiana — making perhaps five sixths of its population — held in subjection by a handful of Spanish troops and ruled by hard Spanish officials; they saw their own vital right to navigate the Mississippi haughtily denied them by Spain; they believed, and had much reason to believe, this country was about to join France in the war with Spain; and that war they looked upon as a holy one. No one then doubted that Louisiana, under an independent French republic, would be a far more congenial neighbor than under the rule of the Spanish King; nor could any one foresee that the Republic in France would be supplanted by the despotism of Napoleon, or that Louisiana would be purchased by the United States.

It was during the height of the American enthusiasm for war with Spain that General Clark, in a letter to the French minister, offered to lead an army of western volunteers to free the French and Americans in Louisiana. The proposal was promptly accepted. Many Kentucky and Tennessee men flocked to his standard,[1] and far more were ready to join him. Genêt promised needed funds to equip the expedition, but the ill-ordered French Republic failed to supply them. Had they been forthcoming, it seems almost certain that Spain's rule in Louisiana would have been quickly ended. Her force there was small, ill-supplied, and alarmed, while the French revolutionists were many and ardent; but time was lost, Genêt's high-handed conduct and the excesses of the revolutionists in France dampened the ardor of many Americans, and finally President Washington issued a proclamation of neutrality prohibiting the expedition. Thereafter Clark ceased recruiting and abandoned the project.

Few episodes in the history of the Revolutionary west have been more misunderstood than this projected movement to liberate Louisiana. As Winsor says, 'The grand aim of all was to set up Louisiana as an independent ally of both the United States and France.'[2] The western Americans also aimed, of course, to secure their right to navigate the lower Mississippi. Their attitude is indicated in Governor Shelby's reply to the federal Secretary of State, who wrote him to stop the expedition. This the Governor declined to do, saying:

'If it is lawful for any one citizen of the state to leave it, it is equally so for any number of them to do it. It is also lawful for them

---

[1] Amongst them Colonels Benjamin Logan and John Montgomery.

[2] *Western Movement*, 538; *American* *Historical Association Report* (1896), i 933.

to carry any quantity of provisions, arms and ammunition; and if the act is lawful in itself, there is nothing but the particular intention with which it is done that can possibly make it unlawful; but I know of no law which inflicts a punishment on intention only, or any criterion by which to decide what would be a sufficient evidence of that intention, even if it was a proper subject for legal censure. ...I shall also feel but little inclination to take an active part in punishing or restraining any of my fellow-citizens, for a supposed intention only, to gratify the fears of the minister of a power who openly withholds from us an invaluable right, and who secretly instigates against us a most savage and cruel enemy.'[1]

The expedition to liberate Louisiana was in fact very far from being a chimerical one, as some writers have thought. This is made evident by the official reports of Baron Caron- delet, the Spanish governor, who wrote (January 1, 1794) that if Clark's expedition

'is carried into effect, the whole of upper Louisiana from [St. Louis] as far as Nogales [Vicksburg], that is an extent of 380 leagues, will fall into the hands of the enemies in Spring, since the forces that can be collected for the defense of the forts of [St. Louis] and of New Madrid do not amount to 90 men of regular troops and 200 militia; and even these can be but little trusted. If at the same time we have to face an attack by the mouths of the Misisipi, as their papers an- nounce, it is evident that all Louisiana will fall into their hands with the greatest rapidity and facility, since we cannot count on more than 800...to man so many points, ...it being certain that few of the American inhabitants will side against an army composed of their countrymen, and, as the French inhabitants will still less offer to take arms in our favor, both from their leaning toward France, and because all their estates situated on the upper part of the river will remain undefended when once Nogales and Natchez are lost, I shall have no other resource than an honorable surrender, or to perish in defense of the redoubt of San Carlos with my regular troops, as I shall not find myself sufficiently in force to defend the plaza. ...

'I do not doubt their success, if helped by the inhabitants of upper Louisiana, and their Indians, who are well affected toward the French. ...I have no further hope than in the faults the enemy may commit, and in accidents which may perhaps favor us.'[2] [Caron- delet's apprehensions were amply justified by the facts as they appear in many other letters written at the time.]

Although it was not prohibited by any statute, certainly the expedition was not technically justifiable under inter- national law, for the United States had not declared war on

---

[1] English's *Conquest of the Northwest,* 821.

[2] *American Historical Association Re- ports,* 1896, I, 1027-28.

Spain; but it is preposterous to impute disloyal or unworthy motives to the men engaged in it, or encouraging it. We do not brand as traitors Americans who went to free Texas from the rule of Mexico, or to free Cuba from the rule of Spain, or to fight in the World War against Germany, when those powers were at peace with us. However irregular may have been the project to free Louisiana, the patriotic and humane motives of the westerners engaged in it were beyond question; yet some reckless writers have represented it as a mere free-booting venture for personal profit, and even as treasonable![1]

The movement to liberate Louisiana having been abandoned, General Clark never afterward took part in any public affair. Any noteworthy incidents occurring during the twenty-four remaining years of his life were nearly all personal ones mentioned in family letters. That comparatively few of these letters have been preserved is doubtless mainly due to two circumstances. After the Revolution first one and then another of the Clarks removed from Virginia to Kentucky. The journey was long, difficult, and usually dangerous. Bad roads, rugged mountains, and numerous streams to ford, made it unwise to overload wagons or pack-horses, and many essentials had to be put on them, such as provisions, clothing, bedding, tents, cooking utensils, horse feed, and other articles in variety. Then, too, room in the wagons had to be left for the young and infirm who were unable to ride horseback or walk. Under these circumstances old letters were oftenest left behind or burned, although many of them would be very interesting now, and some of much historic value.

Again, the dearth of letters passing between the members of the Clark family, after their removal to Kentucky, is explained by the fact that they were neighbors, who visited one another frequently and seldom had occasion to correspond. Shortly after the Revolution, General Clark's oldest sister, Ann, and her husband, Owen Gwathmey, removed with their children to Louisville, where he became a merchant.[2] The next sister, Lucy Clark, married Major William Croghan, a comrade of Colonel Jonathan Clark in the Continental Army; and they

---

[1] Roosevelt's *Winning of the West*, vi, chap. ii; Archibald Henderson's address, November 3, 1921, *Virginia University Alumni Bulletin*.

[2] Two of their sons and a daughter married children of Colonel Aylett Booth.

settled on a fine tract of land called 'Locust Grove,' overlooking the Ohio River some six miles above Louisville.[1] The third sister, Elizabeth, married Colonel Richard Clough Anderson, also a native of Caroline County. Their Kentucky home, 'Soldier's Retreat,' lay on the Ohio a short distance above the Croghan's.[2] The youngest sister, Frances, married three times — Dr. John O'Fallon, Charles Mynn Thruston, and her cousin, Dennis Fitzhugh—and lived at Louisville.[3] When later General Clark's brothers, Jonathan and Edmund, came west they also made their homes in or near Louisville.

In 1798 an interesting letter was drawn from General Clark concerning events on the upper Ohio twenty-four years earlier, during Cresap's War. In his *Notes on Virginia*, Mr. Jefferson had attributed the murder of Logan's family to Cresap, and gave Logan's famous speech to Lord Dunmore as a noble example of Indian eloquence. Luther Martin of Maryland, a bitter political and personal enemy, published a savage attack on Jefferson, asserting that the *Notes* slandered Cresap, and denying that Logan ever made the speech. As a number of men lived in Kentucky who had taken part in Cresap's War and might know about the events in dispute, Mr. Jefferson wrote Dr. Samuel Brown, medical professor in Transylvania University at Lexington, and asked him to get their statements.[4] He said:

'I suppose it probable that General Clarke may know something of the facts relative to Logan or Cresap. ...I am told you are preparing to give an account of the General, which for its matter I know, & for its manner I doubt not, will be highly interesting. I am in hopes, in connection with it, [for] some account of Kentuckey, that your information & his together will be able to correct & supply what I had collected relative to it in a very early day. Indeed it was to Genl. Clarke I was indebted for what degree of accuracy there was in most of my statements. I wish you to attend particularly to the overflowage of the Mississippi, on which I have been accused of

[1] One of their daughters, Eliza, married George Hancock, another, Elizabeth, General Thomas Jessup of the United States Army. Their son, Colonel George Croghan, won distinction in three wars, particularly by his defense of Fort Meigs in the War of 1812, when barely twenty-three years of age.

[2] By a second wife — a cousin of General Clark's — Colonel Anderson left numerous descendants, amongst whom were Colonel Robert Anderson, defender of Fort Sumter in the Civil War, Charles Anderson, governor of Ohio, General McArthur of the United States Army, and Nicholas Longworth, Speaker of the United States House of Representatives.

[3] By each marriage she had two children. Many of her descendants have been people of note.

error. Present me affectionately to the General & assure him of my constant remembrance & esteem.'[1]

Dr. Brown accordingly wrote General Clark, saying:

'I remember to have had some conversation with you respecting the affair when at your house; and, although the variety and important nature of the events which your conversations suggested, have in some degree effaced from my memory that distinct recollection of this particular event, which I ought to have before I should attempt to communicate your account of it to Mr. Jefferson, yet still I am pretty certain that as you related the story, any mistakes that have crept into the Notes on Virginia are not attributable to Mr. Jefferson, but to Logan himself, or to those by whom his speech was originally published. I think you informed me that you were with Cresap at the time Logan's family was murdered, that Cresap was not the author of the massacre, that Logan actually delivered the speech as reported in the Notes of Virginia.'[2]

In reply General Clark wrote a lengthy and clear account, exonerating Cresap, who, Logan believed, was the murderer, and concluding as follows:

'When a treaty of peace was held, ...Logan did not appear. ... Logan's Speech to Dunmore now came forward, as related by Mr. Jefferson. It was thought to be clever, though the army knew it to be wrong as to Cresap; but it only produced a laugh in camp. I saw it displeased Captain Cresap, and told him, 'that he must be a very great man, that the Indians palmed every thing that happened on his shoulders.' He smiled and said 'that he had an inclination to tomahawk Greathouse for the murder.'

'What I have related is fact. I was intimate with Cresap; Logan I was better acquainted with, at that time, than with any other Indian in the western country. I was perfectly acquainted with the conduct of both parties. Logan was the author of the Speech as alleged by Mr. Jefferson; and Cresap's conduct was as I have here related it.'[3]

On receipt of this statement Dr. Brown wrote Jefferson:

'I am...happy in having it in my power to transmit to you an interesting letter from your friend General Clarke, which indeed appears to me to render further investigation quite unnecessary. ... The incidents in General Clarke's narrative follow each other in a manner so simple & so natural as to afford to every liberal & candid enquirer the highest internal evidence of their reality. To those who

---

[1] P. L. Ford's *Works of Jefferson* (Federal Edition, Putnam, 1904), VIII, 390.
[2] *Maryland Historical Society Publications*, II, 1844–51; *Draper MSS.* 48 J 2.

[3] *Id.*; English's *Conquest of the Northwest*, 1029.

have the happiness of being acquainted with that truly great man, his statement will bring the fullest conviction. His memory is singularly accurate, his veracity unquestionable. To such respectable authority I can suppose no one capable of objecting, except Mr Luther Martin. I have shewn General Clarke's letter to Major Morrison, the Supervisor of the Ohio District, who resided near Pittsburg, when the transaction respecting Logan occurred. He asures me that he knows most of them as stated in the letter to be true, for they are within his own recollection.'[1]

This letter was written over eleven years after General Clark's condemnation by the Virginia executive, and nearly as long after his 'Memoir' was written, and the high estimate of his mentality by this very able physician, who knew him well, differs widely from that of writers who, without investigation, have represented him as mentally incapacitated when he wrote the 'Memoir.'[2]

In April, 1799, General Clark's mother died at Mulberry Hill, and, only three months later, his father. By his will[3] Mr. Clark made specific devises of seven thousand and forty acres of Kentucky lands and twenty-four slaves to members of his family. Jonathan and George Rogers were named amongst the executors of the will; but Jonathan, who already had large means, was left nothing, while George Rogers — evidently because anything given him was liable to be seized to pay the state's debts — was only left two slaves, a man and a woman. William received virtually all the rest of the estate, including the personalty and lands north of the Ohio, as well as the home farm, 'Mulberry Hill.' General Clark for a time continued to live there, but William was often called away

---

[1] *Jefferson Papers*, 5th Series, I. (Library of Congress.)

[2] Roosevelt, after strangely asserting that Clark wrote the Memoir 'some thirty or forty years after the events of which it speaks' (in other words, between 1809, when Clark was paralyzed, and 1819, when he was dead!), says: 'The Memoir [was] written by an old man who had squandered his energies and sunk into deserved obscurity'! (*Winning of the West*, II, 176, 198.) Careful investigation, it is believed, will show that in every instance where this brilliant but reckless writer criticizes the *Memoir* he was wrong.

Of Dr. Brown, the accomplished naturalist Michaux wrote in his Journal: 'During my stay at Lexington I fre-

quently saw Dr. Samuel Brown from Virginia, a physician of the College of Edinburgh, a member of the Philosophical Society to whom members of that society had given me letters of recommendation. A merited reputation undeniably places Dr. S. Brown in the first rank of physicians settled in that part of the country; receiving regularly the scientific journals from London he is always in the channel of new discoveries and turns them to the advantage of his fellow citizens.' (Thwaites' *Early Western Travels*, III, 205.)

[3] Jefferson County, Kentucky, Clerk's Office; English's *Conquest of the Northwest*, 46.

for long periods, for he was now twenty-nine years of age and, like all his brothers, a soldier.[1]

With both his parents gone, William so much absent, and his sisters all married and living elsewhere, General Clark's life at Mulberry Hill, with only negro servants about him and occasional visitors, must have been a very lonely one. He found a much needed occupation, however, in performing his duties as president of the Board of Commissioners which had been created after the Revolution to distribute amongst the soldiers of his 'Illinois Regiment' a body of land which the state had granted. The land lay on the north side of the Ohio opposite the Falls, and was commonly called 'The Illinois Regiment Grant,' and sometimes 'Clark's Grant.' A brief notice of its history may be found interesting.

It will be remembered that as the success of Clark's expedition against Kaskaskia depended on its secrecy, Governor Henry dared not ask the Assembly to pass an act to pay the volunteers on the expedition. They would naturally expect some reward, however, and therefore the governor's advisors, Mason, Jefferson, and Wythe, gave Clark their written statement that 'each volunteer entering as a...common soldier in this expedition should be allowed three hundred acres of land, & the officers in the usual proportion, out of the land which may be conquered in the country now in possession of [the enemy.]'[2] The Virginia government repeatedly recognized its obligation to make this assurance good.[3] In January, 1781, the Assembly passed an act reciting that 'Colonel George Rogers Clark planned and executed the secret expedition by which the British posts were reduced, and was promised, if the enterprise succeeded, a liberal gratuity in lands in that country for the officers and soldiers *who first marched thither*.'[4] The promise had been much more definite, and was for *three hundred acres* for each common soldier and for officers in the

---

[1] Ten years before, in 1789, when only nineteen, William took part in Hardin's expedition against the northwestern Indians, the next year went on a mission to the Creeks and Cherokees, in 1791 was lieutenant in the expeditions of Generals Scott and Wilkinson, and two years later was serving as a captain with General Wayne. (*William Clark's Journal, Missouri Historical Society Collection*, St. Louis.)

[2] *Ante*, page 45, n. 3; English's *Conquest of the Northwest*, 102–03 (facsimile).

[3] Virginia State Library, *Journal House of Delegates for 1780* (July 8), 80; *id. for 1781* (Dec. 11), 35; *id. for 1783* (May 21), 15.

[4] Hening's *Statutes*, x, 565; xi, 10–26; Dillon's *Indiana*, 180. Author's italics.

usual proportion. The assembly act gave them no such quantity, but only provided that 'a quantity of land, not exceeding one hundred and fifty thousand acres, be allowed and granted to the said officers and soldiers *and the other officers and soldiers that have since been incorporated into the said regiment*, to be laid off in one tract...in such place on the northwest side of the Ohio as the majority of the officers shall choose.'[1] 'The officers and soldiers who first marched thither,' in 1778, were thus required to share the granted lands with all others who joined the regiment afterward, *at any time during five later years of war*. The result of this long division was that instead of receiving *three hundred acres* promised to the common soldier, he was allowed only *one hundred and eight;* and the officers' shares were diminished in the same proportion. In effect, the state paid its new troops with nearly two thirds of the lands it had promised to 'those who first marched.' Even this reduced allowance, however, was long but a hope deferred. The unpaid soldiers of the Illinois Regiment were yet to wait years before any of them got an acre of the promised lands.

In 1783 the Virginia Assembly essayed to redeem the state's promise to them without waiting longer. It passed an act appointing General Clark, and nine others, a board of commissioners, and directing them to locate and survey the land, lay off one thousand acres for a town opposite the Falls, and allot the rest amongst the officers and soldiers. He was chosen president of the board, the records of which are preserved and show a great amount of business transacted, much of it judicial.[2] The town was laid off by the Falls, extending to navigable water above and below them, and was called Clarksville. Peace with Great Britain being assured, a rapid development of the western country was confidently expected, and it was generally thought that the town would soon be a thriving city. In that case the town lots and outlying lands would prove valuable and relieve the unpaid soldiers from want.

The law creating the board made the commissioners trustees of the land and required them to survey it before a given

---

[1] Hening's *Statutes*, x, 565; xi, 10–26; Dillon's *Indiana*, 180. Author's italics.

[2] Jefferson County (Kentucky) Court Clerk's Office; R. C. Ballard Thruston's *MSS.*, photostat copy.

day, and thereafter, 'as soon as may be,' to allot it amongst the claimants.[1] In obedience to the act, the trustees proceeded with the survey, little suspecting they could be censured for doing exactly what the law commanded. Had they failed to make the surveys promptly they would have wronged the claimants and become personally liable for any ensuing damages.

Congress finally, on March 1, 1784, accepted Virginia's deed of cession to the Northwest territory with all its conditions — amongst them the reservation of the one hundred and fifty thousand acres for Clark and his soldiers. Many eastern men and syndicates were looking for profitable land grants in the ceded territory and hoped there would be no Indian war to impair land values there. Almost immediately after Virginia's cession, a Pennsylvania officer, seeking to better his fortunes, went west on a tour of inspection, spent two months at the Falls, and determined to settle there. He wrote to the president of Congress: 'The gentlemen who rec'd the Illinois grants of 150,000 acres opposite Louisville, on the west of Ohio, have already laid off a town in that district, which is settling fast & this will probably give rise to an immediate Quarrel,' meaning a war with the Indians.[2] The president promptly sent a copy of this letter to Governor Harrison, and it elicited a reply which, for the governor's reputation, had better never have been written. After expressing his own objection to the survey as being likely to provoke an Indian war, Governor Harrison said he was embarrassed 'to find a mode that can be carried into effect to stop the evil complained of, as we have positive acts of Assembly to contend with, which put it into the power of Clark and his officers... to survey lands on both sides of the Ohio that never have been ceded or purchased from the Indians. That their proceeding to survey immediately would bring about a war, I never doubted, and [I] communicated my sentiments to the Assembly on the subject... which had no other effect that I

---

[1] Hening's *Statutes*, x, *supra*. The act provided that the officers and soldiers entitled to a share of the lands should present their claims 'on or before the first day of April' ensuing (1784) and 'that from and after the said first day of April ...the commission or a majority of them should proceed with the surveyor to lay off the said lands and divide the same by fair and equal lot among the claimaints, ...and as soon as may be, ...upon application, execute good and sufficient deeds for conveying the several portions of land to the said officers and soldiers.'

[2] Library of Congress, *Papers Continental Congress*, no. 56, 113–15.

know of but hastening the act & resolutions. You may rest assured that everything will be done by me, that my cramped situation will admit of, to stop Clark's progress; but I am pretty confident he will turn a deaf ear to my orders, as he has the sanction of a much higher power for going on with his work & perhaps may have some secret motives for wishing to bring about what you & I think will be so extremely prejudicial to this state in particular & to America in general.'[1] Here was the man who for eight years had devoted himself and his estate and risked his life to protect Virginia's people from the Indians, being virtually charged by Governor Harrison with the unspeakable baseness of seeking, for personal and selfish aims, to bring upon those people the horrors of savage war.

In truth the survey neither did, nor was likely to, provoke war. The territory embraced by it (a little over twelve miles square) was never claimed by any hostile Indians, but was within the undisputed country of the one tribe which had always remained friendly to us, the Piankeshaws. Furthermore, that tribe had long before voluntarily conveyed to General Clark some seven and one half miles square of it, including the town site, which grant he only took in trust for the state of Virginia.[2] They probably neither knew nor cared that the survey was to cover twelve miles square instead of the seven and one half they had already conveyed; for either area made but a negligible part of the millions of acres within their country. Had it been deemed necessary to get a grant of the rest of the land it could probably have been had for the asking, or for a trifle in trinkets and rum.

Soon after his unworthy insinuation, Governor Harrison wrote General Clark himself, complaining of the survey and 'building & settling the town of Clarksville.' He said: 'You must excuse me for saying that there is a degree of cruelty in the proceedings to your Country which was never expected from General Clark, as he must well know it would involve us in a most bloody and expensive war, which we are at this time not in any degree able to support.[3] Soon after this the governor secured from the assembly power to suspend the survey Act and did suspend it.[4] Again the unpaid soldiers of the

[1] Virginia State Library, *Governor's Letter Book*, 374–75.
[2] *Illinois Historical Collections*, VIII, 151–53.

[3] *Draper MSS.* 53 J 14.
[4] Although the legislative act plainly required the survey to be made promptly, and fixed the time for it, Governor Harri-

Illinois Regiment were kept out of their promised land. Many of them, losing hope of ever getting any of it, sold their claims for trifling sums to speculators.

Three more years passed, when the act suspending the survey was rescinded and the commission resumed its work of surveying and allotting the lands.[1] As president, General Clark directed its work for over fifteen years. The town of Clarksville was laid out, numberless claims to lots and outlying tracts were adjudicated — some few of them presented by original volunteers, many more by later-enlisting men, many by heirs of those who had died, but far the greater number by speculators in the claims.

About 1803 General Clark removed to Clarksville and became a citizen of the Northwest Territory. No doubt he did this mainly because his duties so often called him to the north side of the river, and perhaps partly because the old home at Mulberry Hill had become so lonely. He selected for his new home a point of land jutting into the Ohio beside the Falls, and there built himself a small log house and continued to live for some years with three black servants, Kitt, Cupid, and Venus. Josiah Espy visited the place in 1805 and in his Journal described it thus:

'At the lower end of the falls is the deserted village of Clarksburgh [Clarksville] in which General Clark himself resides. I had the pleasure of seeing this celebrated warrior at his lonely cottage seated

son adds a labored argument to show General Clark that 'the legislature never meant that the lands should be possessed, or entered on, till Congress should have obtained them from the Indians, either by treaty or purchase.' He should have known that the located Illinois Grant was not within the treaty-making power of Congress. It had been expressly reserved in the cession of the Northwest Territory, and Virginia for many years afterward exercised jurisdiction over it.

In his *Winning of the West*, IV, 48, Roosevelt grossly misinterprets the significance of Harrison's letter and makes General Clark, in the performance of his duties under the law, appear as a buccaneer robbing the Indians of their lands! He says: 'While the Federal Government sincerely desired peace — the northwestern tribes were resolutely bent on war; and the frontiersmen themselves showed nearly as much inclination to hostilities

as the Indians. They were equally anxious to intrude on the Government and on the Indian lands, for they were adventurous, the lands were valuable and they hated the Indians and looked down on the weak Federal authority. They often made what were legally worthless "tomahawk claims." ... Even the men of note, men like George Rogers Clark, were often engaged in schemes to encroach on the land north of the Ohio; drawing on themselves the bitter reproaches not only of the Federal authorities, but also of the Virginia Government, for their cruel readiness to jeopardize the country by incurring the wrath of the Indians.' In support of this he cites the letter of Harrison to Clark. Blundering could hardly be more reckless!

[1] Governor Randolph's Proclamation, Jan. 25, 1787, Hening's *Virginia Statutes*, XI, 447.

on Clark's Point. This point is situated at the upper end of the falls, particularly the lower rapid, commanding a full and delightful view of the falls, particularly the zigzag channel which is only navigated at [high] water. The general has not taken much pains to improve this commanding and beautiful spot, having only raised a small cabin, but it is capable of being made one of the handsomest seats in the world.

'General Clark has now become frail and rather helpless, but there are the remains of great dignity and manliness in his countenance, person, and deportment, and I was struck, on seeing him, with perhaps a fancied likness to the great and immortal Washington.'[1]

At this place General Clark was in full view of the rapids over which he had carried his men on their way to take Kaskaskia, of Corn Island where they had embarked, and of the town of Louisville — now a great city — which he had founded on the Kentucky shore. Here he spent the few years remaining before he became totally disabled.[2]

By the first years of the nineteenth century nearly all the Clark family had migrated to Kentucky. Captain Edmund Clark, who never married, settled by the Ohio a considerable distance below the Falls. In 1802 Jonathan (who had been made a major-general by Virginia) also moved west and made his home on a fine tract of land called 'Trough Spring,' lying just east of Mulberry Hill.[3]

For years before he came to Kentucky he had made repeated efforts to get the Virginia Assembly to settle the state's account with George Rogers, and relieve him from her debts. Year after year he went to Richmond and attended the Assembly sessions on this business, but all in vain. In the west, also, the youngest of the brothers, William, labored hard to rid General Clark of law suits and those debts. In 1797, seven years before going on his expedition to the Pacific, he wrote Jonathan: 'Our bro G's business is in a disagreeable sitution three or four heavy suits pending, one with Mr. [Humphrey] Marshall for the first payment of the land at Tenn[essee], one

---

[1] *Ohio Valley Historical Series, Miscellaneous,* 14 *et seq.* (R. Clarke & Co., Cincinnati, Ohio, 1871.) A number of others were struck by Clark's resemblance to Washington — perhaps impressed more by their similiar size and dignified bearing than likeness of features.

[2] On Silver Creek, near his home, General Clark erected a stone grist mill and is said to have operated it so long as he lived at Clarksville. The writer saw the remains of it in 1862.

[3] 'The finest inland seat in Kentucky without exception,' wrote George Rogers to Jonathan, when arranging to purchase it. (*Author's MSS.*)

of 8000£ with Shannon's heirs in this country, one for 24000 against him in the Illinois brought by a Spaniard [Bazadone] for something about the taking of a Boat at the time the Militia was there under him. I have been, agreeable to his request, surveying his lands and doing what part of his business I could, which I found in a very unfinished situation.'[1] Later he said: 'I have rode for Bro Geo in the course of this past year upwards of 3000 miles, continually on the pad, attempting to save him and have been serviceable in several instances; got Spanish suit dismissed — secured his property on that side of Ohio.'[2]

[1] *Draper MSS. 2 L 45.*

[2] (*Draper MSS. 2 L 46; id., 1 C 11.*) Years later he sent a copy of General Clark's account for only three items of his claim against the state — namely (1) officer's pay, $10,080; (2) the flour purchase, $4375, and (3) payment of Shannon's bill and interest, $6138.07, making in all $20,593.07 — and said: 'You will perceive, by this account which was rejected in 1790 or /91 Gen. G. R. Clark had paid in specie $7336 and an interest of $3177, which compelled him to sacrifice all his negroes, his pay for 5 years and the greater part of the lands he had acquired by his exertions and for his services; and for which advances of $10513 in specie he received in depreciated certificates $535 77/100, leaving a balance which he should have received in justice of $9977 25/100 in specie in 1790. This loss blasted all his hopes, as he had individual debts which he had no active means to pay.' (*Draper MSS. 10 J 174a–175.*) Besides these claims were the many and far greater supply bills on which he was bound as endorser for the state and was being sued by the holders — usually speculators. In one case he was imprisoned (for imprisonment for debts was then common), but on some legal ground was released. (*Order Book, Kentucky General Court,* 309. *Kentucky State Historical Society Collections,* Frankfort, Ky.)

CHAPTER XXXIII

LAST DAYS

WHEN Napoleon acquired Louisiana from Spain, President Jefferson and his cabinet, fearing trouble with the rapacious despot, planned to fortify the mouth of the Ohio. The plan was not carried out, but the Secretary of War wrote Captain William Clark for information concerning the best site for a fort. The letter was turned over to General Clark, who wrote Jefferson giving his observations of the lands about the mouth of the Ohio in 1780 when he was selecting a site for Fort Jefferson, and concluded his letter thus:

'I suggest to you Sir, if worthy your attention, any farther information, and the best perhaps that can be obtained of that Country, may be got from my brother William, who is now Settled at Clarksville in the Indian Territory. I have long since laid aside all Idea of Public affairs. By bad fortune, and ill health I have become incapable of persuing those enterpriseing & active pursuits which I have been fond of from my youth — but I will with the greatest pleasure give my bro William every information in my power on those or any other points which may be of Service to your Administration. He is well qualified almost for any business — If it should be in your power to Confer on him any post of Honor and profit, in this Country in which we live, it will exceedingly gratify me — I seem to have a right to expect such a gratification when asked for, but what will greatly heighten it is that I am sure it gives you pleasure to have it in your power to do me a Service.'[1]

Jefferson complied handsomely with this request by appointing Captain William Clark, jointly with Captain Meriwether Lewis, to lead the famous Lewis and Clark Expedition to the Pacific shortly after the purchase of Louisiana. Lewis had served under Captain Clark in Wayne's campaign and afterwards was Jefferson's private secretary. In this connection it is interesting to recall Jefferson's letter to General Clark in 1783 suggesting that he lead such an expedition. At that early time few thought of that vast western region becoming part of the United States, or the danger of its becoming British. It is interesting also to note the similarity of the

[1] *Draper MSS.* 11 C 27.

method of exploration adopted in the Lewis and Clark Expedition and that which General Clark had recommended to Jefferson twenty years earlier.

On October 8, 1803, Captains Lewis and Clark with their little party started down the Ohio from Clarksville on their way to the Pacific, embarking a short distance below General Clark's home. His brother Jonathan's diary for that day says: 'At Clarksville, Capt Lewis and Captain Clark set off on a Western Tour. Went in their boat to Mr Temple's' — the farm of his son-in-law, the Reverend Benjamin Temple.

Nineteen years earlier, William had been brought as a lad of fourteen to Mulberry Hill. From that time General Clark had been his closest companion, sharing with him many interests of many kinds. No doubt the younger brother gained, from the rare experience and judgment of the elder, much that qualified him for his after life — not only as a soldier and explorer, but as Superintendent of Indian Affairs in the newly acquired region west of the Mississippi, and later as governor of Missouri Territory. One may imagine the feelings of the old warrior as he waved him farewell and, after the departing boat was lost to sight, turned back to his lonely home. How vividly·he must have recalled the time when he too, flushed with the confident enthusiasm of youth, had gone down the same river for glorious service; but the laurels he then won had since turned to thorns.

Ten days after this, he sent to his friend, United States Senator John Breckenridge, a petition praying Congress for a grant of land somewhere in the Northwest Territory to relieve him of the state debts, which the United States had assumed.[1] In writing Breckenridge he said:

[1] His petition prayed for land equal in quantity to the tract the Piankeshaws had conveyed to him in 1779, but to which he had always disclaimed title. The petition, after setting forth the history of the Indian grant, said: 'My reason for not soliciting Congress before this, was the great Number of petitions before them, and the prospect I yet had of a future support; [meaning by Virginia's payment of his claims] but those prospects are vanished. I engaged in the Revolution with all the Ardour that Youth could possess. My Zeal and Ambition rose with my success, determined to save those frontiers which had been the seat of my toil, at the hazard of my life and fortune. At the most gloomy period of the War, when a Ration could not be purchased on Public Credit, I risked my own, gave my Bonds, Mortgaged my lands for supplies, paid strict attention to every department, flattered the friendly and confused the hostile tribes of Indians by my emissaries — baffled my internal enemies (the most dangerous of the whole to Public Interest) and carried my point. Thus at the end of the War I had the pleasure of seeing my Country secure, but with the loss of my Manual activity, and a prospect of future indigence — demands of very great amount were not

'Although the quantity called for is considerable, it will not more than compensate me for the losses I have actually sustained by my involving myself so imprudently in the publick expenses which I doubt, without assistance, I never shall get clear of. But a country was at stake, and if it was imprudence, I suppose I would do the same again, should I again have a similar field to pass through.'[1]

Considering the return his services and sacrifices had received, it would be hard to find a nobler expression of patriotism than this in the annals of America.

The treatment his petition met from Congress should make Americans blush. Although the debts he prayed to be relieved from were debts of the United States — and Congress never denied the obligation — yet on various pretexts it evaded paying them.[2] His petition was rejected; he was denied so much as an acre in the vast territory he had won for the United States. Had his prayer been granted, the Federal Government would have given him — not as a gift, but in payment of the debt it owed him — less than one five-thousandth part of the land it had acquired through his services.

This was General Clark's last effort to get relief from the state debts. Henceforth his time was largely devoted to running a small mill which he had erected near his home, and in superintending the varied business of the Illinois Regiment Grant.

paid, others with depreciated Paper — Suits commenced against me for those sums in Specie — My Military and other lands, earned by my service, as far as they would extend were appropriated for the payment of those debts, and demands yet remaining to a considerable amount more than the remains of a shattered fortune will pay. This is truly my situation — I see no other resorce remaining but to make application to my Country for redress — hoping that they will so far ratify the Grant as to allow to your Memorialist an equal quantity of land now the property of the United States, or such other relief as may seem proper.' (Library of Congress, *American State Papers, Public Lands*, I, 274; *Draper MSS.* 54 J 50.)

[1] *Draper MSS.* 54 J 49.

[2] Because the petition told of the Piankeshaw conveyance to him of the tract of land at the Falls, the committee to which the petition was referred affected to understand that he was claiming title to that particular tract and was asking the United States to confirm his title to it. The committee must have known that he made no such claim or request. The United States did not own that land, for Virginia had reserved her right to grant it to the Illinois Regiment soldiers and had done so with General Clark's recorded consent. His petition clearly disclaimed title to that tract, and only prayed '*an equal quantity* of land, now the property of the United States, or such *other* relief as may seem proper.' The committee's report — evidently written by a pettifogger — ignored all this; and, after arguing at length to show that he had no title to the land conveyed by the Piankeshaws, said: 'The committee therefore, on this ground alone, independent of any arguments drawn from the policy of practise of the general government, have no hesitation in giving it as their opinion that the prayer of the petitioner ought not to be granted.'

On November 5, 1806, there was great rejoicing in the little towns at the Falls, for on that day, as an entry in Jonathan Clark's diary said: 'Captains Lewis and Clark arrived at the Falls on their return from the Pacific Ocean after an absence of a little more than three years.' They had encountered great difficulties and dangers, but had succeeded completely in their extraordinary undertaking. To no one else, perhaps, did their safe return and glorious achievement mean so much as to General Clark; for he both loved and was proud of his young brother, and knew the risks he had run. Many an hour during those three long years he must have endeavored to calculate the progress of the expedition, hoping and fearing; and now to his great relief and joy the young explorer was back safe, with an imperishable record of skill and endurance.

The following year Jefferson, then entering his seventh year as president, wrote the General the following gratifying letter:

WASHINGTON, *Dec* 19, '07

Dear General:

As I think it probable your brother will have left you before the enclosed comes to hand, I have left it open and request you to read it and do for me what it asks of him and what he will do should he be still with you — that is to say to have the bones packed and forwarded for me to William Brown Collector at New Orleans who will send them on to me.

I avail myself of this occasion of recalling myself to your memory & of assuring you that time has not lessened my friendship for you. We are both now grown old, you have been enjoying in retirement the recollection of the services you have rendered your country and I am about to retire without an equal consciousness that I have not occupied places in which others could have done more good; but in all places & times I shall wish you every happiness and salute you with great friendship and esteem.

TH JEFFERSON

Genl George Rogers Clark.[1]

The next two years, 1808–09, proved eventful ones in General Clark's life. He was gradually growing frail with advancing years, but was still active enough for fowling, although unequal to the more strenuous sport of deer-hunting.[2] He read much. In July, 1808, his request of his nephew George Gwathmey to send him some books brought the following reply: 'I have

---

[1] English's *Conquest of the Northwest,* 57 (facsimile).   [2] Edmund Clark's letter, May, 1808, *Author's MSS.*

sent you the life of Fred^k the 2nd, but I suppose you have Read them. We have no Other Books that will Suit you as you are not fond of [MS unintelligible]. I will try and get some for you — perhaps I will be down this afternoon.'[1] About this time Clark was visited by Audubon, who was then engaged in bird study in the western country. As the General had been a life-long and close observer of wild life, and could not only share the ornithologist's interest in birds, but give him much information about many of them, their talks could not fail to give mutual pleasure. In his notes Audubon refers to Clark as authority; but unfortunately most of them concerning the period when he resided at the Falls were destroyed.[2]

The members of General Clark's family realized his failing health and regretted his living alone at Clark's Point with only negro servants. During the summer of 1808 he went with his brother Jonathan for a stay of some weeks at the mineral springs near Jeffersonville. Soon afterward his brother-in-law, Mr. Gwathmey, wrote him this letter:

Sept 16, 1808

Dear Genl
I really intended this day to have been at your house, but I have been in constant pain for Six or Eight days past with Boils and have three at this time tormenting me. When I saw you at the Springs the other day, you told me you were busily engaged in finishing your house. That is well enough, but I sh^d feel better satisfied if you would come & spend the Winter with me. Every thing that is in my power to make your situation comfortable shall be done & think you had better come.

Y^{rs} with Esteem
OWEN GWATHMEY[3]

If convenient you'l please send the Gun by Isaac.

This invitation, however, General Clark declined, preferring to remain at Clark's Point, where he was interested in building an addition to his house. October 15, 1808, he wrote his last extant letter, a short one, to one of his nephews.[4] Early

---

[1] *Draper MSS.* 55 J 63.

[2] Audubon and his young wife were several times guests of General Jonathan Clark at Trough Spring, and once she remained there while her husband was away so long on one of his bird-hunting trips that it was feared he was lost. The author knew Mrs. Audubon — a beautiful, sweet-mannered, white-haired old lady — and well remembers, one occa-

sion when she was visiting his mother, her smiling and saying: 'Ellen, I do think no wife ever had so many causes of jealousy, for every bird was my rival.'

[3] *Draper MSS.* 55 J 63.

[4]   1808 Oct 15
Jn Clark Esqr
     Merchant Louisville
Pr Kitt
DEAR SIR — The finishing my house hath

the next year, while he was in his room with his nephew, Dr. John Croghan, he was stricken with paralysis of his right side. The stroke does not seem to have been a very severe one, although it impaired the use of his right limbs; and such was the original vigor of his constitution, that he steadily improved. Members of his family became more solicitous about him, however, and soon another affliction compelled him to go to Louisville, where he remained for some time with Mr. Gwathmey. An infection of his right foot and leg alarmed his physician, who called two surgeons into consultation, and they agreed that to save the General's life the leg should be amputated about the middle of the thigh.[1]

Antiseptics and nearly all modern surgical appliances for such an operation being then unknown, a fatal result was not unexpected. Excruciating pain was of course inevitable, for anæsthetics also were then unknown. While the surgeon's knife cut round to the bone, his saw severed it, and a red-hot iron seared the bared flesh and bleeding arteries, the patient had only to bear the pain. To do so without flinching, Clark sent for a drummer and fifer; and, during the two hours of the operation, stirring strains of martial music, such as he and his men had heard when he led them through the deep waters against Hamilton, steeled him to endure the torture. Tradition says one of the musicians was his 'antic drummer boy' of the Wabash. General Clark's namesake, young George Rogers Clark Sullivan, thus described the occasion in a letter written a few weeks later: 'Your Uncle George is with us and in high spirits and the wound healed up. I have stayed with him every night since he has been in town, that is about 5 weeks. I never new a man in my life to stand it so well as he did the day it was taken off. he sent for the drummer and fifer to come and play. Floyd then took the hint and had all the men placed around the house with two drums and two fifers and played for about two hours and his leg was taken off in the mean time. In the evening they returned and played for about an hour,

been more expensive than I expected. I yet owe the hands some money. I am at present run short. If you could conveniently lend me about fifty dollars for the purpose of paying the hands alluded to you will do me a favour. I can return you the money by New Year.

I am Yours Affectionately
G R CLARK

P.S. If you can honour this note send it by Kitt.

(*Author's MSS.*)

[1] Dr. Galt was the physician, Drs. Ferguson and Collins the surgeons. Their bills are given in *Draper MSS.* 55 J 66.

and then ten at night four elegant violins two drums two fifes marched around the house for about an hour playing elegant marches.'.[1]

Soon after this letter was written, General Clark was removed to Locust Grove, the country residence of Major Croghan. Here, with every kind attention, he lived the nine remaining years of his life. During the first part of this period, although writing with difficulty and needing crutches to walk, he was by no means so helpless as one might suppose. He was provided with a carriage for riding to town, and had a wheel chair in which he moved about the first floor of the house; for his paralysis probably made it difficult to use his crutches. Three times during the year that his leg was taken off, the record books of the Illinois Grant Commissioners show him still attending their occasional meetings and signing their minutes as president. His last signature was on March 14, 1810, and was evidently written with difficulty by his paralyzed right hand; but he continued to attend the meetings for several years afterward.[2] In 1811 he was greatly shocked to learn of the sudden death of his brother Jonathan, the playmate of his childhood, and a most devoted brother. When told of it he said: 'It was hard that he, who wanted to live, should die, while I, who wanted to die, should live.'[3]

Of the many true friends General Clark had made amongst the Creoles in the Illinois towns and Vincennes, none was more loyal to him, or the American cause, or was a worthier man, than Francis Vigo. The following beautiful tribute to his character by General William Henry Harrison was given in support of a petition to Congress for Vigo's reimbursement for losses incurred by him for Virginia:

'I have been acquainted with Colo. Francis Vigo of Vincennes for thirty nine years, and during the thirteen years that I was the Governor of Indiana, I lived in the same town with him, and upon terms of the most intimate friendship. I have often heard him speak of the draft which had been given him by General Clark for supplies furnished to the army, and that it had never been paid. . . . With respect to the credibility of Colo. Vigo's statement, I solemnly declare, that I believe him utterly incapable of making a misrepresentation of the facts, however great may be his interest in the matter, and I am also

[1] *Draper MSS.* 12 C 1.
[2] The minutes are in the office of the Jefferson County (Kentucky) Clerk. A facsimile of this signature is given by

English in his *Conquest of the Northwest,* 858.
[3] *Draper MSS.*

confident that there are more respectable persons in Indiana who would become the guarantees of his integrity, than could be induced to lay under a similar responsibility for any other person. His whole life, as long as his circumstances were prosperous, was spent in acts of kindness and benevolence to Individuals, and his public spirit and attachment to the Institutions of our Country proverbial.'[1]

M. Vigo, having learned of General Clark's misfortune, sent him this touching letter:

VINCENNES *July* 15, 1811

Sir:
Permit an old man who has witnessed your exertions in behalf of your country in its revolutionary strugles to address you at the present moment. When viewing the events which have succeeded those important times, I often thought that I had reasons to lament that the meritorious services of the best patriots of those days were too easily forgotten & almost taxed my adopted Country with ingratitude. But when I saw that on a late occasion, on the fourth of July last, the Citizens of Jefferson County and vicinity, from a spontaneous impulse of gratitude and esteem had paid an unfeigned tribute to the Veteran to whose skill and valor America and Kentucky owe so much, I then repelled the unwelcome idea of national ingratitude and my sentiments chimed in unison with those of the worthy Citizens of Kentucky towards the saviour of this once distressed Country. Deprived of the pleasure of a personal attendance on that day, I took this method of manifesting to you, Sir that I participated in the general sentiments.
Please Sir to accept this plain but genuine offering from a man whom you honoured once with your friendship, and who will never cease to put up prayers to heaven that the evening of your days may be serene and happy.
I have the honour to be Sir Your most obed Sert

VIGO[2]

To this letter General Clark dictated the following reply:

LOCUST GROVE, NEAR LOUISVILLE, *August* 1, 1811

Dear Sir:
A letter from a man who has always occupied a distinguished place in my affection and esteem must insure the warmest and most cordial reception — an affection, the result not so much of being associates in the placid stream of tranquillity and the benign sunshine of peace, as companions amidst the din of war and those struggles when the indefatigable exertion of every muscle and nerve was demanded.

---

[1] Dec. 22, 1834. Virginia State Library, *Box 'Special'*; *'Illinois Papers 1833–5,' Commissioners' Report*, x, 95.

[2] *Draper MSS. 55 J 77.*

But may it be enough to remark that while the one is the effect of your uniformly discreet and irreproachable conduct in the intricate path of civil and domestic life, the other is wrought by a strong sense of that gratitude due from your adopted country, having myself both witnessed and experienced the signal advantages flowing to our common country from your inestimable conduct, and what is more enhancing to such services, having rendered them at a time when the cloud on which our fate hung assumed the most menacing aspect.

When I contemplate the glowing affection with which your letter is fraught, and only the revival of such you in past times, (ah! better times, troublous as they were) were wont to evince for me, I am so filled with correspondent feelings that I am at a loss for words to express them. How happy would I be could those sentiments of entreaty to a trustful Providence, in the conclusive part of your letter, for a serene and happy evening be realized. But that, Providence (submitting as I do with manly patience to his decrees) has long since denied me that boon. He has cut asunder the life's tenderest string.

With sentiments of the warmest regard, I remain,

G. R. CLARK[1]

By those words — 'Providence...has cut asunder the life's tenderest string' — General Clark doubtless referred to the long hidden tragedy in his life — the breaking off of his betrothal with the beautiful Terese de Leyba. That they were engaged, and that, when he found himself financially ruined, he told her he could not marry her, has not only always been a family tradition, but one which appears to be supported by the statements of several trustworthy contemporaries, and by what he himself told one of them. Six months after the capture of Vincennes, John Todd, evidently knowing of Clark's tender regard for her, though apparently not of their betrothal, wrote him a newsy letter from the Illinois, saying: 'Madam'le Terese is still a maid.'[2] No correspondence between her and Clark has been discovered, and it is not known when, or in what manner, he informed her that their marriage was impossible. Her brother having died about a month after the British and Indian attacks on Cahokia and St. Louis, she shortly afterward, according to a note of Draper, returned to New Orleans, where she had friends, but no relatives, and

[1] Virginia State Library, *Illinois Papers* (*Vigo MSS.*), x, 102; English's *Conquest of the Northwest*, 785–86. The letter shows Clark's peculiar style of composition in some parts, but in others a departure from it by the amanuensis.

[2] *Illinois Historical Collections*, v, 128.

thence sailed to Spain, entered a convent there, took the nun's veil, and died in 1821.[1]

General Clark's helpless condition soon became known in the east. In the Virginia Assembly was one young member who appreciated the mistreated old soldier's services to his state and determined to urge a belated recognition of them. This was Charles Fenton Mercer, then entering upon a distinguished career as soldier and statesman.[2] He introduced in the Assembly, and succeeded in having adopted, the following act:

'Whereas, the General Assembly of Virginia have ever entertained the highest respect for the unsullied integrity, the valor, the military enterprise, and skill of General George Rogers Clarke, to whom, and to his gallant regiment, (aided by the justice of their cause, and the favour of Heaven), the state of Virginia was indebted for the extension of her boundaries from the Atlantic to the Mississippi; and whereas the General Assembly have been informed that the hand of misfortune has overtaken this veteran chief; and that he, whose name was once a host, filling his friends with confidence, and his foes with dismay, is now, himself, a victim of age and disease, and a dependent on the bounty of his relatives.

'1. *Be it therefore enacted*, That the Governor of this Commonwealth shall be, and is hereby, authorized and requested to have manufactured, at the Armory of this State, a sword, with Suitable devices engraved thereon; and to cause the same to be presented to General George Rogers Clarke, accompanied with an expression of

---

[1] *Draper MSS.* 7 J 109. Clark's niece, Diana Gwathmey — herself locally noted for loveliness of person and character — said in reply to an inquiry from Mr. Draper: 'I learned from Gen. Clark's mother all I ever knew about his love affair. I was quite young, only fifteen at the time, and I have no doubt that Uncle Wm. Clark's memorandum about the relationship of the lady to the Spanish Gov[ernor] is correct. I was with Gen. Clark a great deal until I was twenty years of age when I was married; I never heard him allude to the lady or the affair except when he was intoxicated. He would then frequently say to me that if he had been properly treated I would have had an elegant aunt whom I would have loved very much. His reflections about her appeared to distress him very much; I have often seen him shed tears when he would make the above remark to me. He never mentioned her name, and indeed, the forgoing is the most he ever said to me on the subject.' (*Draper MSS.* 10 J 177.)

General Clark's first cousin, Mrs. Semple, the daughter of his aunt, Mrs. Donald Robertson, also wrote Mr. Draper: 'In the Spring of 1797 we removed to Ky. and came to my Uncle Clark's. Gen. Clark lived there at that time. He seemed to be fond of my society, and conversed with me often. He would point out to me his Battle Grounds, on the Maps, &c. Aunt [his mother] said she had heard that George had seen a Spanish Nun somewhere and fallen very deeply in love with her. Why he could not get her, or what became of her, she did not, or could not tell. She said that was the reason why he took no notice of Ladies, and was surprised to see him pay me so much attention.' (*Draper MSS.* 10 J 45. For interesting notices of Mrs. Semple and her mother, Rachel Clark Robertson, see Anderson's *Donald Robertson and Family,* Detroit, 1900, Winn & Hammond.)

[2] *Appleton's Cyclopædia of American Biography,* IV, 300.

the gratitude and friendly condolence of the General Assembly of Virginia.

'2. *And be it further enacted*, That General George Rogers Clarke shall be, and he is hereby, placed on the list of pensioners; and that he shall be entitled to receive annually from the public treasury, one half of the full pay which he received as Colonel of the Illinois Regiment; that is, immediately after the passage of this Act, the sum of four hundred dollars; and annually, thereafter, on the first day of January of every year, the sum of four hundred dollars, And the Auditor of Public Accounts is required to issue his warrants therefor, payable out of any money in the treasury.

'3. This act shall be in force from the passing thereof.'[1]

In the following letter to Major Croghan, Mercer tells how the passage of this act was procured:

RICHMOND *February* 21st 1812

Dear Sir:

The inclosed certified copy of a law which passed both branches of the Virginia legislature yesterday, I hasten to forward, thro' you, to General Clark. I can truly declare that no event in my life has given me more pleasure than I derived from being the instrument of Justice and Honor, in preparing, presenting, and urging the passage of the inclosed act. Whether I may be permitted to congratulate you and General Clark upon the success which attended my efforts, I know not; but, of this, I am persuaded, that had you been present, you would have approved of the course which I pursued, which sustained the honor and dignity of General Clark, while it interested the tenderness, the generosity, and the magnanimity of the General Assembly of Virginia. Our house was dissolved in tears: my voice was almost drowned in my own emotion. I told them the Story of the Sword, and urged as a reason why they should present to the gallant veteran another, that he had, with a haughty sense of wounded pride and feeling, broken and cast away that which this state formerly gave him. As I have not, therefore, in any respect departed from that course which the reputation of General Clark demanded of me, I hope the whole transaction of yesterday will afford to your illustrious friend the pleasure which it gave, not to me alone, but to more than two thirds of the Virginia legislature. For their credit, too, let it be remarked, that the bill not only passed into a law in one day, but that that day was expected to be the very last of the longest session which we have had since the foundation of the Commonwealth, and, consequently, when the members were very impatient to return to their respective homes, and regarded with very ill will, whatever might, in any degree, tend to protract their stay. It is due also to their motives to state that the sum of four hundred dollars was the only sum with which it was proposed to fill the blank in the engrossed bill, and in justification of myself to

[1] Virginia State Library, '*Acts passed at a General Assembly of Virginia, 1812,*' 140.

add that I supposed it to be about one half of a Colonel's full pay,
and that I knew it exceeded any annuity ever granted by the commonwealth for past services.

I write in great haste, that my letter may not be delaid and with it
the enclosed bill. Be pleased to present my most respectful compliments to General Clark and to Mrs Croghan, and your gallant son
if he is with you, and permit me to subscribe myself with my best
wishes for your happiness,

Your friend and very Hum^{ble} Servt,

CH^s FENTON MERCER [1]

After some months the new sword — the third which had
been ordered by the Virginia Assembly for General Clark —
and a copy of the act were sent to him with a handsome tribute
from Governor Barbour.[2] While the crippled old soldier sat in

---

[1] *Draper MSS 55 J 79.* In behalf of
General Clark Major Croghan thanked
Col. Mercer for his kind exertions as fol-
lows:

Near Louisville Kentucky
March 17th, 1812

DEAR SIR:

Your friendly letter of the 21st Ult
Inclosing the Act of assembly which you
was so Eminently Instrumental in Get-
ing passed which Gives Gen! Clark a
pension Came duly to hand, I immediately Communicated it to the General,
who will ever with Gratitude, Remember
your very Friendly attention to him. he
wishes me to Inform You that, had he it
in his power, he would Write to You and
endeavor to Express his Gratitude & feelings. — The Generals friends and Relations are, and have every Reason to Be
highly pleased at the very honorable
Manner You have Mention(ed) him in the
Law, and will at all times take pleasure
in acknowledgeing themselves Indebted
for your Exertions in procuring for the
General what he Deserved from the State,
but probably Never would have got had
he not been so happy as to Meet with a
friend in You who knew his present Situation and was well Informed of the Great
Services he has Rendered the U.S. — My
Son George whom You Mentioned in your
letter is now with me & Requests I will
offer his Compliments to You, — his Volunteer trip to the Wabash has gave him a
taste for the Military, so much so that he
has applyed for and is promised the Command of a Company.

W. CROGHAN

To
Charles Fenton Mercer.
(*Draper MSS.* 55 J 81.)

George Croghan mentioned in the
above letter, the next year won great
fame by his brilliant repulse, with a small
force, of the British General Proctor's
'500 regulars and 700 Indians' attacking
Fort Stephenson. A great monument
there now commemorates the event.

[2] Council Chamber, Richmond October 29, 1812.

SIR:

The ... general assembly, duly appre-
ciating the gallant achievements during
the Revolutionary War of yourself, and
the brave regiment under your command,
by which a vast extension of her empire
was affected, ... have assigned to me the
pleasure duty of announcing to you the
sentiments of exalted respect they cher-
ish for you, and the gratitude they feel
at the recollection of your unsullied integrity, valor, enterprise and skill. Having learned with sincere regret that you
have been doomed to drink the cup of
misfortune, they have requested me to
tender you their friendly condolence.
Permit me, sir, to mingle with the discharge of my official duty an expression
of my own feelings.

'The history of the Revolution has always engaged my deepest attention. I
have dwelt with rapture upon the distinguished part you acted in that great
drama, being always convinced that it
only wanted the adventitious aid of numbers to make it amongst the most splen-
did examples of skill and courage which
any age or country has produced. I feel a
conspicuous pride at the recollection that
the name Clark is compatriot with my
own. I, too, most sincerely sympathize
with you in your adverse fate, and deeply
deplore that the evening of your life,

his wheel-chair on the front piazza of the Croghan residence, overlooking the Ohio and the great country north of it which had been the field of his achievements, the governor's representative came to make a formal presentation address and deliver the new sword. What a scene for an artist! While the address was being made, General Clark sat silent. When it ended he received the sword, laid it across his lap and said: 'Young man, when Virginia needed a sword, I found her one. Now I need bread!'[1]

Several months after this dramatic episode, in February, 1813, he attended for the last time a meeting of the Board of Commissioners of the Illinois Regiment grant. Soon afterward a second stroke of paralysis not only destroyed his speech and the use of his limbs, but left him mentally wrecked. In this sad condition he lived five years longer. Weather permitting, he was wheeled every morning to the front piazza, where a great

whose morning was so brilliant, should be clouded with misfortune. The general assembly of Virginia have placed among their archives a monument of their gratitude for your services, and, as a small tribute of respect, have directed that a sword should be made in our manufactory, with devices emblematic of your actions, and have also directed that four hundred dollars should be immediately paid, as also an annual sum to the same amount. I lament exceedingly that any delay should have occurred in this communication. You will readily believe me when I assure you it arose from the tardiness of the mechanic employed in completing the sword. It is now finished and is sent herewith. I shall take pleasure in obeying your commands as to the transmission of the money to which you are entitled. You will have the goodness to acknowledge the receipt of this as soon as your convenience will permit. I am, sir, with sentiments of high respect,

Your obedient servant

JAMES BARBOUR

General George Rogers Clark
   Louisville, Kentucky

(Virginia State Library, 'Box Executive Communications, Nov. 30, 1812–May 26, 1813; English's Conquest of the Northwest. 880.)

[1] Various accounts of Clark's reply appear in print. Draper gives it thus: 'When Virginia needed a sword, I gave her one. She sends me now a toy: I want bread.' (English's Conquest of the Northwest, 874.) The language in the text was that given the author by his father, who had it from the maker of the presentation speech (Colonel Hancock, according to the writer's recollection) but probably the precise words of General Clark's reply have never been correctly given.

English in his Conquest of the Northwest discusses at great length the question of how many swords General Clark received and what became of them. The inscription appearing on the sword pictured on pages 405, 872, and 873 of his book certainly were never inscribed on the sword voted and sent to Colonel Clark in 1779, for the inscription reads: 'presented by the State of Virginia to her beloved son General George Rogers Clark' etc. He did not become a general until 1781 (Jefferson to Clark, Draper MSS. 51 J 18.) The inscription was evidently put on this sword long after Clark had received the one sent him by Lieut. Governor Page in September 1779. (Page to Clark, Draper MSS. 49 J 68.) If the pictured sword was ever ordered by the Virginia Assembly, or was ever seen by General Clark, the inscription gives no satisfactory evidence of it. The date inscribed on it — June 12, 1779 — was probably inserted as being the date of the passage of the Assembly resolution ordering it made. In fact, however, the resolution was passed June 14th, not 12th. (Virginia State Library, Journal House of Delegates, 48.)

part of his time was passed. His niece, Miss Gwathmey, went regularly every two weeks to see him, and afterward told of 'his stroking down her hair and attempts at speaking.'[1] In 1815 he made known his wish to make a will, and was so intent upon doing so that, to relieve his mind, one was drawn for him by his brother, William. It was formally executed, with a cross mark for the testator's signature; but the beneficiaries named in the will treated it as a nullity and declined to take anything under it.'[2]

Three more years passed and then, on February 13, 1818, while sitting in his wheel-chair on the piazza at Locust Grove, the worn-out old hero passed into the great beyond. A stroke of apoplexy had at last released him from his troubles. 'The death of General Clark,' said Governor English, 'cast a gloom over the whole community and steps were promptly taken at Louisville to honor his memory by general attendance and suitable ceremony at his funeral. The newspapers of the day paid glowing tributes to his merit.'[3] The members of the Louisville Bar in meeting resolved to attend the funeral in a body and 'wear crepe on the left arm for thirty days,' and appointed Judge Rowan 'to deliver a funeral oration at the place of interment.'[4] On the 18th — 'a very stormy, snowy day,' — funeral services were held in the Croghan house, and the remains carried thence to the family burying ground near by. There Judge Rowan, then famed as an orator, made a short funeral address of which only one sentence was afterward reported: 'The mighty oak of the forest has fallen, and now the scrub oaks may sprout all around.'[5]

[1] *Draper MSS.* 10 J 188.

[2] English, *Conquest of the Northwest,* 893, 1128. A portrait from life of General Clark, painted about this time by the talented artist Joseph Bush, contrasts painfully with Matthew Jouett's, which represents him in the prime of manhood — strong and handsome, though somewhat saddened. In Bush's portrait an old man is seen sitting wrapped in a loose black broadcloth cloak, with short yellow-fringed cape and a broad standing collar flaring open in front and exposing a red plush lining. His teeth are gone, the once fine mouth now showing only flabby and expressionless lips; the massive head is bald, except at the sides and rear, where long silvered sandy hair falls to the shoulders; the eyes, which once shone with intelligence unmistakably show senility. It is a distressingly realistic picture of a great ruin.

To Clark's niece, Mrs. Henry C. Pindell of Louisville, Bush said his portrait of General Clark, although painted when he was quite young and far from being of his best works, was the best *likeness* he ever painted. The author has her written statement to this effect when she gave him the portrait. It had been given her by her uncle, Colonel Isaac Clark, son of General Jonathan Clark, and for many years hung in his house, the old Clark home, at Mulberry Hill.

[3] English's *Conquest of the Northwest,* 887.

[4] *Draper MSS.* 55 J 84.

[5] *Id.,* 188.

Under the trees in the quiet little graveyard at Locust Grove, General Clark's remains lay for over fifty years. The Croghan family scattered, the place passed into other hands, the monuments were neglected, and some of them lost — amongst them that which had marked the resting place of George Rogers Clark. In 1869 the remains were removed to Louisville's beautiful cemetery. 'Cave Hill.' There they rest to-day beside those of his brothers, General Jonathan and Captain Edmund Clark. Each of the three graves is marked only by a small headstone about two feet high. One of them bears this simple inscription:

Gen'l George Rogers Clark

Born O.S., November 9, 1752;

Died February 13, 1818

Surrounded by hundreds of costly and imposing monuments to other dead, below that obscure little headstone have lain for over half a century, unknown to his countrymen, the remains of the hero who labored and sacrificed and suffered and achieved so much for them. Eminent men have declared him, next to Washington, the greatest builder of this great empire; but probably not one in a thousand of its citizens knows who he was. They know Paul Revere, Israel Putnam, and Ethan Allen; they know Marion and Sumter and Daniel Boone — but will ask: 'Who was George Rogers Clark?' While Senator Hoar of Massachusetts and Senator Sherman of Ohio were championing a bill in the United States Senate to erect a national monument in his honor, Senator Sherman said that a great New York daily objected, asserting that there had never been any such person as General George Rogers Clark — that the senators must have meant General William Clark of the Lewis and Clark Expedition to the Pacific!

Such ignorance of the very existence of one who played so important a part in the Revolutionary War seems strange indeed; but for over a hundred years historians of the Revolution rarely mentioned the western phase of the war, and the truth about Clark nearly all lay buried in the unpublished records of his time. He had no contemporary biographer. His movements were little known where the printing press ran. His career was in the distant west, whilst our historians and publishers were nearly always eastern men, interested in recording the events and portraying the heroes of their own sections, but not in the exploits of a handful of pioneers and soldiers in the far western wilderness.

Many signs, however, indicate a fast growing interest in western Revolutionary events and men, and particularly Clark. A considerable number of the contemporary source materials necessary to an understanding of him and what he accomplished are already published; many times more soon will be. The many great states west of the Alleghenies have successively passed from rude frontier conditions to peaceful and prosperous civilization. As leisure and culture in these states increase, their citizens will more and more seek to learn their historic beginnings; and not one of them, from Ohio to Oregon or Texas, but must trace its origin, as a part of the United States, to the winning of the Revolutionary West and to Clark's part in winning it. The day will surely come — and it may be near — when, from the unerring contemporary records, some Prescott or Irving will reach the American public with the true story of his career and its national significance. Then, on Corn Island at the head of the Falls of the Ohio — midway between his last resting place on one side and his last home on the other, and midway between the five great northern states that he won for us and the five states south of them that he saved for us — will rise a monument piercing the skies, and every school child will know who George Rogers Clark was.

AFTERWORD: CLARK AND HISTORIANS

IT may be doubted whether any other American, credited with great services to his country, has been more cruelly misrepresented in history than George Rogers Clark; and it was the author's intention, in a concluding chapter, to show at length by whom and how this has been done. Because of the space required, however, and because this book is not intended only for historians, who alone are likely to be interested in the subject, it has been thought best to treat it in another publication.

Any one familiar with the facts about Clark shown in the unerring records of his time, will read with amazement what some historians have said of him. Misrepresentation of him has usually been attributable to ignorance of the facts concerning his career and character, but not always. It was his fate to be first portrayed in history by a malignant and adroit contemporary. This was Humphrey Marshall, whose untrustworthy polemic, entitled *The History of Kentucky*, has been heedlessly copied by a surprising number of later writers. Some of them display no less hostility toward Clark than Marshall — for example, the latter's kinsman and violent partisan, Thomas Marshall Green.[1] It has been left, however, for a living descendant of Colonel Henderson, whose Transylvania land scheme Clark upset, to go furthest in defaming the hero of Vincennes. In a recent work this writer lauds his ancestor as the great leader in the conquest of the South-west, and describes Clark as an 'unscrupulous,' self-seeking revolutionist.[2] In a recent address at the dedication of a statue of Clark at the University of Virginia, near the spot where he was born, he said Clark 'sullied his honor by selling his military services to a foreign power; and like Burr, Blount, and Wilkinson dallied with projects verging upon treason.'[3]

Very different was the estimate of Clark by one who knew far more of him. No man, living or dead, has been so inti-

---

[1] *The Spanish Conspiracy.* As to both of them see Introduction to *Littell's Political Transactions,* Filson Club Publications, no 31.

[2] *Conquest of the Old Southwest,* 257, by Prof. Archibald Henderson, of North Carolina.

[3] November 3, 1921, Virginia University *Alumni Bulletin.*

mately acquainted with the source materials of western history as Dr. Lyman Draper, whose wonderful collection of manuscripts in the Wisconsin State Historical Society constitutes the richest existing mine of information for the historians of the west — rivaled only by the State Archives of Virginia. No man was more unbiased in judging events and men. To a correspondent he wrote: 'I do not wonder that you sh^d have your heart's memories and affections deeply stirred within you when such a man's worth & services were brought to your notice. The life services of Gen! Clark have so long been a subject of profound study with me, that I have long learned to reverence him as I never have any other public character. It is my earnest desire, that I may be spared to complete the work devoted to his memory and services, for which I have been over thirty years gathering materials.'[1]

[1] *Draper MSS.* 10 J 312, holograph.

APPENDIX

WILKINSON'S PLOT AGAINST CLARK

THE reader will perhaps be aided to a clearer understanding of Wilkinson's plot against Clark by reading the present writer's introduction to *Littell's Political Transactions in Kentucky*, where the traitor's western political career and hitherto unpublished writings are set forth much more fully than can be done here.[1] His plot was carried out almost entirely by elaborately fabricated writings — some of them anonymous, most of them forged — some sent to Congress and others to Governor Randolph. Nearly all were mere pretended *copies* of originals which never existed. Seemingly they came from widely scattered sources with which he could not be thought connected; but all reached their intended destinations. They were most ingeniously dovetailed to supplement one another and were designed to alarm the governor and Congress with the fiction about Clark's gathering a great army to invade Louisiana. As Wilkinson doubtless anticipated, Randolph and Congress promptly forwarded to one another copies of the writings each received.

The use the adroit schemer made of unwitting men of character to further his ends, the fear he aroused at Richmond and New York of a Spanish war, the panic he caused amongst northern delegates in Congress lest the commercial treaty be defeated, and finally, the amazing success of his whole plot, make one of the most interesting and historically important chapters in that most critical period of American history. His effort to destroy Clark has been suspected by several historians,[2] but, doubtless for lack of reliable information about it, no one has attempted to unravel it. To lay it bare properly would require the detective acumen and the constructive and analytic skill of a master advocate like Erskine, Webster, or Choate.

Although the style of Wilkinson's writings varied greatly, their authorship is easily recognized by any one familiar with them. His public addresses, suiting the popular taste of his time, were verbose and grandiloquent; but he was quite capable of lucid and strong writing, as witness his 'Memorial.'[3] When writing to men of character, his letters abounded in professions of high principles and undying personal devotion; but to coarser intimates his language was often vulgar, and, when necessary for his ends, shamelessly bared his rascality. He was ever as cunning as an Indian in covering his tracks, and they are often hard to find; yet, cunning as he was, many of them remain — some obscure, others unmistakable — and nearly

---

[1] *Filson Club Publications*, no. 31, (John P. Morton & Co., Louisville, Ky., 1926.)

[2] E.g., Winsor's *Western Movement*, 347.
[3] Given in full in *Filson Club Publication*, no. 31, *supra*.

all of them, during 1786, point in the line of his elaborate plot to over-set and supersede Clark. He was most careful to destroy every pro-curable shred of evidence that might later incriminate him, but he lost or overlooked some of his innumerable writings which fortu-nately have been preserved; for, fitted to one another, they make a surprisingly complete exposure of the plot.

To assist the reader to follow the steps by which he carried it out, his general plan, as interpreted by the author, will first be briefly outlined, and afterward the means used to effect it will be explained.

General Clark, it will be remembered, after recruiting his small garrison at Vincennes, returned to Louisville, where in the fall of 1786, he received Colonel LeGras' written report of the bril-liant negotiations and speeches by which they had brought the hos-tile Indians to sue for peace and agree to a truce until the next April. Soon after this, Wilkinson appeared in Louisville, where he managed to get from Clark both LeGras' report and the minutes of the Vincennes military court ordering the impressment of Baza-done's goods. Wilkinson's object in getting them is made plain by the use he soon made of garbled parts of them. At Louisville he will be found sending anonymous and forged communications to Congress and Governor Randolph to prepare them to credit the falsehoods he would afterwards send over his own signature to the governor.

From Louisville he went to Danville, where the convention dele-gates-elect were then slowly gathering. The Virginia Assembly act, authorizing the Convention to consider Kentucky statehood, had directed it to be called for the preceding September, 1786; but, no quorum appearing, it was not really convened until in January, 1787. Let this fact be noted, for Wilkinson will soon be found de-ceiving Governor Randolph with a 'report' from a fictitious 'com-mittee of members of the Convention convened at Danville...on the nineteenth day of December' 1786 — which was weeks before there was any convention at all!

It will presently appear, from letters and papers he sent the governor, that he first deceived some of his friends amongst the delegates-elect into believing that General Clark was utterly inca-pacitated for military leadership by drink, and alarmed them with reports of a powerful impending invasion by the confederated In-dians unless some more competent man were appointed to handle them — and who more competent than Wilkinson? With the dele-gates thus fearful for the safety of their homes and families, and made distrustful of Clark's leadership, the plotter next tricked them into signing two cunningly framed letters to Governor Randolph. He was himself the first signer of one letter,[1] which, although it made no charge whatever against Clark, referred vaguely to 'testi-monials which accompany this'; and it was these 'testimonials,' (which Wilkinson evidently fabricated and sent with the letter),

---

[1] The order of signatures is erroneously given in every printed copy. His name headed the first (right-hand) column of names, T. Marshall the left. The letter is still in the Virginia State Library, pho-tograph in *Author's MSS.*

which contained the falsehoods about Clark and represented him and one Thomas Green of Natchez as raising a great army to invade Louisiana and wrest the Yazoo region from Spain. To the governor the 'testimonials' *seemed* to be vouched for by all the signers of the letter; but it is morally certain that none of them, except Wilkinson, knew what they contained. The false statements in them about Clark's great army and violent seizure of Spanish goods at Vincennes were well calculated to alarm Randolph.

The other letter, which was also signed by some of Wilkinson's friends, but not by him, urged Randolph to nominate him to Congress for appointment to succeed Clark as Indian Commissioner, — a position which would give him military ascendency in the west.

Having now broadly outlined Wilkinson's plan for deceiving his fellow-delegates and Governor Randolph, let us next see the shrewd methods he used to carry it out. He knew that when these papers reached the east they would cause grave fear of a Spanish war and of the doom of the coveted commercial treaty. Before making them up, however, he was careful to prepare both Congress and Randolph to credit the falsehoods in them. While he was in Louisville, three anonymous writings, bearing his almost unmistakable earmarks, found their way to them. One purported to be 'A Copy of a Letter from a Gentleman at the Falls of Ohio, to his Friend in New England, Dated December 4, 1786.' It was much less explicit about Clark than the others, but was well calculated to prepare uninformed eastern men for the later and more direct charges against him which Wilkinson would send Governor Randolph. It read as follows:

Dear Sir: — Politics, which a few months ago were scarcely thought of, are now sounded aloud in this part of the world, and discussed by almost every person. The later commercial treaty with Spain, in shutting up, as it is said, the navigation of the Mississippi for the term of twenty-five years, has given this western country a universal shock, and struck its inhabitants with an amazement. Our foundation is affected. It is therefore necessary that every individual exert himself to apply a remedy. To sell us, and make us vassals to the merciless Spaniards, is a grievance not to be borne.

The parliamentary acts which occasioned our revolt from Great Britain were not so barefaced and intolerable. To give us the liberty of transporting our effects down the river to New Orleans, and then be subject to the Spanish laws and impositions, is an insult upon our understanding.

Do you think to prevent the emigration from a barren country, loaded with taxes, and impoverished with debts, to the most luxurious and fertile soil in the world? Vain is the thought, and presumptious the supposition. You may as well endeavor to prevent the fishes from gathering on a bank in the sea which affords them plenty of nourishment. Shall the best and largest part of the United States be uncultivated —a nest for savages and beasts of prey? Certainly not. Providence has designed it for nobler purposes. . . . Shall all this country now be cultivated for the use of the Spaniards? Shall we be their bondsmen, as the children of Israel were to the Egyptians? Shall one part of the United States be slaves, while the other is free? Human nature shudders at the thought, and free men will despise those who could be so mean as to even contemplate on so vile a subject.

Our situation is as bad as it possibly can be; therefore every exertion to retrieve our circumstances must be manly, eligible, and just. We can raise twenty thousand troops on this side the Allegheny and Appalachian mountains; and the annual increase by emigration, from other parts is from two to four thousand.

We have taken all the goods belonging to the Spanish merchants of Post Vincennes and the Illinois, and are determined they shall not trade up the river, provided they will not let us trade down it. Preparations are now making here (if necessary) to drive the Spaniards from their settlement, at the mouth of the Mississippi. In case we are not countenanced and succored by the United States (if we need it) our allegiance will be thrown off, and some other power applied to. Great Britain stands ready, with open arms, to receive and support us. They have already offered to open their resources for our supplies. When once reunited to them, 'farewell, a long farewell to all your boasted greatness.' The province of Canada, and the inhabitants of these waters of themselves, in time, will be able to conquer you. You are as ignorant of this country as Great Britain was of America. These hints, if rightly improved, may be of some service; if not, blame yourselves for the neglect.[1]

This anonymous letter was received by Governor Randolph from none other than General Clark's old enemy, Colonel Arthur Campbell;[2] and, especially when read with the 'testimonials' Wilkinson would send him, it could hardly have been better designed to create alarm lest the westerners precipitate the country into a war with Spain. It was addressed from the Falls of Ohio, and Wilkinson was there. Like him, Campbell was agitating separation of the western counties from the parent state, and he too was ambitious to be appointed Commissioner of Indian Affairs in the southern department,[3] as Wilkinson was in the northern; and both were keen to undermine Clark.

About this time two other papers — both anonymous and of import like the letter just quoted — found their way to Congress. Both represented Clark as 'constantly drunk' and as planning to invade Spanish Louisiana. One purported to be an '*Extract from a letter from a gentleman in North Carolina to a gentleman in Congress.*' It represents Clark at Vincennes as 'retaliating on the Spaniards for some of the Seizures and Confiscations of the property of our citizens at the Natchez,' and concludes by saying 'They add that Clarke is constantly drunk.'[4] The other was '*An extract of a letter from a person in Kentucky to a delegate from Pennsylvania.*'[5] Of this anonymous extract, it has been truly said: 'The circumstances point unerringly to Wilkinson as the author.'[6] It was written in his familiar, lively style, and it may be strongly suspected that it was at his request that the 'delegate from Pennsylvania' communicated it to Congress. It reads as follows:

'Clarke is playing Hell. He is raising a Regiment of his own and has 140 men stationed at Opost already, now under command of Dalton. Seized a

---

[1] In full in *Secret Journal of Congress*, IV, 320.

[2] *Virginia Calendar State Papers*, IV, 242.

[3] *Virginia Calendar State Papers*, IV, 375.

[4] *Id.*, IV, 189.

[5] Virginia State Library, '*Box Executive Papers Continental Congress.*'

[6] Green's *Spanish Conspiracy*, 72.

Spanish boat and 20,000 Dollars, or rather seized three stores at Opost worth this sum, and the Boat which brought them up. J. R. Jones, Commissary General, gets a large share of the plunder and has his family at Opost. Platt comes in for snacks. He brought the Baggage and a thousand pounds of small furs to the Falls the day I left it. Plunder-all means to go to Congress to get the Regiment put upon the establishment. He is the 3rd Captain. The taxes, he tells his associates, are necessary to bear his expenses; but he doesn't return. I laid a plan to get the whole seized and secured for the owners, and Bullet and Anderson will execute it. Clarke is constantly drunk, and yet full of design. I told him he would be hanged. He laughed and said he could take refuge among the Indians. A stroke is meditated against St. Louis and the Natchez.'[1]

'Bullet and Anderson,'[2] who, according to this anonymous writer, were to execute his 'plan,' probably never heard of it; but they were two of the many reputable men in Kentucky whose confidence Wilkinson won, and whose names he used on several occasions to give credit to his crooked schemes; for, strange as it now seems, almost all the most highly esteemed men there were at this time his trusting friends, never suspecting that he would lie to them, or use their names for criminal purposes.

That Wilkinson wrote this 'extract' is persuasively shown by five facts: (1), within a few weeks afterward he sent, over his own signature, substantially the same false statements about Clark to Governor Randolph in elaborately devised letters and 'testimonials'; (2) no one else of whom we know had his motive for writing the falsehoods contained in the extract; (3), no other person in Kentucky had so large an acquaintance or correspondence with eastern men, or was so likely to have been on such familiar terms with the 'delegate from Pennsylvania' as the coarse language of the 'Extract' indicates; (4), excepting in the writings he sent Governor Randolph, a diligent investigation has failed to disclose any other writing, from any other person in Kentucky, even intimating that Clark was guilty of the lawless conduct or designs attributed to him in this anonymous extract; and (5) it was certainly well fitted to further Wilkinson's ends, and within eight months afterward he will be found himself telling Miro at New Orleans that he 'was the first and principal factor who destroyed the undertaking Brigadier Clark was meditating against the Natchez, &c.'[3]

Mr. Madison, then a member of Congress, referring to this anonymous extract, wrote Governor Randolph: 'A very dismal account of Clark's proceedings in the Western country has been informally laid before Congress, and will be forwarded to your department. If the information be well founded, you will probably receive a confirmation through other channels.'[4] Wilkinson saw that Randolph did receive such confirmation through other channels.

[1] *Virginia Calendar State Papers*, IV, 202.

[2] Alexander Scott Bullitt, afterward Lieutenant-Governor, and Colonel Richard Clough Anderson.

[3] *Pontalba Papers*, copies in *Author's MSS.* and *R. C. Ballard Thruston's MSS.*, Louisville, Ky.

[4] *Madison Papers*, II, 629.

It seems strange that such an anonymous paper should have been thought worthy of the slightest notice by Congress, but it is hard to realize how ignorant people in one part of the country then were about happenings in another, or how slow and uncertain communication of intelligence then was, especially in the western wilderness. For the transmission of news, Vincennes in western Indiana, or Nashville on the Cumberland, was hundreds of times farther from Danville than it now is from points in central Siberia or Africa. News of events happening in either of those distant western settlements, if it ever reached Danville at all, oftenest did so by mere chance, by word of mouth, by many haphazard carriers, and after many stages and long delays. Thus, unless some one like Wilkinson was specially interested in sending or carrying news quickly, the people at one western settlement would usually hear nothing from another a hundred miles or more away, for weeks or months, if at all. Wilkinson's whole plot was founded on this ignorance at Richmond, New York and Danville, of recent happenings at far-away Vincennes, or on the Cumberland.

To prepare all, whom he expected to deceive, to credit the falsehoods he afterward sent them about Clark, he doubtless wrote many letters of which nothing is now known. While at Louisville he wrote 'a friend in Fayette' — probably his neighbor, Colonel Thomas Marshall, the father of John Marshall, afterward Chief Justice — that 'the sun of General Clark's military glory had set, never more to rise.'[1] What else his letter contained we do not know; but the quoted remark presumably introduced or followed a description of the *débâcle* of Clark's Wabash Expedition, and said it was attributed by the troops to Clark's incapacity from drink.

About the same time Wilkinson wrote the future Chief Justice requesting him to ask Governor Randolph for a passport to New Orleans, and in the letter gave an account of Clark's and Logan's expeditions against the Indians. John Marshall in reply said:

'It is with a great deal of mortification I tell you that I have failed in obtaining the passport I applied for. On my mentioning the subject to the governor, he said he was acquainted with you, and would with great pleasure do anything which was proper to serve you. He took time to consider the subject, and after several applications, told me to-day, that to grant the passport as an official act was entirely improper, because it could only extend to the limits of Virginia, to which you had a right to go without his permit; and that he could not write a private letter of recommendation to the governor without having some acquaintance with him.

'On these reasons sir, my application in your favor was rejected. I am much chagrined at my disappointment — I am much indebted to you for the clear and succinct account you have given me of the two expeditions against the Indians.'[2]

What kind of account Wilkinson gave him may be imagined.

This letter indicates Marshall's and Governor Randolph's esteem

---

[1] Marshall's *History of Kentucky*, I, 249.   [2] Littell's *Political Transactions*, 96, *supra*.

for him — an esteem which seems to have been then general, both in the East and West. Wilkinson probably designed his account of Clark's expedition to reach the Governor and further his plot; for he knew John Marshall had much intercourse with Randolph and other high state officials.

After the several anonymous communications, Wilkinson, being at Danville, after the middle of December, proceeded to construct his masterpiece of deception — the letters (dated December 22) and the accompanying 'testimonials' which he sent to Governor Randolph. To understand his cunning methods in framing the letters and tricking his delegate friends into signing them, one must first know the nature of the 'testimonials.' For that reason the text of the testimonials will first be set forth with explanatory comments, and then the attestations appended to some of them will receive attention. The 'testimonials' consisted of the following papers:

1. An alleged *copy* of a letter, purporting to be signed by one Thomas Green, to the Governor of Georgia, setting forth an imaginary scheme in conjunction with Clark to invade Spanish Louisiana with a great army.

2. A pretended extract from a report of a fictitious convention committee at Danville. This report refers to the Green letter.

3. A pretended *copy* of a paper purporting to be signed by Clark and others and agreeing to pay one Wells for going to Georgia 'on public business.'

4. A garbled quotation from LeGras' report to Clark of their speeches to and dealings with the Indians on the Wabash.

5. A deposition of one Neeves, evidently an ignorant private soldier, about the impressment at Vincennes of the goods of the Spaniard, Bazadone.

That Wilkinson's manner of making up and using these 'testimonials' can be explained at all is largely due to the fortunate finding by Doctor Draper of an old writing, giving what purport to be the 'minutes' of the fictitious committee at Danville on the 19th and 20th of December, 1786. Wilkinson's authorship of the paper, the use he probably intended making of it, and the reason which led him to send Governor Randolph only an excerpt from it will now be considered. He knew the Governor would be more likely to credit the falsehoods about Clark in the 'testimonials' if they came apparently vouched for by a committee of the Kentucky Convention. He knew the governor was aware that the convention had been called to meet in September,[1] but was *not* aware that no quorum had appeared and that the convention was not convened by the 19th or 20th of December, and would not, in fact, convene until in January following. Wilkinson also knew the governor was personally acquainted with the more prominent delegates-elect as men of character, and would likely credit any testimonials apparently vouched for by them.

---

[1] The Virginia Act of Separation had fixed the September date. (Hening's *Virginia Statues*, x; Littell's *Political Transactions*, Appendix, 66.)

As the bogus committee 'minutes' throw strong light upon Wilkinson's method of constructing his 'testimonials' (so that each seems to explain one or more of the others, and all seem to be vouched for by the other signers of the letters to the governor) they will now be copied in full, with italicizing and bracketed comments to call attention to significances which might otherwise be overlooked. They read as follows:

'A committee of the Gentlemen *members* of the *convention convened* at Danville in the County of Mercer in the District of Kentucky on the *Nineteenth day of December* One Thousand Seven Hundred and Eighty Six, to take into consideration and make enquiry into the Cause of Certain Commotions within this District. Which Committee consist*ed* of the Members whose names are *hereafter subscribed* hereunto. —
'Mr. Thomas Marshall was unanimously elected Chairman, who took his seat accordingly.
'Resolved, that a committee be appointed to wait on General Clark [who was not at Danville, but at the Falls of Ohio] and receive from him such information as he may think proper to make respecting the establishment of the Corps at Post St. Vincents, of the Seizure of Spanish property made at that place, and such other matters as they may consider necessary to give satisfaction to the members of this committee and make report tomorrow.
'And a committee was accordingly appointed of Mr. Wilkinson, Mr. Innes, Mr. Brown, Mr. Garrard, Mr. Greenup and Mr. Lyne. The Committee then adjourned till tomorrow. T— of the Clock.'

[A miraculous 'committee' this, which could elect a chairman, pass a resolution, appoint a sub-committee, and adjourn, although it 'consist*ed* of the members whose names are *hereafter* subscribed' to the minutes! None of the foregoing statements in the 'minutes' showing Wilkinson's part in the proceedings were sent to Governor Randolph. He was never informed that any of the other persons named had any connection with them. Wilkinson doubtless concluded that this might expose his fraud, since some of them might soon see the Governor and be asked about the proceedings, when they would disclaim any knowledge of them.]

'*Wednesday the 20th day of December* 1786
The Committee met according to adjournment.
Mr. Wilkinson made report from the Committee appointed Yesterday to wait on General Clarke and receive such information as he may think proper to make respecting the establishment of the Corps at Post St. Vincents, of the Seizure of Spanish property made at that place, and such other matters as they may consider necessary to give satisfaction to the members of this committee; that the Committee had according to order, waited on General Clarke [when Clark was not in Danville, but a four or five days journey away, at his home by the Falls of Ohio!] and collected such facts, as he [Wilkinson] read in his place and delivered at the Clerk's Table where they were again read and are as follows :

[This statement by Wilkinson — showing Clark at Danville — is the *only one* disclosed by a long and careful search of the innumerable extant letters of the time, although Clark's movements were oftener mentioned in them than those of any other man.]

'That they find by inquiry from General Clarke, and from sundry papers by him submitted to their inspection, that a board of Field Officers, composed from the Corps employed on the late Wabash Expedition, did in council held at Post St. Vincents the 8th of October 1786 unanimously agree that a Garrison at that place would be of essential Service to the District of Kentucky, and that Supplies might be had in the District more than sufficient for their support by impressment or otherwise, under the direction of a Commissary to be appointed for this purpose, pursuant to the authority vested in the Field Officers of the District by the Executive of Virginia. The same board appointed Mr. John Craig Junior a commissary of purchases and Resolved that one Field officer and a hundred and fifty men, exclusive of the Company of artil[lery] to be commanded by Captain Valentine Thomas [Dalton — MSS torn] to be recruited to Garrison Post St. Vincents, That Colo. [MSS torn] Holder be appointed to command the troops in this service. In consequence of these measures it appears to your committee that a Body of men have been enlisted and are now recruiting for one year; that General Clarke hath taken the Supreme direction of the Corps, but by what authority doth not appear, and that the Corps has been further officered by appointments made by the General, who acknowledges that the seizure of Spanish property was made by his order for the sole purpose of Cloathing and subsisting the troops and that the Goods seized were appropriated in this way. That John Rice Jones, who acts as Commissary to the Garrison, had passed Receipts for the Articles taken.

The General Alledges that the Troops were raised for the security of the District, that he considers them subject to the direction of the Committee who may discharge them if they think proper, but conceives this measure may prevent the proposed Treaty and involve this country in a Bloody war.

He denies any intention of depredating on the Spanish possessions, or property at the Illinois, and declares that he never saw the intercepted letter of Thomas Green — [which will appear in full presently] — that he understood Green's object was to establish a settlement at or near the Garo [Yazoo] River under the authority of the state of Georgia; that his view was, by encouraging the settlement, to obtain a small grant of land and that he had no idea of molesting the Spaniards, or of attending Green in person. He informed the Committee that the Garrison now at Post St. Vincennes is about one hundred strong [it had already dispersed for want of food] and that the Merchants at the Illinois had determined to support it, for which purpose they had sent for the Commissary Jones to receive Provisions;[1] that Major Bussaron was sent to the Illinois to advise settlers there of certain seizures made at Natchez of American Property by the Spanish Command-[ant] and to recommend it to them to conciliate the minds of the Indians and be prepared to retaliate any outrage the Spaniards might committ on their property, but by no means commence Hostilities.

[General Clark, at the Falls, not suspecting Wilkinson's sinister motives, evidently gave him all the information he asked, including the LeGras report and a copy of the minutes of the Vincennes court-martial ordering Bazadone's goods impressed; for one will be found quoted, word for word, in one of Wilkinson's testimonials — so far as suited his purpose — and the substance of the other given. Doubtless Clark also told him of the goods having been used to support the troops, of his recruiting men to garrison the town, of his nego-

[1] See Vallinière to Congress, *Illinois Historical Collection*, v, 425–27.

tiations with the Indians, and of the imperative need of a treaty of
peace with them to prevent a destructive invasion of Kentucky; for
Wilkinson's committee report states these things correctly.[1] In all
other respects it is pure fiction. Excepting in this fictitious report,
there is not a shred of evidence that there ever was any 'inquiry
from General Clarke,' or that there were ever any 'papers by him
submitted'; or that he ever stated 'that he considers [his troops]
subject to this committee'; or that he ever heard of the Green letter;
or that he ever said anything to the 'committee,' or to anybody else,
about that letter; or that he ever heard of such a committee! These
'minutes' were never sent to Governor Randolph, nor were they
referred to in the letters to him. So far as can be learned from anything any of the signers of those letters, other than Wilkinson, ever
wrote or said, not one of them ever heard of Clark's being then at
Danville, or of any such 'committee...to wait on General Clarke!'
Even those mentioned as its members never heard of it! But it was
very important for Wilkinson's purpose that Governor Randolph
should be led to believe that a convention was in session and that a
Committee really did wait on Clark and found him utterly unqualified for business of any kind; and it will soon be seen how adroitly
this purpose was effected. The pretended committee minutes continue
as follows:]

'*Mr. Wilkinson reported* also that the *Committee* had taken the deposition
of a Certain Daniel Neeves which he read in his place and is as follows:
' "The Deposition of Daniel Neeves, being first sworn on the Holy Evan-
gelist of Almighty God, Deposeth and saith that he this Deponent was enlisted by a Captain Thomas Mason as a Soldier in the Wabash Regiment;
that he was summoned as one of a Guard by Capt. Valentine T. Dalton and
was by him marched to a store and he the said Dalton by an Interpreter
demanded of a Spanish Merchant to admit him the said Dalton into his
cellar; the Spaniard asked what he wanted and the said Dalton replied he was
sent by the Commanding Officer to search his cellar, it being at a late hour in
the night the Spaniard lighted a candle and opened his doors and went and
opened his Cellar door, the said Dalton came with several others and entered
the Cellar; after some time he came out and placed Deponent as a Guard
over the Cellar and took the rest of the guard to another store. That on the
succeeding day the said Dalton came with a number of others and plundered
['plundered' was a favorite word with Wilkinson] the Cellar of a large
Quantity of Peltry, Wine, Taffy, honey, Sugar, Tea, Coffee, Cordial, French
Brandy and several other Articles, together with a Quantity of dry goods.
the particular Articles this Deponent doth at present [not] recollect. part of
the goods was made use of to cloathe the Troops the remainder, with the
other articles, was set up at public auction and sold. That the sale was conducted by a certain John Rice Jones, who marched in the Militia Commanded by General Clarke as a Commissary General; and farther this De-

---

[1] At first blush it may seem strange
that Wilkinson should have given so
truthfully Clark's explanation of parts of
the occurrences at Vincennes; but if, as
he probably planned when he wrote them,
he intended to call some sort of meeting
of delegates-elect and get their signatures
to these minutes, perhaps he feared that
some of them might have heard of Clark's
version of the facts. Repeating it, too,
would give an air of fairness to the proceedings and could do no harm.

ponent saith he obtained a furlough dated the 24th day of November 1786 signed Valentine Thos. Dalton Captain Commandant Ouabache Regiment of which following is a copy: "Daniel Neeves a Soldier in the Ouabache Regiment has liberty to go on furlough for two months from the date hereof, at the expiration of which he is to return to his duty, otherwise looked upon as a deserter. November the 24th 1786 Valentine Thos Dalton Captain Commandant Oubache Regiment. To all whom it may concern." And farther this Deponent saith not.' [1]

[So far from Bazadone's goods being 'plundered,' the records show they were taken under formal order of the military court, that they were duly receipted for by the commissary, and that all of them were either distributed among the soldiers to meet their needs, or sold at public auction by the commissary and the proceeds used for their support. Bazadone himself afterwards so stated under oath; so also did worthy Francis Vigo.[2] Indeed, Neeves' deposition itself dispels the idea that the goods impressed were 'plundered' when it says 'part of the goods was made use of to cloathe the troops; the remainder, with the other articles was set up at public auction and sold.' This was the usual course in lawful military impressment. Plunderers would never have exposed the plundered property to public auction, but would have kept it, or disposed of it privately. Wilkinson's subcommittee report then says:]

'Resolved that a Committee be appointed to State to the Executive the Facts set forth in the Report of the Committee who were appointed to wait on General Clarke and receive from him information respecting the establishment of the Corps at St. Vincent, the Seizure of Spanish property made at that place and such other matters] as they consider necessary to give satisfaction to this Committee And in behalf of this Committee disavow the mode adopted for the establishment at Post St. Vincents, reprobate the Seizure of Spanish property and solicit the interference of the Executive; but at the same time urge the absolute necessity of Supporting a Military Post at St. Vincents and at the mouth of Eagle Creek on the North West side of the

---

[1] Aside from being part of the bogus 'minutes,' this Neeves deposition bears significant signs of Wilkinson's authorship. If Neeves, whose name cannot be found anywhere else in Kentucky history, himself signed the deposition (which seems decidedly questionable) he was evidently an ignorant man, barely able to scrawl his name. The wording of the deposition was certainly by some one else, and almost certainly by Wilkinson. The straggling signature — without the separation of letters usual in the signatures of illiterate men — indicates that it was written by some more facile writer pretending unfamiliarity with the pen. But for the use of the word 'plundering' in describing the impressment of Bazadone's goods, the deposition is doubtless substantially correct, though quite immaterial, excepting as pointing to Wil-

kinson as its author. In describing the impressment Neeves would hardly have been so particular to enumerate 'wine, taffy, [rum], cordial, French Brandy' — suggesting wherewiths for carousals of plunderers rather than for soldiers' needs; but Wilkinson would naturally emphasize them to suggest plundering.

The deposition is in the Virginia State Library; a photograph in *Author's MSS.* A copy was sent by Governor Randolph to Congress and appears in the *Secret Journals of Congress*, IV, 309. That it was copied in full in the pretended minutes is additional convincing evidence that the paper in the *Draper MSS.* containing the minutes is a genuine contemporary document.

[2] Virginia State Library, *Bazadone Papers.*

Ohio about Seven miles below the mouth of Limestone and carry into effect the Treaty proposed by General Clarke. [Wilkinson particularly desired, as Indian Commissioner, to command that post and hold that treaty.] And a committee was appointed of Mr. Innes, Mr. Wilkinson, Mr. Muter, Mr. Garrard, Mr. Greenup, Mr. Brown and Mr. Lynne.

'Resolved, as the Opinion of this committee, that it [be] Certified that Mr. John Craig Junior did not act [MSS. torn] der or accept of the Appointment of Commissary of Purchases.

'The Committee then adjourned till Tomorrow Ten Oclock.'[1]

Thus end these extraordinary 'minutes' of this fictitious committee. That the old paper containing them was concocted by Wilkinson can hardly be doubted. Not only is it inconceivable that any one of a later period would have had either the motive or the detailed knowledge to write it, but an extract — copied word for word from his sub-committee report — is found in the contemporaneous *Secret Journal of Congress* as one of the 'testimonials' he sent Governor Randolph.[2] This conclusively proves the bogus 'minutes' a genuine historic document — despite the tissue of falsehoods in it.

How Wilkinson at first designed using the 'minutes' will probably never be known. They were never finished, nor was any part of them used except the extract from them already mentioned as one of the testimonials sent to the governor and by him forwarded to Congress. The opening sentence — the 'Committee consist*ed* of the members whose names are *hereafter* subscribed hereto' — seems to indicate that Wilkinson at first designed having the names — genuine or forged — of other delegates added and sending them to the governor. To get the other delegates to sign such false minutes might seem impossible to one unacquainted with Wilkinson and his genius for plot-construction. Any one who has often attended business meetings of men who have verbally agreed on what shall be stated in some paper they are to sign, knows how readily they accept the statement of a trusted man who offers it for signature, and how they come forward to sign it, one after another, without reading it; and it must be remembered that amongst these men Wilkinson was a trusted leader.

Passing now from the bogus 'minutes' which were *not* sent with the letters to the Governor, let us see the 'testimonials' which *were* sent him.

Here it is important to observe that, excepting the Neeves deposition, not one of them was more than a mere alleged *copy*, and that, before sending them to the Governor, Wilkinson evidently had ample opportunity to fabricate them to suit his own ends. He needed no genuine originals; his fertile imagination could invent them.

---

[1] *Draper MSS.* 53 J 59. Craig's father was one of the delegates Wilkinson had sign the letters to the governor, and this possibly explains the exoneration of the son.

[2] *Secret Journal of Congress* (Waite, Boston, 1821), IV, 311.

APPENDIX

The only part of the bogus 'minutes' which was sent to Randolph was a copy of Wilkinson's report of a pretended interview with General Clark; and as a testimonial it began with these significantly vague words: 'A committee appointed to wait on General Clarke.' What committee was so appointed is not disclosed; who appointed the committee is not disclosed; but it will presently appear how both committee and report were made to seem genuine to the Governor.

Another of the 'testimonials' purported to be a copy of a letter to the Governor of Georgia from Thomas Green, whom Governor Randolph described as 'of indifferent character.'[1] It was to play the chief part in alarming the Governor about General Clark's great army; but it is pretty certain that Green never signed, saw, or heard of any such letter, and that it was wholly Wilkinson's invention. If so, the use of Green's name as the apparent author of the letter was shrewd; for it was generally known that both Georgia and Spain claimed to own the Yazoo region, on the east side of the lower Mississippi; that the Georgia legislature had in 1785 declared it a county of that state, and had appointed Green and other Natchez residents commissioners to negotiate with the Spaniards for peaceable possession; and that this had been refused. Much to the disgust of his fellow citizens, Green had taken it upon himself to conduct the negotiation, but had accomplished nothing. He was evidently a man of small education, as the following excerpt from one of his letters will show:

'This...is to inform you that the Spaniards will not give up the garrison and that they have sence I Demanded it have Reinforsed it and is daly so Doing and sayes that there clame is as far as the tennesee if not further. ... The Spanards is a Drawin the Intrust of the Indens from us and has admitted Turnbull and others to bring goods to Mobeal and pencecola where thare Ships is to Land thare goods which cums under the Spanish Trade and has by the influence of the Creeks Stopt ower trade that way and Even sent after our people that Came from Georga as Commisheners to have them Murderd but mist them and I am Informed that it was the Creeks that did the mistch about Cumberland and Canetuck this Spring. ...
I am Dear Sir Your Most Sencear frind and Hbl Sarvent
Thos Green[2]

From this letter it is evident that Green's style of writing was very different from that in the copy of the letter, purporting to be his, which Wilkinson sent as his chief testimonial to Randolph and which read as follows:

Louisville, Falls of Ohio, *December 23,* 1786
Honored and Respected Sir,
Since I had the pleasure of writing my last, many circumstances of alarming nature have turned up to view. The commercial treaty with Spain is con-

[1] *Madison Papers,* Library of Congress, Ac. 1081.
[2] *American Historical Review,* xv, 334

et seq. Original in Bancroft Library, Berkeley, Cal.

sidered to be cruel, oppressive and unjust. The prohibition of the navigation of the Mississippi has astonished the whole western country. To sell us and make us vassals to the merciless Spaniards is a grievance not to be borne. Should we tamely submit to such manacles we should be unworthy the name of Americans, and a scandal to the annals of its history. It is very surprising to every rational person that the legislature of the United States, which has been so applauded for their assertion and defence of their rights and privileges, should so soon endeavor to subjugate the greatest part of their dominion even to worse slavery than even Great Britain presumed to subjugate any part of hers. Ireland is a free country to what this will be when its navigation is entirely shut; we may as well be sold for bondsmen as to have the Spaniards share all the benefits of our toils. They will receive all the fruits, produce of this large rich and fertile country at their own prices, (which you may be assured will be very low) and therefore will be able to supply their own markets and all the markets of Europe on much lower terms than what the Americans possibly can. What then are the advantages that the inhabitants of the Atlantick shores are to receive? This is summed up in a very few words: their trade and navigation ruined, and their brethren labouring to enrich a luxurious, merciless and arbitrary nation. Too much of our property have they already seized, condemned and confiscated, testimonies of which I send you accompanying this. Our situation cannot possibly be worse, therefore every exertion to retrieve our circumstances must be manly, eligible and just. The minds of the people here are very much exasperated against both the Spaniards and Congress. But they are happy to hear that the state of Georgia have protested against such vile proceedings; therefore they have some hopes, looking up to that state, craving to be protected in our just rights and privileges. Matters here seem to wear a threatening aspect. The troops stationed at post St. Vincent by orders of general George R. Clarke have seized upon what Spanish property there was at that place, also at the Illinois, in retaliation for their many offences. General Clarke, who has fought so gloriously for his country, and whose name strikes all the western savages with terrour, together with many other gentlemen of merit, engages to raise troops sufficient, and go with me to the Natchez to take possession, and settle the lands agreeable to the lines of that state, at their own risk and expense; provided you in your infinite goodness will countenance them, and give us the lands to settle it agreeable to the laws of your state. Hundreds are now waiting to join us with their families, seeking asylum for liberty and religion. Not hearing that the lines are settled between you and the Spaniards, we therefore wish for your directions concerning them, and the advice of your superior wisdom. At the same time assuring you that we have contracted for a very large quantity of goods, we hope sufficient to supply all the Indians living within the limits of Georgia. Trusting that we shall be able to make them independent of the Spaniards, wean their affections and procure their esteem for us and the United States, as we expect to take the goods down with us. We earnestly pray that you would give us full liberty to trade with all those tribes, and also to give your agents for Indian affairs all the necessary instructions for the prosperity of our scheme. The season for the Indian trade will be so far advanced that I wait with very great impatience.

General Clarke, together with a number of other gentlemen, will be ready to proceed down the river with me on the shortest notice, therefore hope and earnestly pray that you will despatch the express back with all possible speed with your answer, and all the encouragement due to so great an undertaking. As to the farther particulars, I refer you to the bearer Mr. William

Wells, a gentleman of merit who will be able to inform you more minutely than I possibly can of the sentiments of the people of this western country.

Sir, I have the honour to be your honours, &c,

THOMAS GREEN [1]

Let it be understood that all we know of this letter is what *Wilkinson* said of it in his pretended 'committee' report, where he simply mentioned it as 'the intercepted letter of Thomas Green.' That he did not show the other delegates any such Green letter as he sent Governor Randolph, is strongly indicated by the fact that, although it discloses an exceedingly dangerous design on Green and Clark's part to precipitate the country into a war with Spain, it was *not once mentioned in the letter they signed and with which it was enclosed.* Yet this Green letter was the very kernel of Wilkinson's whole array of 'testimonials,' and was the only one which said anything about Green and Clark's design to invade Louisiana. The others were sent merely to support it.

Again, as will presently appear, the Green letter, as sent to Governor Randolph, was nothing more than a copy — a pretended copy. Why was not the *original* 'intercepted letter of Mr Green' forwarded to the governor? Is it conceivable that the reputable 'gentlemen members of the committee,' having intercepted such a letter, disclosing so dangerous a scheme, would not have sent *the original* to Randolph, proving Green's guilt over his own signature, and not sent a mere copy? The answer, we may be sure, is that there never was an original, but Wilkinson fabricated the alleged copy. If there had really been any such original, written and signed by Green, its style of composition would hardly have been so like Wilkinson's florid one.

Next let us see somewhat of the contents of this Green letter. The falsehoods it contains about Clark's great army of invasion; about his readiness to 'proceed on the shortest notice'; about the vast quantity of goods *already* contracted for — sufficient to supply all the Indians living within the state of Georgia, a vast number — conclusively prove that if Green contrived the letter, either for his own purpose, or as Wilkinson's confederate, his audacity in lying was surprisingly like Wilkinson's. On its face the letter shows that Green did not even know but that Georgia had '*given up...claim*' to the disputed Yazoo region; yet, despite this uncertainty, it makes him say that he and 'General Clarke and many other gentlemen of merit...*have contracted* for a very large quantity of goods, we hope sufficient to supply all of the Indians living within the limits of Georgia!' It is inconceivable that Green would have written so palpably absurd a statement to the governor of Georgia, with any expectation of its being credited; but the statement sufficed for Wilkinson to fool Governor Randolph.

Again, such contracts for so vast a quantity of goods would pretty certainly have excited lively curiosity and widespread comment

---

[1] *Secret Journal of Congress,* IV, 315–17.

amongst the people of Kentucky, where nearly everybody was poor, would have created a great stir among many who had similar goods to sell, and would have greatly inflated the market price for them. Yet, amongst all the numberless letters of Kentucky people written during that period, not one has been found referring either to such purchases, or to any such rise in prices, or to Clark's alleged design to invade Louisiana! Nowhere is that design mentioned, except in the 'testimonials' Wilkinson sent to Governor Randolph, and the anonymous 'extracts' already mentioned. Whether the Green letter was written by Green, or concocted by Wilkinson, or by the two in collusion, the conclusion seems irresistible that it was designed to be used as a part of Wilkinson's scheme against Clark; and it is certain that it was so used by Wilkinson.

That it was prepared by the same hand that wrote the anonymous letter sent to the governor by Arthur Campbell, and that the hand was Wilkinson's, are persuasively shown by several remarkable coincidences. The Green letter says: 'The prohibition of the navigation of the Mississippi has astonished the whole western country. *To sell us and make us vassals to the merciless Spaniards is a grievance not to be borne.*' The anonymous letter says: 'The commercial treaty...has given the western country a universal shock and struck its inhabitants with amazement. .... *To sell us and make us vassals to the merciless Spaniards is a grievance not to be borne!*' Again, the Green letter said: 'Our situation cannot possibly be worse; *therefore every exertion to retrieve our circumstances must be manly, eligible and just.*' The anonymous letter Campbell sent likewise says: 'Our situation is as bad as it possibly can be; *therefore every exertion to retrieve our circumstances must be manly, eligible and just!*'

The repetition of these peculiar expressions in the two letters, in style so much like Wilkinson's and so utterly unlike Green's; their nearly identical dates and place of address — at the Falls of Ohio;[1] the like falsehoods contained in them, exactly serving Wilkinson's ends; and, lastly, the fact that Wilkinson sent the Green letter as one of his 'testimonials' against Clark, seem unerringly to fasten the authorship of both letters on him.

It is impossible to determine from the handwriting who wrote or signed the Green letter, for no original of it can be found amongst the Georgia archives; and, like all the other 'testimonials' Wilkinson sent (excepting only the unimportant Neeves deposition) it disappeared early from the Virginia state archives at Richmond! How they disappeared is not known; but, as Wilkinson the next year returned from New Orleans to Kentucky by way of the sea and Virginia, and visited Richmond,[2] it is no violent inference that he got them — probably by asking the governor, or his clerk, to let him see

---

[1] The anonymous 'Clarke is playing hell' letter was also dated from the Falls.

[2] Randolph to Madison, Dec. 27, 1787 (*Madison Papers*, Library of Congress, Ac. 1081), says: 'General Wilkinson from Kentucky, who is now here, is not to be appeased in his violence against the Constitution.'

them. They evidently could not be found by the careful compilers of the *Calendar of Virginia State Papers* over fifty years ago. That elaborate publication was intended to embrace all papers of historic value in the state archives. In it appear many of the letters and other documents written by, or to, or concerning General Clark. Amongst them are the two anonymous 'extracts,' one beginning 'Clarke is playing hell'; but the alarmingly important Green letter and all Wilkinson's other testimonials are missing, except the harmless Neeves deposition.[1] They would have exposed the plotter's villainy.

Another one of the 'testimonials' was the paper purporting to be an agreement by Green, Clark, and others to pay one William Wells for going to Georgia. It was evidently sent to Governor Randolph to connect Clark and Wells with the 'intercepted' Green letter referred to in the extract from Wilkinson's fictitious committee report which was also one of the testimonials. It reads as follows:

LOUISVILLE, *December* 4, 1786

Jefferson County SS.

Whereas William Wells is now employed by Colonel Thomas Green and others to go to Augusta, in the state of Georgia, on public business, and it being uncertain whether he will be paid for his journey out of the public treasury, should he not be, on his return we subscribers do jointly and severally, for value received, promise to pay him on demand the several sums that are affixed to our names, as witness our hands.

Thomas Green	£ 10.
John Williams	1.
George R. Clarke	10.
Lawrence Muse	3.
Richard Brashears	5.
James Patton	3.
James Huling	1.
David Morgan	1.
John Montgomery	1.
Ebenezer S. Platt	1.10
Robert Elliott	.10
Thomas Stribbling	1.10
	£38.10 [2]

Evidently the missing copy of this subscription paper was sent as a 'testimonial' to be read in connection with the Green letter and the sham 'committee' report, in order to show, over Clark's own signature, that he was a confederate of Green in his great scheme. If we could assume that there was any such scheme, then the tremendous importance of its discovery by Wilkinson's 'committee' plainly demanded that the *original* of this paper, no less than of Green's 'intercepted' letter, should be forwarded to the governor, and not a

---

[1] The author had an extended examination of the archives made, by careful searchers and extending over nearly a year, to find every paper bearing on Wilkinson's plot, but has failed to discover any of these missing 'testimonials.'

[2] *Secret Journal of Congress*, IV, 318–19.

mere *copy.* If Wells was really entrusted by Green with the letter, his apparent willingness to permit it and the contribution paper to be copied indicates a bad character, or a dull dupe. If, as seems far more likely, the whole paper — signature and all — was fabricated by Wilkinson, Wells, as the letter bearer, may be dismissed as a myth.

That the paper was a fabrication pretty clearly appears in the form of Clark's signature. Amongst many hundreds of his extant genuine signatures, not one has been found written, as in that paper, 'George R. Clarke,' — none with the name 'George.' His invariable practice was to sign his name 'G. R. Clark.' Wilkinson, however, greatly needed Clark's signature and actually used it as an important link in his chain of fabrications for Governor Randolph, and this addition of five letters, converting the initial 'G' into the full name 'George,' certainly raises strong presumption that it was written by him or somebody for him, and not by Clark. Again, Clark always wrote his surname 'Clark' — not 'Clarke'; but in every one of the 'testimonials' — in this Wells paper, in the Green letter, in the pretended committee report, in the Neeves deposition — every time General Clark's name appears it is misspelled with a final 'e' — 'Clarke,' instead of 'Clark.' Even in what purports to be his own signature it is thus misspelled. It also appears as 'Clarke' in all the foregoing anonymous letters sent to Congress and Randolph.

The next 'testimonial' to be considered is the garbled quotation from LeGras' written report to Clark, giving an account of their dealings with the Indians on the Wabash. The facts about their brilliant negotiations with the savages have already been seen in the text, and they show Clark at his very best — cool, clear-headed and prompt, amidst all the dissension and confusion following upon the mutiny and return to Vincennes, enlisting a garrison to defend the town, showing a brave front to the Indians, arresting the one who dared assume that the war hatchet had been laid down, defying them all with his bold speech offering them peace or war, but sending with it LeGras' adroit appeal to them, and finally, bringing fifteen hundred warriors to sue for peace and agree to a truce. But not one of these facts is disclosed in Wilkinson's 'testimonials'! They would have exposed the falsehoods he was sending the governor about General Clark's incapacity for military command. Instead, he sent the Governor merely the following:

'Extracts of general Clarke's speeches to the different nations of Indians on the Wabash, and their answers, in October, 1786.

GENERAL CLARKE

I send you today some strings of white, inviting you with sincerity to come to a grand council which will be held at Clarkesville, of the 20th November next, to see if we can come to terms, and make a treaty of peace and friendship,' &c.

The Goose and Fusil

'My elder brother, Thou oughtest to know the place we have been accustomed to speak at, it is at post St. Vincennes, there our chiefs are laid, there our ancestor's bed is and that of our father the French, and not at Clarkesville where you required us to meet you; we don't know such a place, but at post St. Vincennes where we always went when necessary to hold councils. My elder brother, thou informest me I must meet you at the place I have mentioned, yet thou seeist, my brother, that the season is far advanced, and that I would not have time to invite my allies to come to your council, which we pray to hold at post St. Vincennes,' &c.

The Loon

'My elder brother, Thou invitest us to a grand council at Clarkesville; we don't know that place; it is at post St. Vincennes that our fathers used to go to speak, and we hope you will not refuse it to us, that place being the bed of our ancestors and of monsieur de Vincennes. In the spring of the year we will repair at your pleasure to post St. Vincennes,' &c.

General Clarke

'I propose the last of April for the grand council to be held at this place (St. Vincennes) where I expect all those who are inclined to open the roads will appear, and we can soon discover what the Deity means.' [1]

The manifest purpose of thus garbling LeGras' report was to represent Clark as a mental weakling in dealing with the hostile savages, by suppressing all that would show his masterful handling of them, and making him appear as begging peace from them.

Having now set forth the *contents* of all the 'testimonials' Wilkinson sent the governor, let us next consider the *attestations* added to them. Since all the papers, except the Neeves deposition, have disappeared from the Virginia archives, there is not a single attesting signature whose genuineness can now be tested by expert examination, or determined otherwise than by reasonable presumption and inference.

(1). The pretended report of 'A committee appointed to wait on General Clarke' bore these attesting words: 'A copy. Thomas Todd, Clk. Com.' Were they written by Todd, or by Wilkinson, or by some one else by Wilkinson's procurement? Although no inspection can be made of the handwriting, circumstantial evidence points pretty plainly to Wilkinson. It is morally certain that Todd never made any such attestation, unless he was tricked into it by some falsehood or sleight-of-hand. He was an honorable man, was appointed justice of the Supreme Court of the United States, and always bore an honored name; and he could not honestly have given any such attestation. He knew there was no such convention, or 'committee,' or 'report,' and certainly knew he was not clerk of any such committee; yet he is made to appear as attesting its report as Clerk of the Committee — 'Clk. Com!' Which is the more reasonable

---

[1] *Secret Journal of Congress*, IV, 313.

presumption: that an honorable man like Todd would have made a false attestation of this bogus committee report, or that Wilkinson wrote it, or got some one else to do it for him? Another feature of this attestation, common to all the others, will be mentioned presently.

(2). Wilkinson's next 'testimonial' was the garbled copy from Le-Gras' report, with the added words 'Copied from General Clark's papers by Harry Innes.' To an unwary reader this may seem to be a certificate *by Innes*, and to the effect that *he* copied the papers; but it is not. It is no more than a mere memorandum, which any one (with no forgery of Innes' name), could have written, at the top, or at the bottom, or on the back of the paper, reciting that Innes had copied it from Clark's papers. The word 'by' here makes all the difference between a mere memorandum and a legal forgery.

But Innes was well known to Governor Randolph, and a seeming attestation *from him* that he had copied Clark's papers was very important for Wilkinson's purpose. When read along with the bogus committee report, this endorsement, seeming to be by Innes, was well calculated to make Clark appear as Green's confederate.

(3). On the Wells contribution paper, purporting to be signed by 'Thomas Green, ... George R. Clarke,' etc., appears this attestation:

DANVILLE, *December 22, 1786*

We do certify the foregoing papers to be true copies of the papers shown to us by William Wells, the person referred to by Thomas Green in the said letter.

HARRY INNES
J. BROWN
CHRIS. GREENUP

The same presumption of fabrication by Wilkinson, applicable to the other missing testimonials, applies to this one; but, even waiving that and assuming the certificate and signatures genuine, what did the signers certify? Only that 'the foregoing papers are true copies of the papers *shown to us by William Wells.*' They do not certify the genuineness of the contribution paper, or of the subscribing names, or of the Green letter. Wells may innocently have shown them papers faked by Wilkinson; and that they were so faked has already persuasively appeared.

(4). There is no attestation directly affixed to the Green letter, which therefore appeared to Governor Randolph to be an original, signed by Green himself, and that was precisely what Wilkinson wanted. The certificate on the Wells contribution paper, however, shows pretty plainly that the Green letter was the other one of 'the foregoing papers' certified 'to be true copies of the *papers* [note the plural] shown us by William Wells,' and was no more than a copy; for the certifiers add that Wells is 'the person referred to by Thomas Green in the *said letter.*' That letter and the contribution paper are the only 'papers' referred to by the certifiers.

There was little danger of Green's learning that such a letter, with his name forged to it, had been sent to the Virginia Executive (and none after it disappeared from the executive archives); but even if Green had been informed that such a letter had been sent, and by Wilkinson, that worthy would have been in no danger of prosecution for forgery. Wells would have been the man presumably responsible for any forgery when he showed the letter to the certifiers of the contribution paper. Wilkinson could have disclaimed any knowledge other than what he learned from Wells and from the reference to it in the certificate on the contribution paper.

Here two peculiar features of these 'testimonials' should be noted. One is that all are *copies;* the other that, however plainly false the statements in them and the attestations added to some of them, both contents and attestations were so framed that Wilkinson could not have been convicted of forgery on any one of them; not only because he was too shrewd to let his handwriting appear on any of them, but because no one of the testimonials, save the Green letter, could well be said to 'prejudice another's right,' which is an essential of the crime.[1] Each gained its significance by mere *juxtaposition* with others! Yet, when read with one another and the letters they accompanied, the falsehoods they contain dovetail with and support each other too well not to have been part of a scheme to overthrow Clark and make way for Wilkinson to succeed him as Indian Commissioner.

Having now seen all of the 'testimonials,' let us next see how ingeniously the *letters* to Governor Randolph were framed to deceive, first the signers other than Wilkinson, and then the governor. That Wilkinson framed them seems morally certain. That he showed some sort of 'testimonials' to the other signers appears from the reference in one letter to 'the testimonials which accompany this.' What sort of testimonials he showed them is not known, but may be imagined. No doubt some of the Lincoln mutineers were quite ready to sign statements that it was generally reported and believed (amongst the mutineers) that Clark had caused the mutiny by being constantly drunk, and that he was wholly incapable of handling the Indians. Some of the delegates had doubtless heard and believed these false reports. It was probably easy also for Wilkinson to get both verbal and signed predictions of an overwhelming Indian invasion of Kentucky unless the savages were handled at the coming treaty gathering at Vincennes by a more capable man than Clark. Wilkinson could easily concoct some story for his fellow delegates about Green's design, without once mentioning any 'intercepted letter,' or naming Clark as a confederate; but he could not safely mention such a *letter* lest he be asked to show it. Then, if it contained any such false statements as in the Green letter sent the governor about Clark's great army and contracts for supplies, Wilkinson's whole plot would have been exposed. Most of these delegates

[1] *Abbott's Law Dictionary:* "Forgery."

were Clark's friends, and always remained such — a fact which affords strong evidence that when they signed the letters to Randolph none of them knew anything whatever of the Green letter, or about 'a committee appointed to wait on General Clarke.'

In reading the letter to Governor Randolph which was first signed by Wilkinson and then by fourteen of his delegate friends, the reader will note: (1) it does not profess to be from the 'gentlemen members of the convention convened at Danville,' but simply from 'a few *private individuals*.' They evidently never heard of Wilkinson's fictitious 'committee report.' (2) It makes *no charge whatever of misconduct on General Clark's part*. His friends among these men could therefore sign it without suspecting that it would be used to ruin him. It does not even charge 'the *officers appointed* by General Clark' with more than an 'attempt...to augment the banditti at Saint Vincennes by delusive promises of lands, bounty and clothing'; but who the 'officers' were it does not state. (3) It says no more of Clark than that 'the testimonials which accompany this will give your excellency a general idea of...the negotiation which has taken place between General Clarke and the Wabash Indians.' (4) Of Green it only says those testimonials 'will give your excellency a general idea...of the *illicit views* of Mr Green and his accomplices' (a significantly vague description!) and that 'We are fearful that Green will find no difficulty in levying *auxiliaries* in the titular state of Frankland, and the settlements in Cumberland'; (5) It does not indicate who Green's 'accomplices' were, or even intimate that General Clark was one! That was to appear only in the 'testimonials' Wilkinson would send the governor. (6) The *letter* makes no mention whatever of any army to invade Louisiana, or of troops being raised by Clark, or of any being raised in *Kentucky*, where all the signers well knew none were being raised; but only of 'auxiliaries' in Frankland and Cumberland where, for all the other signers of the letter knew, Green might be raising them. The word 'auxiliaries' was shrewdly used; for, when read by Governor Randolph in connection with the Green letter, he would be sure to think the *main* army was being raised by Green and Clark in Kentucky, on the Wabash, and in the Illinois. (7) Finally, the letter to Randolph shows the signing delegates greatly fearing that the Indians would 'overwhelm' the Kentucky settlements, if not skillfully handled at the coming treaty meeting, and demanding the holding of the treaty with them which Wilkinson, as commissioner, was anxious to control.

With this preface to point out the adroit construction of the letter — leaving Clark's friends amongst the signers entirely ignorant that any charges were being made against him — the letter, with some italicizing and bracketed comments, follows. Its literary style is almost unmistakably Wilkinson's.

DANVILLE, *December 22, 1786*

SIR:

'Whatever general impropriety there may be in a few *private* individuals addressing your excellency on subjects of publick nature, we cannot resist those impulses of duty and affection, which prompt us to lay before the honorable board at which you preside a state of certain unwarrantable transactions [what transactions Wilkinson's testimonials alone would explain], which we are apprehensive may, without the seasonable interposition of the legislature, deeply affect the dignity, honour and interest of the commonwealth.

The testimonials which accompany this will give your excellency a general idea of the outrage which has been committed at post Saint Vincennes, [this letter gives none] of the *illicit views* of Mr. Green [the *testimonials* alone would disclose them] and his accomplices [Clark is not mentioned as one], and the negotiation which has taken place between general Clarke and the Wabash Indians. We beg leave to add, that we have reason to believe property has been plundered to a very considerable amount [by whom, the *letter* does not say] and that it has been generally appropriated to private purposes.

We are fearful that Green [Clark is not mentioned] will find no difficulty in levying *auxiliaries* in the titular state of Frankland, and the settlements in Cumberland; in the mean time attempts are daily practised to augment the banditti at Saint Vincennes, by delusive promises of lands, bounty and clothing, from *the officers* appointed by General Clarke.

We beg leave to suggest to the serious consideration of your excellency, the necessity of carrying into effect the treaty proposed in April; for we fear that the savages, when assembled, if they are not amused by a treaty, or kept in awe by a military force at Saint Vincennes, will form combinations among themselves hostile to this country, and before they disperse may turn their arms against our scattered settlements in such force as to overwhelm them. To the superior wisdom and the paternal care of the heads of the commonwealth we take the liberty of submitting the matters herein mentioned, in full confidence, that every necessary measure will be immediately adopted. And have the honour to be, with every sentiment of respect,

Exc. yr. mo. ob.

T. MARSHALL	JAMES WILKINSON
GEORGE MUTER	J. BROWN
HARRY INNES	CALEB WALLACE
EDMUND LYNNE	JOHN CRAIG
RICHARD C. ANDERSON	JAMES GARRARD
RICHARD TAYLOR	CHARLES EWING
	JOHN LOGAN
	JOHN EDWARDS [1]

The second letter, sent to the Governor along with the other one and the 'testimonials,' was signed by ten of Wilkinson's deluded friends. He did not sign it himself, for its object was to secure his appointment as Indian Commissioner in lieu of General Clark, and as a person 'well qualified for the purpose and against whom no exception can be taken!' It is hardly less cunningly constructed than the first letter. Nine tenths of it are devoted to the double purpose

[1] Virginia State Library, '*Box Executive Papers*'; photostat, *Author's MSS.* The order of the names is incorrectly given in *Secret Journal of Congress*, IV, 309, and Green's *Spanish Conspiracy*, 77.

of appealing to the prejudice of the intended signers against the hated generals Parsons and Butler, and to show their unfitness for dealing with the Indians. In a single concluding sentence (which if Wilkinson *read* the letter to the other signers we may be quite sure he passed over without reading) Clark is regretfully represented as utterly disqualified, by his 'unfortunate habit,' for business of any kind. As already seen, too, however preposterous this charge, Wilkinson was undoubtedly able to produce to any signer who might demand to read the letter, plenty of hearsay statements from the Lincoln mutineers supporting it; and he knew the old false report about Clark's drinking following upon the Blue Licks disaster four years earlier, was still believed at Richmond and would make Governor Randolph receptive to this repetition of it. This second letter, recommending Wilkinson, reads as follows:

DANVILLE, Decr 22^d 1786

Sir:

We flatter ourselves your Excellency will admit the peculiarity of our situation, as an apology for the liberty of this address, circumstanced as we are, we unfortunately find ourselves obliged to dispense with common forms, & to transcend the bounds of strict propriety.

In the progress of the American Republic, it is but too frequent, that we have beheld men wriggled into office by their own act at the influence of their friends, without regard to public interest; from this cause it has frequently happened that we have seen characters appointed in remote quarters of the States to transact business on ground, adjacent to which men better qualified could be found.

In the late treaty at the Miami, which cost the Continent many thousands without effecting one Solitary purpose, it was extremely distressing to us, to behold the Commissioners under the influence of two gentlemen, one from a Distant Northern State, & the other embittered by ancient prejudices against the frontier citizens of Virginia. These gentlemen so far from shewing that Sympathy & Consideration for our young country, which are the characteristics of liberality, candor & good sense, took pains to magnify trifling transgressions into deadly crimes — the cause, one or two disorderly persons, from whence is not known, retook two or three horses which the Indians had previously stolen from the District, — they consigned its soil, climate, & inhabitants to infamy, and missed no occasion to load them with opprobrium.

The Settlement of Kentucky is formed by an assemblage of characters from almost every quarter of the Union, among whom may be found old, faithful & respectable servants of their country; had the Eyes of Congress been directed hither, they might have selected Commissioners better qualified for their purpose, and by that means have saved to the Continent the thousands which have gone into the pockets of Generals Parsons & Butler.

To save to Congress a repetition of these expenses, & to place the negotiation in those who are most deeply interested in the issue, should any treaty be proposed on the Wabash we implore your Excellency to exert your influence, that the commission may be filled by gentlemen from this District; and as persons well qualified for the purpose, and against whom no exception can be taken, we beg leave to recommend Genl James Wilkinson, Col.^{os} Richard Clough Anderson & Isaac Shelby.

We lament that the unfortunate habit to which Gen! Clark is addicted, obliges us to observe, that we consider him utterly unqualified for business of any kind.

We repeat our hopes, that you will pardon the liberty we have taken — a liberty dictated by the general, as well as local interest of our country. We have the honor to be,

Your Excellency's mo. ob. Servants,
T. MARSHALL
EDMUND LYNE
RICH^D TAYLOR
J. BROWN
HARRY INNES
GEORGE MUTER
CALEB WALLACE
JOHN CRAIG
BENJ. POPE
CHARLES EWING [1]

To the Governor of Va.

Both these letters contain too many falsehoods to have been wittingly vouched for by any of the signers other than Wilkinson; and these falsehoods are too cunningly fitted to supplement one another and to further his aims to have been concocted by any other man.

As already seen in the text, the result of his sending them to Governor Randolph was that they were ordered to be 'forthwith transmitted to our delegates in Congress, with an earnest request to communicate them, in whole or in part, according to their discretion, immediately to that body, to urge the speediest arrangements for a treaty to be holden with the Indians in April next, under the sanction of the federal government; and to propose as commissioners, general *James Wilkinson*, colonel Richard Clough Anderson, and colonel Isaac Shelby.' [2] Not only was Wilkinson named first, but he doubtless had reasons for knowing that neither Anderson nor Shelby would be appointed, or would accept the position he coveted. Furthermore, the mere fact of his being recommended by leading Kentuckians and the Virginia executive would be persuasive evidence of his great influence to show to Miro.

For sake of argument it has been thus far assumed that the signers of the letters to Randolph, other than Wilkinson, actually read them; and the letters themselves have been analyzed only to show that they do not say what the testimonials make them *seem* to say. In all probability, however, not one of the signers, save Wilkinson, ever read the letters, but only heard him read them, with such omissions and additions as suited his aims. His audacity and cunning in such false reading was shown in the Kentucky Convention of November, 1788, when he pretended to read to the members all of his infamous 'Memorial,' to the Spanish King, but left out every treasonable feature in it and received the unanimous thanks from the Convention for the patriotism it displayed! [3]

Here it should be said that in view of the anonymous character of

---

[1] *Draper MSS.* 14 S 88–91.
[2] *Secret Journal of Congress,* IV, 306–07.
[3] See author's introduction to *Littell's Political Transactions, supra.*

the preparatory communications to Congress and Randolph, and of the disappearance of all the 'testimonials' sent to the governor (except Neeves' harmless deposition) Wilkinson's fabrication of them can only be proved by circumstantial evidence and reasonable presumption; and error is of course quite possible in some of the interpretations here given. It is a judicial axiom, however, that cumulative circumstantial evidence, which may depend little or not at all on the veracity or accuracy of witnesses, may be the strongest possible evidence; and the cumulative and dovetailing evidences of Wilkinson's fabrication of the 'testimonials' and accompanying letters certainly seem overwhelming. '*Falsus in uno, falsus in omnibus*' is a maxim in the law of evidence which may perhaps be more fairly applied to Wilkinson than to any other man noted in American history. Certainly, too, although another legal axiom is that 'every man is to be presumed innocent until proven guilty,' no such presumption is applicable to Wilkinson. In the absence of direct evidence, a strong presumption of deceit fairly attaches to every act, paper, and signature he used in furtherance of his elaborate plot. 'The trail of the serpent is over them all.'

This detailed explanation of Wilkinson's complex plot has been deemed necessary in order to correct a perfectly natural, but wholly erroneous belief that Governor Randolph must have had just grounds for his proclamation condemning General Clark. Without knowing how Wilkinson framed the letters and testimonials and got them signed by his reputable friends, any unsuspecting reader would be almost sure to think the condemnation proper.

BIBLIOGRAPHY

ALVORD, CLARENCE W.: *Mississippi Valley in British Politics* (Arthur H. Clark Co., Cleveland, 1917); Volume V, *Illinois Historical Collections, — Kaskaskia Records* — (Illinois State Historical Society, Springfield, Illinois, 1909.)

AMERICAN HISTORICAL ASSOCIATION REPORT. (Washington, Government Printing Office.)

AMERICAN HISTORICAL REVIEW. (Macmillan Co., Lancaster, Pa.)

ANDERSON, ...*Donald Robertson & Family.* (Detroit, 1900, Winn & Hammond.)

APPLETON'S CYCLOPÆDIA OF AMERICAN BIOGRAPHY. (New York, 1888, D. Appleton & Co.)

BRACKENRIDGE, HENRY M.: *View of Louisiana.* (Pittsburg, 1814, Cramer, Spear & Eichbaum.)

BROWN, JOHN MASON: *Political Beginnings of Kentucky.* (Louisville, 1889, John P. Morton & Co., Filson Club Publication No. 6.)

BURK, JOHN: *History of Virginia.* (Petersburg, Va., 1804–16, Dickson & Pescud.)

BUTLER, MANN: *History of Kentucky.* (Louisville, 1834, Wilcox, Dickerman & Co.)

CARTER, CLARENCE E.: *Great Britain and the Illinois Country.* (American Historical Association, Washington, 1910.)

COLLINS, LEWIS: *History of Kentucky.* (Covington, 1882, Collins & Co.)

COMANS, KATHERINE: *Industrial History of the United States.* (Macmillan Co., N.Y., 1911.)

CONGRESS: see Journal of.

CONWAY, MONCURE: *Writings of Thomas Paine.* (G. P. Putnam's, New York, 1894–96.)

CRESSWELL, NICHOLAS: *Journal of Nicholas Cresswell.* (Dial Press, New York, 1924.)

CRUMRINE, BOYD: *Old Virginia Court House at Augusta Town.* (Washington County Hist. Soc., Washington, Penna., 1905.)

DAILY SCIENCE SERVICE BULLETIN. (May, 1923, Washington, D.C.)

DENNY, MAJOR: *Record of Upland, ...Denny's Diary.* (Lippincott, 1860, Philadelphia.)

DILLON, J. B.: *History of Indiana.* (Bingham & Doughty, 1859, Indianapolis.)

DUNN, J. P.: *Indiana.* (*American Commonwealth Series*, Houghton, Mifflin & Co., Boston, 1900.)

ELLIOTT, J.: *Debates on the Federal Constitution, — Virginia —* (Philadelphia, J. B. Lippincott & Co.; Taylor & Maury, 1863, Washington.)

ENGLISH, WM. H.: *Conquest of the Northwest.* (Bowen-Merrill Co., 1896, Indianapolis.)

FILSON CLUB PUBLICATIONS: *Political Beginnings of Kentucky* (J. M. Brown, Publication No. 6); Centennial Address (R. T. Durrett, Publication No. 27); *Littell's Political Transactions* (Reprint, Publication No. 31) — (All by Jno. P. Morton Co., Louisville, Ky.)

FITZMAURICE, EDMOND G. (Petty-Fitzmaurice): *Life of William, Earl of Shelburne.* (London, 1875–76.)

FORD, P. L.: *Works of Thomas Jefferson.* (G. P. Putnam's, N.Y., 1904 — Federal Edition.)

GAYERRE, CHARLES: *History of Louisiana, — Spanish Domination.* (Wm. J. Widdleton, 1866, N.Y.)

GREEN, NELSON: *History of Mohawk Valley.* (S. J. Clarke Pub. Co., 1924, Chicago.)

GREEN, THOS. M.: *Spanish Conspiracy.* (Cincinnati, O. Robt. Clarke & Co., 1891.)

GROTIUS: *Rights of War & Peace.* (Cambridge Law Library Classics, M. Walter Dunne, N.Y., 1901.)

HARPER, LILLIE (DU PUY): *Colonial Men & Times.* (Innes, 1915, Philadelphia.)

HART, ALBERT BUSHNELL: *Formation of the Union.* (Longmans, Green & Co., 1915, New York.)

HASSLER, E. W.: *Old Westmoreland.* (Pittsburg, 1900, J. R. Weldon & Co.)

HENDERSON, ARCHIBALD: *Conquest of The Old Southwest.* (The Century Co., N.Y. 1920.) *George Rogers Clark and the Conquest of the Northwest.* (Alumni Bulletin, University of Virginia, Address at the Unveiling of George Rogers Clark Memorial, Charlottesville, Va., November 3, 1921.)

HENING, WM. WALLER: *Statutes of Virginia.* (Richmond, Va., 1819–23.)

HENRY, WM. WIRT: *Life of Patrick Henry.* (Charles Scribner, 1891, New York.)

HINSDALE, BURKE A.: *Old Northwest.* (Silver, Burdett & Co., 1899, New York.)

HOLMES, W. H.: '*Moundbuilders,*' Bulletin No. 60, Bureau of Ethnology, Smithsonian Institution, Washington.

ILLINOIS HISTORICAL COLLECTIONS. (Illinois State Library, Springfield, Ill.)

JAMES, JAMES ALTON: *Financing of Clark's Conquest (Mississippi Valley Historical Review,* Volume IV, Cedar Rapids, Ia., 1917); Volume VIII, *Illinois Historical Collections,* Illinois State Library, 1912, Springfield, Ill.

JAY, JOHN: *Peace Negotiations of 1782–3.* (New York Historical Society, 1884.)

JEFFERSON, THOMAS: *Notes on Virginia* (David Carlisle, 1801, Boston); Ford's *Works of Thomas Jefferson* (G. P. Putnam's, 1904, N.Y.); H. A. Washington's *Writings of Jefferson* (Congressional Edition, Washington, 1853, Taylor & Maury); *Life of Jefferson (American Statesmen Series,* Houghton, Mifflin & Co., Boston, 1883.)

JOURNAL OF CONGRESS. (David Claypoole, 1779, Philadelphia.)

JOURNAL CONTINENTAL CONGRESS. (Library of Cong., Government Printing Office, 1904–22.)

KELLOGG, LOUISE PHELPS: *Frontier Advance on Upper Ohio* (Wisconsin Hist. Soc. 1916); *Frontier Retreat,* etc. (Wis. Hist. Soc. 1917); Thwaites & Kellogg: *Revolution on the Upper Ohio; Dunmore's War,* see THWAITES, R. G.

KENTUCKY HISTORICAL SOCIETY REGISTER, Frankfort, Ky.

LEE, RICHARD HENRY: *Life of Arthur Lee.* (Boston, 1829, Wells & Lilly.)

LITTELL'S POLITICAL TRANSACTIONS: see Filson Club.

LOUISIANA HISTORICAL SOCIETY PUBLICATIONS: *Proceedings 1916.* (New Orleans, La., 1917.)

McELROY, ROBERT McN.: *Kentucky in the Nation's History.* (Moffat, Yard & Co., 1909, N.Y.)

McKEAN PAPERS. (Historical Society of Pennsylvania, Philadelphia.)

MAGAZINE OF AMERICAN HISTORY. (A. S. Barnes & Co., New York, 1877.)

MARSHALL, HUMPHREY: *History of Kentucky*. (Frankfort, Ky., 1824, George S. Robinson.)

MARYLAND HISTORICAL SOCIETY PUBLICATIONS. (Baltimore, Md.)

MICHIGAN PIONEER COLLECTIONS. (Report of Pioneer Society of Michigan, State Printer, Lansing, Mich.)

MISSISSIPPI VALLEY HISTORICAL ASSOCIATION REVIEW. (Cedar Rapids, Ia.)

MISSOURI HISTORICAL SOCIETY PUBLICATIONS: *William Clark's Journal*. (St. Louis, Mo.)

MORSE, J. T.: *Life of Jefferson*. (*American Statesmen Series*, Houghton, Mifflin Co., Boston, 1883.)

NEW YORK HISTORICAL SOCIETY PUBLICATIONS: *Peace Negotiations of 1782–3*, by John Jay. (New York, 1883.)

OHIO VALLEY HISTORICAL SERIES. (Cincinnati, R. Clarke & Co., 1871.)

PARKMAN, FRANCIS: *Montcalm and Wolfe*. (Little, Brown & Co., 1905, Boston.)

PENNSYLVANIA ARCHIVES. (Harrisburg, Pa., 1878, Lane S. Hart, State Printer.)

PENNSYLVANIA PACKET: August 12, 1783. (Philadelphia Library Co.; Library of Congress; Historical Society of Pennsylvania.)

PERKINS, JAMES H.: *Western Annals*. (Cincinnati, 1847, James R. Albach.)

PETTY-FITZMAURICE: see Fitzmaurice, Edmond G.

PIONEER SOCIETY OF MICHIGAN REPORT: see Michigan Pioneer Collections.

POPE, JOHN: *Tour of the Western & Southern Territorys, 1790–1*. (J. Dixon, 1792, Richmond.)

QUAIFE, MILO M.: *Conquest of the Illinois* (R. R. Donnelley & Sons Co., Lakeside Press, Chicago, 1920); *Royal Navy on the Upper Lakes* (Burton Historical Collection Leaflets, Volume 2, No. 5, May, 1924, Detroit Public Library).

RECORD OF UPLAND...DENNY'S DIARY. (Lippincott, 1860, Philadelphia.)

REPORT OF REGENTS OF UNIVERSITY ON BOUNDARIES OF NEW YORK. (University, State of New York, Albany.)

ROOSEVELT, THEODORE: *Winning of the West*. (Current Literature Publishing Co., N.Y., 1906.)

ST. CLAIR PAPERS, edited by Wm. G. Smith. (Cincinnati, 1882, Robt. Clarke & Co.)

SATO, SHOSUKE: *History of the Land Question in the United States*. (Johns Hopkins University Studies in Historical & Political Science, Baltimore, 1886.)

SCHOOLCRAFT, HENRY R.: *Indian Tribes*. (Lippincott, Grambo & Co., 1852–57, Philadelphia.)

SECRET JOURNALS OF CONGRESS. (Thomas Waite, Boston, 1821.)

SEMPLE, ELLEN G.: *American History and Its Geographic Conditions*. (Houghton, Mifflin Co., Boston, 1903.)

SMITHSONIAN INSTITUTION, Bulletin No. 60, Bureau of Ethnology.

SPARKS, JARED: *Writings of Washington*. (Boston, 1837, American Stationers Company.)

THWAITES, REUBEN GOLD: *Early Western Travels*. (Cleveland, 1904, A. H. Clarke Co.)

THWAITES & KELLOGG: *Revolution on the Upper Ohio* (Wisconsin Historical Society, Madison, 1908); *Dunmore's War* (Wis. Hist. Soc. 1905); *Frontier Defense on the Upper Ohio* (Wis. Hist. Soc., Madison, 1912).

TURNER, FREDERICK J.: *Frontier in American History*. (Henry Holt & Co., 1920, N.Y.); *Policy of France in the Mississippi Valley* (American Historical Review, 1904, Volume X, Macmillan Company, Lancaster, Pa.).

UNIVERSAL CYCLOPÆDIA. (D. Appleton & Co., N.Y., 1905.)

UNIVERSITY, STATE OF NEW YORK: see *Report of Regents*, etc.

VIRGINIA CALENDAR STATE PAPERS. (Richmond, Va., Supt. of Public Printing, 1875–1884.)

WASHINGTON, H. A.: *Writings of Thomas Jefferson.* (Congressional Edition. Washington, 1853, Taylor & Maury.)

WHARTON, FRANCIS: *Diplomatic Correspondence of the Revolution.* (Washington, Government Printing Office, 1889.)

WINSOR, JUSTIN: *Westward Movement* (Houghton, Mifflin & Co., Boston, 1899); *Narrative and Critical History* (Houghton, Mifflin & Co., Boston, 1884–89).

WISCONSIN HISTORICAL SOCIETY PROCEEDINGS. (Madison, Wis., 1893.)

WITHERS, ALEXANDER SCOTT: *Chronicles of Border Warfare.* (Clarksburg, Va., 1831, J. Israel; Reprint, edited by R. G. Thwaites, 1912, Stewart & Kidd Co., Cincinnati.)

INDEX

INDEX